Fiction and the Languages of Law

Contemporary legal reasoning has more in common with fictional discourse than we tend to realize. Through an examination of the U.S. Supreme Court's written output during a recent landmark term, this book exposes many of the parallels between these two special kinds of language use. Focusing on linguistic and rhetorical patterns in the dozens of reasoned opinions issued by the Court between October 2014 and June 2015, the book takes nonlawyer readers on a lively tour of contemporary American legal reasoning and acquaints legal readers with some surprising features of their own thinking and writing habits. It analyzes cases addressing a huge variety of issues, ranging from the rights of drivers stopped by the police to the decision-making processes of the Environmental Protection Agency—as well as the term's best-known case, which recognized a constitutional right to marriage for same-sex as well as different-sex couples. *Fiction and the Languages of Law* reframes a number of long-running legal debates, identifies other related paradoxes within legal discourse, and traces them all to common sources: judges' and lawyers' habit of alternating unselfconsciously between two different attitudes toward the language they use, and a set of professional biases that tends to prevent scrutiny of that habit.

Karen Petroski, St Louis University School of Law, USA, has been teaching law since 2008 and is trained in both literary analysis and law. She has published several articles and book chapters on legal fictions and the relationship between fictional and legal discourse, including chapters in *Legal Fictions in Theory and Practice* (ed. Maksymilian Del Mar & William Twining, Springer, 2015) and *The Nature of Legal Interpretation: What Jurists Can Learn About Legal Interpretation from Linguistics and Philosophy* (ed. Brian Slocum, Univ. of Chicago Press, 2017).

Law, Language and Communication

Series Editors: Anne Wagner, Université du Littoral Côte d'Opale, France and Vijay Kumar Bhatia, formerly of City University of Hong Kong

This series encourages innovative and integrated perspectives within and across the boundaries of law, language and communication, with particular emphasis on issues of communication in specialized socio-legal and professional contexts. It seeks to bring together a range of diverse yet cumulative research traditions in order to identify and encourage interdisciplinary research.

The series welcomes proposals – both edited collections as well as single-authored monographs – emphasizing critical approaches to law, language and communication, identifying and discussing issues, proposing solutions to problems, offering analyses in areas such as legal construction, interpretation, translation and de-codification.

Titles in the series

Synesthetic Legalities
Sensory Dimensions of Law and Jurisprudence
Edited by Sarah Marusek

Legal Persuasion
A Rhetorical Approach to the Science
Linda L. Berger and Kathryn M. Stanchi

International Arbitration Discourse and Practices in Asia
Edited by Vijay K Bhatia, Maurizio Gotti, Azirah Hashim, Philip Koh and Sundra Rajoo

Phraseology in Legal and Institutional Settings
A Corpus-based Interdisciplinary Perspective
Edited by Stanislaw Gozdz Roszkowski and Gianluca Pontrandolfo

Fiction and the Languages of Law
Understanding Contemporary Legal Discourse
Karen Petroski

For more information about this series, please visit: www.routledge.com/Law-Language-and-Communication/book-series/LAWLANGCOMM

Fiction and the Languages of Law

Understanding Contemporary Legal Discourse

Karen Petroski

Routledge
Taylor & Francis Group
LONDON AND NEW YORK

First published 2019 by Routledge

2 Park Square, Milton Park, Abingdon, Oxfordshire OX14 4RN
52 Vanderbilt Avenue, New York, NY 10017

Routledge is an imprint of the Taylor & Francis Group, an informa business

First issued in paperback 2020

British Library Cataloguing-in-Publication Data
A catalogue record for this book is available from the British Library

Library of Congress Cataloging-in-Publication Data
Names: Petroski, Karen, author.
Title: Fiction and the languages of law: understanding contemporary legal discourse / Karen Petroski.
Description: New York, NY: Routledge, 2018. | Series: Law, language and communication | Includes bibliographical references and index.
Identifiers: LCCN 2018027096 | ISBN 9780815350118 (hardback)
Subjects: LCSH: Law—United States—Language. | Judicial opinions—United States—Language. | United States. Supreme Court.
Classification: LCC KF250.P48 2018 | DDC 340/.14—dc23
LC record available at https://lccn.loc.gov/2018027096

ISBN: 978-0-8153-5011-8 (hbk)
ISBN: 978-0-367-51988-9 (pbk)

Typeset in Galliard
by codeMantra

Contents

Acknowledgments

Much of this book was written during a sabbatical leave from teaching at the Saint Louis University School of Law. I developed some of the ideas presented here in papers delivered at the "Inference, Intention, and 'Ordinary Meaning'" conference at the University of the Pacific-McGeorge School of Law in 2015; the "Law and Fictional Discourse" conference at the Whitney Humanities Center in 2015; the "Issues of Fact" conference cosponsored by Erasmus University and Leiden University in Rotterdam in 2015; the "American Legal Fictions" conference hosted by the Savannah Law School in 2016; the 2016 meeting of the Law, Literature, & Humanities Association of Australasia; the 2017 meeting of the Association for Law, Culture, and the Humanities; and the 2017 International Roundtable for the Semiotics of Law at Cardozo Law School. I thank participants at these conferences for their questions, suggestions, and input. For offering me the opportunity to share my ideas with others, I thank the organizers of these conferences, in particular Brian Slocum, Hans Lind, Jeanne Gaakeer, Frans-Willem Korsten, Caprice Roberts, Peter Goodrich, and Angela Condello.

For their helpful input, I thank David Caudill, Maksymilian Del Mar, Robert Ferguson, Simon Stern, and Laura Portwood-Stacer, as well as my colleagues Matt Bodie, Miriam Cherry, Monica Eppinger, Chad Flanders, Joel Goldstein, John Griesbach, Jeff Redding, and Anders Walker. For their help in the editorial process at Routledge, I thank Alison Kirk, Alexandra Buckley, Ting Baker, and Philip Stirups. For his helpful input, encouragement, optimism, and partnership, I thank T.J. Bross.

1 Three ways of reading a term

1.1 The big day

Friday, June 26, 2015: the plaza below the wide steps of the Supreme Court building in Washington, DC, holds a crowd of hundreds. Many in the group wear rainbow flags and wave banners bearing the equals-sign insignia of the marriage-equality movement. Just after 10 a.m., the news the crowd has been hoping for is carried out of the courthouse by a stream of young interns sprinting to their media sponsors. As the information they bear spreads through the crowd, so does the chant, "Love has won" (Liptak 2015).

The Court's decision in *Obergefell v. Hodges*, recognizing a fundamental constitutional right to marriage for members of same-sex couples, was expected this morning but stirs great excitement anyway. Within minutes, the news has spread widely: in the first hour after the decision, 3.8 million people made 10.1 million Facebook posts or shares about it, and tweets within the first four hours after the announcement averaged 20,000 per minute (Corasantini 2015). Many online communications reproduced text from the justices' opinions, especially the final paragraph of Justice Anthony Kennedy's opinion for a five-justice majority:

> No union is more profound than marriage, for it embodies the highest ideals of love, fidelity, devotion, sacrifice, and family. In forming a marital union, two people become something greater than once they were. As some of the petitioners in these cases demonstrate, marriage embodies a love that may endure even past death. It would misunderstand these men and women to say they disrespect the idea of marriage. Their plea is that they do respect it, respect it so deeply that they seek to find its fulfillment for themselves. Their hope is not to be condemned to live in loneliness, excluded from one of civilization's oldest institutions. They ask for equal dignity in the eyes of the law. The Constitution grants them that right.
>
> (*Obergefell*, 28)[1]

This passage, along with the #lovewins hashtag, was among the most circulated content about the case in the days after the decision. The passage itself became a symbol of the right it described; social-media users treated it almost like a decree or proclamation.

Justice Kennedy's *Obergefell* opinion was not universally welcomed. Four justices—Chief Justice John Roberts and Associate Justices Antonin Scalia, Clarence Thomas, and Samuel Alito—wrote passionate dissents, and the Chief Justice read his from the bench after the announcement of the majority's decision. The dissenting justices' words also circulated online. Justice Scalia's dissent stood out for its focus on the *language* of Justice

Kennedy's opinion, not just the opinion's legal, logical, or practical shortcomings. In addition to criticizing the substance of the *Obergefell* majority opinion, Justice Scalia also attacked its "style":

> [Justice Kennedy's] opinion is couched in a style that is as pretentious as its content is egotistic. It is one thing for separate concurring or dissenting opinions to contain extravagances, even silly extravagances, of thought and expression; it is something else for the official opinion of the Court to do so. Of course the opinion's showy profundities are often profoundly incoherent. "The nature of marriage is that, through its enduring bond, two persons together can find other freedoms, such as expression, intimacy, and spirituality." (Really? Who ever thought that intimacy and spirituality [whatever that means] were freedoms? And if intimacy is, one would think Freedom of Intimacy is abridged rather than expanded by marriage. Ask the nearest hippie. Expression, sure enough, *is* a freedom, but anyone in a long-lasting marriage will attest that that happy state constricts, rather than expands, what one can prudently say.) . . . I could go on. The world does not expect logic and precision in poetry or inspirational pop-philosophy; it demands them in the law. The stuff contained in today's opinion has much [sic] to diminish this Court's reputation for clear thinking and sober analysis.
>
> (*Obergefell*, Scalia, 7–9; second interpolation in original)

To Justice Scalia, and to the public celebrating the decision, *Obergefell* amounted to more than the Court's 5-to-4 vote and a change in the behavior of public officials across the country. *Obergefell* was also a linguistic performance: a set of statements to be circulated, brandished, and contemplated—or mocked. *Obergefell* marked one of the rare occasions when the language used by judges matters to an audience other than lawyers and law students, and when the justices themselves, anticipating that attention, paid especially close attention to the language they were using.

Yet the language of the *Obergefell* opinions was, in fact, not extraordinary. As this book will show, many of the techniques Justice Kennedy used in his majority opinion—some of them, though not all, criticized by Justice Scalia—are standard elements of judicial prose. Despite their legal disagreement, the majority and dissenting opinions in *Obergefell* are remarkably alike in many of the ways they discuss the acts and thoughts of people and groups, the possibilities and traditions that inform legal decisions.

It becomes easier to see patterns of the kind considered here—and their existence as patterns becomes harder to deny—the larger the body of writing one considers. Demonstrating both this point and the patterns themselves, this book explores rhetorical commonalities among all of the merits opinions the Court issued during the term that included *Obergefell*, that is, the 2014–15 term. (A merits opinion addresses at least some of the parties' arguments and explains the basis for the Court's ruling.) The term began in early October 2014, with oral argument in *Heien v. North Carolina*, a case arising out of a police officer's traffic stop of a driver based on a broken taillight. It ended formally a year later, with the beginning of the next term, although the Court issued its last merits opinion of the 2014 term, *Glossip v. Gross*, on June 29, 2015. Over those nine months, the Court issued 74 merits opinions, more than 2,000 pages of text. Only a handful of the opinions have received much attention, even from legal commentators; many are likely to be read closely only by specialists. Normally, the patterns described here would escape attention.

During the months over which the Court issued these opinions, a series of dramatic events occupied public consciousness in the U.S. These included the spread of the Black Lives Matter movement following, in particular, the choking death of Eric Garner by a police officer in Staten Island in July 2014 and the shooting death of Michael Brown by a police officer in Ferguson, Missouri, in August 2014, as well as the deaths at police hands of Walter Scott in North Charleston, South Carolina, and Eddie Gray in Baltimore in April 2015. In October 2014, a brief panic followed confirmation that patients were carrying the Ebola virus in the United States. The spring of 2015 brought political news that would turn out to be fateful for Hillary Clinton's 2016 presidential bid: the revelation that she had used a private email server during her time as Secretary of State. Civilian shootings of Muslim students and African-American churchgoers in Chapel Hill, North Carolina, in February 2015 and Charleston, South Carolina, in June 2015 reignited debates about gun control and hate crime. The spring of 2015 also saw controversies over the honesty of two white women as spokespeople for African-American experience; critics questioned the academic bona fides of white sociologist Alice Goffman's personal ethnographic study of a mostly Black Philadelphia neighborhood, issued in paperback in April 2015, and in June 2015, public criticism prompted Rachel Dolezal's resignation as president of an NAACP chapter due to her misrepresentation of her racial identity.

The Court's 2014-term opinions do not mention these events, but they would have been on the minds of many of the justices and their clerks during the year. Many of the term's cases reflect anxieties about racial identity, personal and government power, and the mutual incomprehension of individuals belonging to different cultural worlds. The discussion of the opinions in this book is informed by this context and considers these ongoing cultural anxieties from time to time, but the book mainly focuses on the opinions themselves. It explores regularities in the opinions' language and construction that have not previously been noticed or, if they have been noticed, have not been thought to merit discussion. The book also examines the potential effects of these regularities on readers of the opinions. Seeing the patterns *as* patterns, bringing them out of the unnoticed background of "standard legal usage" and into awareness, suggests both new critiques and new defenses of contemporary legal, judicial, and legal-educational practices.

The book's approach is also informed by classic accounts of legal discourse offered by observers such as James Boyd White, Robert Cover, and Ronald Dworkin. Like these critics, the book draws on other disciplines to examine legal discourse, and like them it explores how lawyers' thinking and writing are shaped by the experience of reading legal materials. But this book also draws on more recent work on language and mind by philosophers, cognitive scientists, and literary theorists. Scholars in these fields have been interacting productively and generating new insights since the heyday of the study of law and literature in the 1970s and 1980s, and even since the first efforts at marrying the study of legal discourse with the mind sciences in the early 2000s (Amsterdam & Bruner 2000; Winter 2003). The focus in this recent work, and in this book, is not just on general theories of what language looks like and how it works but also on more fine-grained aspects of its relations to the world it presupposes and to its users and readers.

The implications of this study are broader than its focus on a year's worth of Supreme Court opinions might suggest. First, as later sections of this chapter explain, the Court's opinions have a uniquely powerful effect on reading, writing, and thinking habits across the legal profession, including on law students of the future, advocates, clerks, and justices. Second, this book identifies some striking commonalities in legal discourse across practice areas. Because of legal–professional specialization, these commonalities have become increasingly difficult to see in the wild. Their persistence suggests, among other things, that we might be able to expect some degree of legal consistency even in the absence of lawyers' or judges' deliberate efforts to maintain it. This book explores some of the arguments supporting such a conclusion.

While there are no studies exactly like this one, the legal academy and the profession have to some extent institutionalized the practice of reading Supreme Court terms as unified legal events. The next two sections of this chapter (1.2 and 1.3) consider two high-profile accounts of the same term studied by this book: one from the *Harvard Law Review*, the other from the online SCOTUSblog. Section 1.4 then addresses in more detail the motivation and methods for studying the term's opinions as a single, albeit multiauthored, text. Brief descriptions of some of the term's decisions appear throughout this discussion. Summaries of all of the term's merits opinions appear in the Appendix.

1.2 The old school

Since the late nineteenth century, Harvard Law School has exercised an outsized influence over U.S. legal education and professional activity (e.g., LaPiana 1994, 3–28). Each year for almost a century, the student-edited *Harvard Law Review* has published an annual survey of the Court's activity in the previous term. In November 2015, for the first time, this review included a survey of surveys, a retrospective account of the overviews dating back to their beginning (Lazarus 2015).

Because of their source, these surveys have impact. But they are also selective. Although the Court decided more than 70 cases on the merits during the 2014 term, the Harvard survey of the term addresses just 28, some only in passing. The professor-authored portions of the survey consider only three decisions in any detail (*Obergefell* being one); student case notes address another 20. Although the professors' and students' contributions take a variety of perspectives on the cases they discuss, these contributions also (and understandably) share a mostly instrumentalist attitude toward the opinions, treating them as tools for the promotion of academic work, the reform of legal practices, or the shaping of policy. In the process, they also display what this book calls the "wordsmith's fallacy," a kind of professional bias in lawyers' thinking about and discussion of what they do with language.

1.2.1 The professors: the wordsmith's fallacy

The professor-authored contributions to the Harvard survey come from seven professors (one of whom, Richard Posner, was also a federal judge in 2015). All seven are prominent academics, most well advanced in their careers. They represent a handful of elite institutions.[2] Although each author advances a different argument, each argument takes one of two basic approaches, one concerned with scholarly impact, the other with legal impact. The professors' contributions are consistent enough to present a fairly coherent example of excellence in legal analysis to law students and other legal academics. One of the consistencies among the contributions is their focus on the justices' treatment of legal texts and legal discourse.

The most prominent pieces in the survey treat the term's opinions as evidence for a particular account of judicial behavior with respect to texts. These pieces discuss the Court's work from an academic perspective, not from the perspective of a legal practitioner. The survey's centerpiece is David Strauss's Foreword, "Does the Constitution Mean What It

Says?" (2015). Strauss uses *Obergefell* as an occasion to discuss a series of "anomalies" in constitutional law: situations in which "constitutional law" as understood by lawyers "'contradicts' the text of the Constitution" (3). For example, the standard legal understanding of the First Amendment, developed by the Court over time, regards the amendment as prohibiting restraints on speech by any government body, including, for example, local governments—even though the "amendment, by its terms, applies only to 'Congress'" (3). In this sense, according to Strauss, the Constitution does not "mean what it says." In other work, Strauss has described this process of gradual judicial development of constitutional meaning as "common-law constitutionalism" (1996, 2010). He sees *Obergefell* as another instance of the phenomenon (2015, 8), an example of how judges are and should be judging issues of constitutional law. *Obergefell*, and other opinions like it, are evidence that U.S. legal culture is committed to a view of the Constitution as something more than the words that make it up (61); according to Strauss, the truly central texts of U.S. constitutional law are the decisions of the Supreme Court, not the Constitution itself.

Abbe Gluck, another academic contributor to the survey, also reads an important case from the term as vindicating a position she has taken in other work. Gluck discusses the term's other blockbuster decision, *King v. Burwell.* In this case, Chief Justice Roberts's majority opinion approved an interpretation of the Affordable Care Act ("Obamacare") that seemed hard to square with the Act's text but ensured that the Act would continue to function. Gluck describes the decision as a heartening step toward "recognition . . . of modern statutory complexity" (64), a recognition Gluck had advocated in previous work.[3] Like Strauss, she describes the Court's activity during the term as confirming the utility of her suggested approach, which involves looking beyond the text of statutes to the institutional activities surrounding their drafting and enactment, in order to understand how they should properly be implemented.

Richard Fallon's response to Strauss's Foreword likewise draws on Strauss's piece as support for a theory about the kind of "meaning" judges should seek, one that Fallon has advocated elsewhere (Fallon 2015a, 2015b). Richard Posner's response to Gluck's comment similarly describes *King v. Burwell* as support for Judge Posner's account of statutory interpretation, which he describes as a "natural, instinctive, and unsystematized . . . activity" (Posner 2015, 15), not a theoretical one, as Gluck sometimes seems to suggest (Gluck 2015, 111). Judge Posner questions the "'complexifying'" of law by "judges and law professors," and particularly their generation of "rules" for interpretation of legal texts (Posner 2015, 14).

Although these commentators all address some aspect of the justices' activity in interpreting either statutory or constitutional language, the commentators seem to take a variety of positions on that activity. Posner's argument, in particular, draws on a familiar tradition, one implicitly critical of the kind of work done by Strauss, Gluck, and Fallon. Recent versions of this argument cast U.S. legal scholarship and legal education as impractical, self-indulgent (on the part of professors and administrators), and heedless of students' and professionals' needs (see, e.g., Posner 2016; but see Scalia 1982). Despite the popularity of this critique, much of law professors' and their students' ostensibly scholarly writing, in fact, directly addresses lawyers and judges, making fairly specific recommendations to them (cf. Newton 2012). This kind of legal–academic writing identifies conflicts between legal rules, proposes legal arguments for their resolution, and explains how to handle specific kinds of situations using legal, rather than academic, reasoning.

The three remaining professor-authored pieces in the 2014-term Harvard survey are of this kind. One is the comment on *Zivotofsky v. Kerry* by Jack Goldsmith, a Harvard law professor who worked in the George W. Bush White House. *Zivotofsky* required the Court to decide the relative authority of the federal executive branch and Congress on the question of Jerusalem's status vis-à-vis Israel. The Court concluded mostly in favor of the executive branch; although the Court's conclusion is complex and qualified, Goldsmith anticipates that lawyers advising the President are likely to "construe *Zivotofsky*['s] . . . holding dicta, and ambiguities in the President's favor" (2015, 134) and describes several specific settings in which they might do so (136–45). Significant parts of his comment provide guides for practicing lawyers' use of the *Zivotofsky* decision.

Kenji Yoshino's comment on *Obergefell* is similar. Written in the analytical style of an appellate brief, the comment presents the *Obergefell* majority opinion as offering a new approach to identifying fundamental rights, superseding the approach established in the Court's 1997 *Washington v. Glucksberg* decision (2015, 151–64). Yoshino calls the new approach "antisubordination liberty" (174) and packs his comment with common-law-style synthesis of authority to support this characterization of the decision.[4] Like Goldsmith's comment, Yoshino's is a resource and guide for practitioners as well as a scholarly assessment. Laurence Tribe's reply to Yoshino's piece is similar. Tribe describes the legal pedigree of "dignity" as a protectable right, both worldwide and in Justice Kennedy's previous opinions (2015, 19–23). Like Yoshino (and Strauss), Tribe argues that *Obergefell* was a conventional legal decision, conventionally justifiable. Both Yoshino and Tribe rebut criticism of the *Obergefell* majority opinion as unlawlike and unjudicial by demonstrating, and not just stating, the consistency of the opinion with legal-justification conventions.

Between them, these seven pieces address a small subset of the term's opinions. Strauss (2015) mentions a handful of decisions from the 2014 term other than *Obergefell*[5] but devotes more than a few words to only one—*Ariz. State Legislature v. Ariz. Independent Redistricting Commission* (discussed below in Chapter 4.2.2.2).[6] Gluck likewise cites a few 2014-term opinions besides *King v. Burwell*[7] but discusses at length just one, *Yates v. United States* (discussed in Chapter 2.4.3).[8] Tribe cites only two 2014-term cases aside from *Obergefell*.[9] Goldsmith, Yoshino, and Posner mention no cases other than those on which they respectively focus, and Fallon does not mention any cases from the term by name at all.

The professors' accounts thus offer a limited view of the Court's output over the year. Among the cases about which the professors say little or nothing are several that have had important implications for federal criminal sentencing (*Johnson v. United States*), for city sign regulations (*Reed v. Town of Gilbert*), and for police practices (*Heien v. North Carolina*), to name just a few examples. Some of the gaps in coverage are filled by student notes (discussed in the next section) and the "Statistics" included in the same issue (discussed in section 1.3.1). But those materials do not supply a comprehensive survey either.

There are other gaps in the professors' contributions. The professors cite support for many of the legal, historical, political, and moral assertions in their pieces.[10] They are less scrupulous about supporting other kinds of assertions, including assertions about matters of language, meaning, and communication. Yet such matters are central to many if not most of the arguments in the professors' pieces, including Strauss's Foreword, whose title declares this centrality: "Does the Constitution Mean What It Says?"

Strauss answers that question, "not always." He explains this counterintuitive conclusion by pointing out a number of legal conventions that are inconsistent with the law we would have "[i]f we read the text of the Constitution in a straightforward way" (5). Fallon notes, accurately, that Strauss's argument depends on "somewhat casual references to ordinary, natural, and straightforward meaning" (Fallon 2015b, 5) and offers a more structured account of several varieties of meaning that, he argues, judges and lawyers should treat differently (10). But Fallon does not do much more than identify these categories; his piece suggests that, once they are distinguished, the appropriate treatment of each kind of meaning will be evident. Judge Posner, in turn, seems to criticize approaches of this kind: according to him, the "elaborate conceptual structure that has arisen [within legal doctrine] to enable meaning to be assigned to . . . statutory provisions" is unnecessary (Posner 2015, 14); "[c]onfronted with a novel issue to resolve, one [i.e., a judge] often will have an intuitive, even an unconscious response" (15). Strauss makes a similar point when he suggests that it will often be clear to everyone what the Constitution "says." Goldsmith likewise contends that "[w]e can be sure" how lawyers in the Office of Legal Counsel will use the *Zivotofsky* decision (Goldsmith 2015, 136).

This book calls such a view of lawyers' unparalleled facility with language and insight into its uses the "wordsmith's fallacy." It is, the book suggests, a kind of cognitive bias common to legal professionals in the contemporary United States. It emerges from the interaction of several well-studied cognitive biases—such as the overconfidence effect (Oscamp 1965), the illusion of control (Langer 1975), "functional fixedness" (e.g., Adamson 1952), the "curse of knowledge" (Camerer et al. 1989), and the bias blind spot (Pronin et al. 2002)[11]—with the following beliefs and commitments, among others:

- An awareness that most legal practices involve language use and arguments about language use (e.g., the meaning of language in a statute, the legal effect of everyday communications).
- An awareness that, beyond this, legal professionals—especially judges—may have the power to decide what particular verbal formulations are going to "mean" for nonprofessionals, that is, that legal power includes a power over the practical consequences of certain choices of language (cf. Putnam 1975).
- An awareness that competent legal professionals usually communicate with one another successfully, including in arguments about language meaning and use.
- And a conviction that, as a result, legal professionals are unusually skilled at analyzing the operation and effects of language (cf. Galanter 2005, 31–63; Mellinkoff 1963).

The fallacy is committed when a legal analyst assumes that a legal perspective is a uniquely privileged perspective on the structure and working of linguistic communication, or that lawyers' conventional ways of analyzing matters of language can be improved upon only at the margins. It is visible when a lawyer's argument presupposes that legal materials, together with lawyers' professionally honed intuition and a bit of reflection, provide all that is needed to understand every feature of language use worth noticing. Historically, the fallacy has been abetted by the late twentieth-century flowering of legal instruction on statutory and constitutional interpretation (e.g., Manning 2017) and the attention given to these matters by an increasing number of judges, developments to which this book will repeatedly return.

A couple of decades ago, Lawrence Solan diagnosed a related phenomenon in judicial discourse in his linguistic study of *The Language of Judges* (1993). Solan concluded that "linguistic principles frequently do not operate as the courts say they do" (29) but that judges are "under pressure to sound authoritative," leading them "to create the illusion that interpretation of language is more definitive than it really is" (134). The 2015 Harvard survey shows law professors succumbing to a similar temptation. The phenomenon does not prevent academics (like Strauss, Gluck, and Fallon) from proposing incremental changes in the ways lawyers think of and use language, but it does limit the kinds of insight and recommendations they provide.

As noted in the previous section, although this book focuses on a single Supreme Court term, the implications of the discussion are much broader. The professors' pieces and the justices' opinions do not just display the wordsmith's fallacy; both opinions and commentary also perpetuate it powerfully. Some *Harvard Law Review* Forewords have shaped the terms of legal-academic debate for decades. (Chapter 5.4 will explore the implications for the 2014-term opinions of a Foreword from 1983.)

This "shaping" can be literal: the structure of the professors' pieces, especially those addressed to practitioners, echoes that of the justices' opinions. The professors also echo the justices' characterization of the opinions as linguistic performances. Goldsmith (2015), for example, describes the *Zivotofsky* majority opinion as an unfolding "story" of justification (e.g., 118). "Knowing how the play ends," he writes, "the Court finally glanced at Article I [of the Constitution] on the last page of its opinion" (127). Judges also often liken judicial reasoning to storytelling, as in the following passage from Justice Scalia's dissent in *Williams-Yulee v. Florida Bar*, a 2014-term case addressing whether candidates for judicial election could be disciplined for soliciting donations to their campaigns:

> As its opinion unfolds . . ., [the majority's] concept of judicial integrity turns out to be "a mere thing of wax in the hands of the judiciary, which they may twist, and shape into any form they please." . . . When the Court explains how [judicial candidates'] solicitation [of campaign donations] undermines confidence in judicial integrity, integrity starts to sound like saintliness. . . . When the Court turns to distinguishing in-person solicitation from solicitation by proxy, the any-possible-temptation standard no longer helps and thus drops out. The critical factors instead become the "pressure" a listener feels during a solicitation and the "appearance that the candidate will remember who says yes, and who says no." . . . This is not strict scrutiny; it is sleight of hand.
>
> (Scalia, 4–5)

Another trope common to judicial and academic writing presents the judicial opinion not as a story, but as a character. Yoshino writes, for example, that *Obergefell*:

> made explicit what had remained implicit in *Glucksberg* [an important precedent] by invoking *Poe* [another precedent] directly. In doing so, it indicated that it was departing from the *Glucksberg* approach (though it waited until later in its analysis to raise *Glucksberg* directly).
>
> (Yoshino 2015, 163)

In this account, the opinion itself makes decisions and waits for the right moment to announce them. To a legal reader, this presentation is unlikely to seem strange. Indeed, the notion that opinions are agents, in a sense, is a central premise of much of the student writing considered in the next section.

1.2.2 The students: opinions as instruments

The law professors who contributed to the Harvard survey are also (or have been) teachers. Their students look to the professors' writings as models of academic writing and legal communication. Some of the best of the students contribute to the Harvard survey through "notes" on "Leading Cases." Their notes exemplify the kind of precision verbal performance considered excellent in legal education. They display a strikingly instrumentalist perspective on the Court's opinions; the students treat the opinions as tools assessed for their utility. The features of the opinions that students identify as bearing on this utility are mostly linguistic features, and the students generally treat these features as self-evident.

Each of the 20 student notes in the 2014-term survey discusses a single decision from the term in exactly ten pages. Each note also has an identical structure. One paragraph introduces the case the note addresses (only one of the 20 notes does this in two paragraphs). Each note then, clone-like, presents a "background," a "procedural history," a description of the justices' opinions, and an analysis showcasing the student's skill at explaining the relationship of the decision to its legal context and making confident predictions, often along the lines of Goldsmith's forecast of executive-branch lawyers' use of the *Zivotofsky* decision. The notes are a remarkable set of exercises in communicative discipline.

The notes are unsigned, so none makes a plug for the author's theoretical "brand." Rather, almost all of the notes explain how the decision in question could or will be used by judges or counselors in future legal conflicts. Seven of the 20 authors argue that the decisions they address created uncertainty and may be read or used in various ways, of which the note writer usually recommends one.[12] These authors criticize the Court, or particular justices, for creating the possibility of divergent uses of their work product. Of course, the ambiguity the authors find in these decisions gave the authors something to write about; the students had an incentive to seek such ambiguity, and their notes model methods for establishing ambiguity as well as resolving it. Chapter 5 will return to this important legal activity. These student notes also support and promote an understanding of the Court's decisions as tools or instructions for other decision-makers. The notes criticize the Court for producing faulty or incomplete tools; in some cases, the note writers try to repair the shortcoming, that is, to state more clearly the legal significance of the case.

Four other notes focus not just on the rules provided in 2014-term decisions but also on the justices' justifications for those rules. Authors of notes following this model argue that particular opinions insufficiently justify their conclusions or inadequately explain the relationship of a holding to other law.[13] The authors of these notes criticize the Court not for issuing ambiguous pronouncements but for what might be called "incompletely theorized" holdings whose logical and legal premises are not fully spelled out (cf. Sunstein 1995). Authors of another two notes similarly use their analyses to supply justifications that the Court could have, but did not, provide in its decisions.[14] Like the kinds of notes discussed above, these critiques of and proposed alternative rationales for the Court's output treat the decisions as means to an end. The students describe their verbal recommendations as "add[ing] benefit" to the Court's contributions to the law and making those contributions more "impactful" (Note 2015s, 370).

A different student approach points to other potential consequences of the Court's decisions. Three notes focus on the perverse results, beyond simple uncertainty or unpredictability, that some decisions might have.[15] Another three suggest that other decisions might have more positive large-scale effects.[16] Despite their varying evaluations, all of these notes, like all of those mentioned above, assume that the Court's opinions are worth discussing because of the ways they can and will be used in future legal arguments or judicial justifications.[17] With one exception, the notes consider the possible future uses of the Court's decisions by judges, lawyers, legislators, and regulators.[18]

The consistent format of the notes also makes clear the reproducibility of their approach. Not only do they provide models for students at other law schools, but their authors are the legal power players of the future—the large-firm lawyers, law professors, and Supreme

Court clerks of years to come.[19] The notes teach current and future students and professors how to use judicial opinions as tools for the construction of certain standard arguments, both academic and legal, and they teach their writers and readers which aspects of the opinions' presentation it is worthwhile to point out.

The Harvard survey is in many ways the "authoritative annual survey of the Court's leading cases" (Garrow 2004, 64). But as this section has explained, it offers only a partial account of the Court's output during the term. For one thing, it addresses in detail fewer than half of the cases the Court decided by written opinion during the term.[20] The students' consideration of the cases they do analyze is also, as this explanation has sought to show, extraordinarily focused and selective. Other parts of the Harvard survey seem to address other aspects of the Court's activity during the term, but these overviews, as the next section explains, also fail to consider significant aspects of that activity.

1.3 The new old school: terms as units

Since the 1920s, the Harvard survey has included, in addition to discussion of particular cases, an overview of the "Statistics" of the term. On top of this, the 2014-term survey presented a retrospective of these overviews (Lazarus 2015). The acclaimed SCOTUSblog has offered similar quantitative digests of the Court's annual work for more than a decade. This section considers the limitations of these term-wide overviews and their relation to the wordsmith's fallacy.

1.3.1 The statistics, authorship, and content

Before becoming a Harvard professor, Richard Lazarus was a Supreme Court advocate, and he has continued to write about the Court's practices as a scholar. To the 2014-term Harvard survey, he contributed a piece looking back at the periodical's reviews of the Court's work since 1925 (2015, 34 & n.7). Although Lazarus does not stress the point, the main continuity in this nearly century-long history is the quantitative ("statistical") focus of the Harvard overviews. Neither the issue's "Statistics" nor Lazarus's "gloss" (37) on them addresses much of the content of the Court's opinions.

The tradition of Harvard Supreme Court surveys began with an eight-part series published between 1925 and 1927 by then-professors Felix Frankfurter (later a Supreme Court Justice) and James Landis. As Lazarus explains, the early retrospectives "sought . . . to survey the work of the Court from its early years to the present," that is, the 1920s (34 n.7). They included tables of figures showing such things as the increases in the size of the Court's docket that led to successive congressional restructurings of the federal judicial system in the nineteenth and early twentieth centuries. After bringing their account up to the then-present day, Frankfurter and Landis launched a series of annual articles "reviewing the Court's statistics" (Lazarus 2015, 34 n.7; Frankfurter & Landis 1928). Until the early 1970s, these tables of figures (first called "The Statistics" in 1971) appeared at the beginning of the survey issue, rather than (as now) following the professor and student pieces (Lazarus 2015, 36–37).[21]

Lazarus frames his contribution to the 2014-term survey as, in part, resurrecting a vanished practice: he proposes to "add some analytical gloss to the current *Review*'s un-Frankfurter-like practice of providing bare statistical tables without also gleaning 'a deal of the tale' that a plumbing of these numbers could tell" (Lazarus 2015, 37). The tale Lazarus reads from the 2014-term statistics concerns Chief Justice Roberts's approach to assigning opinion-writing duties among the justices, an approach Lazarus describes as revealing the Chief Justice's attitude toward his institutional role.

Lazarus explains that as of the 2014 term, the practice seemed to be for the Chief Justice to assign each opinion to a justice voting with the majority on that case when the justices vote informally about its disposition at conference (38–39 & n.40, 45–46). Over time, Lazarus finds, Chief Justices have apparently striven for "greater parity in the number of opinion assignments that each Justice receives" (41), and Chief Justice Roberts has achieved this goal more successfully than any of his predecessors (46–47). But his assignments do not seem random. Lazarus concludes that the Chief Justice "assign[s] the more high-profile and . . . closely divided cases disproportionately to certain favored Justices, including himself, with little regard to seniority," and "place[s] a premium on opinion writers who can write more narrowly" (47).[22]

Lazarus concludes with 17 tables of figures supporting these hypotheses.[23] Lazarus also ventures more substantive explanations for the tendencies the numbers suggest. For example, he proposes that Chief Justice Roberts assigns high-profile cases more often to Justice Alito than to Justice Scalia because "Justice Alito has . . . displayed a willingness, unlike Justice Scalia, to carve the more middle-ground, less absolute positions that the Chief favors" (2015, 60). In support of this claim, Lazarus offers the following footnote:

> For example, the Chief assigned Justice Alito the plurality opinion in *Hein v. Freedom from Religion Foundation, Inc.* . . . (2007), a significant taxpayer-standing opinion that Justice Scalia harshly criticized for exhibiting "minimalism." *See id.* at 633 (Scalia, J., concurring in the judgment) ("Minimalism is an admirable judicial trait, but not when it comes at the cost of meaningless and disingenuous decisions. . . .").
>
> (60 n.163)

Elsewhere in his piece, Lazarus similarly draws on justices' assertions about opinion content and style as a kind of "evidence" (see 56, 59, 61, 62, 65–69). Although Lazarus's study *appears* to consider characteristics of judicial language in such discussions, he gets his information about that language from the justices' own account of it. Very much like the student note writers, he treats the opinions as containing ready-made analysis of the justices' discursive habits, analysis provided by the justices themselves. His independent analysis of those habits is limited.

The figures Lazarus presents, like most of the annual "Statistics," also concern features of the Court's opinions other than their language. None of his 12 tables presents information about the *content* of the Court's output, with the possible exception of the final table, a breakdown of the subject matter of the term's cases.[24] That table displays the number of cases in each of 60 categories and tallies the number of decisions "for" and "against" the government, in cases where the government was a party. To compile these statistics, neither Lazarus nor the *Law Review*'s editors needed to read the opinions—they just needed to count pages, record the alignment of justices (information available at the end of the Syllabus that opens each slip opinion), and note the origins, disposition, and general subject of each case (also available in the Syllabus).

The *Law Review*'s "Statistics" look comprehensive—indeed, six of the tables record Court activity that did not involve issuing opinions with any content—but they do not provide a complete picture of the term. The "Statistics" treat the language in the opinions as largely invisible, suggesting that it is either immaterial to or not suited for large-scale analysis and evaluation. The "Statistics" also do not include any information about two sets of opinions issued by the Court during the term and appearing among the slip opinions on the Court's website; these opinions decided cases arising within the Court's original jurisdiction, rather than in review of lower-court decisions. One set of such opinions, in the interstate water dispute *Kansas v. Nebraska*, is 67 pages long; it is a more substantial written product than the opinions issued in many other cases addressed by the "Statistics."

Lazarus explains his "analytical gloss" on the term as correcting for the assumption that the "Statistics" speak for themselves. But Lazarus also treats the language in the Justices' opinions as if it *does* speak for itself. The frame in which he places his statistics does not, in the end, inform us about, but rather depends on assumptions about, how the justices present their conclusions in prose. In this way, Lazarus too succumbs to the wordsmith's fallacy. As the next section will explain, this fallacy seems to be a professional and not just an academic phenomenon.

1.3.2 SCOTUSblog and professional accounts of the term

Launched in 2002, the award-winning SCOTUSblog now vies with the *Harvard Law Review* for the title of highest-profile, most authoritative coverage of the Supreme Court. SCOTUSblog offers commentary throughout each term on cases the Court might review, oral arguments, and the Court's opinions, and like the *Law Review*, it offers statistical overviews at the end of each term. The blog is an essential resource for anyone researching a particular case. It offers free access to material, such as amicus briefs, that affects the content of the justices' written opinions. SCOTUSblog is in many respects far more comprehensive than the Harvard survey.[25] But it too tells only part of the story of each term.

One of the blog's founders, Supreme Court advocate Tom Goldstein, has been generating summaries of Court activity since 1995. These summaries migrated to the blog when it went online in 2002 and are now available as downloadable "Stat Packs." The Stat Pack for the 2014 Term is 52 pages long, but for each opinion, it records minimal information: authoring justice, outcome, and extent of the Court's agreement with other justices and lower courts. While the Stat Pack does collect information not included in the *Harvard Law Review*'s "Statistics" or Lazarus's augmentation, such as the number of opinion pages produced by each justice, it treats all pages as interchangeable.[26] SCOTUSblog's statistics do not tell us, for example, whether particular justices tend to specialize in writing opinions addressing particular areas of law, or the extent and nature of any common ground between justices that we might consider ideologically opposed.

To a limited extent, the commentary appearing on SCOTUSblog addresses these matters. The site includes a page for every case decided by the Court during the term, not just the 28 addressed in the *Law Review*. Each page contains links to copies of all of the briefs filed with the Court, copies of the lower-court decisions in the case, transcripts of oral arguments when they become available, and some commentary. SCOTUSblog also presents significantly more commentary from practicing lawyers than does the Harvard survey. Two out of six "symposia" the blog hosted on 2014-term cases featured contributions from a greater number of practitioners than academics.[27] And the commentary reflects the blog's less academic orientation; even the academics' contributions are footnote-free and more journalistic than scholarly or even legal in tone.

Still, most of the commentary broadly resembles the student notes in the Harvard survey. Many contributors move quickly and confidently from observations about linguistic or rhetorical features of the justices' opinions to conclusions about the moral or legal implications of those features. In a comment on *Obergefell*, for example, Michael Dorf, a professor at

Cornell's law school, responds to Justice Scalia's scathing attack on Justice Kennedy's prose (part of which is quoted in the first section of this chapter). Dorf (2015) calls the opening sentence of Justice Scalia's dissent "perhaps the most intemperate line in the U.S. Reports" and notes that Justice Scalia has a habit of using language just as extreme as the language he "mocks" in the *Obergefell* majority opinion. In fact, Dorf suggests, Justice Kennedy's rhetoric in *Obergefell* was admirable: even if his "style . . . sometimes bordered on poetry," "Justice Kennedy's opinion fittingly solemnized the occasion." Dorf seems to agree with Justice Scalia that Justice Kennedy's *Obergefell* opinion was an atypical piece of judicial writing; Dorf simply evaluates the opinion positively rather than negatively. But he does not explain in what sense Justice Kennedy's opinion "bordered on poetry" or what its style teaches lawyers about acceptable ways of discussing rights in legal writing. Dorf takes the opinion's departure from the conventions of legal discourse to be self-evident.

Another contributor to the *Obergefell* symposium was Judith Schaeffer, vice president of a progressive legal think tank. Schaeffer also defends Justice Kennedy's opinion, but she defends it from the criticisms issued by Chief Justice Roberts rather than by Justice Scalia. The title of her comment, "The Constitution has everything to do with it," responds directly to the last lines of the Chief Justice's dissent, which read, "If you are among the many Americans . . . who favor expanding same-sex marriage, by all means celebrate today's decision. . . . But do not celebrate the Constitution. It had nothing to do with it" (*Obergefell*, Roberts, 29). According to Schaeffer, it is Chief Justice Roberts who misunderstood—or willfully misread—the relevant legal authority in his *Obergefell* dissent: "it was clear from Roberts's [2005] confirmation hearing that he correctly understood the proper [legal] analysis applicable to a case involving the fundamental right to marry" (Schaeffer 2015). In *Obergefell*, Schaeffer explains, inconsistently with that testimony, "Roberts premised his dissent on the erroneous assumption that the 'definition of marriage' was at issue, rather than the application of fundamental [constitutional] principles." Justice Kennedy's opinion is praiseworthy, she suggests, because its conclusions are indeed consistent with precedent, including precedent that Chief Justice Roberts himself endorsed. Schaeffer's discussion presupposes that the justices' statements and writings offer straightforward access to the justices' convictions, and that their words are important mainly because they offer such access.

The wordsmith's fallacy has a strong hold on contemporary U.S. legal education and practice; the justices' opinions model and reinforce it. The following pages will consider some possible causes and consequences of this phenomenon. They will also show that the 2014-term opinions contain a great deal of information about the justices' linguistic practices and understandings of their role that tends to go unremarked.

1.4 A fresh look at opinion content

Like the Harvard and SCOTUSblog surveys, the following chapters are sensitive to the ways lawyers would read the 2014-term opinions (and the ways law professors might teach students to read them). But these chapters are also sensitive to features of the opinions' content that lawyers and law students are not trained to notice. This approach starts from a premise that is also basic to the Harvard and SCOTUSblog overviews: we can learn important things from a body of texts that we might not see were we to consider the writings separately. Unlike those overviews, however, it looks carefully at the content of the term's opinions. "Content" here just means the words in the justices' opinions—including both linguistic form and the informational, logical, and rhetorical import of the justices' language. To the intensive discussions of the Harvard survey and the quantitative overview of the "Statistics" and Stat Pack, this book adds a third model for reading a term, one attentive to the linguistic regularities in the justices' opinions and alert to the potential significance of those regularities for the opinions' readers—including the ways the regularities might structure readers' assumptions and expectations beneath readers' conscious awareness.

The next two sections explain the importance of opinion content, and the approach to be taken in later chapters, in more detail. The first section considers some of the ways opinion content shapes what legal theorists call the "internal" point of view—the perspective of legal practitioners—and previous accounts of U.S. lawyers' relationship with language. The following section reviews major theoretical accounts of legal discourse from the past several decades, by legal academics and others, which this book builds on and extends.

1.4.1 Why content matters

The words and sentences that make up judicial opinions matter because, for one thing, opinion content is often the content of the law. Opinions can also be read as Judith Schaeffer read Chief Justice Roberts's confirmation testimony, as records of their authors' beliefs and commitments. Reading them carefully can thus help scholars and practitioners predict judges' future behavior. Beyond this, however, opinion content—like all language use—also affects those who generate and consume it. Lawyers and legal scholars are attuned to some of the effects of language on its readers, to be sure, but they are unaccustomed to discussing that attunement systematically; to the extent law students are trained to consider this aspect of language, they are usually trained to rely on rhetorical intuition. Seeing and discussing these effects on readers of legal language requires a shift to a partly "external" perspective and a suspension of the assumption that lawyers understand language uniquely well because their job is to use and manipulate it. This section explores some of these familiar and unfamiliar understandings of the content of judicial opinions.

The most obvious reason that the content of judicial opinions matters is that this content often has direct legal effect (e.g., Mertz 2007, 25; Schauer 1995). In the 2014-term opinions, the justices do often show awareness of the potential legal import of their words. Sometimes they express concern about the possible future uses of a colleague's language. Justice Scalia's *Obergefell* dissent, quoted at the beginning of this chapter, is an example. Justice Alito offers another in his dissent in the 2014-term case *Brumfield v. Cain*, which concerned the standards for showing that a criminal defendant has the level of "intellectual disability" making it unconstitutional, under the Court's precedent, to sentence the defendant to death. Criticizing the content of Justice Thomas's dissent, which had recounted the life story of the woman killed by the defendant and her family, Justice Alito observes,

> The story recounted in that Part [of Justice Thomas's dissent] is inspiring and will serve a very beneficial purpose if widely read, but I do not want to suggest that it is essential to the legal analysis in this case.
>
> (*Brumfield*, Alito, 1)

With this remark, Justice Alito acknowledges the potential import of any justice's words and tries to undercut it with respect to part of his colleague's opinion.

Judges also use their opinions to supply models of legal language to other lawmakers. Justice Alito's concurring opinion in the 2014-term case *Reed v. Town of Gilbert*, along these lines, includes a list of sample sign-posting restrictions that municipal governments could adopt without fear of constitutional challenge (Alito, 1–2). Most of the student authors in the Harvard survey treat the opinions in a similar way, as legal raw material. The note authors recognize that subsequent lawyers, judges, and lawmakers will recontextualize that material and may transform it, but that the justices' linguistic presentation of their opinions will constrain such transformations (cf. Tiersma 2013).

In a few areas, academics have considered how judicial opinions reflect patterned language practices and may have systemic effects. Some of these scholars have studied the content of groups of opinions. Political scientists, for example, have examined the effect of briefing by parties and amici on Supreme Court opinion content (e.g., Corley 2008; Kearney & Merrill 2000; Spriggs & Wahlbeck 1997). Comparing the content of briefs and opinions across cases, these studies show that some justices borrow language from briefs more than other justices do (Corley 2008, 473), and that some kinds of briefs tend to contribute more language to opinions than others (476). Opinion content is, then, in some cases generated not by justices, their clerks, or previous judges, but by parties and their lawyers (469). But the content of briefs is in turn shaped by their drafters' legal education—by how they learned to read and write legal analyses as students and novice practitioners. Much of that education focuses on reading judicial opinions and internalizing the models of analysis those opinions supply.[28] Studies of sources of opinion content do not examine those models.

The political scientists and legal scholars who study the sources of opinion content tend to share a set of assumptions with a long pedigree in U.S. legal scholarship. The legal realists of the early twentieth century initiated a school of thought that continues to influence legal education, as well as public and academic discourse about the courts. The realist perspective (1) doubts that the reasons a judge offers in an opinion to justify a decision exactly match the "real" reasons for the decision; (2) considers other factors, usually psychological and ideological, that might have a better claim to be "real" reasons; and (3) infers from the mismatch between stated reasons (opinion content) and postulated real reasons that the judge writing the opinion could have decided otherwise and therefore that the legal principles cited by the writing judge lack the compelling force the judge ascribes to them (see, e.g., Cohen 1935; see also Baum 2006). This understanding of judicial activity has broad implications, not only for judicial and legal practice, but also for scholarship. The realists' perspective casts the contents of opinions—the reasons judges provide for their conclusions—as untrustworthy or even deceptive. And this view also contributes to the wordsmith's fallacy. By discounting the significance of opinion content, it encourages analysts to look elsewhere for useful information. And by training readers to "see through" the judges' stated reasons, it encourages in those readers a sense of control over their own processing of judicial language.

Despite the skepticism fostered by this perspective, lawyers and law professors still take the language appearing in judicial opinions to be meaningful and to tell readers something about the opinions' authors. Legally trained readers are aware that the justice whose name appears at the beginning of an opinion was probably not personally responsible for all of the contents of the opinion.[29] But lawyers pay attention all the same to the language of the justices' opinions (as do the justices themselves). Lawyers often take the language of an opinion to indicate the authoring judge's commitments, as Judith Schaeffer did in her commentary on Chief Justice Roberts's *Obergefell* dissent.

In law school, students learn to read judicial opinions in both of these ways: with skepticism about the sincerity of opinion language, on the one hand, and on the assumption that the language indicates its authors' commitments, on the other. Self-awareness about the ability to perform this kind of skeptical-and-credulous reading can deepen a reader's sense of control over the language the reader is alternately believing and disbelieving. The skill and the self-awareness are manifestations of a specific relationship to language, and to judicial opinions in particular, that U.S. legal education cultivates in lawyers-in-training. In her ethnography of U.S. legal education, Elizabeth Mertz (2007) explains how this education, a kind of "socialization" (21–22), turns largely on reorienting students' "approach [to] written legal texts" (4–5). Students learn the law mostly by reading edited judicial opinions and discussing their implications in class. This process creates "a new relationship . . . for legal readers with language and text" (95). The familiar description of legal education as training in how to "think like a lawyer," Mertz explains, "glosses over the degree to which what is changing is as much how students read and talk as how they think" (98). The "linguistic ideology" of law, she concludes, plays a "central role . . . in law school socialization" (215).

Mertz argues that most law students start their education with a "referentialist" view of language, an "ideology [that] . . . views written texts as . . . carrying determinate meaning that inheres in the written words themselves" (46). Law school, she explains, "pulls students away from referentialist approaches, which treat the text as transparent and view its core meaning as its referential content" (94). Students' new relationship with language involves, first, detachment; they "learn a style of reading that filters and frames the story of the case in a new way" (59). Students learn new ways of categorizing events and objects, according to a "legal logic [that] defies common everyday understandings" (64). This detachment and decontextualization enables the skepticism and eventually the self-awareness mentioned above.

Law students' new relationship with language also involves acquiring "metalinguistic" skills (59, 83, 88–89, 110, 135). Students learn to "decipher[]" "authority . . . [by] unpacking metalinguistic connections among legal texts and authors" (59). They learn to read in a way that

> runs events as well as social and moral concerns through a complex filter structured around the interrelation of precedential texts, text-based analogies, repetition of key phrases and terms from text to text, and layers of legal authority related through and in layered legal texts.
>
> (83)

Legal education continuously reiterates this "metalinguistic emphasis on language forms as the actual source of epistemological certainty" (110). Describing a phenomenon akin to the wordsmith's fallacy, Mertz notes that the linguistic ideology inculcated in law school "can easily lend itself to a form of methodological arrogance, in which . . . practitioners feel themselves able to master any material with which they are presented by running it through a legal reading" (219).

This book substantiates and builds on Mertz's conclusions, investigating how the language of the 2014-term opinions, some of which have already been incorporated into legal educational material, documents and reinforces the linguistic ideology Mertz identifies. This book also considers the possibility that Mertz's account might have some blind spots. She focuses primarily on students' classroom experiences, not their silent, private encounters with text, and she describes the linguistic ideology instilled in law students as tending to displace a "referentialist" understanding of a more stable relation between language and the world. The following pages will explain how legal language also *preserves* a referentialist understanding—and not just at its peripheries. As suggested earlier in this section, being able to maneuver between referentialist and metalinguistic perspectives on language—or to assume both perspectives at once—is an important legal skill, although neither law professors nor lawyers are in the habit of considering or discussing it explicitly.

Reading the 2014-term opinions can help to clarify these points. The opinions provide lessons in the kind of metalinguistic performance described by Mertz, including lessons in how to present different kinds of information, how to make arguments about the meaning of language, and how to construct an argument that a judge can accept as sound. Precisely because law students and lawyers are unlikely to read all of any given term's opinions, or even to hear of many of them, those readers learn that any features shared by opinions across subject-matter areas are both so basic as to be required components of legal communication and so uncontroversial that there is no point in paying critical attention to them. By redirecting attention to these features, this book seeks to reveal important patterns in legal discourse—some of them positive, others troubling—that are difficult to see in ordinary classroom or practice settings.

Mertz conducted the research for her book in the 1990s, and her book appeared in 2007. Since then, legal education has been in turmoil; tuition rates have risen and enrollment has fallen, and educators have scrambled to respond (see, e.g., Tamanaha 2012). It is possible that the practices Mertz describes will disappear within another decade. More likely, however, they will change only slightly. Criticism of legal education is decades old (see Spencer 2012), yet organizational and curricular change in law schools has been very slow. Most schools still offer a mandatory first-year curriculum that has been mostly fixed since the early twentieth century (see Gordon 2007), along with a core set of upper-level electives addressing subjects covered on bar exams or recommended for students with particular interests. The format of instructional materials has been equally slow to change. A few law-textbook authors have adopted a problem-based format, but most textbooks still consist mostly of edited opinions from appellate courts, especially the Supreme Court, and synopses of other decisions in "notes." So Mertz's account is still largely accurate and is likely to remain so indefinitely; law students at schools across the U.S. have a mostly uniform educational experience and learn a uniform vocabulary. That vocabulary includes the elements Mertz describes, but also more specific patterns of presentation common to the justices' (and other judges') opinions and explored throughout the following chapters.

1.4.2 What kind of content? Language, ontology, mind

> The single most useful tool of judicial certitude involves the deliberate conflation or, sometimes, confusion of the actual world as a source of representation with the world represented in the text.
>
> (Ferguson 1990, 211)

This book is not the first examination of the content of judicial opinions from a partly "external" perspective.[30] Over the past half-century, scholars have suggested a variety of models for considering the content of judicial opinions, often borrowing from the study of related issues in other disciplines: how people process written exposition and narrative; how language is related to its users, on the one hand, and their environment, on the other; and how language creates a "reality" of its own. As the sentence above from Robert Ferguson's essay "The Judicial Opinion as Literary Genre" suggests, legal language practices often capitalize on readers' preexisting habits and on the "actual world" that legal conventions create. This book builds on the insights of Ferguson and a number of other scholars concerned with these issues. Reviewing some of the landmarks in this tradition, this section focuses on work from three disciplinary streams: literary criticism and theory, Anglo-American philosophy, and psychology and cognitive science.

The law-and-literature tradition, largely launched by the work of James Boyd White (1973), likens judicial opinions to poems, orations, or novelistic installments (see White 1973; see also Dworkin 1986; Ferguson 1990). Work in this tradition often examines extended textual patterns, rather than the smaller bits of content (words, phrases, or propositions) typically studied by linguists and philosophers. But traditionally, law-and-literature scholarship has not closely examined issues of reference, that is, how language "hooks up" with the world and its readers. Although some *literary* scholars have examined the relationship between the referents of literary texts and the referents of nonliterary texts (e.g., Gallagher 2018; Pavel 1994; Ronen 1994), their work remains mostly unknown to legal audiences, even though it is highly relevant to legal practices.

Instead, the main source of insight for those interested in the semantics of legal texts has been the philosophy of language developed in the Anglo-American academy over the past half-century. This work, produced by scholars such as Michael Moore (1980), Ronald Dworkin (1986), and others (see Marmor & Soames 2011), has generated some sustained discussions among legal theorists. But most of these discussions have addressed issues in a fairly narrow slice of the philosophical tradition, marked out by the work of H.L.A. Hart (1961) in legal theory, on the one hand, and of H. Paul Grice (1984) in the philosophy of language, on the other. Another stream of philosophical work, less often discussed in legal circles (but see Doerfler 2017), speaks more clearly to the concerns voiced by Ferguson about the conflation of textual and actual "worlds": this tradition, which spans the philosophy of language and metaphysics, has investigated the properties and implications of fictional discourse, or discourse about nonexistent things. Chapter 2 introduces some of this work, and subsequent chapters explore it further.

The dominant philosophical approaches to legal language have also tended not to address how legal language interacts with (and may be limited by) the capacities of the people who generate and use it: lawyers, judges, and law students, as well as, to a lesser degree, members of the public. This relation between legal discourse and its users has, however, received attention from a handful of scholars who have examined what might be called the cognitive linguistics of law, including Anthony Amsterdam and Jerome Bruner (2000) and Steven Winter (2003). This work offers a far more detailed account of the mechanisms behind the human generation of meaning than does either literary theory or philosophy. But this work has focused mainly on how legal language reflects writers' and readers' biological and cultural limitations, rather than on how that language shapes its users' minds. Indeed, by treating language mainly as a vehicle for concepts, rather than an environmental feature in its own right, some work in this vein displays the same referentialist bias Mertz describes as characteristic of American nonlegal culture.

The perspective taken in the following chapters draws on all three of these traditions: literary-theoretical, philosophical, and cognitive-scientific. In particular, it seeks to show how recent work bridging these disciplines supports new perspectives on judicial discourse in general and the content of the 2014-term opinions in particular. The rest of this section reviews some of the basic insights of traditional law-and-literature, legal philosophical, and cognitive-science scholarship underlying the discussions in the chapters that follow. Readers familiar with work in these fields might wish to skip ahead to section 1.5.

1.4.2.1 Law and literature

James Boyd White's *The Legal Imagination* (1973) inaugurated the modern study of law and literature and anticipated Mertz in several ways. "[A] legal education," White writes, "could be defined by saying one learns to read and write the professional language of the law, to master a set of special ways of thinking and talking" (xxi). White himself uses language to stimulate his readers' imaginations, more than to argue for any specific theoretical position. His exploration of the "professional language of the law" has the dichotomous form common to literary criticism of the 1960s, '70s, and '80s. The contrasts he emphasizes include those between fiction and reality[31] and between "narrative and theory" (244), which he also describes as a contrast between "story" and "reasons" (243).

As the title of White's book suggests, the contrast that concerns him most is that between "reality" and "imagination." White encourages his readers to appreciate the role of both forms of experience in legal practice: "Can these tensions between story and theory, fact and fiction, particular and general, and so on," he asks, "be regarded in more general terms, as instances of a conflict . . . between the demands of reality and those of the imagination?" (268). White conceives of the "imagination" psychologically, to some extent, but his psychology is a folk psychology, not a rigorous functional description of the imagination. In his account, imagination has something to do with personal experience, inventiveness,[32] and empathy,[33] but it is not clear whether, for White, "imagination" is a phenomenological state, a modality of communication, or a capacity for action. The relation of imagination to pretense and authenticity is also ambiguous in his account. Imagination, he suggests, allows indirect access to truth and justice through a kind of imaginative detour (208).

Robert Ferguson's much-cited 1990 essay reaches similar conclusions, although Ferguson's tone is less optimistic. Like White, Ferguson stresses the importance of narrative in legal discourse:

> The courtroom . . . takes the complexity of event—the original disruption that provokes legal action . . . —and transfers aspects of that complexity into a narrative, the written form of which is a literal transcript of what has been said. The judicial opinion then appropriates, molds, and condenses that transcript in a far more cohesive narrative of judgment. . . .
>
> (211)

Ferguson's overall emphasis is on the severe constraints of the opinion form, which uses and promotes what he calls "the rhetoric of inevitability" (204). This rhetoric relies on the "monologic voice" of the judge as oracle or insurer of meaning (206). And it is inimical to the acknowledged use of imagination in White's sense: Ferguson notes, "The one thing a judge never admits in the moment of decision is freedom of choice" (206–07). Ferguson's account remains accurate and compelling. As this book will show, today's justices still use the techniques Ferguson described 25 years earlier (in an essay about judicial opinions from the 1940s).[34] But Ferguson's focus on common features of the opinion form and on constitutional-law decisions means that he pays little attention to the microstructural alternatives within the genre for achieving the ends he identifies.

Much subsequent scholarship addressing the language of law in general and judging in particular has, like Ferguson, adopted a rhetorical approach or, like White, emphasized the dependence of legal discourse on "stories" (Weisberg 2016, 2). Illustrative of the rhetorical perspective is the recent crop of responses to the work of Philip Bobbitt (1982) on the "modalities" of constitutional argument (see, e.g., Balkin 2011; Greene 2013). This work emphasizes the "rhetorical regularities" (Levinson 1996, 191) making up the conventions of legal argument about constitutional meaning. Like Ferguson's essay, this work tends to treat judicial opinions addressing constitutional-law issues as a genre (or genres) unto themselves, that is, as forms perpetuating a limited set of law-specific rhetorical traditions, rather than as devices requiring judges and readers to rehearse writing and reading techniques that they also use in other settings.

Other scholars, more sensitive to this crossover, have explored the place of story rather than rhetoric in legal discourse. This approach has been especially popular in certain subfields lacking the traditional institutional status of constitutional law: work on trial advocacy (e.g., Gaines 2016, 182–97; Meyer 2014; Sherwin 1994) and critical race theory (as pioneered by, e.g., Delgado 1989; Williams 1992). In this work, using familiar narrative forms allows legal actors to speak to legal outsiders (the advocate's storytelling to the jury) or allows those who have historically lacked access to state power to make their experience felt by legal insiders (critical race theory). Perhaps because of its concern with accessibility, work in these traditions tends to treat "narrative" mostly as a given—a way of using language that engages and transports—rather than a phenomenon to be explored critically. The present book, in contrast, follows the model of some approaches to the study of literature (e.g., Gerrig 1993; Herman 2013) that have hesitated to take narrative as a given in this manner. Drawing in particular on work in cognitive science, these approaches seek a more precise description of how narrative language—including legal language, and even judicial opinions—has the effect on us that it does.

1.4.2.2 Philosophy of legal language

Another interdisciplinary tradition of scholarship examining legal discourse has drawn on academic philosophy. The philosophically informed study of legal language in the U.S. has been heavily influenced by the mid-twentieth-century work of Henry Hart (1958) and Lon Fuller (1958), who focused not on judicial opinions as such, but on judicial decision-making. With the partial exception of Ronald Dworkin (1986), most legal philosophers—including those who specialize in analyzing language—have likewise examined how judges do and should *conceive* of language, rather than how they *use* it.

A good example is Michael Moore's influential law-review article "The Semantics of Judging" (1980). Moore's stated goal in the piece is to "extract . . . the kind of knowledge of language upon which a judge may draw in deciding cases under any theory" (153). Moore investigates a set of issues much debated by philosophers, including different conceptions of meaning[35] and the phenomena of linguistic ambiguity,[36] vagueness, and open texture. Moore explains that judges grapple with these phenomena, whether they realize it or not, whenever they make decisions about the legal effect to give particular linguistic formulations. But Moore focuses exclusively on judges' assessment of legal language, not on judges' legal *use* of language. He also deliberately declines to discuss any referential functions of legal language: how that language orients its readers in the world or coordinates readers' activity. According to Moore, "in most cases legal fact-finders are burdened with word/word relationships, not word/thing relationships" (283), so it is not necessary to worry about whether or how legal terms relate to the "real world." In this respect, Moore's perspective on judicial activity is fully "internal," even though his disciplinary perspective is partly external. He is not trying to render legal experience comprehensible to nonlawyers or to reveal new aspects of legal practice to lawyers. Rather, he offers lawyers new and better tools for familiar problems.

Moore's article set the agenda for much later work on law and language. Philosophically informed approaches to legal language over the past few decades have tended, like him, to examine how judges do and should conceive of language rather than how they do and should use it. This work has also tended to discount questions about the ontology presupposed or generated by legal practices, especially legal language practices (for recent examples, see the essays collected in Marmor & Soames 2011).

Similar limitations are present in Ronald Dworkin's landmark *Law's Empire* (1986). Dworkin's influential account of "law as integrity" examines the "constructive interpretation" of legal tradition that judges perform in common-law systems like those of the U.K. and U.S. (10, 13–14).[37] Dworkin presents this account as written from an "internal, participants' point of view" (14). Nevertheless, he considers only a handful of texts generated by judges themselves (e.g., 229–50).

Dworkin's argument, like Moore's, is ambivalent about the ontological implications of judicial language practices. On the one hand, *Law's Empire* is studded with the invented scenarios typical of Anglo-American philosophy, including an imaginary community Dworkin presents to introduce the notion of "constructive interpretation" (47–49, 87); his famous "chain novel" metaphor, offered to capture the feel of common-law reasoning and conveyed partly through a thought experiment (229, 232–35); his insistence that practicing "law as integrity" requires a legal practitioner to personify a normative community (167–71, 187–88, 343); and, of course, "Hercules," Dworkin's "imaginary judge of superhuman intellectual power and patience," posited to "exhibit th[e] complex structure of legal interpretation" (239; see also 242, 245, 265, 313–16, 342–54). These devices suggest that Dworkin, like Moore, is not concerned about finding real-world referents for legal terms. Indeed, Dworkin contends that metaphysics is irrelevant to interpretation; he argues that we do not need to consider what does and does not exist in order to determine what a judicial opinion or other legal source says or means (79, 87, 238).

On the other hand, Dworkin is critical of accounts of legal practice that describe judges' activities as detached from real-world phenomena and concerns (e.g., 37, 152, 155–56, 159–60). Dworkin's approach in *Law's Empire* was an important contribution to a scholarly and theoretical variation on the wordsmith's fallacy. By placing "interpretation" at the center of his account of judging, Dworkin suggested that interpretation is both an intuitively accessible activity and mostly immune to analysis, beyond the conceptual and quasi-phenomenological tests of "fit" and "justification" that he proposes. This view of lawyers' and judges' relationship to language has become part of the tacit knowledge of legal scholars and practitioners. It is an implicit premise of almost all of the contributions to the Harvard survey of the 2014 term.

1.4.2.3 Legal cognition

A third and more recent interdisciplinary tradition has not yet been as deeply absorbed into the legal academy. This tradition draws on psychology and cognitive science to explain the activities of legal practitioners—including their language practices—from both a familiar "internal" perspective and a less familiar external one. A landmark work in this tradition,

Anthony Amsterdam and Jerome Bruner's *Minding the Law*, appeared in 2000. Amsterdam and Bruner describe their influences as including "psychology, linguistics, anthropology . . ., literary theory, neurology, and the computational sciences" (3). Their study addresses three aspects of legal cognitive–linguistic practices: categorization, narrative, and persuasion. Amsterdam and Bruner trace the effects of these practices on the "linguistic microstructures" of a handful of key Supreme Court opinions (91–93; see also 156–74) and, like the scholars of advocacy and critical race theory mentioned above, stress the ubiquity of storytelling in legal practice (110, 141). "Telling and hearing stories comes as second nature to us," they observe, so we should not be surprised to find stories permeating legal practice and communication (112).

Like White and other scholars of legal storytelling, however, and in a manner reminiscent of Dworkin's treatment of "interpretation," Amsterdam and Bruner suggest that storytelling and its effects are not susceptible to analysis past a certain point (120, 170). Similarly, like Moore and Dworkin, they insist that law is not concerned with "representing something 'out there' in the world" (13–14). Yet they also express concerns about legal rhetoric that suggest otherwise. For instance, Amsterdam and Bruner are critical of what they call judicial techniques of reification and "ontologization," the postulation of abstractions as somehow existing outside of legal discourse (97, 177–81).

Still, in many ways, Amsterdam and Bruner go further than their predecessors in analyzing the peculiarities of legal discourse. Anticipating Elizabeth Mertz, they note that although legal language mostly looks like "ordinary language" (173), practitioners use it in a distinctive way: "Law-talk . . . is always susceptible to shattering without warning, as one or another of its users suddenly questions assumptions that had been accepted a moment before" (173–74; see also Solan 1993, 15–16). This practice of questioning assumptions is taught in law school and generates, for many practitioners, a pervasive and only partly conscious ambivalence about language:

> What a speaker says in legal discourse needs to be made only reasonably and revocably clear to the reader; and what the speaker *means* by what is said needs to be made only reasonably, revocably, and partially clear. . . . This partial masking of the litigator's intended meanings is necessary in order to *keep up the appearance of using language in an ordinary way.*
>
> (175–76; emphasis in original)

In this account, lawyers use language as a kind of mask of precision allowing behind-the-scenes contingency planning; lawyers who do this know tacitly, if not explicitly, that language is an instrument (able to be put to all of the uses described by Mertz, White, Ferguson, and the others) but that its utility also depends on its being *taken to be* referential, a stable pointer to things in the world, often at the same time.

In the decades following Amsterdam and Bruner's work, legal academics in the U.S. have taken increasing interest in the findings of cognitive scientists, especially as those findings suggest flaws in traditional assumptions about perception, decision-making, and judgment both in and outside law (e.g., Anderson 2014; Kahan et al. 2009; Maroney 2011). Scholars of literature have also increasingly been drawing on cognitive science during this period (e.g., Elfenbein 2018; Herman 2013; Spolsky 2015; Vermeule 2010; Zunshine 2006). These two trends have not converged, however; in the legal context, further development of the path suggested by Amsterdam and Bruner has mostly focused on specific decision-making issues rather than on the dynamics and effects of legal discourse.

The most sustained study of the cognitive structures of legal practice, Steven Winter's *A Clearing in the Forest* (2003), is, like Michael Moore's "Semantics of Judging," a study more of legal cognition than of legal language practices. Winter explicitly focuses on mechanisms of thought, deemphasizing "mere language" (13). He explains the content of legal language as determined by mental mappings (13, 30–33) and downplays the importance of the symbols we sometimes consider carriers of significance (e.g., 214). Winter rejects an "objectivist" view, according to which physical phenomena ground our perception, thought, and language; he cautions his readers against this "ontological fallacy," a form of "reification, in which we treat our projection as external reality" (341). It leads, he argues, to an "empowerment fantasy," a "false sense of freedom that seems to arise from the recognition of this fallacy" (341; see also 310). Winter does not, however, draw any direct connection between the illusions he describes and lawyers' idiosyncratic relationship with language, as opposed to perception and reasoning.

The scholars mentioned throughout this section have all addressed aspects of the issues this book explores, but each has presented only part of the picture. Like the blind men investigating the elephant in the Buddhist parable, they have mapped complementary but disconnected features of lawyers' peculiar relationship with language and with the world beyond the legal profession. Their accounts have been converging on a common insight concerning these relationships, which are ordinary in some ways—lawyers in the U.S. do use the same English language that nonlawyers do—and unusual in others. And while U.S. lawyers and judges are aware that their relationship with language is unusual, that awareness is, for even the most sophisticated, often distorted by the wordsmith's fallacy. The rest of this book begins to map some of these relationships and distortions, investigating how lawyers' relationship with language both incorporates and transforms the language-processing capacities shared by most members of the cultures of the United States.

1.5 Plan of the book

The chapters that follow build on the work described throughout this chapter, and more. Recent challenges to received legal wisdom about how lawyers and judges read statutes (e.g., Nourse 2016; Slocum 2016) have begun to unseat some of the assumptions underlying the theoretical work described above. And the same disciplines legal scholars have been mining for decades for insights—literary theory, linguistics, philosophy, and cognitive science—have also recently been in productive conversation on matters bearing directly on the wordsmith's fallacy, such as the discursive techniques for presenting mental phenomena and the metaphysical commitments made by writers and readers. Getting behind and underneath the wordsmith's fallacy, however, requires sustained attention to some ordinarily unnoticed patterns in the surface of judicial language as well as reflection on our own responses to these patterns.

Each of the following chapters addresses a different set of related legal conundrums. Chapter 2 considers some of the ways the justices' opinions oversimplify the referential function of legal language and wrestle with the status of "fact." Chapter 3 explores how the 2014-term opinions address human agency and mental activity, showing how the justices tend to present the minds of others as both inaccessible *and* subject to authoritative description. Chapter 4 examines the justices' tendencies to take for granted the experience of role performance by individuals and to avoid considering the internal dynamics of group agents, such as corporations and government agencies. Chapter 5 discusses the justices' conflicting attitudes toward speculative language and offers an initial map of the alternative "universe" inhabited by legal professionals. Chapter 6 continues this mapping, considering the different temporal structures implicit in the justices' opinions and how legal analysis layers those structures in a way that reinforces the wordsmith's fallacy.

The guiding theme of these investigations is a complex analogy between legal discourse and fictional discourse. Together, the chapters show how lawyers' intricate and conflicted but only partly self-aware relationship with language—as diagnosed by, for example, Mertz, Amsterdam, and Bruner—parallels the relationship with linguistic constructions developed by readers of fictional narrative. A reader of fictional narrative must keep in mind two varieties of reference at once. One is aligned with the ordinary "referentialist" function of language, the function we use to discuss matters of mutual interest, including ourselves and our relationships. The other is a more metalinguistic dimension of reference, which permits the contemplation and construction of new realities that we do not take to preexist their first presentation in language. When we read a novel, we use the same language and inferential skills that help us communicate with others and understand referential discourse; at the same time, we always bear in mind that the language we read is referential in a limited and qualified sense—that the matters we take to "real" within the narrative are real within that narrative's universe only, and only because they have been linguistically presented as real.

This mode of engagement can be described as a kind of doubled awareness, doubled vision, or doubled consciousness. One useful analogy might be to the phenomenon of multistable perception—familiar to most in the form of so-called "illusions" like the Necker cube, the duck-rabbit, or the Rubin vase. Once we grasp the possibility of controlled shifting between the two views of each of these ambiguous images, we gain not only the ability to shift at will between views, but also the ability to see the image as affording both views. Perceiving discourse as fictional is a culturally specific skill that enables a reader (or viewer) to approach a linguistic or visual phenomenon that unfolds over time as similarly inherently "readable" in multiple ways (cf. Smith 1995). Legal practitioners approach discourse in a very similar way, although they are not explicitly trained to recognize this aspect of their activity.

The ability to engage with language in either of these complex ways is a sophisticated and often underappreciated capacity that depends on several more basic abilities, including the ability to use language at all and the ability to pretend, make believe, and imagine (linguistically or otherwise). This ability is, moreover, and contrary to some widely held beliefs, far from solipsistic. Like the ability to use language and to make believe, it is a fundamentally social activity, one that allows us to learn, to share understandings of what is real, to agree on what is true, and to coordinate our activity.

The doubled relationship with language involved in legal activity is also fundamentally social. The broadest aim of this book is to clarify this analogy and to draw out the parallels between these two sophisticated human institutions. The following chapters trace how the analogy can help to explain, among other things, lawyers' characteristic vacillation between denial and acceptance of the referential function of language, the popular view of lawyers as "corrupters of discourse" (Galanter 2005, 17), the enduring difficulty of articulating the relationship between law and truth, the peculiar avoidance of any training in the establishment of "fact" in U.S. legal education, and the ways justices (and lawyers) often and apparently unconsciously borrow narrative devices well-studied by literary theorists, sometimes with unfortunate consequences. By shedding new light on these puzzles, the book also hopes to demonstrate the continued importance of traditionally humanistic inquiry—such as the study of fiction—to our legal, political, and social well being.

Notes

1 Throughout this book, citations to the Court's opinions are to slip opinions posted on the Court's website. If no justice's name appears, the citation is to the majority opinion.
2 When the issue was published, David Strauss and Richard Posner were on the faculty at the University of Chicago's law school; Posner was also a federal appellate judge. Jack Goldsmith, Richard Fallon, and Laurence Tribe were faculty members at Harvard Law School. Abbe Gluck was a faculty member at Yale Law School, and Kenji Yoshino was on the faculty at New York University's law school.
3 These articles, coauthored with Lisa Bressman (Gluck & Bressman 2013; Bressman & Gluck 2014), report the results of surveys of congressional legislative drafters. Gluck and Bressman argue that scholars and judges discuss statutory meaning in ways that do not match how drafters talk (and presumably think) about their activity.
4 Echoing Judge Posner's contribution, Yoshino closes his piece by observing, "Discerning new liberties has always been, and will always be, more an art than a science" (Yoshino 2015, 179).
5 See Strauss 2015, 9, 26 n.141, 27 n.150, 27–28.
6 Strauss 2015, 9–12, 18, 19, 30, 59.
7 Gluck 2015, 67 n.18, 90 n.169, 94 n.194, 108 n.275, 110 n.288, 111 n.290.
8 Gluck 2015, 73–74.
9 Tribe 2015, 19 n.25, 22 n.49, 26 n.72.
10 The "internal" contributions (Goldsmith, Yoshino, Tribe, Posner) draw mainly on legal materials. The more academic pieces also cite books written by legal scholars, as well as historical sources, political-science sources, and philosophical works.
11 The overconfidence effect breeds excessive confidence in one's own judgment. The illusion of control names individuals' tendency to overestimate the extent of their influence on events. Functional fixedness is the tendency to use tools only in the way one is accustomed to seeing them used. The "curse of knowledge" names the difficulty of "un-knowing" information, and experts' difficulty in considering problems from a non-expert perspective. The bias blind spot names the tendency to see oneself as less cognitively biased than others.
12 Seven of the notes take this approach, including notes addressing *Wynne* (Note 2015c, 181); *Armstrong* (Note 2015f, 211); *Patel* (Note 2015p, 241); *Heien* (Note 2015o, 251); *Horne* (Note 2015k, 261); *Elonis* (Note 2015j, 331); and *N.C. State Bd.* (Note 2015t, 371).
13 Notes take this approach to the decisions in *Wellness Int'l* (Note 2015e, 201); *Williams-Yulee* (Note 2015m, 231); *Ass'n of Am. Railroads* (Note 2015q, 341); and *Holt v. Hobbs* (Note 2015r, 251).
14 One of these notes addresses *Walker* (Note 2015l, 230); the other addresses *Yates* (Note 2015s, 361).
15 Notes in this category include analyses of *Glossip* (Note 2015h, 271); *Perez* (Note 2015a, 300); and *Michigan v. EPA* (Note 2015g, 311).
16 The first of these addresses *Ariz. State Legislature* (Note 2015d, 200); the second considers *Johnson* (Note 2015b, 301); the third considers *Texas Dep't of Housing* (Note 2015i, 321).
17 The only note not included in any of these categories also fits this broader description. That note addresses *Alabama Legis. Black Caucus*, in which the Court held that an organization representing minority voters in Alabama could challenge the state legislature's redistricting plan. The author describes the decision as a well-intended but useless tool given "the great harm to voting rights in the South resulting from [the Court's 2013 decision in] *Shelby County*," in which the Court invalidated an important provision of the Voting Rights Act (Note 2015n, 281).
18 The nineteenth note, on *Yates*, mentions the decision's possible "benefit of organizing public resistance to an ever-expanding federal code" (Note 2015s, 370).
19 During the 2014 term, ten of the justices' 36 clerks were graduates of Harvard Law School.
20 Other periodicals offer term surveys; for example, since 2001 the Cato Institute has offered a libertarian take on each term's cases in the *Cato Supreme Court Review*. But it, too, is a selective review.
21 Statistical analyses authored by professors continued through the 1930s; the student-edited review issues began appearing in 1949 (Lazarus 2015, 35).
22 Lazarus finds that Chief Justice Roberts assigns big cases less often to Justices Alito, Scalia, and Breyer, and least often to Justices Ginsburg and Thomas (Lazarus 2015, 58–59).

23 The tables record such matters as the numbers of opinions assigned to each justice per month, 2005–14 (74–79) and the Chief Justice's assignment opportunities and assignments in several categories of cases (84–87).

24 The "Statistics" include tables summarizing the number of opinions written by each justice during the term (381; Justice Thomas wrote the most, 37); the number of cases in which seven different sets of justices composed five-justice majorities (387; the most common coalition, in ten cases, included Justices Kennedy, Ginsburg, Breyer, Sotomayor, and Kagan); the average length of each justice's slip opinions and each justice's total page output (388; Justice Thomas had the highest output, more than 403 pages); and the number of opinions issued in each of 60 categories (393–95; the most popular category—with five cases—was bankruptcy).

25 The SCOTUSblog Stat Pack includes information, for example, about which lawyers presented oral argument (but not briefs) in the term's argued cases (39–40), as well as the justices' questioning activity during oral arguments (38).

26 The 2014-term Stat Pack tabulates such matters as the number of opinions authored by each justice by monthly sitting (2, 26–27), as well as the "average number of days between argument and opinion for [each] Justice's majority opinions" (7; see also 32–33) and the number of pages released by each justice each week (13).

27 SCOTUSblog hosted symposia for *Obergefell*, *King*, *Texas Dep't of Housing*, *Glossip*, *Zivotofsky*, and *Williams-Yulee*. In the symposia addressing *King* and *Texas Dep't of Housing*, practitioners (including clinical professors and authors from think tanks) made more contributions than academics did.

28 The question of what makes judges' decisions come out as they do has long preoccupied legal scholars. Attempts to answer this question often focus on outcomes, as in the "Statistics" and Stat Pack. The research described in the text is part of a wider body of political-science research seeking to explain the drivers of judicial decision-making, especially Supreme Court decision-making.

29 Clerks play an important role in the drafting process. The justices' opinions often contain language from the briefs of parties and *amici*. Justices also may revise opinion drafts after circulating them to colleagues.

30 The approach taken here tries to bridge internal and external perspectives—to understand, from outside, the peculiarly legal perspective on language. In this way it differs from more thoroughly external approaches to the study of legal discourse, such as those of Marianne Constable (2014) and Ellen Spolsky (2015).

31 White (1985) contends, for example, that legal communication "maintains a false pretense that it can be used as a language of description or naming" (112–13). Sometimes he suggests that these practices are not necessarily troublesome: "[T]hose who deal with judges had better realize the extent to which [their discourse] is a deliberate pretense, a way of talking, by which we say one thing and mean another" (224).

32 "The lawyer's imagination," White writes, "must work in the past as well as the future. 'If I had been there. . . .'" (1985, 209).

33 "To argue well," White writes, "you must imagine another mind and have some sense of how someone else might look at your client and his case" (1985, 208–09).

34 Ferguson focuses explicitly on Supreme Court opinions, especially two from the 1940s, *Minersville Sch. Dist. v. Gobitis* (1940) and *W.V. State Bd. of Educ. v. Barnette* (1943).

35 Moore maintains that the realists did not have a sophisticated view of language (162) and that Hart also did not have a semantic theory (273–74).

36 Moore addresses, for example, intentional ambiguity (183 n.80, 182–83, 208–14; see also Chapter 3.2.2).

37 Like Moore, Dworkin argues that legal theorists should not waste energy on developing and refining lists of criteria for the correct application of legal terms, a preoccupation he describes as the "semantic sting" (45–46).

2 Fear of fiction

2.1 Before post-truth

Outsiders to the legal system might consider it obvious that lawyers' language is like make-believe. On one popular view, lawyers are out of touch with ordinary people, playing a game that makes little sense (see Galanter 2005). Lawyers, in contrast, might find the suggestion that their language is like make-believe not just wrong but insulting. To them, legal activity clearly has important consequences in the real world. This book seeks to show how both reactions capture part of the truth, as well as to explain why many lawyers might resist seeing their activity this way.

The Court issued its 2014-term opinions during a period of growing anxiety about the reliability of assertions of "fact" and "truth" (e.g., Manjoo 2008). The Oxford Dictionaries, in their role as barometers of English usage, named "post-truth" the 2016 "word of the year," noting a "roughly 2,000 percent increase in its usage [that year] over 2015" (Wang 2016). This trend had been under way for a while. Concerns about the stability of assertions of fact, about what qualifies as an assertion of fact, about what to call assertions that do not quite qualify, and about how to distinguish such assertions from assertions that do qualify appear throughout the Court's 2014-term opinions. Those concerns are the focus of this chapter.

In the term's opinions, the justices promote the alignment of legal discourse with "fact" and distance it from "fiction." But they seem to work with conceptions of "fact" and "fiction" that are simplified and a bit distorted. In particular, the legal understandings of these notions tend to ignore the role of communication in making it possible for us to conceive of "fact" and "fiction." The standard lawyerly conception of "fact" understands facts as real-world states of affairs preexisting and informing legal activity. The law is responsive to facts but does not, at least not admittedly, generate or create them. Thus, although legal activity involves using language, facts about the world and about language preexist that activity. And although some facts are more challenging to identify than others, agreement on the facts is always in principle possible. The standard legal conception of "fiction," in contrast, associates fiction with the products of individual imaginations. Such products, to the extent they exist, exist only in imagination, which is by definition a matter of private, subjective, individual experience. So no agreement about imaginary things is possible, even in principle. Nevertheless, references to imaginary things are often seductive, and we need to be on our guard against them.

This chapter suggests a more nuanced account of "fact" and "fiction" that can explain how popular culture's equation of law with fiction and lawyers' aversion to that equation might both be justified. Section 2.2 addresses the approach taken in the 2014-term opinions to "fiction," an approach that matches the legal aversion to identifying legal with fictional discourse hypothesized above. Section 2.3 considers the justices' approach to "fact," assessing the uses to which the justices put that notion and some of the inconsistencies in their account of it. Section 2.4 further develops these points, describing the justices' only partly successful efforts to stabilize their discussions of "fact" in the 2014-term opinions. The chapter shows how a more sensitive view of fictional discourse and of its specific kinships with legal discourse might have the desirable side effect of making visible new ways to think and talk about fact (cf. Appiah 2017).

2.2 The many faces of "fiction"

The justices—and lawyers more generally—rely on two flawed and partly overlapping notions of "fiction." One is specific to law: legal fictions are communicative and reasoning devices by which lawyers agree to treat one situation as if it were another one. The other notion of "fiction" is not specific to law but seems to be regarded as particularly antithetical to appropriate legal activity: this is the view described above that aligns fiction with imagination and solipsism. The first of these notions is more sophisticated, but its implications are rarely acknowledged; indeed, when the justices must address the real-world use of fictional discourse, they seem to forget about the legal-fictions tradition.

2.2.1 Traditional legal fictions

Lawyers have used the term "legal fiction" for centuries to describe a specific kind of situation: when everyone involved in a legal dispute agrees on one description of the real world (to take a famous example, that the island of Minorca is located in the Mediterranean) but lawyers agree to act as if a different state of affairs were the case (in this example, as if Minorca were located in London; see Miller 1910, 629–30). Such legal fictions involve a kind of collective consensual "pretending" by lawyers. This pretending has much in common with more everyday instances of pretending, as section 2.2.3 will begin to explain. In particular, it involves a kind of double consciousness: lawyers who treat Minorca as if it were in London are committed to non-pretend, real-world facts concerning Minorca, as well.

This kind of pretending can look like duplicity, especially to those not aware of the reasons for treating one situation as if it were another. Such reasons are usually available, even when they are not expressly mentioned. One recurring defense of legal fictions describes them as a way for the law (judges, legislators, lawyers) to accommodate old rules to new situations (e.g., Maine 1861, 21–22). Still, when they use legal fictions, lawyers are indeed engaging in a pretense. They know things are really one way but deliberately act as though things are different.

Although Supreme Court justices sometimes use the term "legal fiction" to refer to these practices, they did not do so in any of the 2014-term opinions. (Justice Thomas did use the phrase "legal fiction," but with a different implication, and he and other justices referred just to "fiction" several times; the next section addresses these instances.) In several cases, however, the Court did address legal practices that are equivalent to traditional legal fictions. Such practices permeate legal activity.

Some legal fictions are so familiar to lawyers that they are no longer called "fictions," but are labeled in a less provocative way. One example is the term "constructive." When a lawyer says that someone had "constructive knowledge" of something, the lawyer means that person will be treated legally as if he or she had knowledge of the thing, even though it is possible the person did not actually know about it. In his opinion in the 2014-term case *B&B Hardware v. Hargis Industries*, Justice Alito mentions an example of this concept used in trademark law. When a person registers a trademark with the federal Patent and Trademark Office, the registration "serves as 'constructive notice of the registrant's claim of ownership' of the mark" (8). Another user of the mark cannot successfully claim ignorance of the registrant's claim to ownership of the trademark, even if the second user really did not know about that prior claim to ownership.

Constructive possession is a similar idea. This doctrine was central to the 2014-term case *Henderson v. United States*. Because of a federal statute forbidding a felon's possession of firearms, Tony Henderson, who had a felony conviction, asked a federal judge to oversee the transfer of Henderson's guns to a friend. All nine justices agreed that the statute in question forbade not only "actual possession" ("direct physical control") of the guns but also "constructive possession" ("the power and intent to exercise control") of them (3–4). All of the justices also agreed that in some cases, though not all, a felon who gave his or her guns to a friend might retain constructive possession of them (1, 4, 7–8). In any given case, the Court explained, whether a felon retains constructive possession depends on the circumstances: whether the recipient will agree to keep the guns out of the felon's control, whether the recipient is credible, and so forth. *Henderson* perfectly exemplifies how judges use legal fiction–like devices to deal with situations where a law does not seem to apply, strictly speaking, yet it seems fair to apply the law anyway. If Henderson's friend has the guns, it does not make sense to say that Henderson "possesses" them, but if Henderson's friend will hand the guns over to Henderson on request, Henderson might as well "possess" them.

Another term indicating the presence of a legal fiction is the label "deemed" (see, e.g., Scheppele 1990, 54–55). This label indicates that a term is being used in a technical legal way that might differ from its everyday use. Such a technical sense might have been established by the legislature, or it might be a matter of judicial practice, as in the 2014-term case *Gelboim v. Bank of America*, which dealt with the timing of appeals in civil cases. Normally, a party in a civil case can appeal a trial court's decision only after the court issues a "final order." Since there will be only one final order in a case, the rule helps to limit the number of appeals and speed up the resolution of cases. But trial courts sometimes make pre-"final order" rulings that are important enough for it to make sense for an appellate court to weigh in on them immediately. In such cases, as Justice Ginsburg explains in *Gelboim*, "an order [of the trial court] may be deemed 'final'" (8 n.5).

Sometimes judges call similar namings "doctrines." The 2014-term case *Hana Financial v. Hana Bank*, for example, involved the "doctrine . . . called 'tacking'" in trademark law, a rule used when, despite some changes in a trademark, "the original and revised marks are 'legal equivalents' in that they create the same, continuing commercial impression" (1). Deeming can be indistinguishable from simple definition. The 2014-term case *Kerry v. Din*, for instance, concerned a federal statute instructing U.S. officials to deny U.S. visas to anyone who had engaged in "terrorist activities." Like many statutes, this one includes a definition section identifying conduct that can count as "terrorist activity" and including in that identification conduct that might not ordinarily seem to merit that label (Scalia, 3).

Deemings, deeming doctrines, and definitions are routine practices that most lawyers do not regard as particularly artificial. It is hard to imagine what the law would look like without them, and they are seldom criticized as general practices. In contrast, the term "legal fiction," although it refers to a similar practice, often does imply criticism. For decades, discussion of legal fictions by lawyers, judges, and law professors has followed a recurring pattern. Lawyers who want to argue for abandonment of a doctrine label the doctrine a "fiction," calling on all of the negative connotations of that label—disengagement from the real world, disrespect for the facts, mystification of the public.[1] Using the "fiction" label instead of one of the more innocuous synonyms can help a sympathetic judge justify departures from legal convention. As the next section explains, the negative connotations of "fiction" also attach to associated terms that judges and justices treat as its synonyms, like "pretend," "imagine," and "invent."

2.2.2 "Fiction" as epithet

Although the justices do not always refer to "fiction" disparagingly, usually the term is an apology at best. Like many related terms, it almost always implies an undesirable departure from reality or the "facts." The justices often use these terms to justify rejection of other judges', justices', or parties' arguments.

A justice may, for example, accuse other judges of letting their imaginations run wild by charging them with indulging in "speculation," with being "fanciful," or with deciding a "hypothetical" case. To accuse a judge of making a legal mistake—applying the wrong legal rule—a critic may say that the misbehaving judge "imagined," "invented," "created," or "made up" the rule, implying an intentional departure from consensus reality. Sometimes a justice accuses a judge of dissimulation, or "pretending" to do one thing while really doing another. To stress the futility of a misbehaving judge's illegitimate activity, the critic will say that the judge has created or gotten lost in a "world" of his or her own creation.

Justice Thomas was the 2014 term's most prolific dissenter, and he repeatedly used this kind of rhetoric in his 2014-term opinions. In *Teva Pharmaceuticals v. Sandoz*, for example, he describes the governing legal standard—a perspective that patent law requires judges to assume, the perspective of the "skilled artisan"—as contrived, to support his broader point that applying the standard does not involve deciding any questions of "fact." "[T]he 'fact' of how a skilled artisan would understand a given term… is a legal fiction," he writes:

> it has no existence independent of the [patent] claim construction process [the process in which a judge determines a patent claim's scope based on the claim's language]. There is no actual "skilled artisan" who . . . formed an understanding of the terms of the claim.
>
> (Thomas, 10)

Although Justice Thomas uses the term "legal fiction" here, he is not calling the "skilled artisan" a traditional legal fiction. Rather, he is describing the perspective as detached from actuality to support his point that appellate judges can inhabit the perspective despite their own detachment from the evidence presented in trial-court proceedings.

Justice Thomas does not always use the "fiction" label this neutrally. Dissenting in *Obergefell*, for example, he criticizes the majority's reasoning in this way:

> I have elsewhere explained the dangerous fiction of treating the Due Process Clause as a font of substantive rights. . . . It distorts the constitutional text. . . . Worse, it invites judges to do exactly what the majority has done here—"'roa[m] at large in the constitutional field' guided only by their personal views" as to the "fundamental rights" protected by that document.
>
> (Thomas, 2)

This "fiction," unlike the legally appropriate "skilled artisan" fiction, is illegitimate, according to Justice Thomas. Labeling the doctrine a "fiction" helps him to communicate his disapproval of it as a manner of speaking that allows judges to indulge their "personal views" and make up new rules.[2]

Justice Thomas is not the only justice to have used the "fiction" label this way during the 2014 term, nor is he the only justice to criticize others for departing from reality. In his majority opinion in the "skilled artisan" patent case, Justice Breyer quotes similar language from the opinion of the lower-court judge who took a position contrary to Justice Thomas's (*Teva*, Breyer, 9). Justice Alito often criticizes other judges and justices for wandering away from reality. In his 2014-term opinions, a dissenting justice's assumption that voters can effectively control legislators by voting them out of office is "fanciful" and infected by improper "speculation" (*Wynne*, 12); an appellate court inappropriately indulged in a "flight of fancy" (*Davis v. Ayala*, 24); the majority's claim that members of the public have come to rely on a particular Supreme Court decision is also "fanciful" (*Kimble*, Alito, 5); and a majority's decision is "unnecessary, impractical, and arbitrary," because it "addresses a purely hypothetical question" (*Rodriguez*, Alito, 1).

Other justices use similar language in 2014-term opinions to criticize other judges for creating or willfully misconstruing legal rules. Justice Sotomayor criticizes the majority in *Heien v. North Carolina* for "imagin[ing] a holding that is not rooted in the logic of the opinion" on which the majority relies (Sotomayor, 8). She criticizes Chief Justice Roberts's dissent in *T-Mobile South v. City of Roswell* for "invent[ing] a process that turns judicial review on its head" (10). Chief Justice Roberts, dissenting in *Obergefell*, describes the constitutional right to state-recognized same-sex marriage as "a right imagined by the majority," contrasting it with rights "actually spelled out in the Constitution" (Roberts, 27).

Justice Scalia was, of course, especially fond of colorful denunciations of this kind. A majority opinion "imagine[s] . . . a legal utopia . . . —a world in which all lawyers are responsible and no lawyers make mistakes" (*Dart Cherokee*, Scalia, 6). Dormant Commerce Clause doctrine is "brazen invention," a "judicial fraud" (*Wynne*, Scalia, 2), based on an "Imaginary Commerce Clause" that "lead[s] to imaginary benefits" (7). A majority's "make-it-up-as-you-go-along approach . . . has no basis in the Act [governing the case] . . . and will prove unworkable in practice" (*ONEOK*, Scalia, 1). These critiques all describe other judges' activity as illegitimate because of its deviation from "reality," "actuality," or "fact" and its resulting susceptibility to personal preference and unpredictable variation.

Sometimes, when a justice accuses another judge or justice of "pretending," the accusation is of even worse conduct, amounting to deception. A majority opinion "pretend[s] to review the appellate court's exercise of discretion while actually reviewing the trial court's legal analysis" (*Dart Cherokee*, Scalia, 2). A majority's fidelity to controversial precedent involves the "pretense that" the precedent "was legitimate" (*Texas Dep't of Housing*, Thomas, 1). In these instances, justices describe judicial activity as involving something close to deliberate falsehood. Pretense in this sense involves not just a judge's imposition of his or her personal preferences but also the judge's deliberate concealment of that activity.

The justices used similar language on other occasions during the 2014 term.[3] The following pages will revisit many of the examples cited here and introduce others as well. To be sure, the justices sometimes use similar language more neutrally or even positively. As Chapter 5, in particular, will explain, some justices explicitly instruct readers of their opinions to "imagine" or "suppose." And most of the justices will cite works of literature, usually prose fiction, now and then in support of a point.[4] Still, the label "fiction" usually imparts a negative tone to a justice's description of another judge's activity, suggesting departure from a solid, public world of fact into a private, often shifty world of imagination.

The justices' use of this family of terms is consistent with legal scholars' use of them. In her majority opinion in *Los Angeles v. Patel*, Justice Sotomayor cites a 2011 law-review article by Richard Fallon, "Fact and Fiction About Facial Challenges" (4). As the article's title suggests, Fallon wrote it to correct misperceptions about such challenges, in particular what he considered a tendency to underestimate the frequency of successful facial challenges to the constitutionality of statutes. He describes these misperceptions ("fictions") as a misunderstanding of practice, a kind of illusion. He attributes the illusion both to judges themselves, who describe facial challenges as disfavored, and to observers of the Court, who take the descriptions at face value. In this argument, fact is to fiction as truth is to (possibly understandable) mistake. Scholarly discourse, like judicial discourse, should aim at the former and seek to unmask the latter (see also Harrison 2001, 22; Hempfer 2004, 308). This kind of argument depends on understanding fiction as detached from reality and impractical.

Somewhat like Fallon, this book argues that understanding fiction in this way involves misconceiving it. This understanding oversimplifies the structure and functioning of fictional discourse, and the oversimplification has implications for our understanding of other modes of discourse, including legal discourse. Unlike Fallon, however, this book does not define "fiction" in absolute opposition to "fact." Recent work on the dynamics of fictional discourse supports a more nuanced understanding of the relationship between fiction and fact. As the next section explains, interdisciplinary work over the past several decades has been converging on an understanding of fictional discourse and practices of "make-believe" that acknowledge their utility, instead of condemning them as frivolous and deceptive, and—unlike similar earlier accounts like that of Hans Vaihinger (1911)—explain their operation in some detail.

2.2.3 Taking fiction seriously

The conception of "fiction" that most lawyers and judges seem to work with today was developed in the nineteenth and early twentieth centuries and has remained mostly unchanged since (compare Ogden 1932 with Smith 2007). Over the same period, researchers in other fields have been refining their understandings of the phenomena we call fiction in ways that challenge the mostly negative view still so potent in legal discourse. The following two sections trace some of these developments.

2.2.3.1 *Accounting for fiction through the twentieth century*

A century ago, the scholarly study of fiction as such was mainly the province of philosophers who studied humans' use of language to refer to nonexistent people, things, and events (e.g., Meinong 1904; Russell 1905; see also Currie 1990). Philosophers examined these practices as posing questions of metaphysics (do fictional characters exist?) and of the logical analysis of language (is the name of a fictional character the same kind of name as the name of a real person?). A new wave of literary scholars began theorizing about fictional language use in the 1970s; around the same time, scholars in the mind sciences started to investigate how people imagine and process imaginary scenarios.[5] Legal scholars and educators have taken little notice of these developments, and as a result, most contemporary lawyers are also unfamiliar with them.

American lawyers tend to think of the first third of the twentieth century as a period when a nineteenth-century formalist paradigm yielded to a modern realist mode of legal argument and judging (see, e.g., Tamanaha 2009). As the "realist" label suggests, legal realists glorified the "real" and devalued the non-real, often using the term "fiction" to refer to the latter. An influential showcase for this position, still dear to legal academics, is Felix Cohen's law-review article "Transcendental Nonsense and the Functional Approach" (1935). Cohen championed his new-school functional approach against old-school transcendental nonsense. He described nineteenth-century formalism as an "apparatus for creating fictions" (809) and emphasized the pernicious effect of the "vivid fictions and metaphors of contemporary jurisprudence" (812). According to Cohen, these devices functioned as a kind of smokescreen, "dull[ing] our understanding of what courts do in fact" (816) and making it possible for judges to conceal the actual grounds of their decisions (820, 833, 841).

If this argument sounds familiar, that is because Chapter 1.4.1 described a variation on it, and because much contemporary legal scholarship, as well as popular discourse about law, takes a similar debunking stance. Fallon's (2011) article about facial challenges is a perfect example. Neither Cohen nor any of his legal-scholarly descendants, however, have been too clear about exactly what fiction *is*, beyond being undesirable. The "transcendental" fictions Cohen discussed in 1935 included legal arguments about the location of corporations (809–14) and the value of trade names (814–17). Cohen's objection to these matters seemed to have something to do with the fact that they concern intangible phenomena that come to exist only through discussion by lawyers. But Cohen does not clarify how these matters differ from the questions of moral and political value that he encourages lawyers to focus on.

Not all early twentieth-century legal thinkers used the term "fiction" so casually. Lon Fuller published his influential three-part series of law-review articles on legal fictions in 1930 and 1931 (Fuller 1968). These articles would be republished as a book in the late 1960s, and they are still taken to be the authoritative treatment of legal fictions today. But Fuller's focus was mainly on the kinds of traditional legal fictions discussed in section 2.2.1 above. When Fuller broadened his focus—as when he discussed the work of the German philosopher Hans Vaihinger—his account became more impressionistic.

In part, the shortcomings of Fuller's more general account of fiction matched the limitations of other then-current discussions of fiction. For many decades, philosophers' approaches to the topic were dominated by a debate over the existence of fictional characters and the truthfulness of sentences referring to them that Bertrand Russell (1905) and Alexius Meinong (1904) mapped out in the early twentieth century. Russell argued that such imaginary entities do not exist, so sentences referring to them are false; Meinong argued that they do exist in a sense, so sentences referring to them can be true.

Lawyers today seem to subscribe to Russell's position, mostly without realizing it. A number of intellectual developments in the mid-twentieth century, however, set the stage for the emergence of a less dismissive understanding of fiction toward the end of the twentieth century. New philosophical approaches to linguistic reference made the Russell–Meinong debate potentially irrelevant, or at least less dominant (see, e.g., Gale 1971; Kripke 1980; Thomasson 1999). New approaches to logic and metaphysics proposed understanding and analyzing statements of possibility and prediction in terms of "possible worlds" (e.g., Goodman 1955; Kripke 1963; Rescher 1964). This approach could also be used to analyze fictional discourse, and other scholars, to be discussed shortly, have taken it up for that purpose.

In the mind sciences around the same time, philosophers, psychologists, and organizational theorists began to notice how their interests and findings overlapped, and to study how people develop understandings of others' thoughts and beliefs, as well as how people develop the ability to expect and to plan (e.g., Simon 1969). In literary studies, a group of (mostly European) scholars began borrowing from linguistics, anthropology, and hermeneutics to develop the subfields of narratology (e.g., Barthes 1970; Genette 1983) and reader-response theory (e.g., Holland 1975; Iser 1980), which would supply frameworks for the more systematic analysis of fictional discourse in future work.

From this point (the 1960s and 1970s) on, understandings of "fiction" inside law and outside it developed along very different paths. Neither the work on legal fictions discussed in section 2.2.1 above nor the law-and-literature scholarship discussed in Chapter 1 has taken any account of much of the work just mentioned (for a recent partial counterexample, see Doerfler 2017). Yet cross-pollination among these other fields has continued and increased over the final three decades of the twentieth century and into the twenty-first.

Philosophers, for example, continued to debate the properties of fictional discourse. Initially, this work focused on individual propositions containing names of fictional characters (Sherlock Holmes being a favorite; see, e.g., Gale 1971; Donnellan 1974; Searle 1975; Lewis 1978), but philosophers later turned to analysis of extended fictional narratives (e.g., Walton 1993; Thomasson 1999). Philosophers even adopted the term to name a group of philosophical positions, "fictionalism" (see, e.g., Doerfler 2017; Sainsbury 2010).

Some philosophers drew on understandings originally developed by cognitive scientists to build theories of what pretending involves (Walton 1993) and how we understand both each other and verbal representations of people (Dennett 1987). Behavioral scientists and psychologists also investigated phenomena related to the experiences of writing and reading fictional discourse, such as the role of mental "simulation" in planning (Kahneman & Tversky 1982); the development in children of a concept of others' false beliefs (Wimmer & Perner 1983); and the relationships between retrospective explanation and deliberate planning, as well as the dependence of both on counterfactual reasoning (e.g., Roese & Olson 1995). Much of this work confirmed that people process written, spoken, or viewed accounts of imaginary actions and events in regular, consistent ways, rather than entirely idiosyncratically (see also Elfenbein 2018).

In literary studies, scholars working in the narratological and reader-response traditions began to look to vocabularies developed in philosophy, cognitive science, and linguistics to advance new accounts of narrative processing and character comprehension (e.g., Fludernik 1992; Palmer 2008). Other literary scholars have drawn on the possible-worlds frameworks originally developed in philosophy to examine narrative dynamics (e.g., Doležel 2000; Harshaw 1984; Herman 2013; Ryan 1991).

Now, scholars in all of these fields borrow freely from one another to explain why people create fictions, why we find them appealing, how we process them, and what regularities they have (e.g., Bogdan 2013; Everett 2013; Herman 2013). Debates persist on some of these questions, of course, but simply asking the questions has led to consensus on some matters and a more nuanced understanding of fiction than was available to earlier legal scholars such as Felix Cohen and Lon Fuller. The next section will sketch some general features of this understanding, which later sections and chapters of this book will develop further.

2.2.3.2 Contemporary views

The early twentieth-century work of thinkers such as Cohen and Fuller did not make a number of distinctions whose importance can seem self-evident in hindsight. For example, even though these authors were explicitly concerned with understanding the characteristics of statements about fictional things, they did not always clearly distinguish between such statements and the things to which they referred. A similar blurring occurs in contemporary judicial discussions of both fiction and fact, as the examples in section 2.2.2 suggest. These authors also often failed to distinguish between the conceptions formed by a reader of statements about fictional things, on the one hand, and the referents of the statements, on the other, as well as between the generation of such statements and their comprehension.

Most of the more recent discussions of fictional discourse discussed in the previous section are more careful about such distinctions. A key characteristic of fictional discourse, for many recent theorists, is that it does not refer directly to anything tangible outside language itself, even though we treat it as if it refers to things in the world that we jointly occupy (or in some world that we jointly extrapolate from our own).[6] Fuller (1968) did recognize that readers of fiction are usually aware of its fictional quality, making fictional discourse distinct from lying and other forms of deception. But Fuller did not clearly describe another equally important characteristic of fictional discourse: its metalinguistic (or metarepresentational) character (cf. Graziano 2013; Tomasello 2001).

Most current accounts of this aspect of fictional discourse take one of two approaches. They are not necessarily incompatible. The first regards fictional discourse as involving a distinct kind of speech act (e.g., Doležel 1988, 490 & n.4) in which language is used to create its own referents (see, e.g., Azzouni 2010; Schiffer 1996, 154–59; Thomasson 1999). According to this view, a fictional character—like Sherlock Holmes or Harry Potter—does not exist before it is initially written about, but it does exist afterward as a special kind of real-world entity, similar in this regard to theories, ideologies, and maybe laws as well (see, e.g., Popper 1986). The other approach focuses on the conventional and consensual dimension of fictional discourse, the way it enables people to align their understandings and conduct. On this view, fictional discourse involves a communicative "contract" or language game (e.g., Ryan 1997, 166, 168) or, more narrowly, a set of "instructions" for imagining or make-believe (Scarry 1999; Walton 1993). This perspective emphasizes how fictional discourse builds on widely shared cognitive capacities that most children naturally develop, involving the semiautomatic use of their imaginations.

This overview suggests some of the shortcomings of the simplified conception of fiction implied by the justices' use of that term and related ones in the 2014-term opinions. Fictional discourse does involve a departure from the real world, but the discourse itself, as well as the understandings of its participants, remains very much a part of the real world. And fictional discourse is not a purely private phenomenon. Because fictional discourse can be read by multiple people, who can then discuss their experiences (and will often spontaneously agree about them), it is misleading to describe fictional accounts as yielding inherently idiosyncratic conceptions of the fictional entities described. Nor is the creation of fictional discourse entirely unconstrained. For readers to use a piece of fictional discourse as a set of instructions for imagining, the language of the discourse must be comprehensible; to be comprehensible, the language must in general work similarly to the way it works in discourse about real-world phenomena. All of these features of fictional discourse explain undeniably real phenomena associated with such discourse, like fan culture (see, e.g., Jenkins 1992), as well as the justices' use of literary allusion (see also Henderson 2008).

Fictional discourse is distinct from both deceptive discourse and factual discourse. But fictional discourse can also *include* statements that are factually accurate. It is also possible to make factual statements about fictional matters; indeed, factual statements about fictional things (such as the history of Sherlock Holmes fans, see Saler 2012) are not only possible but common. As the discussion in section 2.2.2 suggested, however, legal writers seem to view fiction (and related phenomena) in a far more simplified way than this. The simplification has two unfortunate consequences. It leaves the justices unequipped to handle cases involving actual fictional discourse, cases in which the human capacity to generate fictions plays a role (see the next section). More troublingly, it may also contribute to the justices' difficulty in agreeing on the characterization and identification of "fact," the subject of sections 2.3 and 2.4 of this chapter.[7]

2.2.4 Some pitfalls of a simplified view

The justices' opinion-writing practices sometimes contradict their pejorative references to fiction. Occasionally the specifics of a case make it necessary for the justices to consider what makes discourse fictional or how readers interact with such discourse. In these cases, the drawbacks of an oversimplified conception of fiction become clear. Two sets of opinions from June 2015—in *Kimble v. Marvel Enterprises*, a patent case, and *Elonis v. United States*, a criminal prosecution—exemplify the justices' peculiar approach to such cases.

The dispute in *Kimble* concerned the authority of a case the Court decided in 1964, *Brulotte v. Thys Co.* The Court held in *Brulotte* that a patent owner cannot receive payments from a licensee (one who buys the right to make or use the patented invention) after the patent expires, even if the owner and licensee agree otherwise. Commentators criticized *Brulotte* for decades. They pointed out that the parties to a license agreement might want to spread payments out over a longer period of time—to reduce upfront investment by the licensee, for example. The parties in *Kimble* seemed to prove the point, since they (apparently unaware of *Brulotte*) had entered into a license agreement with no expiration date. Chapter 6.2.2.1 discusses some of the reasoning in the *Kimble* opinions in more detail. For the purposes of this chapter, the case is notable because of the invention that was the subject of the parties' agreement.

This invention was, as Justice Kagan described it in the second paragraph of her opinion, "a toy that allows children (and young-at-heart adults) to role-play as a 'spider person' by shooting webs—really, pressurized foam string—'from the palm of the hand'" (1, quoting U.S. Patent No. 5,072,856). In other words, the invention was what Kendall Walton (1993) would call a "prop" designed for making believe one is Spider-Man or a similar figure. The invention had commercial value because people might, in fact, want to pretend in this way, as Justice Kagan acknowledged. Marvel Entertainment licensed the right to make and sell this toy from its inventor, Stephen Kimble, and was willing to go to court over Marvel's right to keep making it without paying Kimble. The case would never have arisen, much less made it to the Supreme Court, were it not for the real-world ramifications of our practices of make-believe engagement with well-known fictional characters.

Justice Kagan's opinion plays on these themes, offering several puns on Spider-Man's features and presentation. Kimble and Marvel "set no end date for royalties" in their agreement, "apparently contemplating that they would continue for as long as kids want to imitate Spider-Man (by doing whatever a spider can)" (2). Introducing the principle of patents' limited terms, Justice Kagan writes: "Patents endow their creators with superpowers, but only for a limited time" (3). *Brulotte* has a "close relation to a whole web of precedents" (11). Most dramatically, the penultimate paragraph of Justice Kagan's opinion begins:

> What we [the Court] decide, we can undecide. But *stare decisis* teaches that we should exercise that authority sparingly. Cf. S. Lee and S. Ditko, Amazing Fantasy No. 15:

"Spider-Man," p. 13 (1962) ("[I]n this world, with great power must also come—great responsibility").

(18)

This quote from the concluding frame of the comic book issue in which Spider-Man first appeared might seem to trivialize the dispute or the Court's decision, if "fiction" is understood in the simplified way described in section 2.2.2. Justice Kagan's decision to conclude her opinion this way (and the absence of any criticism of her choice by other justices, in a term in which the justices criticized others' opinion styles fairly often) suggests an understanding that figures like Spider-Man carry not only a set of characteristics that opinion readers presumably know about, but also that readers regard those figures as in some sense exemplary (cf. Eco 1972). Tongue-in-cheek or not, Justice Kagan presents Spider-Man/Peter Parker's quip (attributed to his uncle in later tellings of his origin story) as appropriate guidance not just for the character, but also for the justices.

Of course, none of this is explicit in the *Kimble* opinion; all of Justice Kagan's references to Spider-Man could be removed from the opinion without altering its legal implications. In this sense, her allusions are purely ornamental, personal touches expressing her cultural literacy. Sometimes, however, a case can ask the parties and judges to consider the functioning of fictional discourse more directly. This was the case in *Elonis v. United States*, decided three weeks before *Kimble* in a confusing set of three opinions written by Chief Justice Roberts (for the majority) and Justices Alito (concurring in part) and Thomas (dissenting for himself alone).

The defendant in this case was prosecuted for violating a federal statute that criminalizes the transmission of "threat[s]," or threatening language, in interstate commerce (1). This defendant, Anthony Elonis, had turned to the Internet after his marriage broke up:

> Eventually, Elonis changed the user name on his Facebook page from his actual name to a rap-style nom de plume, "Tone Dougie," to distinguish himself from his "on-line persona." . . . The lyrics Elonis posted as "Tone Dougie" included graphically violent language and imagery. This material was often interspersed with disclaimers that the lyrics were "fictitious," with no "intentional resemblance to real persons." . . . Elonis posted an explanation to another Facebook user that "I'm doing this for me. My writing is therapeutic." . . . Elonis's co-workers and friends viewed the posts in a different light.
>
> (2)

Chief Justice Roberts's opinion contains lengthy quotations from Elonis's posts under the Tone Dougie name. Indeed, in the "factual background" section of the majority opinion, the Chief Justice devotes more lines to block quotes from Elonis's posts than to judicial exposition (2–4; 75 lines of exposition, 84 of quotation), and the account of the underlying events in the opinion is gradually swamped by the quotations as the account proceeds.

These quotes from Elonis's Facebook posts, like Justice Kagan's puns in *Kimble*, are not strictly necessary for analysis of the legal issue. The parties' dispute concerned the instructions given to the jury during Elonis's trial, specifically the instructions jurors received about how to decide whether Elonis's posts qualified as "threats." As Justices Alito and Thomas point out in their separate opinions, Chief Justice Roberts's majority opinion concluded that these instructions were erroneous but did not provide any guidance about what a jury instruction *should* say (Alito, 1, 2; Thomas, 1, 2). The majority opinion just holds that a jury must be instructed to find that Elonis made the statements in question with some (unspecified) culpable mental state, such as recklessness or intention to cause harm. As the separate opinions observe, Chief Justice Roberts's *Elonis* opinion avoids addressing most of the issues presented, which had been dividing lower courts and commentators in similar cases and were likely to recur in future cases (Calvert et al. 2014).

Elonis's characterization of his posts as "fictitious" might partly explain the justices' difficulty in converging on an appropriate response to the issues presented in *Elonis* and the strange way in which quotes from his posts take over the majority opinion without much analysis. None of the justices disputed the characterization of the posts as "fictitious," but the significance of this detail remains largely unexamined even in the separate opinions. In his separate opinion, Justice Alito suggests—but does not clearly conclude—that use of a pseudonym generally should not affect the legal significance of a person's statements:

> If [a] celebrity can utter such words, Elonis pleads, amateurs like him should be able to post such things on social media. But context matters. "Taken in context," lyrics in songs that are performed for an audience or sold in recorded form are unlikely to be interpreted as a real threat to a real person. . . . Statements on social media that are pointedly directed at their victims, by contrast, are much more likely to be taken seriously. To hold otherwise would grant a license to anyone who is clever enough to dress up a real threat in the guise of rap lyrics, a parody, or something similar.
>
> (Alito, 6)

This discussion notes the possibility that wrongdoers might falsely claim a "fiction" label for their threats and suggests that individuals' claims to create fictional characters DIY-style should be viewed skeptically. But Justice Alito presents these possibilities as musings rather than considered doctrine (and in other opinions, as later discussions will show, Justice Alito is willing to be quite explicit in such ancillary musings). Justice Thomas, too, argues that "serious" threats should be treated differently from uses of language involving something other than full commitment (such as "hyperbole," Thomas, 2). But like Justice Alito, he refrains from directly discussing how to make any such distinction.

The *Elonis* opinions are a kind of circumstantial evidence of the sway that the wordsmith's fallacy and one of its corollaries, a simplified conception of fiction, has over the justices' (and their clerks') thinking. That conception generates quandaries when the justices must address the real-world phenomenon of make-believe. If fictional discourse is fundamentally subjective and idiosyncratic, then it does not make sense to develop standards for its analysis. On the other hand, if fictional discourse is by definition nonfactual or false, then it would seem that a threat made by a fictional persona should not be prosecuted under the threat statute. Yet the deception inherent in such a threat means that it nevertheless involves an element of wrongfulness. The simplified conception of fiction thus points toward incompatible resolutions of Elonis's case. In the absence of any alternative to this conception, the justices seem to have been unable even to discuss, much less agree on, the properties and functions of Elonis's communications.

If the simplified conception of fiction is so problematic, what explains its persistence? Section 2.2.3 offered some suggestions. The rest of this chapter explores another, tied to the wordsmith's fallacy introduced in Chapter 1. The simplified conception of fiction is useful rhetorically as a foil for a corresponding simplified conception of "fact." That term, and the cluster of ideas for which it stands, plays a variety of very important roles in Supreme Court discourse and in legal discourse (not to mention public discourse) more generally. But its operation is unsteady. In the justices' opinions, "fact" means sometimes one thing and sometimes another; sometimes the same phenomenon will count as "fact" in one setting and not in another.

In contrast to the practices discussed up to this point in this chapter, the justices often seem all too aware of the simultaneous importance and instability of their references to "fact." One of the main functions of the simplified conception of fiction, then, might be to mark an even more unreliable way for language to operate. The radical lack of seriousness of "fiction" under the simplified conception makes references to "fact" seem, in comparison, authoritative and stable. On a better understanding of fiction, this conceptual scapegoating might be unavailable. That unavailability, in turn, could force clarification of a more obviously important issue: what we mean when we talk about "facts."

2.3 The many functions of fact

This section turns to the justices' references to "fact" in the 2014-term opinions, as well as their use of related labels, such as "actual," "real," and "concrete," serving similar functions, including being often contrasted with "fiction." The justices' discourse relies heavily on these notions as signs of the links between the Court's activity and the nonlegal world (section 2.3.1). But references to "fact," as all lawyers know, are manipulable and contestable; the justices' opinions give lawyers tools for classifying and reclassifying statements as fact or non-fact, providing or demanding backing for statements of fact, and contesting the validity of statements of fact (sections 2.2.3, 2.3.3., and 2.3.4).

2.3.1 Fact as foundation, field, and force

Legal conventions sometimes require judges to define "fact" explicitly; section 2.4 considers some such attempts in the 2014-term opinions. But judges also often refer more casually to "fact" or to what is "actual" in the service of a different point. Casual references to "fact" serve at least three purposes in the 2014-term opinions. Facts are presumed to be the necessary starting point for legal activity. (The "factual background" section appearing at the beginning of virtually every brief and opinion, sometimes labeled as such, underlines this role.) Legal decisions also operate in a factual field—the "real world" the decisions affect. Decisions can thus become foundational facts for further legal activity. Finally, an appeal to fact can be a rhetorical trump card. A standard way to reject an adversary's contention is to describe the contention as concealing or oblivious to the facts. Often, parties on both sides of a disagreement play this card.

The justices consistently describe an account of basic "facts" as a required ingredient of a full legal analysis. In the 2014-term case *M&G Polymers v. Tackett*, Justice Thomas justifies rejecting a lower court's conclusion in part because it had a "shaky factual foundation" (11). In *Rodriguez v. United States*, Justice Ginsburg explains that the reasonableness of a police officer's seizure of a person "depends on what the police in fact do" and that a court examining this issue must "not[e] what the officer actually did and how he did it" (8). And by considering the "foundational" facts of a case, a deciding court may be able to better estimate the effects its decision will have. As Justice Ginsburg explains in *Ariz. State Legislature*, this principle is the basis for the Court's justiciability doctrines, which discourage judicial action when case-specific facts are too difficult to identify: "This dispute . . . 'will be resolved . . . in a concrete factual context conducive to a realistic appreciation of the consequences of judicial action'" (14).[8]

Judicial disregard of "reality" is grounds for criticism. In *Zivotofsky*, Justice Scalia describes Justice Thomas's concurrence as "overlook[ing] the reality" concerning the specific authorities historically responsible for issuing passports (Scalia, 16). Chief Justice Roberts uses this tactic at least three times in his *Obergefell* dissent. He writes, for example, that the Court sacrifices legitimacy if the "perception" of its "humility and restraint" is not matched by the "reality" of these virtues, which the majority has failed to exhibit (Roberts, 24).[9]

When the justices refer to "fact," "reality," and what "actually" happened or will happen in these and similar ways, they do not usually acknowledge that such labels might be contested. But, of course, statements about what "actually" happened are often contested in legal proceedings. In some cases, this is because the dispute concerns phenomena that different people perceived or interpreted differently. In others, it is because of disagreement about the rules for establishing what counts as "fact" and deciding which disputed facts can serve as the basis for inferences. These possibilities generate a standard repertoire of stock challenges to matters presented as "fact."

2.3.2 *Adjudicative, legislative, and metalinguistic fact*

Lawyers understand the Supreme Court to have a different relationship to "fact" than most other U.S. courts. The Court has some power to dictate what kinds of determinations can count as factual in other courts, as well as to dictate how some such determinations are to be made and by whom. But in most cases, the Court does not itself directly find facts, or determine what "actually" happened. Nevertheless, as the previous section suggested, the justices often inquire into or assert matters they call "factual." These assertions do not always map neatly onto the categories of "fact" that the justices identify for the guidance of other courts.

The justices are most self-conscious about their special relationship to what lawyers and judges call "adjudicative facts" (or "historical facts"). These are facts relating to the parties in a case and their past activities—the concrete events that generated the dispute. Like other federal appellate courts in the United States (and unlike appellate courts in some other legal systems), the Supreme Court is not set up to find, or evaluate claims about, such facts in most of the cases it decides.[10] The Court does, however, review lower courts' handling of party-presented adjudicative facts, especially (but not only) in review of criminal proceedings. In the 2014-term case *Brumfield v. Cain*, for instance, the Court held that a trial court erred when it refused to give a criminal defendant a chance to establish the fact of his intellectual disability (see, e.g., 16–17).

Justice Sotomayor, who wrote the *Brumfield* majority opinion, also dissented in *Glossip v. Gross*, arguing similarly there that the petitioners (prisoners on death row) had offered sufficient support for the facts they sought to establish, and that the trial court was mistaken not to find in their favor (see, e.g., Sotomayor, 10). The main "fact" at issue in *Glossip* concerned the sedative effects of the benzodiazepine midazolam, part of the "execution protocol" used in executions in Oklahoma at the time. In some ways, the question of midazolam's properties seems like an adjudicative fact: it is an issue about which witnesses could testify, and it concerns the experiences of individuals in specific situations. In other ways, however, the issue in *Glossip* looks like one of "legislative fact." Sometimes called "social facts," these are facts concerning such things as common or widespread practices, the distribution of traits in a population, physical regularities (such as chemical properties), and so forth. A common, though not universal, feature of legislative facts is that it is difficult to be absolutely certain about them (see Davis 1942; see also Yoshino 2016). The question in *Glossip* also concerned a general property of midazolam, not just its action on a particular occasion. Most legislative facts are, or involve, generalizations.

The Court is an avid producer and consumer of legislative facts (e.g., Faigman 2008; Larsen 2014; Petroski 2013). Sometimes justices rely in their opinions on generalizations that seem easy to validate, at least in theory, for instance because they concern statistical matters, such as the number of prisoners in the U.S. in solitary confinement (more than 25,000; *Davis v. Ayala*, Kennedy, 2) or the number of "administrative subpoena authorities held by" federal agencies (approximately 335; *Patel*, 12). At other times, the justices discuss social phenomena and practices with varying degrees of precision: the "rapidity and pervasiveness with which ideas may spread" on the Internet (*Williams-Yulee*, Kennedy, 5); the "well-known" "deleterious harms" "produce[d]" by "prolonged solitary confinement" (*Glossip*, Breyer, 20). As the next section will discuss further, the justices do not recognize many limits on their presentation of such assertions.

A third kind of "fact" appearing throughout the 2014-term opinions is conveyed in assertions about legal practice or rules. These kinds of facts do not have a classic legal label, but they might be called "metalinguistic facts." Examples include assertions about the significance of statutory and constitutional provisions.[11] Lawyers are trained to call such questions legal rather than factual. But the justices (and other U.S. judges) discuss their conclusions about legal meaning very similarly to the ways they discuss other legislative facts (see, e.g., Fallon 2015a).[12] In his dissent in the 2014-term case *Texas Dep't of Housing*, for example, Justice Alito supports his conclusion about the meaning of the term "because of" in the relevant statute with, among other things, a footnote reproducing each sentence using the phrase that appeared in the *Washington Post* on January 21, 2015 (Alito, 4–5 n.2). Similarly, Chief Justice Roberts appends to his *Ariz. State Legislature* dissent, as support for his argument, a list of the seventeen clauses in the federal Constitution that use the word "legislature" (Roberts, 1–2, 28–32).

Section 2.4.3 will return to these sorts of assertions about the "facts" of law. For present purposes, the point is simply that practices like these make it difficult to distinguish conclusions about the meaning of legal terms from determinations more traditionally considered "factual" (this difficulty was at the heart of the disagreements in *Teva*, the "skilled-artisan" case). Such practices seem to be a manifestation of the wordsmith's fallacy, in that they often involve justices' treating "facts" about language as the facts to which they have best access. As the next section will suggest, however, the wordsmith's fallacy can also breed anxieties about the stability of lawyers' and judges' assertions of fact.

2.3.3 The grounding of fact

As noted above, the Supreme Court generally does not directly find adjudicative facts. But the Court is the ultimate arbiter of the rules governing the establishment of such facts in federal trial courts (and some of the rules applying in state courts). Through their practices with respect to legislative and metalinguistic facts, lawyers also demonstrate commitment to the principle that assertions about facts—about how things are or were in the actual world—need to be accompanied by information about how the assertion might be verified. Lawyers' characteristically obsessive insistence on providing such grounding is frustrated by a patchy and largely arbitrary set of conventions for demonstrating it (see Scheppele 1994; Twining 2006).

In trial courts, adjudicative facts are grounded in evidence: witness testimony and exhibits. The law of evidence ostensibly governs the process of providing such grounding. Government actors' gathering of evidence is also regulated by federal constitutional law, especially the Fourth and Sixth Amendments. The Court has been responsible for developing both federal evidence law and evidence-related constitutional law for many decades. No Supreme Court term now passes without several decisions setting out standards for law-enforcement evidence gathering—via, for example, geolocator tracking (the 2014-term case *Grady*) or drug-detecting dogs (the 2014-term case *Rodriguez*).

The justices' discussion of such matters often seems to aspire to comprehensiveness. After stating a legal rule requiring proof of some fact, for example, an opinion may offer guidance concerning the types of evidence that might suffice to prove such a fact. Here is a typical example from the 2014-term case *McFadden v. United States*:

> as with most *mens rea* requirements, the Government can prove the requisite mental state [of knowledge that a substance is a controlled substance or an "analogue" of a controlled substance] through either direct evidence or circumstantial evidence. Direct evidence could include, for example, past arrests that put a defendant on notice of the controlled status of a substance. . . . Circumstantial evidence could include, for example, a defendant's concealment of his activities, evasive behavior with respect to law enforcement, knowledge that a particular substance produces a "high" similar to that produced by controlled substances, and knowledge that a particular substance is subject to seizure at customs.
>
> (5–6 n.1)

This passage, from an opinion by Justice Thomas, looks like a set of instructions. Yet it explains neither how these varieties of evidence would be presented at a trial nor exactly how to derive inferences about a defendant's knowledge from such properly presented direct or circumstantial evidence. This omission is typical. Legal rules are oddly silent about what would seem to be a central concern: how a lawyer or decision-maker is to get from evidence to the facts at which the evidence is supposed to point (e.g., Scheppele 1994, 1010–12, 1022; Twining 2006). This silence is a perpetual source of mystification for law students. They are expected to learn to navigate the legally acceptable paths from "evidence" to "fact," but not given much guidance on doing so. Instead, they must develop the skill by personally recognizing discursive patterns, in a process discussed further in Chapters 3, 5, and 6.

Judicial opinions are similarly silent about the establishment of legislative facts. The Supreme Court is the ultimate U.S. authority on the content of most federal legal rules; as a result, the justices must sometimes assess factual premises for those rules, that is, the real-world states of affairs presupposed by the rules. Legislative facts provide these premises, and the justices seem to consider themselves competent to "find" such facts. But while the justices do tag many assertions of legislative facts with source information, the types of sources the justices cite vary wildly, as commentators have noted critically (Faigman 2008; Larsen 2014).

Sometimes the grounds for newly asserted legislative facts are previous judicial assertions of legislative fact. In one 2014-term case, for example, Justice Alito cites the majority opinion in the Court's 2008 decision in *District of Columbia v. Heller* as support for a generalization about the "typical" purposes of people who "possess[ ]" short-barreled shotguns (*Johnson*, Alito, 17–18). Statutes and regulations can also support factual assertions. In the 2014-term case *Young v. UPS*, Justice Alito cites provisions of the Code of Federal Regulations to support a description of the medical conditions that can cause truck drivers to lose their Department of Transportation certification (Alito, 9–10).

The justices also, more controversially, cite non-governmental materials to support claims of legislative fact. Amicus briefs are a favorite resource, and their popularity seems to be growing (Larsen 2014). Justices cite amicus briefs as support for generalizations about such matters as voter beliefs (*Williams-Yulee*, Ginsburg, 4–5), past practices of the political branches (*Zivotofsky*, 20), and the causes of contemporary racial segregation in housing (*Texas Dep't of Housing*, 5–6). Chief Justice Roberts even mocks this practice in his *Obergefell* dissent (Roberts, 25). The justices cite journalists' accounts as support for assertions about matters such as public awareness of the effects of solitary confinement (*Davis v. Ayala*, Kennedy, 304). Despite some of the justices' public disparagement of the utility of legal scholarship (e.g., Liptak 2013), justices also cite law review articles as support for factual claims as well as legal and policy arguments (see, e.g., *Davis v. Ayala*, Kennedy, 4). The justices commonly cite academic monographs as support for claims about historical trends and social phenomena (e.g., *Zivotofsky*, 20; *Texas Dep't of Housing*, 5–6; *Obergefell*, 3–4).

The justices follow broadly similar practices in their grounding of adjudicative, legislative, and metalinguistic facts. They recite adjudicative facts found by the lower courts, following the recitals with citations to the lower-court opinion or appellate record. They recite legislative facts, too, alongside the kinds of references described above. They support assertions of metalinguistic facts, sometimes, with lists or samples of language use. Like citations to the record, these citations invite readers to verify the propositions they support and seem to mark the propositions as factual (Ryan 1997, 166–67). In all of these areas, however, the justices ground their assertions of fact in further assertions. Citation practices show the importance of demonstrating connections between the justices' textual output and the "real world," but they also show that the demonstration always occurs through a chain of linguistic acts. This built-in distance between judicial discourse and its referents generates a standard set of vulnerabilities for virtually any judicial assertion of fact.

2.3.4 Discounting facts

As became evident in U.S. public discourse in the year following the 2016 presidential election, all assertions of fact are vulnerable. Even when such assertions are sourced or backed up, adversaries can attack the sources or the assertions' presentation. The late-2010s phenomena of "fake news" and "alternative facts" have counterparts and precursors in legal discourse (Rutenberg 2017). In some ways, these public phenomena are popularizations of a set of typical legal discourse practices (cf. Scheppele 2018). Deep skepticism about the determination of "fact" accompanies many assertions of fact by legal professionals (Rosenberg 2014). The justices are no exception. In their 2014-term opinions, the justices often discount factual assertions by lower courts or by other justices in separate opinions. Asserted facts about some matters—especially mental states and complex social phenomena—draw criticism especially often. Other fact-discrediting conventions aim not at specific kinds of facts, but at recurring kinds of problems with the support for putative facts. These practices form some of the basic but largely tacit rules of litigation rhetoric.

As noted, the justices often challenge facts concerning individuals' (and groups') mental states. Chapter 3 will further consider the justices' often confident assertions about what certain real people think or how they feel—assertions that the same justices often accompany with comments about the difficulty of being sure of what anyone feels or what anyone is thinking. Conflicting accounts of different witnesses may highlight this difficulty, as in the 2014-term case *EEOC v. Abercrombie & Fitch*, in which one employee testified that she told another employee that a job applicant "wore a head scarf for a religious reason," but the second employee testified that the first "did not share this belief with him" (Alito, 2–3 n.2). But justices sometimes spontaneously note similar concerns. For example, Justice

Alito stresses the difficulty of knowing exactly what the confederate flag "symbolizes" to any given person in *Walker v. Texas Div., Sons of Confederate Veterans* (Alito, 15). Similarly, in his majority opinion in *Davis v. Ayala*, Justice Alito notes that "[i]t is not at all unusual for individuals to come to different conclusions in attempting to read another's attitude or mood" (28).

Lawyers also use a set of conventional arguments against inconvenient facts of all kinds. One such convention is to describe the fact in question as irrelevant. Justice Alito uses this technique in his majority opinion in *Comptroller v. Wynne*, where he describes a point made by the dissent about Maryland's sources of tax revenue as a "red herring" (24). Another all-purpose technique questions the sources on which a factual assertion is based. Ideally, a user of this technique shows that no sources support an assertion, or that important support is missing.[13] Alternatively, a critic can identify flaws in the methods used to generate a proposed fact. If an issue was not sufficiently "tested" or challenged by an adversary, for example, then a critic may charge that the supposed fact has not been solidly established. Justice Sotomayor uses both of these approaches in her *Davis v. Ayala* dissent (Sotomayor, 5, 6, 13–14).[14]

The rules of evidence are just part of a network of legal devices for discussing and handling "fact." From the Court's perspective, appellate standards of review are at least as important as rules of evidence in this enterprise. Appellate courts are supposed to review trial courts' findings on factual matters deferentially, that is, to assume the findings are correct and to supply special justification for concluding otherwise (Yoshino 2016). This principle supposedly reflects the different capacities of trial- and appellate-court judges. Trial-court judges have personally seen the witnesses and evidence, so they are better acquainted than appellate judges with the materials from which inferences about facts are supposed to be drawn. One consequence of this principle is that appellate courts can usually avoid making the factual determinations that—because of the conventions of challenge described above—are never quite as certain as we might like them to be. The standards of review allow appellate judges to affirm the central role of fact as the basis for legitimate legal judgment without taking responsibility for the stabilization of particular factual determinations. From the appellate perspective, that stabilization is the job of trial courts, who are assumed to be doing their jobs properly unless they obviously are not.[15]

A reference to fact in an appellate opinion is a bit like a sheer curtain—from a distance, it may look solid, but the more closely you examine it, the less substantial it looks. This phenomenon is both a product and a cause of the "metalinguistic ideology" identified by Elizabeth Mertz and the wordsmith's fallacy described in Chapter 1. Lawyers learn how to make assertions about fact and support them with further assertions or other linguistic performances, such as citations. These conventions breed a sense of control over what counts as "fact." But because legal facts are linguistically constructed, they are also always susceptible to deconstruction. Lawyers are thus acutely aware that their control over what counts as "fact" is always at risk. Because legal practice, at least at the appellate level, is so thoroughly discursive, opportunities for escaping this vicious circle are limited.

2.4 Fact and its foils

As section 2.3 explained, judicial references to matters of fact are both an important resource for justification and cause for anxiety. References to "fact" play other roles in legal argument in addition to those outlined above. Sometimes legal rules require judges to distinguish statements of fact from other kinds of statements—of opinion, of law. The shape-changing quality of "fact" reappears in these settings.

Relative to statements of opinion, the justices describe statements of fact as stable and fixed (section 2.4.1); relative to statements of law, however, statements of fact are unpredictable and contingent (section 2.4.2). Yet law is not just the opposite of fact; law also has a factual dimension. The justices assume that some statements of the law are also statements of fact (section 2.4.3). The following sections examine several cases from the 2014 term that illustrate these shifting positions on "fact." The shifts in turn help to explain why a simplified conception of "fiction" remains a useful rhetorical resource for lawyers and judges.

2.4.1 Fact versus opinion (and law versus morals)

Courts must distinguish facts from opinions (or more precisely, statements of fact from statements of opinion) in a handful of settings, most involving wrongs committed by means of language, such as defamation and fraud. The Supreme Court has repeatedly had to address this distinction, thanks to the existence of many federal fraud statutes and to the potential for conflict between defamation law and constitutional free-speech principles. In the 2014 term, this distinction was one of the main issues in a case arising under one of the federal securities-fraud statutes.

The Securities Act of 1933 requires corporations to register with the Securities and Exchange Commission before selling shares to the public. Section 11 of the act makes a corporation liable to people who buy the corporation's shares if the corporation's registration statement contains an "untrue statement of material fact." (Section 11 also creates liability for statements that "omit to state a material fact required . . . to make the statements therein [in the registration statement] not misleading.") Unlike traditional fraud claims, Section 11 claims do not require a plaintiff to show that the defendant (the corporation) intended to mislead anyone.

In *Omnicare v. Laborers District Council Construction Industry Pension Fund*, the defendant's (Omnicare's) registration statement included two brief assertions that Omnicare was in compliance with applicable law. As it turned out, however, Omnicare was at the time being investigated and was eventually sued for violating anti-kickback laws. When they learned of the investigations, Omnicare shareholders sued the corporation, arguing that the statements about legal compliance in Omnicare's registration statement violated Section 11. The corporation defended on the theory that the statements in question—both of which began with the words "We believe"—were statements of opinion and thus not "untrue statements of material fact."

One of the issues for decision by the Court was thus what distinguishes statements of fact from statements of opinion, and when, if ever, the latter can be a basis for Section 11 liability. All nine justices endorsed a sharp distinction between the two types of statement. As Justice Kagan explained in her opinion for the majority, quoting Webster's Dictionary: "A fact is 'a thing done or existing' or '[a]n actual happening.' . . . An opinion is 'a belief[,] a view,' or 'a sentiment which the mind forms of persons or things'" (6). This distinction associates facts with verifiability and mind-independence; it associates opinions with subjectivity and, perhaps, susceptibility to change. Justice Kagan goes on to reinforce these connotations: "a statement of fact ('the coffee is hot') expresses certainty about a thing, whereas a statement of opinion ('I think the coffee is hot') does not" (6). This contrast stresses the lack of certainty of the person expressing an opinion, but it also implies that anyone who reads or hears such a statement is entitled to no more certainty than the speaker about the matter mentioned in the statement.

As Justice Kagan's analysis continues, this clear association of facts with certainty and opinions with skepticism breaks down. Because statements of opinion are statements about "belief" or "sentiment," "every . . . statement [of opinion] explicitly affirms one fact: that the speaker actually holds the stated belief" (7). (Moreover, "some sentences that begin with opinion words like 'I believe' contain embedded statements of fact" (8).) This explicit affirmation of a belief by the person making a statement of opinion, according to Justice Kagan, entitles a listener or reader to rely on the speaker's sincerity; this partial vouching for the sincerity of the opinion may also imply further factual claims. On this point (though not framed exactly this way), Justices Scalia and Thomas, each writing separately, disagree with Justice Kagan's account.

The second issue addressed in *Omnicare*—on which Justices Scalia and Thomas also disagree with the majority—concerns liability for omissions, or when a corporation should be liable for *failing* to say something in a registration statement. (Omnicare's registration statement arguably involved omissions because it said nothing about the then-pending investigations into Omnicare's activities.) For Justice Kagan and for the two justices who wrote separately, this issue boils down to the question of how much an investor may trust the drafters of a registration statement. Justice Kagan suggests that when a statement of opinion expresses a belief in a relatively specific fact, such as a corporation's legal compliance, readers may justifiably assume that the person writing the statement had some reason for holding the belief and did some investigation before expressing the belief (see, e.g., 8, 13 n.8, 18). It follows that if the writer has no such basis, and fails to say so, the writer might mislead readers through omission.

Justice Scalia disagrees on this point. He agrees that the reader of a statement of opinion may assume that the writer is sincerely expressing the opinion, but he does not agree that such a reader may assume anything about the basis for the opinion. He maintains that such statements do not imply any previous investigation—especially if they concern matters on which the speaker has some authority.[16] According to Justice Scalia, a sound opinion might be based on inquiry, but it might just as reasonably be based on the writer's accumulated expertise (Scalia, 3–6). So the reader of a statement of opinion should trust that any endorsement it contains is both sincere and authoritative.

Justices Kagan and Scalia disagree in part about the level of certainty a reader may reach regarding the state of affairs described in a statement of opinion, and in part about the "depth" of such a statement, or how much the speaker is implicitly vouching for by making it. Justice Thomas, in contrast, would not even have considered the omissions question. To him, both opinions—but especially Justice Kagan's—are themselves insufficiently grounded in fact:

> the highly fact-intensive nature of the omissions inquiry provides a[] . . . reason not to address it at this time. The majority acknowledges that the facts a reasonable investor may infer from a statement of opinion depend on the context. And yet it opines about certain facts an investor may infer from an issuer's legal compliance opinion: that such an opinion is based on legal advice, for example. . . . Those inferences may seem sensible enough in a vacuum, but lower courts would do well to heed the majority's admonition that every statement of opinion must be considered "in a broader frame," . . . taking into account all the facts of the statement and the context.
>
> (Thomas, 2–3)

The three *Omnicare* opinions show a spectrum of judicial attitudes toward the legal treatment of statements of opinion. The seven justices in the majority are willing to parse such statements in some detail. Justice Scalia accepts this analysis up to a point but does not approve of reading any implied "basis" into a statement of opinion. Justice Thomas would not consider the question of liability for omissions in opinion statements, at least not in the abstract. Yet all nine justices agree that there is a clear difference between statements of opinion and statements of fact, that it is possible to categorize particular statements definitively as statements of fact or opinion, and that statements of opinion are more "tentative" (19) than statements of fact—even though statements of opinion may, according to at least seven justices, also both contain and imply statements of fact.

How can it be that statements of fact and opinion are fundamentally distinguishable, if opinions also both include facts and imply them? No opinion in *Omnicare* confronts this question directly. The vocabulary available to the justices for discussing the matter, which depends on associating facts with certainty and opinions with unreliability, makes its resolution difficult (although not impossible). Insisting on the dichotomy between fact and opinion is, moreover, rhetorically useful. It allows the justices to affirm that statements of certain, verifiable "fact" are possible and that they can be distinguished from uncertain and relatively unverifiable "opinion." Like the use of "fiction" as an epithet, the fact-opinion distinction helps counteract concerns about the dependability of "fact."

The dichotomy accepted by all of the justices in *Omnicare* is reminiscent of another classic distinction: that between law, on the one hand, and politics and morals, on the other (see Hart 1961; Shklar 1964). Although judicial discourse often contrasts law and fact (as the next section will explain), it just as often identifies law with fact (associating legal matters with certainty and verifiability) and morals and politics with opinion (all three being domains of justified individual difference).

Such a lamination of the fact–opinion distinction onto a law–politics or law–morals distinction appears in opinions throughout the 2014 term. In *Glossip*, for example, Justices Scalia, Thomas, and Sotomayor all rely on the contrast in different ways. Justice Scalia justifies his refusal to consider the constitutionality of the death penalty by describing the calibration of retribution, a quintessential moral question, as "far above the judiciary's pay grade" (Scalia, 4–5). Justice Thomas similarly criticizes Justice Breyer's reliance on academic studies of the assessment of crimes' egregiousness: the studies are silly and offensive because they reduce moral judgments to "pseudoscientific" "cardboard stereotypes" and "cold mathematical calculations" (Thomas, 6). Moral questions, according to Justice Thomas, cannot be discussed in the language of fact, and moral questions that have been assigned to decision-makers other than judges (the framers, legislators, the capital jury) are not judges' concern. Justice Sotomayor, in contrast, stresses the political dimensions of the death penalty. She describes lethal injection as "the latest iteration of the States' centuries-long search for 'neat and non-disfiguring homicidal methods'" (Sotomayor, 30–31). The Court's job, she suggests, is to examine the legal issues presented in a death-penalty case with awareness that each of the relevant actors (the defendant *and* the state) has acted in a way that has moral implications, and not to get distracted by just one of those implications.

Chief Justice Roberts makes a similar point in his *Zivotofsky* dissent. He argues that the majority's interpretation of the statute at issue in the case—an interpretation of the statute as a congressional endorsement of Israel's claim of sovereignty over Jerusalem—"essentially . . . subject[s] a duly enacted statute to an international heckler's veto" (Roberts, 5). In his reading, the interpretation of statutes is not a matter of personal opinion or political preference, but a matter of law—and thus also, paradoxically, a matter of fact. The equation of law with fact in this kind of argument is paradoxical because in other contexts, legal conventions require matters of law to be clearly distinguished from and opposed to matters of fact. In this scheme, the subject of the next section, "law" signifies stability and certainty, while "fact" takes on the qualities of unpredictability and uncertainty.

2.4.2 Fact versus law

For a lawyer or judge, identifying an issue as factual or legal determines the way the issue can be discussed, the way a statement about it can be backed up, and which decision-maker in the legal system will have final say on it at what point. Although it is fundamental, the distinction is notoriously difficult to make, and judges sometimes acknowledge its artificiality. Both the importance of the distinction and its trickiness are evident in two cases from the term: *Teva Pharmaceuticals v. Sandoz* (decided in January 2015) and *Heien v. North Carolina* (decided a month earlier). In *Teva*, all of the justices affirmed the importance of the distinction between factual and legal issues, just weeks after a majority in *Heien* rejected the significance of the distinction in a different context.

In *Teva*, the eight justices joining Justice Breyer's majority opinion, as well as Justice Thomas, dissenting, agreed that it is feasible to distinguish factual from legal questions and can be important to do so. *Teva* concerned the standard of appellate review of a federal trial judge's conclusions about the meaning and scope of patent claims—the parts of a patent document that describe, in (highly stylized) words, what the patent covers. The process of reaching these conclusions in the trial court is known as claim construction.

In a 1996 decision, *Markman v. Westview Instruments*, the Court held that this process should be performed by the trial judge alone—with the parties' help, but without asking a jury to decide anything about the patent's coverage. *Markman* made claim construction an important phase of patent litigation, often allowing the judge to determine an outcome relatively early in the case and prompting settlement in the parties' anticipation of this possibility. At the trial-court level, it is generally the judge's responsibility to decide legal questions and the jury's to decide factual questions. So *Markman* could be taken to suggest that claim construction involved no factual questions. And after *Markman*, the Federal Circuit—the appeals court for all patent disputes—adopted this position, reviewing all claim construction determinations using the *de novo* standard typically used for review of trial-court decisions on questions of law, without deference to the trial-court judge. The issue in *Teva* was whether this practice was appropriate, or whether, as some judges and observers argued, appellate courts should be more deferential in reviewing factual findings made by a trial-court judge during claim construction.

The *Teva* majority endorsed the latter view. Justice Breyer notes that patent claims often use technical terms, and in other contexts, courts consider questions about the meaning of technical terms to be factual questions that can be resolved before reaching final conclusions about a document's legal meaning. The dispute in *Teva* concerned such a question of technical meaning: "how a skilled artisan [the imaginary person from whose perspective patent claims are read] would understand the way in which a curve constructed from chromatogram data reflects molecular weights" of a substance (16).

Justice Breyer suggests that judges can distinguish factual from legal issues of meaning based on the types of evidence needed to decide the issues. If the court "need[s] to look beyond the patent[]" and consult sources such as treatises and expert witness testimony "to understand . . . the background science or the meaning of a term," the conclusions drawn from such evidence are factual (12). Acknowledging that it will not always be easy to decide whether a particular issue is factual or legal (and that requiring courts to make the distinction could encourage bickering about this tangential point), Justice Breyer observes that courts successfully make similar decisions in other legal contexts all the time.[17]

Dissenting, Justice Thomas agrees that it is, in theory, possible to distinguish factual from legal issues, but he is less confident than Justice Breyer about judges' ability to make the distinction. Partly as a result, he concludes that appellate courts should treat trial judges' decisions about the meaning of technical terms in patent claims as legal decisions. For one thing, he notes, the "skilled artisan" perspective is not the perspective of any real human being, but a "legal fiction" (10). Questions about the meanings of terms in legal documents, according to Justice Thomas, are factual questions only when they prompt a "search" for the "'real intention[s]'" of, say, parties to a contract (5). The meanings of technical terms in a patent claim are not "historical facts" of this kind (2–3). Rather, they are general, abstract meanings, "'akin to'" judicial conclusions about the meanings of terms in statutes (2–3).

Justice Thomas's classification of questions about mental states as factual, at least in this context, seems to associate factual matters with more indeterminate conclusions (needing the insulation of deferential appellate review) and legal matters with more public ones. This alignment is inconsistent with the qualities Justice Kagan associates with "fact," as opposed to "opinion," in *Omnicare*, but it is consistent with Justice Sotomayor's account in *Heien*, discussed below. The variable connotations of the "fact" label compromise its usefulness for stabilizing legal pronouncements in anything more than a local and temporary way. Indeed, the label can be used in apparently contradictory ways not only by different justices writing separate opinions in the same case, but even within a single opinion. Justice Breyer's *Teva* opinion, for example, uses "fact" mainly as an adjective ("factual") modifying "finding," "determination," or "question" (see 5–6, 8, 13–14). This usage suggests a notion of "facts" as the linguistically generated contents of findings and determinations. But Justice Breyer also discusses the "general facts" and "technical facts" that public and private parties "consider" before enacting a statute or granting a patent (11), suggesting that facts precede their discussion. Justice Thomas, in contrast, seems to view "fact" mainly in the latter way. "[T]he 'fact' of how a skilled artisan would understand a given term or phrase at a particular point... is a legal fiction," he writes; "it has no existence independent of the claim construction process" (Thomas, 10), so it cannot be accurately labeled "fact." Yet elsewhere, Justice Thomas describes "determinations" as "'akin to a fact'" or to "'a legal conclusion'" (Thomas, 2–3), suggesting an equivalence between legal pronouncements and facts, rather than a distinction between them. These slippages between what might be called referential and metalinguistic conceptions of "fact" rarely provoke comment or criticism.

Heien offers another illustration of this phenomenon, with a different lineup of justices. This case involved a challenge to the constitutionality of a police officer's stop of a car, after the officer's search of the car revealed cocaine and the car's passenger, Nicholas Heien, was prosecuted for its possession. The officer justified his initial stop based on the car's having only one functioning taillight. As it turned out, the state motor-vehicle code was not clear about taillight requirements at the time of the stop. One provision required "a stop lamp," suggesting that only one taillight could be enough. Another, however, required that "all originally equipped rear lamps . . . [be] in good working order" (12). When Heien was stopped, no state court had yet resolved this discrepancy. Heien challenged the prosecution's use of the cocaine as evidence against him, arguing that his stop was unlawful because he had not violated the traffic code—he had a working taillight, as the first provision required. The state Supreme Court eventually validated Heien's position by concluding that the code required only one working taillight. As a result, the officer who stopped Heien had not been legally justified in doing so. Although the officer could not have known it at the time, he was mistaken about what the law (the vehicle code) required.

In earlier cases, the Court had held that a reasonable mistake of fact (such as a police officer's mistaken understanding about whether a person consenting to search of a house was a resident of the house) would not make an otherwise lawful stop or search unlawful. Before Heien's case, the Court had never decided whether reasonable mistakes about the law should be analyzed the same way. In *Heien*, eight justices concluded that they should.

In his opinion for the *Heien* majority, Chief Justice Roberts describes law and facts as comparable "inputs" into an officer's decision to stop or search a person: "Reasonable suspicion [the required basis for a stop] arises from the combination of an officer's understanding of the facts and his understanding of the relevant law" (6; see also 11). Basing this conclusion on an intuitive account of the structure of decision-making and a few cases addressing roughly analogous issues, Chief Justice Roberts avoided the need to discuss explicitly what distinguishes factual issues from legal ones. But his understanding of the relationship between facts and legal activity seems similar to Justice Thomas's position in *Teva*: facts and law alike exist in the world, coordinated with one another but independent of human action. Facts and law inform human action, and both facts and law inform the evaluation of such action, but neither is inherently dependent on human action.

Justice Sotomayor was the only justice to disagree with this position in *Heien*. Arguing that officers' mistakes of law should be treated differently from their mistakes of fact, she points to many other settings in which the Court distinguishes between the two kinds of mistake, and stresses that judges have traditionally taken different approaches to each. She also describes facts as "probabilisitic," varying with each situation as well as, perhaps, with individuals' perspectives and access to information (4). The law, in contrast, is a "fixed . . . yardstick" for assessing behavior, so it must always be "'definite and knowable'" (1, 4). In *Heien*, Justice Sotomayor seems more committed than the majority to the notion that the law is what the courts say it is, not what people think it is. Yet she also insists on the law's stability, and she seems to agree with the majority that facts preexist and inform the decisions of both citizens and judges.

Teva and *Heien* exemplify the flexibility of the fact–law distinction and the "fact" label in particular in legal discourse. Sometimes fact and law must be distinguished (the *Teva* majority, Justice Sotomayor in *Heien*). Sometimes the difference, while theoretically available, is irrelevant (the *Heien* majority). And sometimes it is so difficult to make the distinction that it is not worth the effort (Justice Thomas in *Teva*, possibly the *Heien* majority). Sometimes facts stabilize decision-making, allowing confident action (*Omnicare*). Sometimes they are obscure (the *Teva* majority) or "probabilistic" (Justice Sotomayor in *Heien*). Sometimes the term "fact" refers to states of affairs in the world that preexist their perception and discussion (the *Heien* majority); sometimes "fact" is a label for particular kinds of legal activity or statement (the *Teva* majority).

The presence of these fluctuations in legal discourse is no revelation. The mutability of legal references to "fact" makes possible a whole array of recurring forms of argument and analysis (cf. Fallon 2011, 960, 964; Scheppele 1990, 43). But because these references play such an important role in legal justification, this flexibility can undercut the utility of any given reference. *Teva*, *Heien*, and the cases discussed in the next section suggest that judges often refer to "fact" to communicate the stability of a legal analysis, but that the references

International Trade and the Environment

International Library of Environmental Economics and Policy
General Editors: Tom Tietenberg and Wendy Morrison

Titles in the Series

Fisheries Economics, Volumes I and II
Lee G. Anderson

Green Accounting
Peter Bartelmus and Eberhard Seifert

The Economics of International Environmental Agreements
Amitrajeet A. Batabyal

International Trade and the Environment
Judith M. Dean

Economic Costs and Consequences of Environmental Regulation
Wayne B. Gray

The Theory and Practice of Command and Control Regulation
Gloria E. Helfand and Peter Berck

Property Rights and Environmental Problems
Bruce Larson

Indirect Valuation Methods
Robert Mendelsohn

The Economics of Land Use
Peter Parks

The Economics of Sustainability
John C.V. Pezzey and Michael A. Toman

The Economics of Biodiversity Conservation
Stephen Polasky

The Economics of Environmental Monitoring and Enforcement
Clifford S. Russell

Discounting and Environmental Policy
Joel D. Scheraga

Economics of Forestry
Roger A. Sedjo

Economics and Liability for Environmental Problems
Kathleen Segerson

Experiments in Environmental Economics, Volumes I and II
Jason F. Shogren

Emissions Trading Programs, Volumes I and II
Tom Tietenberg

serve this function only if lawyers and judges agree not to consider their own more general practices in this regard. In particular, in contemporary legal discourse, facts are sometimes discussed as states of affairs in the world, and sometimes as statements about the world. Lawyers are not trained to distinguish between the two understandings; the wordsmith's fallacy discourages any such distinction, since it is not a difference lawyers are in the habit of pointing out. As the next section explains, lawyers often use the term "law" in similar ways.

2.4.3 The facts of law

Legal distinctions between issues of fact and issues of law often stress the particularity and fluidity of facts in contrast to the generality and stability of law. Many legal disputes, however, either arise from or at some point concern changes in legal rules, rather than factual circumstances. Cases that reach the Supreme Court are especially likely to involve disagreements about whether or not, or how, the law has or should be changed. Thus, although lawyers and judges often describe the law as fixed, it is in practice changing all the time.

Cases involving disputes over whether and how the law has changed present judges with a quandary: how does one give content to, or even create, new legal rules without jeopardizing the symbolic stability of "law"? Many, perhaps most, features of Supreme Court decisional language can be explained as rhetorical responses to this quandary (see Ferguson 1990; Solan 1993). Another pair of cases from the 2014 term—*Yates v. United States* and *Dep't of Homeland Security v. MacLean*—illustrate these points. Both *Yates*, a criminal case turning on an evidence-tampering provision, and *MacLean*, a suit involving the meaning of a statutory provision enacted in the same year, concern the relations among legal rules (as embodied in language), the linguistic facts involved in statements of those rules, and the "facts" of those rules' status or action in the world (facts related to their perlocutionary effect; see Austin 1962). The justices' detailed attention to the first and second of these matters helps to distract their readers from their evasion of the third.

Yates arose out of the prosecution of a fisherman. A federal agent boarded John Yates's boat in the Gulf of Mexico for inspection and identified some of Yates's catch as under the size allowed by federal regulations. After the agent left the boat, Yates had a shipmate throw the undersized fish overboard, contrary to the agent's instructions. Prosecutors charged Yates with violation of several federal laws, including a provision of the Sarbanes-Oxley Act of 2002 authorizing punishment (by up to 20 years in prison) of anyone who "alters, destroys, mutilates, conceals, covers up, falsifies, or makes a false entry in any record, document, or tangible object with the intent to" obstruct a federal investigation (1). The government argued that the fish were "tangible objects" that Yates had caused to be concealed, and the trial-court judge, jury, and Eleventh Circuit agreed.

Five Supreme Court justices did not. Both Justice Ginsburg, writing for the majority, and Justice Alito, concurring separately, identify several features of the statutory provision that, they explain, support the conclusion that the fish should *not* be considered "tangible objects." In addition to dictionary definitions, Justice Ginsburg points to the list of verbs in the provision, noting that several do not seem to be suitable linguistic companions for many nouns that might otherwise seem to name "tangible objects": "It would be unnatural . . . to describe a killer's act of wiping his fingerprints from a gun as 'falsifying' the murder weapon" (15). Justice Alito finds this point especially persuasive: "How does one make a false entry in a fish?" (Alito, 3).[18] In dissent, Justice Kagan objects to the majority's departure from the "everyday" meaning of the term "tangible object," whose clarity, she insists, makes the case "easy" (Kagan, 1).

The opinions in *Yates* exemplify competing contemporary approaches to statutory interpretation. The justices' development and discussion of these approaches, together with extensive scholarly commentary on them (see Petroski 2012) and their presentation to several decades' worth of law students, has fortified the wordsmith's fallacy over the past generation or two. Familiarity with the approaches generates a sense that lawyers are specialists in the assessment and analysis of linguistic meaning (see Solan 1993). As of the 2014 term, the principal competing approaches are textualism, pioneered and elaborated by Justice Scalia starting in the 1980s (see Gorsuch 2016; Manning 2017; Scalia 1998), and a more pluralistic and pragmatic approach exemplified by many of Judge Posner's writings and by Strauss's *Harvard Law Review* Foreword (see Posner 2008, 2015; Strauss 2010, 2015).

Justice Kagan appears to write as a textualist in *Yates*. She starts with the statutory text (more precisely, with an isolated term) and consults other texts (including Dr. Seuss, Kagan, 2) and other legal uses of the same term to establish the "ordinary meaning" of "tangible object" (2). Identifying no grounds for doubt in this process, she insists that no other considerations are relevant.[19] Justice Ginsburg's majority opinion exemplifies a pluralist purposivist approach. The most important factor in her explanation is her assessment of the reasons Congress passed the Sarbanes-Oxley Act. Justice Alito's concurrence is less easy to categorize. He rejects the purposivist parts of Justice Ginsburg's analysis but endorses her textual points, ultimately agreeing that Yates could not be prosecuted under the provision. Justice Alito's concurrence suggests a kind of "scorecard textualism": he seems to have looked at all the textual points supporting each of two (or more) readings, without considering any point conclusive, then endorsed the reading with the greatest number of points in its favor.

There are significant limitations to understanding the justices' positions in *Yates* solely in terms of these competing canonical interpretive methods. Focusing on the differences between the methods used by different justices can distract legally trained readers from the basic task achieved in cases like *Yates*, regardless of interpretive method. In such cases, judges must decide what real-world things or activities lawyers should take the term to refer to. The judgment in such a case is always a kind of active linguistic intervention in the behavior of legal officials. Debates about interpretive method focus on protocols for making this decision but do not tend to address the nature of the decision itself. This reluctance in turn promotes a view of lawyers' and judges' decisions as primarily metalinguistic (concerned with word-to-word relationships). In turn, this focus discourages debate about whether lawyers and judges are consistent in their treatment of "fact." The metalinguistic focus of debates about interpretive method, that is, presumes that facts preexist their identification and are simply tracked by language rather than affected by it.[20]

MacLean also illustrates the limits of contemporary thinking about statutory interpretation. This case arose out of a federal air marshal's employment grievance. The Transportation Security Administration (TSA) fired Robert MacLean after learning that he had spoken with reporters and appeared in disguise on a news program to disclose a TSA decision to reduce air marshals' presence on domestic flights shortly after a federal terrorist advisory. MacLean argued that his whistleblowing was protected by a federal statute shielding from punishment government employees who reveal threats to public safety. The government argued that MacLean's conduct was not protected, because the protection does not apply to government employees who reveal information in a way "specifically prohibited by law" (1, 4); in this case, TSA regulations banned disclosure of "'information concerning specific numbers of Federal Air Marshals [or] deployments'" (2). The issue for decision by the Court was, then, whether the TSA regulations counted as "law," making MacLean's whistleblowing "prohibited by law" and therefore legitimate grounds for his termination.

This issue has the same structure as the issue in *Yates*: does the term in the statute ("law") refer to these things in the world (the regulations)? This is mostly how the majority analyzed the issue. Six justices joined Chief Justice Roberts's opinion concluding that the term "law" in the statute did not include regulations, even though in other statutes, "law" might refer to regulations as well as statutory law. Justice Sotomayor, who wrote separately, did not disagree on this point.

But the government also made a backup argument that did divide the justices. Even if "law" did not refer to regulations, the government argued, MacLean's disclosure could still have been "specifically prohibited by" federal statutory (rather than regulatory) "law," namely, by the statute directing the TSA to issue the regulation in question. Since the statute *required* the TSA to issue regulations dealing with protection of sensitive information, according to the government, the *statute* was the source of the ban on disclosing information about air marshal deployment. The majority rejected this argument, concluding that the authorizing statute did not "prohibit" anything, but, "[o]n the contrary . . ., authorizes something": the issuance of regulations (11). Justice Sotomayor disagreed. The statute, she writes, "does not merely authorize the TSA to promulgate regulations; it directs it to do so, and describes what those regulations must accomplish" (Sotomayor, 2).

This disagreement concerns not the scope of a statutory term, like the disagreement in *Yates*, but the kind of action (other than reference) that a legal provision accomplishes. The disagreement does seem to concern an issue of statutory interpretation, but the usual tools of statutory interpretation are not useful in addressing it. To analyze the issue, the opinions use a hodgepodge of techniques, including simple reiterations of their conclusions and descriptions of a variety of analogous provisions. Interestingly, the majority and dissenting opinions do not directly respond to one another in discussing this issue. The justices' inability to settle on a way of considering this question suggests discomfort, or at least unfamiliarity, with it. For all of its sophistication on matters of language and meaning, legal discourse seems to lacks tools for this particular task.

Yates and *MacLean* are not the only places in the 2014-term opinions where such problems appear. Disputes about the significance to be ascribed to prior judicial decisions, for example, recur throughout the term's opinions.[21] Discussion of these matters is challenging because it requires lawyers and judges to mix ways of talking (about law and fact respectively) that legal conventions urge them to keep separate. Those conventions help lawyers talk about law as if it is unchanging, even when arguing for its change, and about facts as preexisting states of affairs to which the law adapts. When lawyers must address legal change, as in many Supreme Court cases, the conventions permit discussion of a certain limited set of factual (broadly linguistic) matters. The resulting analyses attach statutory-interpretation conclusions to the "real world" and promote a view of lawyers and judges as verbal experts, but they keep certain matters unspeakable.

2.5 Double talk

The practices discussed in this chapter—a flexible approach to what counts as "fact," shored up by a simplified and negative conception of "fiction"—are useful for some purposes. But these practices also make some issues, like those raised by the government's backup argument in *MacLean*, hard or even impossible to discuss. As a result, for all their linguistic self-awareness, lawyers and judges generally do not and maybe cannot address important aspects of their own activity. In addition, at the Supreme Court level, responsibility for fact determination is assigned elsewhere—to parties, juries, and trial-court judges. This assignment relieves appellate judges, Supreme Court justices, and the professors and students who use the justices' opinions as learning tools from looking too closely at how facts are established and tested. But it also means that those tasked with finding "facts" or trying to learn what this process involves receive little guidance.

At least part of the cultural function of legal activity in the United States is to provide a model for the authoritative settlement of disagreements (e.g., Levitin 2017, 16, 99, 101, 129, 155). Up close, however, it seems that legal activity is not as well equipped to perform this function as its practitioners might like to believe. In particular, lawyers have little to contribute to public debates about promiscuous misuse of the "fact" label. A clearer view of the analogies and differences between legal and fictional discourse might help to generate a strategy for responding to this deficiency. Such a view is intuitively accessible to anyone willing to suppose, for a moment, that lawyers' conventional ways of discussing facts, law, and language might be in some respects incomplete.

Outside a legal setting, even lawyers can often agree on whether particular statements are factual, fictional, or false. The features we tacitly consider in making distinctions among these categories involve, first, the kind of "fit" involved in any given statement, and, second, the form of commitment expressed by the statement's speaker (or writer) and audience. Factual statements involve what might be called, following John Searle (1985), "word-to-world" fit. A factual statement is made and received as representing nonlinguistic matters (although such an assertion may also concern an aspect of a linguistic matter, such as the frequency of use of a particular term). Factual assertions are in principle verifiable, but this is not their most important feature; *commitment* is. One who makes a statement of fact is committed to explaining how the statement fits the world, if asked, by way of further statements of fact, and also wishes his or her audience to accept the statement as fitting the world. This last feature distinguishes statements of fact from falsehoods. A person who presents a falsehood wants his or her addressee to accept the false statement as fitting the world but lacks the in-principle-unlimited commitment to explaining that fit that characterizes the person who asserts a fact.

Statements of fiction and law differ from statements of fact and falsehoods with respect to their ultimate grounding. Both statements of fiction and statements of law involve what might be called "word-to-word" fit. At least as the law is currently taught in most U.S. law schools, statements of law are accurate or not depending on their consistency with the body of law preexisting the statements, or their consistency with systems of previous legal communication or statements. Assessing this accuracy requires a metalinguistic perspective of the kind Mertz describes in *The Language of Law School*; much of legal education involves training in how to assume this perspective. A statement of law made in what lawyers call "good faith" is one made with the same kind of commitment that characterizes a statement of fact: a commitment to back up one's statement with further statements to the extent needed to win a matching commitment from one's addressee.

Fictional discourse, like legal discourse, involves "word-to-word" fit. But it differs from statements of law in the kind of commitment it presupposes. The commitment to back up a statement about a fictional matter is genuine but limited (see, e.g., Everett 2013). To take an example that is a favorite of philosophers: if I say "Sherlock Holmes lived at 221B Baker Street in London," I can back the statement up by showing you passages from the Conan Doyle stories that support my claim. I cannot, however, back it up by directing you to any location in London (or any historical accounts of 1890s London), and I cannot ask you to base your own action on it outside the scope of conversations about Holmes. The kind of commitment involved in making a statement about a fictional matter is both like and unlike the kind of commitment involved in making a statement of fact. It involves a willingness to back up the statement, combined with a concession that the sources from which that backup might be drawn are limited and a concession that the statement itself has limited force.

The commitment of a speaker or writer to backing up a statement of fact is in principle unlimited, and the commitment of a speaker or writer to backing up a statement about fictional matters is normally limited, but there is significant overlap.[22] We cannot make sense of a statement about a fictional character such as Sherlock Holmes without importing some of our real-world understanding of human beings, detectives and (if the statement is made in English) the English language, all matters to which our commitment is, if not unlimited, at least broader than our commitment to the content of Conan Doyle's stories (e.g., Everett 2013). Things we "learn" from fictional narratives may likewise affect our beliefs, decisions, and actions more broadly (e.g., Gerrig 1993, 16).

Legal discourse differs from fictional discourse only in this last regard. The sources available for backing up, or checking the accuracy of, statements about matters of law are also limited. Unlike fictional discourse, however, such discourse is, at least in the eyes of those who consider the discourse legitimate, supposed to provide a basis for action outside that limited domain. Citing a Supreme Court decision is an acceptable basis for engaging in particular conduct, such as issuing a marriage license to a gay couple, in a way that citing a fictional character's preferences would not be.

This view of the distinction between factual and fictional discourse does not preclude the possibility of mixtures of the two. Fictional discourse is, in a sense, "quarantined" from real-world matters, but as later chapters will explore, because it is ***discourse***, that quarantine is never absolute. Reading fictional discourse and understanding it as fictional requires a kind of split consciousness: one must comprehend the discourse as if it were factual and at the same time, in the background, remember that it is not. In this sense, fictional discourse is always mixed with or layered on top of discourse about matters of fact. Legal discourse shares this quality, but lawyers and judges, for all their linguistic adaptability, often seem to lose sight of the pervasiveness of this kind of doublespeak in legal language. The following chapters explore some implications of this analogy, identifying discursive practices that the justices borrow, possibly unwittingly, from narrative fiction and a series of important insights about lawyers' interactions, with texts and with institutions, that the wordsmith's fallacy tends to keep hidden.

Notes

1 This set of connotations is enabled by a recurring cycle in scholarship. Every so often, a law professor writes an account of a particular doctrine that recommends reconsideration of the issue, while acknowledging that fictions may be necessary for the reasons mentioned in the text (e.g., Harmon 1990; Smith 2007). The scholar reviews earlier work, especially that of Lon Fuller (1968), whose essays on legal fictions first appeared in the 1930s. This cycle of re-instruction of law-review editors and readers in the same basic ideas about "fiction" has not changed significantly in about a century.

2 Justice Thomas makes a similar point in his *Clark* dissent, quoting one of his own previous dissents to underline his unchanged objection to the majority's approach: "The primary purpose test . . . is . . . 'an exercise in fiction . . . disconnected from history'" (Thomas, 1).

3 A justice might quote a law professor's description of legal "worlds" as imaginary (e.g., *Kansas v. Nebraska*, 6 (Kagan)). But a justice will not describe his or her own activity this way. Accusing

another justice of "fashion[ing] a world" (*T-Mobile South*, Sotomayor, 10) is not a compliment (see also *Kerry v. Din*, Scalia, 2; *Wynne*, Scalia, 6).

4 In the 2014 term, Justice Ginsburg cited *Anna Karenina* and Gertrude Stein's "Sacred Emily" (*Williams-Yulee*, Ginsburg, 5); Justice Kagan cited Dr. Seuss and Stan Lee's *Spider-Man* (*Yates*, Kagan, 2; *Kimble*, 18); Justice Kennedy cited Dickens's *Tale of Two Cities* and Dostoevsky's *The House of the Dead* (*Davis v. Ayala*, Kennedy, 4–5); Chief Justice Roberts cited Faulkner's *Requiem for a Nun* (*Obergefell*, Roberts, 22–23); and Justice Scalia cited or alluded to *Alice in Wonderland* (twice), Orwell's *1984*, and the movie *Groundhog Day* (*Zivotofsky*, Scalia, 11; *Patel*, Scalia, 10–11; *Glossip*, Scalia, 1).

5 Although both literary scholars and scientists of mind considered similar questions earlier, their work did not feed directly into a twentieth-century scholarly tradition as the philosophical work did (Dames 2007).

6 On most current understandings of fiction, visual and audiovisual artifacts can be fictional. See Smith 1995; Walton 1993.

7 The justices use "fiction" interchangeably with several other terms, each with different connotations. *Speculation*, like *supposition*, involves the generation of statements about things that might be actual for the purpose of reasoning (Green 2010). *Hypothesis* involves the generation of statements about things that might be actual for the purpose of testing. *Fancy* involves the generation of an alternative to the actual with no ulterior purpose, and perhaps with no attempt to communicate about the alternative (e.g., Bogdan 2013, 51–52; Scarry 1999). *Imagination*, the focus of most psychological research on the comprehension and production of communication about non-actual things, names the cognitive capacity to generate alternatives to actuality and to respond to others' communications about them (e.g., Bogdan 2013, 49–52). *Invention* refers broadly to the generation of something previously nonexistent; that thing might or might not be linguistic and might or might not be intended to deceive. Unlike fiction, invention may occur in the absence of a communicative "contract" and thus may deceive. *Making things up* resembles invention but may suggest concealment or deception more strongly than "invention." *Make-believe* involves engagement with a "prop" (Walton 1993), as in a children's game of "store," in the course of which the players treat certain parts of the world as if they were other things, draw inferences (not necessarily conscious) from the equivalences, and adjust their behavior or attitudes accordingly. This activity can also be called *pretending*, but the latter term may connote deception (e.g., Anscombe 1958, 279, 294). Finally, fictional discourse often creates reference points that can be experienced as "*worlds*" or worldlike (Harshaw 1984; Pavel 1994; Ryan 1991). These worlds always retain ties to the actual worlds within which they are generated.

8 The Court is not always explicit about labeling such facts. The decree in *United States v. California*, updating the Court's previous declarations of the boundary between coastal waters under California's control and those under federal control, creates geopolitical facts without using the term in its 107 pages of longitude and latitude coordinates and a map diagramming the boundary (112).

9 Chief Justice Roberts also writes in *Obergefell* that the majority opinion hides behind a "shiny rhetorical gloss" (Roberts, 10) and seems unaware that what it is "'really discovering'" is its "'own values'" (Roberts, 14–15). Similarly, Justice Sotomayor attacks the *Glossip* majority for approving the lower courts' acceptance of an expert's testimony, which she describes as based in an "alternative scientific reality" (Sotomayor, 13). Justice Scalia's *Williams-Yulee* dissent describes the majority's concerns as disingenuous: "the Court argues that 'the lines Yulee asks [it] to draw are unworkable.' . . . That is a difficulty of the Court's own imagination. In reality, the Court could have chosen from a whole spectrum of workable rules" (Scalia, 8).

10 When the Court is exercising its original jurisdiction, it may find such facts.

11 Judicial assertions of this kind also include assertions about such things as the characterization of a lower court's opinion (*Dart Cherokee*, 9–10) or a party's allegations (*Alabama Legis. Black Caucus*, 11, 21, 24–26).

12 The Court also makes other kinds of "findings" about legal matters, such as the scope of discovery in proceedings before the Trademark Trial & Appeal Board (*B&B Hardware*, 20); the caseload of immigration judges (*Mellouli*, 7); the effectiveness of state health-care reform efforts during the 1990s (*King*, 2); and the extent of public deliberation on state recognition of same-sex marriages (*Obergefell*, 23, 29–34). Justices sometimes challenge assertions about such facts as irrelevant. Judicial conclusions about the meaning of legal pronouncements, in contrast, are

seldom criticized as irrelevant; they are more commonly criticized as based on faulty or mistaken premises.

13 Justice Alito uses this technique in *Wynne* (28, noting the absence of eighteenth-century travel records). Justice Sotomayor uses it in her dissents in *Davis v. Ayala* (Sotomayor, 6, noting the loss of juror questionnaires) and *Glossip* (Sotomayor, 17, noting the nonexistence of studies of the effects of midazolam at the dosage used in executions).

14 *Davis v. Ayala* illustrates the link between many legal rules and perceived or anticipated problems with fact determination. The dispute in the case turned on whether the Court had the capacity to second-guess the lower courts' fact determinations. For further discussion, see Chapter 5.3.2.2.

15 In trial courts, responsibility is similarly divided between trial-court judges and juries; see Chapter 3.3.2. In habeas cases, such as *Davis v. Ayala*, the Supreme Court's deference to lower courts on factual matters is in theory almost absolute. The habeas setting is an extreme form of the more general phenomenon of ascribing crucial importance to "fact" while using an arsenal of techniques for challenging such assertions.

16 Justice Scalia offers the examples of a jeweler's opinion on the value of a diamond and "an attorney['s] upon a point of law" (*Omnicare*, Scalia, 3).

17 Listing all the contexts in which trial and appellate courts make such distinctions would fill a small book. To take one other example from the 2014 term, the dispute between the majority and Justice Thomas in *Brumfield* turned largely on whether the issues presented by the petitioner were factual, as the majority concluded (7–8 n.3), or legal, as Justice Thomas argued (Thomas, 15, 16, 19–20, 24–25). The difference mattered because it determined which of two statutory provisions would apply to the case. At the beginning of the term, in *Lopez v. Smith*, the Court reversed the Ninth Circuit per curiam for applying the factual rather than the legal portion of the same statute.

18 Justice Ginsburg's opinion had also discussed the context of enactment of the Sarbanes-Oxley Act, which was passed following the Enron accounting-fraud scandal and was unquestionably a political response to that event (*Yates*, 2, 6, 12–14; see Chapter 4.2.2.1). Justice Alito explicitly distanced himself from this part of Justice Ginsburg's analysis.

19 Justice Kagan rebuts the majority's points, but her dissent presents the rebuttals as unnecessary to her analysis (see *Yates*, Kagan, 4–15).

20 Justice Alito's *Yates* opinion contains an interesting slip: "Where, as here, each of a statute's verbs applies to some category of nouns [not things, items, or phenomena], there is some reason to think that Congress had that category in mind" (Alito, 3). Judges do not usually describe statutory terms as applying to parts of speech. But if one's focus is on text alone, and if one does not want to think of interpretive conclusions as determining reference, then text might be all one can see.

21 See *Kimble*, Alito, 1, 7; *Wynne*, 16–17 (Alito); *Dart Cherokee*, 9, 11–12 (Ginsburg); *Wynne*, Ginsburg, 9, 11–12; *Kimble*, 11 n.4 (Kagan); *Ariz. State Legislature*, Scalia, 4–5, 6. This theme recurs in discussions of "clearly established law" in the habeas and qualified-immunity contexts. See, e.g., *Woods v. Donald*, 4 (per curiam); *Sheehan*, 10–11, 13, 14 n.4 (Alito); *Davis v. Ayala*, Thomas, 24. The justices' disagreements in *Mellouli*, discussed in Chapter 5.3.1, also turn on the challenge of making factual assertions about law.

22 Another way to think of this limitation is to conceive of statements about fictional matters as assuming the causal isolation of these matters from factual matters (e.g., Nichols & Stich 2003).

3 Real people, fictional characters, legal phantoms

3.1 Writing minds into being

Distinguishing between truthful statements and lies depends on a particular understanding of human action. We cannot make the distinction by considering statements alone. A statement is a lie only if the person who utters it does so with a certain intention, wanting the receiver of the statement to take it to be truthful and possibly act on it, while the utterer does not share that attitude, but believes the statement not to be a good basis for action. For a statement to qualify as a lie, the beliefs and commitments of the person who utters the lie cannot match those of the person who receives it.

Without this mismatch, a statement is not a lie; it might instead be a mistake, a truthful statement, or a piece of fictional discourse. The latter two kinds of statement, in contrast to lies, involve *aligned* states of mind between the speaker and the recipient. A person making a truthful statement seeks to produce in the recipient a commitment to the truth of the statement that matches the speaker's own. One who makes a statement in a make-believe spirit aims at getting the recipient to share a similarly qualified commitment to the statement's implications. So the truthfulness, falsity, or fictionality of a statement depends not only on the content of the statement and its match with the world, but also on the beliefs and intentions of the person making the statement, including that person's beliefs and intentions about others' beliefs and intentions.

We can often be fairly confident about the beliefs and intentions of those we speak with, or whose words we read, even though we also tend to think of beliefs and intentions as private, individual matters. Many psychologists and cognitive scientists call the ability to assess others' attitudes and intentions "mindreading" (e.g., Nichols & Stich 2003). We "read" others' minds by observing their behavior, including their statements. While some of us are better at this task than others (e.g., autistic individuals seem to have difficulty with it; Baron-Cohen 1995), most children in contemporary Western culture learn to mindread fairly well at a young age and continue to refine the skill, including through play, as they mature (Bogdan 2013; Graziano 2013). The skill is related to, but not identical with, the ability to take another person's perspective (Graziano 2013; Taylor 1988). The precise relationship between these two skills, as well as their connection to the acquisition of other skills, such as language, is the subject of research and debate, but there is no question that skill at mindreading usually accompanies skill at perspective-taking, and vice versa. Both are involved in what is now often called "empathy."

Adults engage in a form of make-believe whenever they read novels or watch narrative film or video programs. Most, if not all, fictional narratives represent mindreading by characters and also prompt readers (or spectators) to mindread the characters. A growing number of scholars, building on psychological research indicating that reading fiction helps hone mindreading skills (e.g., Mar et al. 2006), have been suggesting that a drive to exercise those skills might explain the emergence and refinement of these cultural forms (e.g., Zunshine 2006; see also Kidd & Castano 2013). But while descriptions of fictional characters' actions can provide readers with mindreading practice, in written fictional discourse it is not always necessary to infer a character's mental state from the character's behavior. Instead, we can look directly into characters' minds as described by narrators. Narratologists call this "psychonarration," and some literary scholars have proposed that its presence defines discourse as fictional (e.g., Cohn 1990). One need not accept this position, however, to appreciate the point that psychonarration, or reports of the "contents" of others' "minds," can be irrefutably true only within fictional narrative (Deutsch 2000). This observation might seem both technical and obvious, but it has important and little-discussed implications for legal activity.

Among the reasons it can be tricky to describe the relationship between legal and fictional discourse is that legal discourse, too, depends heavily on presuppositions about and descriptions of humans' intentions, as well as their actions on the basis of those intentions. The states of mind of real, flesh-and-blood people are central to assessments of responsibility in U.S. cultural and legal systems. And the law often demands firm conclusions about the legally relevant mental states of particular individuals. But we do not have direct access to these states in others, and lawyers have not developed any law-specific methods for detecting or determining mental states. Instead, U.S. legal culture calls on lawyers, judges, and juries to use the generalized mindreading skills they initially acquired outside the legal setting.[1]

Throughout the 2014-term opinions, the justices offer examples of and lessons in the discussion and establishment of others' mental states. The lessons they provide are in some ways mixed and conflicting. One approach, used more by some justices than others, treats the intentional states of real people like those of fictional characters, psychonarrating them from the "inside." This approach, which presupposes easy access to or even a kind of authorial control over such states, often makes for engaging reading. But it alternates with a dramatically contrasting discourse of radical skepticism about the accessibility of others' mental states. The justices seem to use these two extreme techniques at least as often as they express a more measured attitude of qualified confidence about mental-state ascriptions. And the justices likewise are mostly unselfconscious about their control over the content of so-called "objective" standards, which (as section 3.4 explains) involve a kind of meta-perspective-taking. Existing legal approaches to questions of subjectivity, mental states, and their representation are locked in a polarized dialectic, between psychonarration on the one hand and protestations of mindblindness on the other, that echoes the fact–fiction polarization discussed in Chapter 2.

Continuing to think through the similarities between fictional and legal discourse takes us to a vantage point from which problems with the judicial narration of individual mental states and judicial articulation of "objective" standards become easier to see and to avoid. These parallels and problems are the subject of this chapter. Sections 3.2 and 3.3 address the ways judicial discourse handles the mental states of real people; sections 3.4 and 3.5 consider the benefits of more explicitly training lawyers to take meta-perspectives.

3.2 Real people and true believers

Legal discourse presupposes an attitude toward human activity that this book, following Daniel Dennett (1987), calls the "intentional stance" (section 3.2.1). This attitude interacts with the discursiveness of legal activity in sometimes problematic ways. Those problems, compounded by the wordsmith's fallacy, are especially pronounced in certain areas of law requiring explicit attention to the mental states of real people, such as criminal law (discussed in section 3.2.2.1) and antidiscrimination law (section 3.2.2.2).

3.2.1 The legal logic of the intentional stance

According to Daniel Dennett (1987), a philosopher heavily influenced by the mind sciences, humans are biologically designed to take the intentional stance toward other people. One need not accept Dennett's scientific premises to appreciate his descriptive point, which is consistent with the research on mindreading mentioned above. The intentional stance allows one who takes it to make sense of and predict others' behavior. Taking this attitude involves assuming that an actor's conduct is driven by the actor's intentions and "reasons," or states of affairs that the actor wants to bring about (Dennett 1987; List & Pettit 2013). The attitude also involves assuming that intentional actors respond to changes in their environment, including the acts of other intentional actors. It does not require assuming that actors always act rationally, but it does require assuming that actors are often rational, in the sense that we can often reliably infer an actor's intentions from the actor's behavior.[2]

The U.S. legal system often requires lawyers and judges to take the intentional stance toward the people and groups on which the system acts (e.g., Boudreau et al. 2005; Ristroph 2008, 1359). Conclusions about actors' mental states may determine who can be subjected to criminal punishment and under what circumstances, as well as who can recover in a civil lawsuit. A judge's or lawyer's skepticism about assessing or understanding others' mental states does not relieve the lawyer or judge of the need to argue about or draw such conclusions.

The legal commitment to these matters also affects the processes of legal reading and writing. The opinions from the 2014-term case *Brumfield v. Cain* illustrate some of these effects. The petitioner in this case, Kevan Brumfield, was convicted in 1995 of murdering an off-duty police officer, then sentenced to death in Louisiana state court. After his sentencing, the Supreme Court decided *Atkins v. Virginia* (2002), which held that "the execution of the intellectually disabled" is unconstitutionally cruel and unusual (*Brumfield*, 1). After the *Atkins* decision, Brumfield's lawyers sought to establish Brumfield's intellectual disability in light of this rule. The Louisiana courts refused the request, but a federal court later concluded that Brumfield's lawyers should be allowed to present evidence of his intellectual disability in state court. Five Supreme Court justices agreed with this conclusion, in an opinion written by Justice Sotomayor; four disagreed and joined a dissent written by Justice Thomas.

The idea driving *Atkins* was that people with cognitive disabilities cannot function as the kind of fully intentional agents that the law typically addresses. In *Atkins* itself and in later applications of its holding, judges turned to medical-clinical criteria for assessing particular individuals' disability; these criteria make the connection of the legal standard to the intentional stance especially clear. To establish cognitive disability satisfying the *Atkins* exception, a defendant's lawyers must show that the defendant has IQ scores below a certain threshold, has "significant impairment in several areas of adaptive skills," and developed the disability as a child (*Brumfield*, 2). Showing "adaptive impairment," in turn, amounts to showing that it is inappropriate to take the intentional stance toward the defendant (*Brumfield*, 12); the intellectually disabled defendant is one who needs others' help to move through the environment successfully, in part because his or her behavior may not conform to others' expectations.

Nevertheless, it will not necessarily be immediately apparent to observers whether a defendant is truly intellectually disabled. A defendant could assert intellectual disability in bad faith. The majority and dissenting opinions in *Brumfield* take different positions on this possibility. Justice Sotomayor's majority opinion presents the question of Brumfield's disability as a fact about Brumfield's mind and thus not a matter that the Court needs to—or can—resolve definitively. Because Brumfield, through his lawyer, was just contesting whether he should have been allowed to offer more evidence on this fact, Justice Sotomayor focuses on whether the evidence he *did* present before the *Atkins* decision seemed generally indicative of the kind of disability his lawyers later wanted to prove.

Justice Sotomayor's opinion also, however, takes an intentional stance toward the participants in the lower-court proceedings in the case, including Brumfield himself.[3] She describes Brumfield as actively participating in his postconviction proceedings. In support of his lawyers' request for a hearing on the disability issue, for example, "Brumfield pointed to mitigation evidence introduced at the sentencing phase of his trial" (3). Of course, Kevan Brumfield himself did not identify that evidence; his lawyers did. In Justice Sotomayor's account, Brumfield is an intentional agent for purposes of his litigation activity, but he might not have been for purposes of his underlying crime. This inconsistency is not at all unusual; it follows the legal convention of attributing lawyers' litigation conduct and reasons for action to their clients. The convention suggests both the controlling force of the intentional stance within legal discourse and how that discourse may depart from nonlegal conventions for describing intentional activity.

Justice Thomas's dissent opposes Justice Sotomayor's on several points. He stresses features of the proceedings in Brumfield's case that he takes to suggest Brumfield's or his lawyers' bad faith. But Justice Thomas also uses many of the same descriptive techniques that Justice Sotomayor does—although he uses them to discuss the underlying story of Brumfield's crime, the story of his victim's children, and the story of his postconviction proceedings.

In each of these stories, Justice Thomas presents Brumfield as an intentional agent. Justice Thomas describes Brumfield's actions during his crime, for example, as elements of a larger antisocial plan: in a confession, Brumfield described how "he had come up with the idea to steal the grocery store's deposit" (Thomas, 2–3). Justice Thomas also suggests a fairly detailed portrait of Brumfield's character:

> Brumfield introduced evidence that his crimes were "beyond his control," a product of his disadvantaged background. . . . His father left the family, and his stepfather would make him sit in the corner on hot rice, whip him, and hit him over the head with a telephone book. His brother eventually decided to go live with their biological father. Brumfield opted to stay with his mother and stepfather.
>
> (5)

In this account, Brumfield is enough of an intentional agent to "opt" to stay with his mother, but deviant enough to want to stay with his abusive stepfather. This portrait of a young Brumfield driven by perversity helps to suggest that Brumfield's later conduct, including his crime, his many postconviction challenges, and his *Atkins* challenge are just further expressions of the same character.

There is another significant difference between Justice Sotomayor's and Justice Thomas's approaches in *Brumfield*. Justice Sotomayor approaches the question of Brumfield's disability as a fact about his mental status. Justice Thomas, in contrast, identifies the central issue in the case as legal. According to Justice Thomas, the Court should not be considering Brumfield's evidence of his capacity; it should be considering whether Brumfield can be placed in the legal category of the "intellectually disabled" (Thomas, 16 n.7). Paradoxically, Justice Thomas's opinion suggests that an appellate court assessing this issue is competent to generate a more confident portrait of a defendant's "mind" than a trial-court judge would be.

Justice Thomas's approach to using descriptions of Brumfield's conduct to imply a complex portrait of his disposition reflects widespread folk-psychological practices in Western culture, as described by Dennett and others. But Justice Sotomayor's more cautious approach is also consistent with widely held attitudes toward the readability of others' minds. Similar assumptions structure any number of other explicit legal rules, ranging from rules protecting individual liberty (as seen in, e.g., Justice Kennedy's *Obergefell* opinion), to those guaranteeing individuals access to information (e.g., *Kerry v. Din*), as well as with the ways lawyers talk and write about legal rules and the people and organizations subject to them. Despite their comfort with certain techniques for describing mental states, lawyers and judges are curiously oblivious to some of the implications of these techniques. The next section considers this phenomenon in more detail.

3.2.2 Judicial mindreading

The intentional stance pervades legal practices, but it is especially central to certain areas of law. The validity of assumptions about human intentions has probably been most fully debated in the criminal-law context (see, for instance, Shen et al. 2014). But lawyers and judges do widely agree that, in general, criminal penalties should only be imposed on blameworthy individuals and that blameworthiness is in part a matter of mental states.

As Justice Sotomayor's *Brumfield* opinion suggests, when a real person's mental states are at issue, caution about the accessibility of these states is always a descriptive possibility. Lawyers and judges are generally aware of this possibility. Nevertheless, judges are generally not similarly cautious about how they *describe* mental states. Their linguistic accounts of actors' intentions, beliefs, and other mental states, like all such linguistic accounts, have a number of odd features much discussed by philosophers of language and mind and by literary scholars. But lawyers do not learn about these matters in law school, and only a few legal scholars have taken notice of them.

The lack of legal awareness of these issues is especially unfortunate in those areas where legal rules themselves refer to mental states. Supreme Court cases addressing federal criminal law, for example, often turn on the interpretation of criminal statutes (and associated jury instructions) containing such references. Section 3.2.2.1 introduces some background concepts in this area and explains their implications for two criminal-law decisions from the 2014 term, *Elonis* (the Facebook-threats case) and *McFadden v. United States.*

Mental states are also pivotal in another area often addressed by the Court: antidiscrimination law. Here, lawyers, scholars, and judges actively debate the extent to which a defendant's liability for discrimination should turn on the defendant's mental state, as well as about just what mental state "intentional discrimination" is. And here, too, lawyers and scholars have mostly ignored some important features of discourse about mental states. Section 3.2.2.2 will address the effects of this avoidance on the opinions in two 2014-term cases, *EEOC v. Abercrombie & Fitch* and *Texas Dep't of Housing.*[4]

3.2.2.1 Criminal mens rea

Early in their training, U.S. law students learn that the appearance of certain words in a statutory or judicial statement of a legal rule is a clue that the rule requires some consideration of mental states. These words are usually verbs or adverbs, such as "know" or "intentionally" (cf. *Elonis*, 7; *McFadden*, 1). They create familiar puzzles. For example, if a jury is instructed that "[a] statement is a true threat when a defendant intentionally makes a statement that communicates an intention to injure or harm another individual" (*Elonis*, 7), must the jury find that the defendant knew others would take the statement to communicate an intention to injure someone? Or would it be enough to find that the defendant intended to communicate, and to find separately that people hearing the statement could have taken it to communicate an intent to harm?

The kind of ambiguity just described has been extensively studied by philosophers and linguists, but little noted by legal writers (with the exception of Jill Anderson (2014)). The study of this ambiguity focuses on unusual properties of mental-state terms, including their creation of something known as opacity. An example of an opaque construction is the sentence "Eli knew he sold a controlled substance." One cannot decide solely from the words of this sentence exactly what it communicates about Eli's knowledge. Is it saying that Eli knew he sold something, and the thing he sold happened to be a controlled substance? Or is it saying that Eli knew he sold something and also knew it was a controlled substance? The sentence could appropriately be used to convey either message. In this, it is unlike apparently similar sentences using different verbs, like "Eli sold a controlled substance."

Opaque constructions also have a characteristic that philosophers call the "nonsubstitutibility of co-referring terms." Because "Ritalin" and "methylphenidate" refer to the same substance, those words are "co-referring terms." If Eli did sell Ritalin, then "Eli sold Ritalin" and "Eli sold methylphenidate" are both true. But if Eli sold Ritalin without knowing that it was also methylphenidate, then "Eli knew he sold Ritalin" and "Eli knew that he sold methylphenidate" might not both be true. Mental-state adverbs have a similar "opacifying" effect on the verbs they modify, as in "Eli knowingly sold methylphenidate."

Opacifying verbs can also block inferences about the existence of the objects of the verb in question. For example, "Eli believes he has unique mesmeric powers" *could* be a true statement if Eli believes he has such powers, even though such powers do not exist. But the sentence remains ambiguous. It does not necessarily amount to a statement that Eli believes himself to have a capability he would call "unique mesmeric powers." (Justice Kagan's opinion in *Omnicare*, the registration-statement case discussed in Chapter 2.4.1, noted a similar phenomenon using different vocabulary.)

The ambiguity these constructions generate is partly an ambiguity about the perspective presented in them. Are the examples above describing things from Eli's perspective, in the language Eli would use? Or are they describing things from an outside perspective, in the language an observer might use? Philosophers call these alternatives *de dicto* ("of the saying," for the version read as if in Eli's voice) and *de re* ("of the thing," for the version from an observer's perspective, which refers directly to the object of the mental-state verb). These alternatives parallel classic techniques for narrating fictional characters' states of mind, discussed further in section 3.3.1. This form of ambiguity also crops up frequently in legal contexts (Anderson 2014; Moore 1980, 182–83, 208–14; Rodes 1998). Yet lawyers often analyze disputes turning on language involving opaque constructions without, apparently, noticing the ambiguity involved.

Elonis, the Facebook-threats case introduced in Chapter 2.2.4, illustrates the point. As decided, the case did not seem to involve ambiguity. Instead, Chief Justice Roberts's opinion for the majority emphasized two points: first, criminal conviction requires proof of a blameworthy mental state, and second, the statute used to prosecute Elonis must be read to require proof of a blameworthy mental state. For decades, U.S. lawyers have conceptualized criminal mental states as falling into four categories: purpose, knowledge, recklessness, and negligence (see Shen et al. 2014; *Elonis*, Alito, 4). Each of the first three of those states requires a different sort of explicit awareness on the defendant's part; to prove purpose, for example, the prosecution must show what the defendant was trying to achieve and how the defendant sought to reach the goal. Proving negligence, however, does not require any proof of mental state. The *Elonis* majority opinion reduces this traditional four-part scale to a dichotomy: no-fault (negligence) versus fault (requiring some proof of a mental state; 8–9, 12, 14). Chief Justice Roberts justifies the reduction by noting that, while the threat statute itself does not specify a mental state, criminalizable conduct has traditionally been distinguished from non-criminalizable conduct on the basis of the defendant's possession of a blameworthy mental state at the time of the act.

In *Elonis*, Justice Alito and Justice Thomas both object that this conclusion does not give much guidance to trial-court judges instructing juries on how to apply the threat statute. In Elonis's case, the trial-court judge had followed the approach previously used by most courts trying cases under the statute (Calvert et al. 2014); the judge told the jury that to convict Elonis it must find that he "intentionally" made "a statement . . . under such circumstances" as those in which "a reasonable person would foresee that the statement would be interpreted" by recipients as "a serious expression of an intention to inflict . . . injury" (7). Unlike the statute itself (which contains no mental-state terms), this jury instruction involves an opaque construction. But the instruction also seems to reflect an attempt (however roundabout) at disambiguation. The instruction is explicit about the perspective from which the defendant's statement should be assessed: it should be assessed from the perspective of a reasonable person. The Chief Justice's analysis, disregarding the ambiguity, seems to read the "reasonable person" component of the instruction as addressing the *defendant's* mental state. Section 3.4, which considers reasonableness standards, will return to this apparent misreading of the *Elonis* instruction.

Although Justice Thomas's dissent does not describe the issue as a matter of ambiguity, his analysis turns mostly on two possible understandings of the jury instruction. Justice Thomas notes, correctly, that the majority seems to have mistaken the trial judge's use of the term "reasonable person" in the instruction for a relaxation of the mental-state standard.[5] Justice Thomas also analyzes a series of Supreme Court decisions addressing questions similar to those in Elonis's case. In each case, the Court had to decide between something like *de dicto* and *de re* understandings of the mental-state requirement in a criminal prohibition. Two cases involved prosecutions for sending obscene material through the mail. In both, the Court directed a more or less *de re* reading, requiring the prosecution to show that the defendant intentionally sent material and knew what it contained, but not that the defendant knew the contents qualified as legally obscene. In *Elonis*, Justice Thomas identifies these two decisions as most analogous to Elonis's case. In another case, relied on more heavily by the *Elonis* majority, the Court directed something like a *de dicto* reading, requiring the prosecution to show that the defendant had knowledge of the precise kind of property he stole (in that case, government-owned property). A third category of cases invoked by the *Elonis* majority took what might be called a "folk *de dicto*" approach.[6] In these cases, the Court required prosecutors to show that the defendant was aware of certain features of the act in question making the act illegal, but not necessarily that the defendant explicitly knew the act was illegal.

The *Elonis* majority discusses these cases in an unstructured way, observing that overall, it seems the Court has historically required defendants to have more rather than less knowledge of the facts surrounding their activity. Although Justice Thomas discusses the cases more systematically, he does not identify the issue as one of ambiguity, either. Jill Anderson (2014) has argued that lawyers' and judges' lack of familiarity with structural ambiguity contributes to analytical puzzles that could be resolved more straightforwardly. The problem she diagnoses also afflicts the *Elonis* opinions and helps to explain their dysfunctionality. Anderson describes the problem as the result of a set of legal cognitive biases; it is also a manifestation of the wordsmith's fallacy.

Attention to the structural ambiguity generated by opaque constructions might also have been useful in *McFadden v. United States*, another criminal case from the term. *McFadden* arose out of Stephen McFadden's prosecution under two federal statutes, the Analogue Act and the Controlled Substances Act. The Controlled Substances Act makes it criminal to "knowingly" sell controlled substances; the Analogue Act "identifies a category of substances substantially similar to those listed on the federal controlled substance schedules" and tells courts "to treat those analogues, if intended for human consumption, as controlled substances" (1).

McFadden admitted that he sold "bath salts" (synthetic drugs) to a video-store owner for resale, but his attorneys argued that he did not know they were "analogues." McFadden's lawyers asked for a jury instruction requiring the prosecution to show such knowledge, while the government asked for the jury to be instructed that McFadden simply needed to have "'knowingly . . . distributed . . . a substance . . . [t]hat was a controlled substance analogue'" (3). Justice Thomas's opinion for the majority in *McFadden* described the instruction given by the trial judge as a "compromise[ ]" (3). On appeal from his conviction, McFadden argued that the instruction did not require enough of the prosecution.

McFadden presented an issue analytically similar to the main issue in *Elonis*: a choice between more or less *de dicto* and *de re* interpretations of a mental-state adverb in jury instructions. The majority's conclusion (choosing something like a *de dicto* reading) is also similar in each case. Yet the *McFadden* opinions—issued a little more than two weeks after *Elonis*—nowhere mention *Elonis*.[7] Moreover, in *McFadden*, Justice Thomas, this time writing for the majority, takes an entirely different approach than he did in *Elonis*. In *McFadden*, Justice Thomas zeroes oddly in on the significance of the indefinite article "a":

> The CSA makes it "unlawful for any person knowingly or intentionally . . . to manufacture, distribute, or dispense . . . a controlled substance." . . . Under the most natural reading of this provision, the word "knowingly" applies not just to the statute's verbs but also to the object of those verbs—"*a* controlled substance." . . . When used as an indefinite article, "a" means "[s]ome undetermined or unspecified particular." Webster's New International Dictionary 1 (2d ed. 1954).
>
> (4)

From this analysis, Justice Thomas draws a conclusion that seems to reproduce the ambiguity in the statute: "The ordinary meaning of [the statute] thus requires a defendant to know only that the substance he is dealing with is some unspecified substance listed on the federal drug schedules" (5; see also 7). Although it is not as open-ended as the *Elonis* majority opinion, Justice Thomas's description of the required mental state, and his guidance to trial judges implementing the decision, are not models of clarity. Chief Justice Roberts's concurrence focuses on this point; he suggests that the jury need not be asked to reach any conclusion about the defendant's knowledge of the status of the substance sold, and that a defendant's lack of awareness about the legal classification of the substance might even be a defense—a marked contrast to the Chief Justice's approach in *Elonis* (*McFadden*, Roberts, 2).

The divergent analyses in *Elonis* and *McFadden* are especially notable because the decisions were issued within weeks of one another. Some basic parallels between the cases seem to have been invisible to all of the justices and their clerks. While the justices sometimes express awareness (or frustration) that *minds* are in some senses "opaque," the justices do not seem to perceive the kind of opacity arising from linguistic description of those mental states. Section 3.3 will further explore how attention to linguistic opacity can help to clarify discussion and thought about access to the mental states of real people. The next section will explore the presence of similar curiosities in antidiscrimination law.

3.2.2.2 Discriminatory intent

During the 2014 term, the Court decided half a dozen cases turning on claims of unlawful discrimination. This area of law is, of course, controversial for reasons other than the difficulty of detecting and describing mental states. But some of the controversy surrounding antidiscrimination law also springs from that difficulty, as the two sets of opinions discussed here will show.

One type of discrimination case is relatively uncontroversial. All of the justices agree that it is and should be illegal for an employer, say, to refuse to hire a job applicant solely because of the applicant's race, and for no other reason. This sort of antidiscrimination law is similar to criminal law, in that legal responsibility depends on an actor's wrongful mental state. But determining actors' reasons for their acts is, of course, not always easy. What kind of mental state counts as a wrongfully discriminatory mental state? Whose responsibility is it to show what was "in" the actor's mind? The first of these questions played an important role in the 2014-term case *Texas Dep't of Housing & Community Services v. Inclusive Communities Project*; the second was key to another case from the term, *EEOC v. Abercrombie & Fitch.*

Abercrombie & Fitch involved a claim under Title VII of the Civil Rights Act, which forbids, among other things, religious discrimination in hiring practices by private-sector employers. In this case, teenager Samantha Elauf had applied for a job at an Abercrombie & Fitch clothing store. After a promising interview, the store managers did not hire her; they cited the retailer's "Look Policy," which prohibits sales associates' wearing any kind of headgear at work (2). Elauf, a Muslim, wore a headscarf in public, including at her interview, but her interviewer did not ask about it, and Elauf did not mention it either. The question the Court was asked to decide was whether it was Elauf's responsibility to show that she told Abercrombie & Fitch that she wore a head covering for religious reasons, or whether she could prevail on her Title VII claim without making this showing.

An employer can violate Title VII by refusing to hire an applicant "because of" the applicant's religion; the statute defines "religion" to include "all aspects of religious practice, as well as belief, unless an employer demonstrates that he [sic] is unable to reasonably accommodate" the practice "without undue hardship" (3). Justice Scalia's opinion for the majority in *Abercrombie & Fitch* concluded that Elauf was not responsible for either informing Abercrombie & Fitch that she wore her headscarf for a religious reason or proving that Abercrombie & Fitch knew why she wore it. He based this conclusion on the absence of any reference to "knowledge" or "notice" in the statute (4–5).[8]

Abercrombie & Fitch fits into a pattern of recent Supreme Court decisions protective of religious observers and making it easier for individuals (and groups) to receive exemptions from general policies on the basis of their religious beliefs (Su 2016). *Burwell v. Hobby Lobby Stores* (2014), decided toward the end of the Court's 2013 term, is probably the highest-profile such case; in *Hobby Lobby*, the Court ruled that a closely held corporation could be exempted from compliance with certain federal laws on the basis of its owners' religious beliefs. Most accommodation cases, in theory, require some consideration of the parties' mental states, including both the "sincerity" of the plaintiff's belief and the defendant's purpose in failing to accommodate the belief or practice (see *Abercrombie & Fitch*, 4; *Holt*, 4, 6–9). Like other cases addressing these questions, however, *Abercrombie & Fitch* mostly skirts the question of how this consideration should proceed.

The lack of received models for addressing these mental states also marks the separate opinions from Justices Alito and Thomas in *Abercrombie & Fitch.* Justice Alito finds meaningless the distinction Justice Scalia draws between a defendant's discriminatory motive and the defendant's knowledge of the plaintiff's characteristics (such as religious belief). He also maintains that the circumstances in Elauf's case supported an inference that Abercrombie & Fitch employees knew she wore a headscarf for religious reasons. Justice Alito's preference for a simplified approach to mental-state analysis in this case is consistent with his practices in other cases, as discussions below will suggest. Justice Thomas, in contrast, approaches the case as an antidiscrimination dispute rather than a religious-accommodation one. He supports a narrow standard that would hold a defendant liable only if the defendant acted with a forbidden motive and knew about the applicant's religious belief, something like a *de dicto* understanding of intentional discrimination.

Justice Thomas's dissent in *Texas Dep't of Housing* contains nearly identical language. In fact, even though the legal issues in this case were very different from those in *Abercrombie & Fitch*, there are several parallels between the two cases. *Texas Dep't of Housing* concerned the viability of disparate-impact claims under the Fair Housing Act (FHA). To be liable on a disparate-impact theory, a defendant must simply have acted in a way that had a pronounced effect on members of a protected group (such as a group defined by race, gender, or religion); the defendant need not have intended to discriminate. Disparate-impact claims are controversial, and some, including Justice Thomas, consider them illegitimate (see, e.g., *Texas Dep't of Housing*, Thomas, 5–12). Although the Court had approved of using a disparate-impact theory under other antidiscrimination statutes starting in the 1970s, it had never addressed the theory's viability under the FHA until the 2014 term.[9]

The FHA contains some of the same language appearing in the Title VII provisions at issue in *Abercrombie & Fitch.* In both settings, the statutory language generates a kind of opacity. The analyses in *Texas Dep't of Housing*, however, are more focused on the statutory text than those in *Abercrombie & Fitch.* This focus helps to make clear that the problems discussed above in the criminal-law context persist in the context of antidiscrimination law.

The FHA makes it illegal "to refuse to sell or rent . . ., or otherwise make unavailable or deny, a dwelling to any person because of race" (11). Justice Kennedy's majority opinion, which concluded that disparate-impact claims are available under the FHA, justifies that conclusion partly by pointing to the phrase "otherwise make unavailable or deny." Justice Kennedy stresses the presence of similar language in other statutes that the Court had previously decided permit disparate-impact claims. He notes, for example, the significance of the term "otherwise," which, he explains, "means 'in a different way or manner,' thus signaling a shift in emphasis from an actor's intent to the consequences of his actions. Webster's Third New International Dictionary 1598" (12). He also stresses the "results-oriented" flavor of the verb "make" (11). These analytical moves, like Justice Thomas's discussion of the meaning of "a" in *McFadden*, perfectly exemplify the wordsmith's fallacy. They show Justice Kennedy relying on familiar linguistic tools (dictionary definitions, judicial precedent) to the neglect of other key linguistic issues—here, the ambiguity generated by the "because of" construction.

Justices Alito and Thomas, in contrast, do focus on "because of," but they do not address the term's ambiguity in terms of intentional states. Justice Alito's analysis of "because of" is especially striking for its zeal and questionable utility. In a footnote, he quotes all 14 sentences using the phrase "because of" that appeared in the *Washington Post* on January 21, 2015, the day of oral arguments in *Texas Dep't of Housing* (Alito, 4–5 n.2). Justice Alito offers the sentences as support for his position on the ordinary meaning of "because of": "When English speakers say that someone did something 'because of' a factor, what they mean is that the factor was a reason for what was done" (Alito, 4). In each of the samples, he maintains, "the phrase ['because of'] linked an action and the reason for the action" (Alito, 4). Justice Alito's examples create an impressive footnote, but several of them do not fit his description. One sentence, for example, reads, "The Postal Service lost $5.5 million in 2014, in large part because of continuing declines in first-class mail volume" (Alito, 4 n.2). This sentence does not describe an *actor's* reasons; it presents a causal explanation for an event. Although Justice Alito's discussion of the term hints at a *de dicto* reading of the statutory requirement, he seems unable to articulate that interpretation clearly.

The justices in *Texas Dep't of Housing* all practice what Victoria Nourse (2016) has called "petty textualism," an approach to statutory interpretation that focuses on the meaning of isolated terms without reintegrating them into the constructions from which they have been extracted. As in the criminal-law context, this practice prevents appreciation and discussion of the structural ambiguity present in some statutory provisions. And as in the criminal-law context, overlooking that ambiguity allows the justices to finesse questions of exactly what mental state a discrimination plaintiff must prove and how that proof might be achieved. In *Texas Dep't of Housing*, for example, the provision at issue could be interpreted to require a defendant to have particular applicants' race in mind when "refusing" or "otherwise making unavailable," or to require a defendant to "refuse" or "otherwise make unavailable" without consciously considering applicants' race. The majority opts for the latter, seemingly *de re* approach; the dissents insist on a more *de dicto* understanding. The meaning of individual terms in the provision does not help resolve the choice between these interpretations. That choice must be made based on a judgment about which type of real-life conduct should be illegal (cf. Rodes 1998).

This is not to say that statutory language is irrelevant. In *Texas Dep't of Housing*, for example, against the dissenters' contention that only a *de dicto* interpretation of the FHA identifies blameworthy conduct, supporters of disparate-impact liability could point to criminal-law precedents to show that a *de re* reading can also capture conduct considered blameworthy. Addressing the statutory ambiguity would, however, have made unnecessary the peculiar textual discussions offered by Justices Kennedy and Alito. In cases presenting less charged questions, attention to the ambiguity arising from an opaque construction in a statute might make a difference. For example, in *Abercrombie & Fitch*, the majority opted for an apparently *de re* interpretation of the relevant provision. That interpretation seems consistent with Title VII's definition of "religion" to include "all aspects of religious practice and observance, as well as belief" (3). That definition of religion does not suggest that mental states are unimportant to Title VII claims, but it does suggest that belief may be manifested in practice, and discriminatory motive therefore might be read simply from a defendant's refusal to accommodate an individual's (evident) practice. This understanding of the statutory language meets the objections of Justices Thomas and Alito to Justice Scalia's analysis in *Abercrombie & Fitch*. Contrary to Justice Thomas's criticism, the reading does not involve strict liability; it takes into account employers' reasons for refusing to hire. But it also does not require the kind of ad hoc distinctions between motive and knowledge that Justice Alito finds unpersuasive.

The need to assess parties' intentions arises in many contexts other than those discussed here.[10] Not all such contexts involve statutes or jury instructions containing opaque constructions, but many do. As the next section will explain, cases raising issues of this sort can also spark disagreement simply because different justices invoke different, incompatible frameworks for addressing the issues.

3.3 There's more to say about mental states

Lawyers' and judges' attitudes toward legal responsibility, shaped by the intentional stance, often reflect an assumption that mental states are "inside" actors and only indirectly accessible to anyone other than those actors. This assumption has a long lineage in U.S. law; Oliver Wendell Holmes's promotion of "objective" standards in his classic *The Common Law* (1881) is a response to the difficulties generated by the assumption. It results in a double bind for legal analysis. On the one hand, lawyers and judges need to be able to discuss and draw conclusions about a variety of mental states. On the other hand, it is often unclear how to detect such states, or even whether they are detectable.

That is, in addition to the legal tendency not to see the kind of ambiguity present in opaque constructions discussed in the previous section, there is a more basic set of difficulties regarding the *referents* of mental-state terms (the actual mental states of actual people). Still, despite those difficulties, lawyers and judges must discuss those mental states—they must use language to refer to them. This necessity generates a distinct and troubling phenomenon. Even in cases not involving any ambiguity in the relevant legal source, the justices' accounts of individuals' mental states sometimes mimic the description and communication of fictional characters' "mental states" in realist and contemporary narrative. This practice sidesteps the double bind mentioned in the previous paragraph at an undesirable cost. As this section explains, it encourages lawyers and judges to take cavalier and opportunistic attitudes toward such matters—to deny their own mindreading abilities when convenient and to deploy them uncritically (and with all the powers of an omniscient narrator) when that course seems desirable. These habits, in turn, tend to disable lawyers and judges from addressing how and when we *do* reliably read others' minds.

The next three sections explore these issues. Section 3.3.1 surveys scholarly approaches to the narrative presentation of fictional characters' mental states in relation to the concerns of this book. Section 3.3.2 examines signs of the justices' skepticism about "mindreading" and assumptions about the messiness of mental states in the 2014-term opinions. Section 3.3.3 addresses the justices' sometimes unwarranted confidence in their mind-describing powers.

3.3.1 Reading fictional minds

The human ability to "read" others' minds—our ability to estimate others' intentions and beliefs—has received a great deal of scholarly attention in recent decades. ("Mind" in this work is a functional term, referring to those aspects of a person that explain the person's behavior, not to a mysterious substance inside the person.) The topic is important partly because, as Dennett argued, we do often successfully predict others' behavior, even though we are not telepathic. That ability seems to be psychologically basic.

Fictional discourse—linguistic depictions of nonactual people and events—provides a model of the activity involved in mindreading and offers its readers practice in that activity (see Herman 2013; Palmer 2008; Vermeule 2010; Zunshine 2006). Characters read each other's minds, just as real people do, and readers draw inferences about characters' motives, emotions, and so on based on characters' narrated conduct. Indeed, many psychological studies of the mindreading abilities of real people use fictional scenarios to assess those capacities (e.g., Gerrig 1993). For instance, a well-known experiment examining children's concept of "false belief"—the understanding that the belief of another person might not incorporate information known to the child—asked children about the beliefs of dolls interacting in a make-believe scenario to identify whether the children had the concept (Wimmer & Perner 1983). Many psychological studies addressing mindreading and imaginative processes in adults ask subjects to read short written narratives and answer questions about them (e.g., Byrne 2005). This approach is partly a concession to the constraints of experimentation on human subjects, but it is also justified by findings that our brain activity is in some respects identical whether we perform an action ourselves, see another person performing it, or read about it (Dovey 2015; Nichols & Stich 2003).

This similarity in processing does not mean represented and actual acts are indistinguishable, of course, but it does mean that we can "rehearse" capacities that we use in our interaction with other people by reading about the use of those capacities and exercising them on represented individuals. Literary scholar Lisa Zunshine (2006) has argued that fictional narrative is especially helpful for refining higher-order mindreading skills—not just conjecturing about the state of mind of another person, but conjecturing about what A thinks B thinks about what A thinks, and so forth. Most of us engage in conjectures like this all the time without noticing it; Zunshine contends that our comfort with the practice is enhanced by our consumption of fictional narratives driven by characters' successful and unsuccessful higher-order mindreading of one another (see also Vermeule 2010). The next time you watch a film or TV narrative, you can investigate the point yourself.

Other features of narrative fictions communicated in language contribute to this skill.[11] Among them are psychonarration (introduced in section 3.1) and the narrative mode known in English as "free indirect discourse" (Banfield 1982; Cohn 1984, 1990). Free indirect discourse is often described as a hybrid of direct discourse (as in "She said, 'This is the spot'") and indirect discourse (as in "She said that was the spot"). Free indirect discourse blends these two forms, mixing pronouns, indexicals ("pointing" words like "this"), and verb forms from both direct and indirect discourse, and dropping quotation marks: "She realized *this* [indexical that would be appropriate in direct discourse] *was* [verb form appropriate to indirect discourse] the spot." Psychonarration, in contrast, describes a character's thoughts directly without borrowing linguistic markers of the character's perspective: "She realized she had found the right place."

Psychonarration and free indirect discourse have several unusual linguistic features. Free indirect discourse, as noted above, mixes linguistic markers suggesting an external perspective ("was") with markers suggesting an internal one ("this"). Free indirect discourse thus accustoms its readers to moving among or mingling perspectives (often between the "perspective" of a narrator and that of a character) without blurring them. It is a kind of narrator-assisted mindreading, or mindreading "under authorial instruction" (Scarry 1999) that instructs readers in the practice of "seeing" a character from inside and outside at the same time. Despite this linguistic complexity, sentences of free indirect discourse are easily processed by most moderately well-educated readers.

The instruction provided by free indirect discourse is a mixed blessing. On the one hand, it accustoms readers to thinking of mental states as readable and perhaps in that way further helps us develop mindreading and perspective-taking skills, as well as capacities for empathy and objectivity (cf. Davidson 2001; Nagel 1984; see also section 3.4.3). On the other hand, when readers come to be narrators, the model provided by narrative fiction may breed overconfidence in their ability to identify and describe the mental states of other real people.

In the 2014-term opinions, as the next two sections will show, the justices veer between fluent and assured mindreading of legal actors (as well as assertions about imaginary figures' mental states) and deep skepticism about the accessibility of other minds. Section 3.3.2 examines the pitfalls of over-indulging in skepticism, focusing on the last set of opinions of the 2014 term, those in the death-penalty case *Glossip v. Gross*. Section 3.3.3 explores the other side of the coin: the many occasions throughout the term in which virtually all of the justices confidently attributed motivation to parties, other actors, and each other, often using psychonarration and free indirect discourse. This section shows how legal discourse resembles fictional discourse not only in the structural ways explored in Chapter 2, but also in more localized ways. There is no reason to think the 2014 term was unique in this respect, and Chapter 6.4 will offer more support for concluding that it was not.

The justices' alternation between "mindblindness" and assured psychonarration appears to be entirely opportunistic. The opinions offer no guidance about when it is appropriate to discuss others' mental states and when it is not. The confusion is problematic not just because it involves inconsistency, but also because it instructs readers of the Court's opinions that decisions about how and when to discuss the contents of others' minds is a matter of lawyerly prerogative or style, not a matter with ethical implications (cf. Mertz 2007). Cavalier treatment of these decisions can have disastrous consequences for real individuals. More careful treatment of them does not require any fundamental alteration of legal training, just minimal familiarity with some features of linguistic accounts of actors' mental states.

3.3.2 Preserves of subjectivity

In the 2014-term opinions, the justices do not seem to be aware of the kind of linguistic opacity discussed in section 3.2. But they do show sensitivity to another kind of intentional opacity: they repeatedly remark on the inaccessibility of mental states to anyone other than the person experiencing them (cf. Robbins & Rumsey 2008). Sometimes the justices even recommend a kind of willed "mindblindness" (cf. Vermeule 2010) as the proper attitude to take toward others' internal states, particularly states of mood, emotion, or unreasoned preference. The handling of such "messy" states is the responsibility of other actors within or outside the legal system authorized to deal with these unruly matters.[12]

Recommendations of mindblindness can resemble the kind of fiction-as-epithet language discussed in Chapter 2. A common judicial criticism of another judge's reasoning involves charging the target with overconfident and overimaginative mindreading. In the 2014-term case *M&G Polymers v. Tackett*, for example, Justice Thomas's majority opinion explains the Court's disapproval of the rule used by the lower court by describing that rule as based on the lower court's "assessment of likely behavior," "derived . . . not from record evidence, but instead from its [the court's] own suppositions about the intentions of employees, unions, and employers" (10). In his dissent in *Williams-Yulee*, Justice Scalia faults the majority for basing its conclusion, by its own admission, on "'intuiti[on],'" without citing any "evidence" for its "happy forecast" about how the public regards elected state-court judges (Scalia, 6).

The justices also sometimes approve of others' skepticism about access to others' states of mind. Justice Alito takes such a position in his majority opinion in the 2014-term case *Davis v. Ayala*. This case turned on whether the outcome of Hector Ayala's criminal trial was affected by the trial judge's meeting with the prosecutor to discuss the reasons for the prosecutor's rejection of several potential jurors, a meeting at which Ayala's lawyer was not present. Several of the jurors stricken by the prosecutor were members of racial or ethnic minority groups; striking the jurors because of their race would have been constitutionally forbidden. The prosecutor explained his strikes as based not on race but on "uncertainty" about the individuals' cooperativeness and willingness to impose the death penalty (14, 25, 27–28). The trial judge accepted the explanation, based partly on the jurors' muddled responses to questions during jury selection. Justice Alito, writing for the Court, found this acceptance appropriate because the prospective jurors' attitudes were so difficult to discern. Indeed, Justice Alito noted the opacity of not only the prospective jurors' minds, but also the minds of the prosecutor and trial-court judge:

> the fact that the trial judge's impression of . . . [a prospective juror's] demeanor was . . . different from the prosecutor's hardly shows that the prosecutor's reasons were pretextual. It is not at all unusual for individuals to come to different conclusions in attempting to read another person's attitude or mood.
>
> (28)

Assertions of judicial mindblindness often accompany the identification of specific settings within which mindblindness is not necessary. Such "preserves of subjectivity" are locations in which either mindreading or the exercise of noncognitive preferences, or both, are appropriate. In U.S. law, the jury is one important such location. The aura of subjective preference surrounding the jury extends to the process of its composition: trial lawyers may strike a limited number of jurors based on the lawyers' "instinct" about jurors' dispositions (*Davis v. Ayala*, 16). Such decisions are "often" appropriately "based on subtle impressions and intangible factors" (*Davis v. Ayala*, 28–29). These characteristics of juries also mostly insulate their decisions from any judicial second-guessing.[13] The limited exceptions to this principle involve situations in which the jury's mindreading and exercise of preference have been hampered, as when external influences have intruded on jury deliberations or jurors have abdicated their role as folk mindreaders (see, e.g., *Warger*, 5 n.1, discussing the appropriateness of reexamining jury decisions in cases in which jurors reach a verdict by nonsubjective methods such as coin tossing).[14]

Two of the five opinions issued in the last case of the 2014 term, *Glossip v. Gross*, use several of these techniques. In *Glossip*, a group of death-row inmates in Oklahoma challenged the state's execution "protocol," three drugs administered in sequence: a sedative, a paralytic, and a drug inducing cardiac arrest. The protocol included the sedative to keep the condemned prisoner from feeling the pain caused by administration of the other drugs. Oklahoma, like other states, originally used barbiturates for sedation; after drug manufacturers refused to supply those drugs for use in executions, a group of Oklahoma decision-makers—not including any doctors—identified midazolam as an acceptable substitute (Berger 2016). Midazolam is a benzodiazepine similar to Valium, not usually used on its own as an anesthetic. The inmates in *Glossip* asked a federal court to order Oklahoma not to execute them using midazolam, arguing that it would not reliably render them unconscious during the execution and therefore violated their Eighth Amendment right to be free from cruel and unusual punishment. Initially, the inmates asked only for a temporary order, which the court could revise if the inmates failed to make their case at trial. The federal trial court, however, denied this request, and the inmates appealed.

In an opinion for the Court joined by four other justices, Justice Alito approved of the trial court's decision. Four justices wrote separately, but only two of the separate opinions were substantial, the dissents of Justices Breyer and Sotomayor, and only Justice Sotomayor's addressed the merits of the inmates' argument. Both Justice Alito's and Justice Sotomayor's opinions turn on the accessibility of two distinct phenomenological states: a decision-maker's cognitive state of certainty (the first state) about the noncognitive state of pain potentially suffered by the condemned (the second state).

Justice Alito's opinion focuses on the first state, emphasizing the trial court's finding "that a 500-milligram dose of midazolam 'would make it a virtual certainty that any individual will be at a sufficient level of unconsciousness to resist the noxious stimuli'" caused by the other drugs (10–11). Although the three experts who testified at the hearing on the inmates' motion qualified their opinions about the "level of unconsciousness" caused by 500 milligrams of midazolam (18 n.3, 19, 21), the trial judge was entitled, according to Justice Alito, to "credit[ ]" the state expert's "central point[:] . . . that a properly administered 500-milligram dose of midazolam will render the recipient unable to feel pain" (24). Justice Alito does not explain the basis for his conclusions that this was the expert's "central point" or that it was pivotal to the district court's decision; he directly attributes to the state expert and to the district judge a state of certainty about the experience of those subjected to Oklahoma's protocol. The attributions suggest that it is appropriate for a justice to "mindread" other legal actors, especially judges, but that it is not appropriate for appellate judges (or Supreme Court justices) to consider the internal, noncognitive states of condemned inmates.

Justice Alito's approach in *Glossip* describes the mental state ultimately at issue through the filter of other actors' assessment. This technique insulates the inmates' mental state from judicial scrutiny. Justice Alito criticizes Justice Sotomayor for disregarding this insulation and describing more directly the inmates' possible experience:

> we find it appropriate to respond to . . . [Justice Sotomayor's] groundless suggestion that our decision is tantamount to allowing prisoners to be "drawn and quartered, slowly tortured to death, or actually burned at the stake." . . . That is simply not true, and the principal dissent's resort to this outlandish rhetoric reveals the weakness of its legal arguments.
>
> (29)

One might expect, from this passage, that Justice Sotomayor's opinion is rhetorically overwrought. But although she does insist that the Court should consider the possibility that inmates might experience severe pain under the midazolam protocol, Justice Sotomayor is generally more cautious in attributing mental states to the petitioners, the testifying experts, and the trial court than Justice Alito in *Glossip*.[15] Regarding the opinion of the state's expert, for example, she notes that none of the scientific materials submitted to the trial court supported the expert's confidence about the effects of midazolam.

It is true, however, that Justice Sotomayor is more willing than Justice Alito to describe the behavior of other inmates executed using midazolam in a way that allows readers to draw inferences about the inmates' "inner" states. In two of the executions conducted with midazolam before the *Glossip* decision, the condemned had apparently not been "insensate" when they received the other drugs. Clayton Lockett, executed in April 2014, had "writhe[d] against his restraints, saying '[t]his s*** is f***ing with my mind,' 'something is wrong,' and '[t]he drugs aren't working'" (Sotomayor, 3–4). Joseph Wood, executed in July 2014, "gasped and snorted for nearly two hours" before being pronounced dead (Sotomayor, 20).

Justice Sotomayor's approach here allows readers to reconstruct the inmates' "inner" states from their described conduct. The approach is more faithful to the folk practices many of us use in drawing inferences about the mental states of other real people than is the blend of deferential confidence and unsupported attribution used by Justice Alito. But Justice Sotomayor's approach in her *Glossip* dissent is not clearly the judicial norm. As the next section will show, the techniques Justice Alito uses in his *Glossip* opinion are at least as typical.

3.3.3 Dangerous tools

Throughout the 2014-term opinions, a variety of justices use techniques commonly associated with fictional narrative, including psychonarration, free indirect discourse, and direct accounts of individuals' "mindreading" of other individuals. Such techniques appear especially often in two contexts: accounts of police activity in constitutional challenges to police action, and arguments rejecting a party's or a justice's proposed conclusion on the ground that it would have surprised the framers of the Constitution or the enactors of a more recent law. But the techniques are not limited to these settings. Interestingly, justices on the Court's conservative wing during the term (Justices Alito, Thomas, and Scalia, as well as Chief Justice Roberts) tended to offer more confident descriptions of others' states of awareness, knowledge, and belief than did justices on the Court's liberal wing (especially Justices Sotomayor, Breyer, and, usually, Kennedy). The latter group of justices tend to—but do not always—qualify their mindreading. This pattern suggests a need to reconsider the standard view (and usual self-presentation) of conservative judges as committed to objective perspectives and cautious minimalism in their analyses.

Supreme Court justices, like many lower-court judges, often produce heavily evaluative narratives of official conduct in opinions addressing claims that police or other government officials violated individuals' constitutional rights. The Court's 2014 term, as is typical of its recent terms, included several such cases. The first opinion issued in the term, for example, addressed the claim of a homeowning couple that police violated the couple's Fourth Amendment rights when the police came to the couple's house in search of a suspect via the back yard, rather than the front door. In an unsigned opinion, the Court describes the officers' approach to the house in detail, ultimately concluding that no previous Supreme Court decisions clearly identified such conduct as "unreasonable." This excerpt is typical:

> The officers initially drove to the front of the house, but after discovering that parking was not available there, turned right onto the side street. As they did so, they saw several cars parked side-by-side in a gravel parking area on the left side of the Carmans' [the plaintiffs'] property. The officers parked in the "first available spot," at "the far rear of the property." . . . The officers exited their patrol cars. As they looked toward the house, the officers saw a small structure (either a carport or a shed) with its door open and a light on. . . . Thinking someone might be inside, Officer Carroll walked over, "poked [his] head" in, and said "Pennsylvania State Police." . . . No one

> was there, however, so the officers continued walking toward the house. As they approached, they saw a sliding glass door that opened onto a ground-level deck. Carroll thought the sliding glass door "looked like a customary entryway," so he and Officer Roberts decided to knock on it.
>
> (*Carroll v. Carman*, 1–2)

This passage includes several examples of psychonarration: "[t]hinking someone might be inside," "Carroll thought the sliding glass door 'looked like a customary entryway.'" It also uses a technique readable as free indirect discourse: "(either a carport or a shed)" signals an ambiguity lacking any obvious relevance to the legal analysis, but suggestive of the officers' uncertainty about their surroundings (the lower-court opinions called this structure a "garage"). The whole vignette, adopting the officers' point of view, implies their helpful frame of mind and understandable confusion about how to get the attention of the house's inhabitants.

Another striking example of these techniques appears in Justice Alito's opinion for the majority in the 2014-term case *San Francisco v. Sheehan*, also a civil case alleging officers' violation of an individual's constitutional rights. Teresa Sheehan sued the police who shot and injured her after being summoned by a social worker to the group home where she lived. Justice Alito's account of the officers' encounter with Sheehan communicates the officers' concern and frustration at their inability to observe Sheehan or assess her intentions after she locked them out of her room:

> The officers were concerned that the door to Sheehan's room was closed. They worried that Sheehan, out of their sight, might gather more weapons—[Officer] Reynolds had already observed other knives in her room . . . —or even try to flee through the back window. . . . Because Sheehan's room was on the second floor, she likely would have needed a ladder to escape. Fire escapes, however, are common in San Francisco, and the officers did not know whether Sheehan's room had such an window. . . . Because the door closed, all that Reynolds and Holder knew for sure was that Sheehan was unstable, she had just threatened to kill three people, and she had a weapon.
>
> (3–4)[16]

Accounts like these position the justices as quasi-omniscient narrators with direct access to officers' attitudes and motivations. The accounts also position the police similarly in relation to the civilians they encounter. The narratives suggest, and sometimes state outright, that when officers' ability to mindread civilians is thwarted, officers have justifiable cause for concern and action (see also, e.g., *Sheehan*, 2; Chapter 6.4.1). The effects of this lesson can be far-reaching; these opinions are thematically and rhetorically indistinguishable from accounts police officers have given—during the 2014 term and since—of the reasons for their use of deadly force against unarmed individuals (see, e.g., Wallace-Wells 2016).

Other frequent targets of judicial mindreading are the people and groups responsible for originating legal commands. Justices' discussion of lawmakers' intentions (discussed further in Chapter 4.2) is a familiar practice, but justices also often assert confidently that lawmakers would be dismayed by a party's, court's, or other justice's position.[17] Justice Thomas offers a good example in his *Obergefell* dissent: "the majority invokes our Constitution in the name of a 'liberty' that the Framers would not have recognized, to the detriment of a liberty they sought to protect" (Thomas, 2; see also *Wynne*, Thomas, 1). A variation on this technique attributes openmindedness rather than dismay to the framers. In his

Obergefell majority opinion, Justice Kennedy similarly attributes humility to the individuals responsible for the due process and equal protection clauses:

> The generations that wrote and ratified the Bill of Rights and the Fourteenth Amendment did not presume to know the extent of freedom in all its dimensions, and so they entrusted to future generations a charter protecting the right of all persons to enjoy liberty as we learn its meaning.
>
> (11)

As suggested above, during the 2014 term the justices on the Court's conservative wing tended to be more categorical in their assertions about what others believe and intend. Often, these justices do not qualify such assertions at all.[18] Justices associated with the Court's liberal wing more often address such matters using hedging language, like "[s]eemingly aware" (*Kerry v. Din*, Breyer, 2), or "likely intends" (*Walker*, 11 (Breyer)).[19] These tendencies are not absolute; conservative justices sometimes qualify their mental-state attributions,[20] and liberal justices are sometimes emphatic in ascribing mental states.[21] But the term's most elaborate and subtle examples of judicial psychonarration appear in opinions signed by Justice Alito, author of the majority opinions in both *Glossip* (the midazolam case) and *Sheehan* (the locked-room case).

One of the term's most memorable examples of this technique appears in Justice Alito's dissent in *Walker v. Texas Division*. In the following passage, Justice Alito sets the scene for an argument against Justice Breyer's classification of specialty license places as a form of "government speech":

> Suppose you sat by the side of a Texas highway and studied the license plates on the vehicles passing by. You would see, in addition to the standard Texas plates, an impressive array of specialty plates. (There are now more than 350 varieties.) You would likely observe plates that honor numerous colleges and universities. You might see plates bearing the name of a high school, a fraternity or sorority, the Masons, the Knights of Columbus, the Daughters of the American Revolution, a realty company, a favorite soft drink, a favorite burger restaurant, and a favorite NASCAR driver. . . . As you sat there watching these plates speed by, would you really think that the sentiments reflected in these specialty plates are the views of the State of Texas and not those of the owners of the cars? If a car with a plate that says "Rather Be Golfing" passed by at 8:30 am on a Monday morning, would you think: "This is the official policy of the State—better to golf than to work?" [sic] If you did your viewing at the start of the college football season and you saw Texas plates with the names of the University of Texas's out-of-state competitors in upcoming games—Notre Dame, Oklahoma State, the University of Oklahoma, Kansas State, Iowa State—would you assume that the State of Texas was officially (and perhaps treasonously) rooting for the Longhorns' opponents? And when a car zipped by with a plate that reads "NASCAR – 24 Jeff Gordon," would you think that Gordon (born in California, raised in Indiana, resides in North Carolina) is the official favorite of the State government?
>
> (Alito, 1–2)

On a first read, this passage seems to encourage readers to take an "objective" perspective, that of a neutral fly on the highway wall. But the passage is, in fact, not neutral.

The thoughts projected into this observer's mind—and from there into the reader's—showcase what Justice Alito describes as the absurdity of the majority's position. The "physical" position in which Justice Alito places his observer is a position many readers are likely to associate with highway patrol surveillance. The passage invites or even instructs its reader to take the perspective of an agent of the state, then shows how this agent could not reasonably consider the license-plate messages to be state-sponsored communications. It cleverly enlists readers in enacting a state agent's disavowal of the license-plate messages.

The authorial instruction in this passage is more explicit than the kind typically found in fictional narrative. But it does not function in a radically different way. As the examples offered throughout this section show, the justices use the same kinds of constructions to ascribe thoughts and attitudes to imaginary figures, as in the above passage from *Walker*, and to real people, especially police officers and those with whom they come into contact. With respect to both kinds of agents, the justices write with an authority approaching that of authors of fictional narrative. Like such authors, the justices offer their accounts not as hypotheses to be tested, but as the final word on the "thoughts" described.

The use of techniques associated with fictional narrative to ascribe mental states to imaginary figures is not necessarily troubling. The apparently unselfconscious use of exactly the same techniques to ascribe mental states to *real* people is more disturbing. Given the importance of real individuals' intentions to assessments of legal responsibility, it is impossible for lawyers and judges to avoid such mindreading altogether, but mindreading does not need to involve psychonarration. A more explicitly reconstructive externalist approach, like Justice Sotomayor's in *Glossip*, makes such direct imaginative dives into others' minds unnecessary.

The danger of a blithe judicial approach to mental-state ascription is not that it involves the exercise of judicial imagination. More troublingly, the technique teaches law students, lawyers, and other judges that it is appropriate to make unsupported yet confident pronouncements about the mental states of other real human beings, even in the absence of any contact with them—to treat them as "creatures" akin to the nonactual figures in a fictional narrative (see van Inwagen 1977). Outside the legal system, most socially competent adults do not define others' mental states by fiat. At least with people with whom we wish to remain on good terms, we usually confirm our mindreading through continued interaction. Lawyers could be taught to retain this skill as easily as they could be taught to abandon it; more cautious mindreading might encourage perceptions of legal activity as principled and constructive, rather than occult and perverse.

3.4 Legal phantoms

An understanding of mental states as only indirectly accessible to outsiders, together with concern that such states might vary greatly from person to person, helped to motivate the development of "objective" standards in law, as in many other areas of professional discourse, since at least the late nineteenth century (see Daston & Galison 2007; Holmes 1881). Among the techniques lawyers and judges have developed to this end are the many legal standards marked by the modifier "reasonable" and its synonyms (see Zipursky 2015). Lawyers contrast such standards with "subjective" standards requiring estimation of real people's actual mental states.

Objective standards are notoriously difficult to define and describe; they are often criticized. A standard critique observes that the "reasonable person" often invoked in connection with such standards is a judicial invention. Because judges "make up" the reasonable person, the argument goes, judges control what counts as reasonable. And more often than not, judges identify their personal perspectives with the "reasonable" perspective. They might do so innocently, because they are just unable to see things from any perspective other than their own (e.g., Thomas 2014). Or they might do so more cynically, using a reasonable-person standard to impose their perspective on others without admitting it (e.g., Moran 2003).[22]

This section reconsiders such arguments, using information about the roles played by objective standards in the 2014-term opinions. The discussion describes application of these standards as requiring a sophisticated kind of meta-perspective-taking. The discussion also explains why—contrary to many critics' contentions—it makes sense to call these standards "objective." The next subsection (3.4.1) surveys the functions of objective standards in the 2014-term opinions. Section 3.4.2 discusses two cases in which the justices explicitly disagreed about such standards—not about the appropriateness of applying them, but about the content of the term "reasonable." Section 3.4.3 presents an alternative account of the standards; drawing on understandings of narrative characterization and focalization, it explains how the application of reasonableness standards requires a cognitive activity similar to that involved in reading the "minds" and taking the perspectives of fictional characters.

3.4.1 The range of the reasonable

Reasonableness standards have been criticized for decades (see, e.g., McNaughton 1955; Moran 2003). But the standards seem unlikely to disappear from legal discourse anytime soon. At least one of the 2014-term opinions suggests that some justices regard reasonableness standards as a relatively safe model for new legal rules. Although the justices do not always endorse the use of these standards,[23] they are without question widespread. Is there a way to reconcile the long-standing criticism of such standards with their continued and perhaps increased use?

Traditionally, critiques of the standards focus on how their application tends to vary from case to case (e.g., Moran 2003). Based on this observation, many critics conclude that the standards are fatally infected with subjectivity—that they cannot operate other than as expressions of their appliers' brute preferences (e.g., Thomas 2014). In a recent reexamination of these standards, Benjamin Zipursky (2015) has helpfully focused on the *language* judges use to articulate and apply them. Following his lead, the discussion here will also consider several adjectival and adverbial equivalents for the terms "reasonable" and "reasonably." Identifying the terms that justices used as interchangeable with "reasonable" in the 2014-term opinions yields valuable information about the semantics of the term.

"Ordinary" might be the term the justices most often use as equivalent to "reasonable." In her opinion for the *Omnicare* majority, for instance, Justice Kagan refers to the "reasonable investor" and the "ordinary investor" as identical perspectives (e.g., 18). Justice Scalia's *Omnicare* dissent uses the phrases "ordinary man" and "reasonable person" apparently as synonyms in two consecutive sentences (Scalia, 3).[24] Justices also sometimes use "typical" as interchangeable with "reasonable" and "ordinary." Justice Scalia's *Omnicare* dissent presents the "typical listener" as equivalent to the "ordinary man" (Scalia, 7). Justice Breyer, describing the messages communicated by specialty license plates in *Walker*, discusses what "issuers of [government] ID[s]" and those who observe them "typically," "routinely," and "reasonably" do, expect, and understand (10). Another stand-in for "reasonable"—"normal"—similarly suggests a descriptive or frequency-based conceptualization of the "reasonable" (Miller & Perry 2012). The per curiam opinion in *Carroll v. Carman* (the case involving police approach to a house via the back yard) uses "normal" this way: the Carmans argued "that a normal visitor would have gone to their front door, rather than into their backyard" (3). But "normal" can also have normative connotations; the "normal" is often preferable to the "abnormal." Other modifiers often interchanged with "reasonable" carry similar implications. When judicial conduct is in question, for example, the justices sometimes require that it be "fair-minded" (e.g., *Davis v. Ayala*, 8, 12). Another synonym suggesting virtuous (and not just predictable) conduct, often applied to government actors, is "rational." The "rational jury" standard, for example, helps judges assess whether a legal error in lower-court proceedings is grounds for reversal (e.g., *McFadden*, Thomas, 10).

The use of these terms as equivalents in the 2014-term opinions suggests that the justices understand "reasonable" to have both descriptive and normative implications. The reasonable is the unexceptional—what Zipursky (2015) calls the "moderate." But it is also conduct that meets minimal levels of positive appraisal, that is socially acceptable, if not commendable—what Zipursky captures in his notion of "mutuality." This is a requirement that an actor's conduct manifest the actor's willingness to take the needs of others into account. If a reasonableness standard carries these moderation-and-mutuality implications, Zipursky argues, perhaps it is not quite as empty a formula as critics maintain.

The critique of reasonableness standards often has as much to do with the "person" part of the "reasonable person" construct as with the "reasonable" part. This "person" admittedly does not exist; because judges invent the figure, the argument goes, they can give it any characteristics they like, including their own (e.g., Moran 2003; Thomas 2014). As Zipursky notes, however, legal references to reasonableness standards are not always references to a reasonable "person." United States law requires all sorts of things to be reasonable, including fees and rates; it also requires many acts to be reasonable, including investigations and interpretations.

The 2014-term opinions make clear that when "reasonable" and its equivalents modify nouns naming kinds of acts, the act in question is invariably an intentional act, and usually an act involving an adjustment in the actor's point of view. In the Fourth Amendment law of search and seizure, for instance, police decisions to proceed with a search along a certain physical path must be "reasonable" (*Carroll v. Carman*, 4). Police decisions to search a place or suspect must be based on "reasonable suspicion," if not probable cause (e.g., *Heien*, 5; *Rodriguez*, Thomas, 12). Suspicion may remain reasonable even if it is based on mistaken understanding of the law, as long as the misunderstanding is reasonable (*Heien*, 1). Once an officer has begun a search, the officer must continue it with "reasonable diligen[ce]" (*Rodriguez*, 8).

Reasonableness is also required of intentional acts outside the Fourth Amendment context. Perhaps the most familiar reasonableness standard is the reasonable-doubt burden of proof. Courts occasionally refer to other proof burdens using similar language. In her *Davis v. Ayala* dissent, for instance, Justice Sotomayor describes the harmless-error standard used by one of the lower courts as involving a "determination that the error was harmless beyond a reasonable doubt" (Sotomayor, 3). Conversely, the Court has described the statutory requirement that a patent claim be "definite" as a requirement that the patent "inform, with reasonable certainty, those skilled in the art about the scope of the invention" (*Teva*, Thomas, 16). More broadly, the majority's conclusion in *Heien*, the police mistake-of-law case, may be summed up as requiring officers to have a reasonable "understanding" of the law (4), a requirement echoed in other decisions addressing different areas of law.[25] The connection between reasonableness standards and perspectives on intentional activity is especially clear in the most specialized subject-matter-specific variants of these standards. The "reasonable investor," for instance, plays a prominent if contested role in the *Omnicare* opinions (10–14, 16 n.11, 18, 20; Thomas, 2; Scalia, 2, 4–7). Another example is the "skilled artisan," which functions similarly in *Teva* (3, 5, 16; Thomas, 10).[26] Yet another is the "prudent fiduciary" of trust law, the standard Justice Breyer describes as dispositive in *Tibble v. Edison Int'l* (5, 7; cf. Stern 2016).

What the law requires to be reasonable, then, is a wide range of intentional activity.[27] Noting this pattern in the justices' use of the term "reasonable" and its stand-ins helps to explain why lawyers refer to the standards as "objective." They do so not to claim authority for the standards, or to claim that they are uncontroversially accessible to all, but to emphasize that the standards require intentional-stance assessment of an action from the outside, with no attempt to read the actor's mind (cf. Holmes 1881). Such standards are objective because they are not "subjective," in the senses discussed earlier in this chapter. But reasonableness standards do not just involve a shift in perspective to one "outside" the actor in question. Rather, the most detailed articulations of the standards indicate that applying a reasonableness standard requires a decision-maker to judge whether the conduct or manifested mental states of the actor fall within the set of the *numerous* acts or mental states that might count as reasonable under the circumstances. This is how applying such standards involves a kind of meta-perspective-taking—a perspective on perspectives. By definition, these standards may be satisfied in more than one way. This feature of reasonableness standards is what makes them necessarily variable in application; it is also why the notion of a "reasonable mistake" is coherent, not an oxymoron (see *Heien*, 1, 4, 13).

It follows that it can be misleading to say that an actor must act reasonably. This way of putting things suggests that in any given situation, there is one particular course of conduct that the reasonable actor would follow. It would be more accurate to describe reasonableness standards as indicating *perspectives* for the assessment of conduct or decisions. The differences among the various reasonableness standards stem from different functional limitations on these perspectives. The conduct of a reasonable police officer is judged from a perspective that regards the officer as an officer, rather than a civilian, but not as a particular officer. Viewed this way, reasonableness standards need not simply mirror their applier's personal preferences. Indeed, they seem to be devices that, ideally, *force* appliers to step *outside* their own perspectives—not only to take another's perspective, but then to repeat that move and take a perspective on multiple perspectives.

Although this account of reasonableness standards is consistent with their use in most cases, not all lawyers and judges seem to understand them this way, so critics' objections may be well founded in some cases. But sometimes the justices do hint at a connection between applying reasonableness standards and taking particular perspectives. The opinions in the 2014-term case *Kingsley v. Hendrickson* offer some examples. *Kingsley* arose from a civil-rights suit by Michael Kingsley, who was arrested and detained before trial. During his detention, Kingsley got into a dispute with four officers over the décor in his cell. The altercation led to a handcuffed Kingsley being Tased by one of the officers while Kingsley laid facedown on a bunk. Kingsley sued, claiming that this treatment deprived him of his due process rights. His claim went to trial, where a jury found for the officers. Kingsley's appeal, and the question presented to the Supreme Court, turned on whether the officers' conduct should be assessed from the perspective of a "reasonable officer" or from a perspective that would consider the actual officers' states of mind. The instructions given to Kingsley's jury alluded to both perspectives, but the Wisconsin appellate court opted for a subjective standard, requiring a finding that the officers actually intended to harm Kingsley, not just subdue him.

Justice Breyer's majority opinion in *Kingsley* concludes that an objective standard—one assessing the officers' conduct from a "reasonable officer" perspective—should be used to assess claims like Kingsley's. The excessiveness of the officers' use of force, Justice Breyer stresses, "must" be made "from the perspective of a reasonable officer on the scene" (6–7; see also 9–10). This conclusion seems consistent with the description of objective standards offered above. Objective assessment of the officers' conduct does not require a decision-maker to read the officers' minds, but it does require the decision-maker to confirm that the officers' conduct was intentional and then to consider whether the officer's conduct was consistent with the conduct that might be displayed by an officer trying to act with consideration for others' interests in a similarly fraught situation (cf. Zipursky 2015).

Justice Scalia, dissenting in *Kingsley*, rejects the feasibility of distinguishing between the intentionality of the officers' conduct and the officers' intention in engaging in that conduct (Scalia, 1–2, 3–4). He describes the standard of "[o]bjective reasonableness of the force used" as "nothing more than a heuristic for identifying" the defendant officer's "intent to punish" (Scalia, 3–4). This equation involves what the next section will call a reductive approach to the objective standard. It is not a critique of the standard in the traditional sense, but a disagreement with Justice Breyer over the relationship between the objective standard and an individual officer's point of view. Justice Scalia seems to see the two as equivalent, at least in this case. As the next section explains, this kind of disagreement about the redundancy of reasonableness standards is a recurring theme in the 2014-term opinions.

3.4.2 Reducing reasonableness

The two sets of opinions considered in this section show the persistence of disputes about reasonableness standards even as the justices also approve of their use in new areas. In making sense of reasonableness standards, the justices often describe them as equivalent to other less controversial standards. But the equivalences often oversimplify, perpetuating the debate over reasonableness standards instead of resolving it.

One of the 2014-term cases involving this dynamic, *Baker Botts v. ASARCO*, arose from a bankruptcy proceeding, the kind of technical dispute that receives little public attention and often does not sharply divide the justices. *Baker Botts*, however, did divide the Court. Justice Thomas wrote the majority opinion; Justice Breyer wrote a dissenting opinion. *Baker Botts* arose from a dispute between ASARCO, a mining company, and two law firms that helped the company through bankruptcy proceedings, one of them the Baker Botts firm. A provision of the Bankruptcy Code authorizes bankruptcy courts to award "reasonable compensation for actual, necessary services" performed by professionals assisting debtors in bankruptcy proceedings (2). At the end of ASARCO's bankruptcy proceedings, the law firms submitted to the company and the court requests for compensation under this provision. ASARCO objected to some aspects of the requests; to respond, the firms had to gather and present more information. Eventually, the bankruptcy judge ordered ASARCO to pay the firms the amounts requested for work during the proceedings (roughly $120 million), as well as "over $5 million for time spent litigating in defense of the fee applications" (2). A federal trial-court judge approved the awards, but the court of appeals reversed as to the $5 million, holding that the statute did not authorize compensation for "litigation defending" an application for compensation (2–3).

The dispute in *Baker Botts* turned on the statutory language "reasonable compensation for actual, necessary services rendered by" professionals. Zipursky (2015) argues that judges tend to read phrases like "reasonable compensation" as describing moderate or unexceptional amounts (e.g., 2135). But the *Baker Botts* majority did not follow this rule of thumb. Justice Thomas instead emphasizes the prepositional phrase following "reasonable compensation": "for actual, necessary services rendered." Because "litigation in defense of a fee application is not a 'service'" to the debtor, but rather an activity in which the lawyer takes an adversarial position toward the debtor, Justice Thomas reasons, "it follows that the contested [part of the] award was not 'compensation' for a 'service'" (9). This approach allowed Justice Thomas to avoid addressing the meaning of "reasonable"; instead he focused on identifying the bounds of the category of "service," a familiar and comfortable statutory-interpretation task.[28]

As Justice Breyer points out in his dissent, Justice Thomas's approach has some perverse implications. Under that reading, a firm that does $5 million worth of work for a debtor, then spends the same amount defending its request for compensation against a bad-faith challenge, could walk away without being reasonably compensated for its services. In fact, Justice Breyer's analysis is consistent with Zipursky's (2015) moderation-and-mutuality account of reasonableness standards, although Justice Breyer does not invoke any rule of thumb for assessing "reasonable compensation." Instead, Justice Breyer treats the term "reasonable" as a kind of trigger for discretionary judicial assessment: "to ensure that each professional is paid reasonably . . ., a court must have the discretion to authorize pay for fee-defense work" (6). Unfortunately, this approach seems to confirm the concerns of the critics of reasonableness standards. Like many critics, Justice Breyer effectively treats "reasonable" as a synonym for "discretionary." This aspect of his argument might explain Justice Breyer's inability to gain the support of more justices for his position in *Baker Botts* (only Justices Ginsburg and Kagan joined his opinion).

The disagreement in *Baker Botts* arose from a kind of statutory ambiguity. Justice Thomas takes "for actual, necessary services rendered" to be the key language in the provision, while Justice Breyer gives "reasonable" that role. This is not the kind of ambiguity that stems from an opaque construction, but it does seem to stem from a difference in perspective. Justice Breyer's insistence that compensation be "reasonable" emphasizes service providers' point of view; Justice Thomas's demand that compensation be "for actual, necessary services rendered" emphasizes the debtor's.[29] But neither opinion explicitly discusses the need to choose between or accommodate these perspectives. Nor does either discuss how the choice might bear on the meaning to give the disputed statutory language. *Baker Botts* thus exemplifies the judicial (and critical) tendency not to examine too closely either reasonableness standards or the linguistic presentation of perspectives on intentional activity.

Elonis, the Facebook-threats case discussed in Chapter 2.2 and earlier in this chapter, involves a different kind of reduction of a different reasonableness standard. As noted earlier, the case yielded a less-than-definitive holding. Chief Justice Roberts concludes that the jury instructions given at Elonis's trial were improper, but he does not specify what an appropriate instruction would say. The instruction given told the jury to consider whether "a reasonable person would foresee that [Elonis's] statement[s] would be interpreted by [recipients] . . . as . . . serious expression[s] of an intention to inflict bodily injury" (7). To explain why this instruction was improper, the Chief Justice first observes that criminal liability requires "awareness of some wrongdoing" (13). Second, he explains, a "reasonable person" standard (as used in the jury instruction) is "a negligence standard" (14).

Negligence standards are by definition objective in the sense that they do not concern a defendant's mental state. It follows from these premises that the reference to a "reasonable person" in Elonis's jury instructions was improper.

The problem with this argument is the second premise, which equates a "reasonable person" standard with a negligence standard. While one formulation of the classic tort negligence standard involves comparing a defendant's conduct to that of a reasonable person, the two standards are not precisely identifiable in the way Chief Justice Roberts suggests. Rather, as Zipursky (2015) explains, the negligence standard is one kind of reasonableness standard. In *Elonis*, both Justice Alito, concurring, and Justice Thomas, dissenting, refuse to equate the "reasonable person" and negligence standards. Justice Thomas wrestles more directly with the issue (cf. Alito, 3). Like Justice Alito, he expressly differentiates the question of a defendant's mental state from the question of whether a communication qualifies as a threat. Justice Thomas stresses the need to decide the latter question objectively; whether a communication qualifies as a threat, he explains, is not something that can

> be determined solely by the reaction of the recipient, but must . . . be "determined by the interpretation of a reasonable recipient . . .," lest historically protected speech [such as political satire] be suppressed at the will of an eggshell observer.
>
> (Thomas, 2–3)

Justice Thomas also offers examples of the Court's use of objective standards in other cases involving the categorization of communications. But Justice Thomas makes this argument indirectly. He explains the error in the majority's reasoning not precisely as presented here, but as a confusion of "general intent" with "specific intent" (7). While the majority does seem to commit this confusion, the confusion alone does not fully explain why the trial judge's use of a "reasonable person" standard was proper; objective standards are "general" in a very particular sense, and not all general-intent standards are objective.

The *Baker Botts* and *Elonis* opinions show the justices struggling to give content to reasonableness standards. The ubiquity of the standards drives the need to discuss and analyze them. Yet the justices still sometimes avoid this task, even when avoidance plays to critics' fears or yields questionable results (as in *Baker Botts*). When they do not avoid the issue, several of the justices seem inclined to reduce reasonableness standards to other standards, such as discretion (Justice Breyer's *Baker Botts* dissent) or negligence (the *Elonis* majority opinion). Even when justices try to give content to these standards—as Justice Thomas arguably does in his *Elonis* dissent—they seem to have trouble doing so.

Zipursky's (2015) "moderation-and-mutuality" account of reasonableness standards goes some way toward addressing these problems but stops short of a full explanation. In particular, it does not directly address the conventional labeling of the standards as "objective." This labeling inspires much of the criticism of the standards. To some critics, calling a standard "objective" is a sure sign of judicial obfuscation. It is obviously impossible to assess conduct from no perspective at all, yet that is what "objective" standards seem to require.[30] If such a standpoint is impossible to assume, it is natural to infer that justices cannot sincerely say that they are assuming it or direct others to do so. Yet the traditions of legal and judicial skepticism about subjective mental states, discussed earlier in this chapter, are surely at least partly well motivated, and they make irresistible a nonsubjective standard of judgment. This tension need not be seen as irresolvable. More careful consideration of how we conceptualize and describe points of view can illuminate why the notion of an objective perspective is not a contradiction in terms. Theorists of narrative technique have developed vocabularies for this very task.

3.4.3 How to make a perspective objective

Section 3.2 outlined the centrality of the intentional stance to legal doctrine and judicial discourse, as well some of the puzzles it generates in the interpretation of legally significant language. Section 3.3 considered the justices' peculiar alternation, in their opinions, between confident ascriptions of mental states to individuals and opportunistic skepticism about the accessibility of those states. Section 3.4, so far, has addressed the popularity of supposedly aperspectival standards that remain oddly difficult for lawyers or the justices to discuss systematically. This section suggests that all of these phenomena stem from a particular manifestation of the wordsmith's fallacy: a tendency for discussions of legal discourse to view choices regarding the linguistic presentation of individual perspectives as trivial.

Scholars of the construction of personality and perspective in narrative fiction have developed several frameworks for examining such choices. Recent approaches to understanding narrative "people" have focused as much on point of view as on individual characters' qualities, the focus of many earlier discussions (e.g., Palmer 2008, 2010; Ronen 1994). Related philosophical discussions have examined characters' ontological or existential status (Everett 2013; van Inwagen 1977; cf. Gallagher 2006). Early twenty-first century scholarship has joined these perspectives with insights from psychologists' and cognitive scientists' accounts of individuation, identification, and mindreading (e.g., Herman 2013; Vermeule 2010; Zunshine 2006).

Two ideas from this work are pertinent to the questions raised throughout this chapter but little discussed in legal settings. One is the necessary incompleteness of fictional characters (Everett 2013; Gallagher 2006; Ronen 1994). Each living human being has many attributes that might never be described or perceived. At the moment you read this sentence, for example, the number of hairs on your head could, in principle, be exactly specified. Fictional characters, in contrast, have only the properties and attributes assigned to them, either by their original creators or by other "authors," such as fans. In this way, fictional characters are much "thinner" than actual human beings.

Given the thinness of fictional characters, and our usual awareness that they are fictional, it can seem odd that we can have emotional reactions to their plights. This oddity has generated sustained scholarly discussion (e.g., Paskins 1977; Radford & Weston 1975; Walton 1993). One explanation for the phenomenon is that narrative fiction in the Western tradition capitalizes on humans' preexisting capacity for perspectival movement or perspective-taking—for "seeing as" a character or "seeing from" different points of view. Some have argued that this capacity is in fact a precondition for language acquisition and abstract thought as well as for more obviously related skills like empathy (see, e.g., Bogdan 2013; Graziano 2013; Tomasello 2001).

Thus, one explanation for our ability to engage with fictional characters, even when we know they are fictional and even, sometimes, when they are "flat," is that we have a similar capacity to engage with real people even when we do not have complete information about them or direct access to their mental states. For example, seeing a real person struggling with a heavy load causes a cognitive-affective response in a normal adult that is physiologically similar to, albeit much more powerful than, reading about a character in the same predicament (Caracciolo 2013; Dovey 2015; Nichols & Stich 2003; cf. Goldman 2006). When we see an actor that we perceive as an intentional agent in a recognizable plight, *regardless* of whether the actor is a real person (or even a representation of a person), we "fill in" the details of the plight and the actor's expected response based on our exposure to similar situations (Heider & Simmel 1944; Scholl & Tremoulet 2000).[31] Because we have these capacities, the incompleteness of fictional characters does not keep us from feeling concern for them.

The *parallels* between fictional characters and real people do not make them equivalent. We take many similar attitudes toward fictional characters and real people, but the objects of our attitudes are fundamentally different in each case. And not all people—not even all Americans, or all graduates of a particular law school—have the same "filling in" resources. Because each of us begins developing these capacities in childhood by interacting with others (Bogdan 2013; Tomasello 2001), differences in our experiences at a young age can provide us with different expectations about the capacities of intentional agents in general and agents in specific situations in particular. Thus, not all readers respond to fictional characters in the same way, nor do they respond to real-life situations involving other people in the same way. This point resembles the arguments made by many critics of reasonableness standards, but those critics tend to draw from the observation the inference that our responses always vary wildly from person to person. That inference neglects the common reasons for the effect of early experiences on our judgments and expectations, an issue to which Chapter 5 will return.

One legitimate consequence of these differences in experience and expectation is that we can and do fail in our attempts to mindread other people. When those other "people" are fictional characters, the failure has trivial implications; we are just surprised by the characters' conduct or fail to see the point of a story. When we *write* a story about fictional characters, in contrast, we cannot fail to mindread them accurately. They have whatever mental states we give them. One risk of inattention to the discursive presentation of mental states is the temptation to write "stories" about the experiences of real people as if their traits and thoughts exist only as we describe them, like the attributes and thoughts of fictional characters.[32]

Scholars of fictional narrative have also examined a related issue: the capacity for perspective shifting that fictional narrative both helps to foster in us and makes so familiar as to be virtually imperceptible. Structuralist narratologists starting in the 1960s devoted considerable thought to analyzing the dynamics of such shifts in narrative point of view. Many narratologists have continued to use the vocabulary of "focalization" first developed for this purpose by Gérard Genette (1967–70; see Ronen 1994; Herman 2013).

The ambiguity present in opaque constructions can illustrate the phenomenon. Consider again the sentence "Eli knew he sold a controlled substance." On one reading (*de re*), the sentence says that Eli knew he sold something, and that thing happened to be a controlled substance. On another (*de dicto*), it says that Eli knew he sold something, and that he knew what he sold was a controlled substance. The *de dicto* reading attributes to Eli the understanding of his conduct described in the noun phrase following the verb "sold." In a way, the *de dicto* reading understands the sentence as if it were uttered by Eli about himself in the third person; it describes Eli's act from Eli's perspective. In Genette's terms, the sentence read this way exemplifies "internal focalization." It describes matters from the perspective of and as known to a character, Eli, even though it does so in the third person. The *de re* reading, in contrast, does not describe matters from Eli's perspective, although it appears to provide access to Eli's mental state—what he "knew." On this reading, the sentence involves "zero focalization," more familiarly known as "omniscient" narration. The final form of focalization distinguished by Genette is "external focalization," which describes events without taking or offering access to anyone's particular perspective.

The vocabulary of focalization suggests some further links among the issues discussed in this chapter. First, as Jill Anderson (2014, 1588–89) has observed, the *de re* understanding of opaque constructions seems to come more naturally to many readers. Although some commentators consider omniscient narration "unrealistic" (Culler 2004), we, in fact, commonly conceptualize others' states of mind in a way that blends what we know and what we believe them to know. Second, our comfort with *de re* readings and zero-focalized narratives further suggests, contrary to the reasonableness-standards critics, that it is not incoherent to talk of external ("objective") perspectives on others' mental states (cf. Davidson 2001; Nagel 1984). Both externally focalized narrative and zero-focalized narrative inform us about characters' mental states, even though such narratives are not presented from the characters' perspectives, and we take such presentations to be natural, not impossible or deceptive. The skeptical notion that mental states are radically inaccessible to "outsiders" is in these ways inconsistent with many of our everyday practices. Of course, there are things about our own subjective experiences that only we know, but there are also things about our mental states that others know better than we do, precisely because others see us from outside (Nichols & Stich 2003; Palmer 2010).

The ability to recognize shifts in focalization can help one see what is going on when one toggles between *de dicto* and *de re* readings of an opaque construction. Having not only names for the two readings but also a way to understand the distinct attitude each involves can make the ambiguity easier to perceive and analyze. The vocabulary also reminds us of the ever-present possibility of describing events from multiple perspectives, and even of conceiving of a meta-perspective on that activity. And it can further remind us that focalization choices affect descriptions not only of mental states but also of "external" matters. Ideally, legal readers, like trained narrative analysts, would be able to spot and challenge mental-state attributions that less informed readers might take to be neutrally descriptive (or simply ineffably "persuasive") accounts of individuals' acts.

A corollary of these points is that it is possible to describe the intentional action of real people without overconfidently ascribing mental states to them. Attributing mental states to real people is *not* like attributing such states to fictional characters, even though the language used in both kinds of attribution can look identical. References to personified reasonableness standards, in contrast, work more like references to fictional characters. Our comfort with the incompleteness of fictional characters shows that the incompleteness of personified reasonableness standards does not make them logically incoherent. This suggestion does not mean that such standards are currently handled especially well in legal discourse. Rather, it suggests that those using the standards should remain aware of their created nature and the need to elaborate them responsibly. While reasonableness standards are constructs, their "authors" are not free to give them any characteristics at all, any more than a fan writing a story about Sherlock Holmes today could give the character any features the fan wanted. The history of the standards, and the practices in the culture in which they are used, limit what can defensibly be said about them. The self-aware assumption and construction of these perspectives, from which lawyers, judges, and juries assess particular legal problems, is what it means to make a perspective objective.

3.5 Thought control

The purpose of writing a judicial opinion is at least partly to establish the legitimacy of the legal consequences announced in the decision. The U.S. legal tradition provides judges with many techniques for this purpose. One technique is to present legal consequences as the result of voluntary activity—intentional choice. Opinions that take the intentional stance toward parties and other actors, and encourage their readers to do the same, allow judges to discharge their opinion-writing obligation in a way that is accessible to their audiences.

At the same time, the justices of the 2014-term opinions seem aware that, as appellate judges, they write at several removes from the parties and that the legitimacy of their judicial pronouncements depends on the justices' successful performance of an impartial role. As Chapter 2 discussed, and as Chapter 4 will consider further, techniques for reassuring readers of an authoring judge's impartiality include accounts of subjective experience as foreign to that activity and as located properly only at certain sites in the legal system. This technique, however, is in some tension with judges' inevitable assumption of the intentional stance, which can seem to require them to consider and confidently pronounce upon others' subjective states in a way that only intentional actors can.

The tension between intentionality and impartiality generates many of the patterns observed throughout this book, some of them long-term subjects of legal concern (for instance, the floppiness with which lawyers address the category of "fact," the neverending controversy over reasonableness standards), others less often noticed (such as the ambiguity generated by opaque constructions and judges' questionable use of psychonarration). The tension is exacerbated by the assumption that because legal practice is a rigorous and highly verbal activity, lawyers and judges already have at their disposal a full arsenal of analytic tools for considering and assessing their own verbal performances.

Lawyers-in-training tacitly learn that legal activity involves new kinds of perspective-taking. They learn, for example, to see discourse both referentially (as given) and metalinguistically (as constructed), and they learn how shifting between these views can help them spot linguistic ambiguity. But they are not explicitly taught to understand these skills as perspective-taking skills, nor are they explicitly taught how perspective-taking can be reflected and prompted by language. The tools of their trade do not include recognition of some of the most economical methods for presenting intentionality and impartiality in language. Lack of familiarity with these methods helps to explain the persistence of certain long-running controversies (e.g., over reasonableness standards), the promotion of undesirable assumptions (e.g., that lawyers can and should "author" parties' intentions), and a failure to perceive desirable alternatives (e.g., structural ambiguity in statutes).

Accepting and understanding the central role of mindreading and imaginative perspective-taking in human decision-making and explanation would be a valuable addition to lawyers' discursive toolkit. Perspective-taking and mindreading are basic to our ability to use language, and it is perfectly possible to consider these skills as intimately related to legal activity rather than inimical to it. If reading narrative fiction allows us to exercise these skills, understanding what happens when we read narrative fiction helps us consider which aspects of those skills are appropriate to use in legal activity. Moreover, perspective-taking is fundamental not only to individuals' interaction and communication, but also to more complex forms of activity such as participation in political, legal, and economic institutions, the subject of the next chapter.

Notes

1 Even as new techniques for making brain states visible become available, the need for human beings to use mindreading skills in interpreting those visualizations is unlikely to disappear soon, if it ever will (e.g., Feigenson 2016).
2 Dennett (1987) defends his account by pointing out that, one, the intentional stance usually works (i.e., successfully predicts action, 21–23) and, two, it accounts for some patterns in behavior that cannot be adequately described otherwise (24–28).
3 Discussing the earlier proceedings in Brumfield's case, for example, Justice Sotomayor describes the state court judges and the entire state of Louisiana as intentional agents. The state court "apparently believed" that Brumfield's reported IQ scores made it impossible for him to show he was disabled (8). After deciding *Atkins*, the Supreme Court "'left to the State[s] the task of developing appropriate ways'" to determine disability in individual cases (2, quoting *Atkins*, 317). Chapter 4 further discusses this kind of ascription of intentions to nonhuman agents.
4 These areas are not the only areas in which issues concerning talk about mental states arise (for discussion of others, see Anderson 2014). But they are two of the most important.
5 Justice Thomas discussed this error by distinguishing between general intent (intent to commit an act) and specific intent (intent to commit an act under a particular description), a distinction partly analogous to the *de re/de dicto* distinction (*Elonis*, Thomas, 8–10), and by distinguishing between a negligence standard and a reference to so-called "objective" meaning (Thomas, 7, 10–12).
6 The label "folk *de dicto*" is suggested because these cases require not that the defendant conceptualize the object in precisely the terms used by the statute (as in a *de dicto* reading), but that the defendant have a conceptualization of the object such that, if the defendant were legally trained, the defendant would regard the object in the statute's terms (so the requirement is not a *de re* reading, which would not consider the actor's conceptualization of the object).
7 The *McFadden* opinions do cite *Staples* and *Liparota*, also discussed in *Elonis* (*McFadden*, 9; Roberts, 2).
8 Nevertheless, Justice Scalia's analysis suggests that a prospective employer might need to suspect that the applicant's practice is religious in order to be liable for violating Title VII (see 5, 6 n.3).
9 The Court had twice before gotten to the brink of deciding this issue, only to be thwarted by parties' settlement (Schneider 2014).
10 For example, in the 2014-term case *Young*, the Court had to decide what an employee must show about her employer's decision-making practices to prevail on a claim of discrimination (in the form of refusal to accommodate, as in *Abercrombie & Fitch*) under the Pregnancy Discrimination Act. The 2014-term case *Clark* turned on the "purpose" of the participants in a conversation, an inquiry required by the Court's recent decisions under the Sixth Amendment's Confrontation Clause.
11 Psychonarration and free indirect discourse are not unique to fictional discourse (see Fludernik 1992, and see section 3.3.3), but they are endemic in fictional discourse and mostly absent from audiovisual narrative forms.
12 The mindreading of represented actors, and the perspective-switching involved in the assisted mindreading of free indirect discourse, operate identically with respect to characters' beliefs and their emotions. The idea that reasons for action often have an emotional component is old news to readers of fiction and to literary scholars. But legal readers and writers often distinguish between emotion, as one kind of reason, and nonemotional reasons for action, on the other. Although a few legal scholars urge attention to the emotional dimensions of mental states (e.g., Greene 2013; Maroney 2011), legal discourse tends to identify emotion with inclinations that lawyers and judges should resist. This contrast partly overlaps with, and tends to reinforce, the law-fact and law-politics distinctions discussed in Chapter 2, as well as distinctions between body and mind, objective and subjective (see section 3.4), and fact and fiction.
13 This "insulation" of juries from review is written into the Bill of Rights. The constitutional protection of juries has made them a logical institution to press into service as a preserve of subjectivity.
14 In Supreme Court adjudication, special masters can play an analogous role. Often appointed in cases brought under the Court's original jurisdiction, masters function like deputy judge-experts, reviewing the filings and recommending a disposition. In the 2014-term case *Kansas v. Nebraska*,

Justice Kagan acknowledged her uncertainty about how the special master had "selected the exact number he did" in recommending an award amount but also admitted that "any hard number reflecting a balance of equities can seem random in a certain light" (19–20) and concluded that the "random[ness]" was no reason not to accept the recommendation (cf. Thomas, 11, criticizing this acceptance). Other reservoirs of subjectivity, from the appellate perspective, include trial judges (e.g., *Davis v. Ayala*, 28–29); officers of the political branches (e.g., *Perez*, Thomas, 10; *Williams-Yulee*, Ginsburg, 2); and individuals in the private sphere (see, e.g., *Obergefell*, 19).

15 Justice Sotomayor indicates that the incommunicable nature of the state at issue—pain—makes it important to consider the motivations of those who risk letting others cause it (Sotomayor, 20–21) and that the inclusion of a paralytic drug in the protocol is meant to make the inmate's suffering invisible (30–31).

16 Justice Thomas offers a similar account in his dissenting opinion in *Rodriguez*, Thomas, 11.

17 Chief Justice Roberts used this trope especially often in his 2014-term opinions. In *Wellness Int'l*, a case addressing the separation of powers, for example, he writes in dissent: "I find it hard to believe that the Framers . . ., who took great care to ensure that the Judiciary was 'truly distinct' from the Legislature, would have been comforted to know that Congress's incursion here could 'only be termed de minimis'" (Roberts, 17–18; see also *Ariz. State Legislature*, Roberts, 1 *Obergefell*, Roberts, 25; and see *Ariz. State Legislature*, Scalia, 6; *King*, Scalia, 3).

18 For other examples, see *Clark*, 8 (Alito); *Williams-Yulee*, 12 (Roberts); *Obergefell*, Scalia, 2.

19 Another approach to qualifying the attribution of mental states is to make it clear that the figure to whom the state is being attributed is imaginary, as in Justice Kagan's *Omnicare* opinion (e.g., 7; see section 3.4.1).

20 See *Bullard*, 7 (Roberts); *Williams-Yulee*, Scalia, 12–13.

21 See *Williams-Yulee*, Ginsburg, 3; *Horne*, Sotomayor, 5–6.

22 Juries are also asked to apply reasonableness standards, but the concerns discussed in the text are less severe in that setting, given the jury's function as a "preserve of subjectivity" (e.g., *Hana Financial*, 4–5).

23 See, e.g., *M&G Polymers*, 4 (Thomas).

24 "Ordinary" is also a familiar alternative to "reasonable" in descriptions of the appropriate reference point for linguistic meaning: the justices conventionally identify the "ordinary meaning" of a provision's language as its presumed legal meaning (see *Texas Dep't of Housing*, Alito, 8; *Perez*, Thomas, 19; Slocum 2016).

25 Further examples appear in references to reasonable "interpretation" of communications by members of the public (*Walker*, 8 (Alito)) or government agencies (*King*, 8 (Roberts); *Michigan v. EPA*, 6 (Scalia)), as well as courts (e.g., *Johnson*, Alito, 9).

26 The skilled artisan is usually not regarded as a standard to which any real person's conduct is compared. One of the difficult issues in *Teva* was that use of the standard in claim construction requires a judge to select one understanding of a disputed term as the understanding a skilled artisan would have of it. Consensus about meaning might be greater within technical communities than among the population at large, but it is rarely absolute. Justice Thomas's labeling of the skilled-artisan standard as a "fiction" might be an effort to point out this procedural artificiality (see Chapter 2.3).

27 The link between reasonableness and intentional activity persists when the "reasonable" label modifies a term naming not a kind of act but a type of actor. Justice Sotomayor cites previous judicial references to a "reasonable minds" standard in her majority opinion in *Brumfield* (8; see also *Davis v. Ayala*, 27 (Alito); *Walker*, 15 (Breyer); *King*, Scalia, 17; *Omnicare*, Scalia, 1, 7). Fourth Amendment reasonableness standards apply to reasonable "officials" (e.g., *Carroll*, 3–4 (per curiam); *Taylor v. Barkes*, 4 (per curiam); *Sheehan*, 10–11 (Alito)). Judges and juries are subject to correction if their decisions are outside the bounds of the "reasonable" (e.g., *Davis v. Ayala*, 8 (Alito); *Heien*, Kagan, 2; *McFadden*, 10 (Thomas)).

28 Justice Thomas's opinion also stresses the "default rule" in U.S. litigation, which has each party bear its own costs of litigation in the absence of an agreement or provision to the contrary (e.g., *Baker Botts*, 4, 11).

29 The part of Justice Thomas's opinion that Justice Sotomayor declined to join addresses incentives for bankruptcy lawyers—the part of the opinion that comes closest to acknowledging those professionals' perspective and includes some fairly confident mindreading of them. See *Baker Botts*, 11–13; Sotomayor, 1.

30 This view is probably more characteristic of academic critics than of the justices, who often refer to reasonableness standards as requiring occupation of a particular "perspective" (e.g., *Kingsley*, 6–7, 9–10 (Breyer); *Omnicare*, 10 (Kagan); *Hana Financial*, 4 (Sotomayor)); "standpoint" (*Heien*, Sotomayor, 2); way of "looking" at affairs (*Rodriguez*, Thomas, 10); "position" (*Heien*, 13 (Roberts); *Omnicare*, Scalia, 2); or "view" (*Clark*, 6 (Alito); *Heien*, Kagan, 2; *Heien*, Sotomayor, 2).

31 The aspects of this "filling in" that have to do with how the actor got into the troublesome situation and might get out of it are often discussed using the language of schemas or scripts, notions relatively familiar to many contemporary lawyers and discussed further in Chapter 5.

32 Our grasp of real people is also always incomplete in a different way. We cannot see all of a perspective from outside, but from inside we are also limited in what we can see (Nagel 1984, 25–27). This is also part of why objective perspectives are not reducible to and do not collapse into subjective perspectives.

4 Big personalities

4.1 Plural minds

We talk about groups of people and institutions, such as corporations and governments, in ways that suggest we habitually take the intentional stance toward those entities (e.g., Schane 1987). Such groups structure the field within which lawyers operate, and lawyers are also often employed by these entities. Although contemporary legal practice presupposes the existence and agency of many such groups, however, they have been a consistent source of legal perplexity. It is not clear exactly how we—even lawyers—should think and talk about them, and lawyers' attitudes toward these agents are often a mystery to nonlawyers.

Confronting these practices—understanding and learning to discuss the dynamics and implications of our activity alongside others in group efforts—is growing increasingly important. In the time between the Court's 2014 term and the publication of this book, Donald Trump's U.S. presidential campaign, election, and administration forced members of the public and academics in the U.S. to reconsider many of their assumptions about the political, legal, and cultural groups and institutions they had believed to be populating their environment. Among other things, this chapter considers how the justices' 2014-term opinions, and particularly their linguistic treatment of group agents, foreshadowed some of the civic and political bewilderment that has followed the term.

The most heated controversies in this area concern corporations and legislatures, both considered in this chapter (sections 4.2.1 and 4.2.2). But the controversies take a similar shape with respect to other groups. Most such controversies concern the legitimacy of treating groups as intentional agents akin to human beings. The model of intentional agency presupposed by U.S. lawyers involves an actor, prototypically a human being, who can perceive the possibility of a choice about how to act, take in information informing the choice, and then make the choice for reasons that can be communicated to others (e.g., List & Pettit 2013). Groups like legislatures and corporations are, of course, made up of, and act through, individual people that we can understand on this model. But if we then treat the group as an intentional agent in its own right, it might seem we are overlooking the agency of the individuals and perhaps also adding to them some super-actor capable of perception, consideration, and decision. Where does this entity come from? What kind of entity is it?

These questions have preoccupied lawyers, theologians, and philosophers for centuries (List & Pettit 2013; Orts 2013). In the past few decades, philosophers and political scientists have begun to ask them again and to reassert their importance (e.g., Dan-Cohen 2016; List & Pettit 2013; Tollefsen 2015; Tuomela 2013).[1] The new generation of thought about group agents, like earlier approaches, insists on the differences between group and individual agents but also, unlike some earlier approaches, tends to describe group agents as real parts of our world, rather than illusions or mystifications. Some of the differences between group and individual agents, such as people, are obvious. Group agents lack physical and emotional states. They do not have a biological instinct for self-preservation; on the other hand, some have attributes that individuals cannot have, such as geographical dispersion and extreme longevity. It is possible for group agents to be nested within one another, something generally impossible with human individuals (see, e.g., Tuomela 2013). Because many group agents—like legislatures and corporations—are the intentional creations of humans, to understand such groups' acts it may be necessary to take not just an intentional stance toward the groups, but also a "design stance," considering the functions the groups were created to serve (Dennett 1987; List & Pettit 2013). Group agents also necessarily act through individuals, although they cannot always be reduced to individuals. And the scope of individuals' agency within groups often depends on the role those individuals play for the group; an individual's ability to affect others may be magnified or diminished by that role (e.g., Tuomela 2013).

Lawyers' treatment of group agents takes little systematic notice of many of these points. Legal discourse is especially deficient in its accounts of individual role performance, and to a lesser extent group design, the main concerns of this chapter. This deficiency might not be unrelated to the wordsmith's fallacy. Many group agents are created and sustained largely by means of language, just as the federal government in the U.S. was created by the federal Constitution and its amendments, and by individuals' behaving subsequently as if that creation occurred. The constructed character of group agents, and their dependence on language (or more broadly on overlapping beliefs and conduct about the significance of language), means that individuals' action within them may involve a kind of make-believe or "as-if" attitude, and perhaps several such interlocking attitudes.

For example, the interaction that sustains group agents depends on some degree of mindreading and perspective-taking by the individuals making up the group (Graziano 2013; Tomasello 2001; Tuomela 2013). In addition, the performance of a role within a group requires a kind of doubled awareness and "quarantining" that is much like pretending. Fully occupying a role within a group involves an agent's intentional suspension of certain considerations; the agent rules out some reasons for action, disregards some sources of information, and suppresses awareness of otherwise relevant states, such as fear and boredom. Just as learning to "play a role" requires (as the idiom suggests) practice through a kind of play, committing to play a role in a group and then playing it requires inhabiting an "as-if" attitude and suspending assumptions and inferences that, outside the role, might be valid. In these ways, playing a role as a member of an institution (such as a business organization or a profession) draws on many of the same skills involved in generating, comprehending, and responding to fiction; playing a role involves a kind of lived fiction.

This chapter explores these themes through the justices' treatment of group agents in the 2014-term opinions. It examines the limits of the justices' self-awareness about their role in the nested institutions they inhabit (section 4.2), the assumptions they make about the existence and characteristics of group agents (sections 4.2, 4.3.1, and 4.4.1), and their struggles to take a "design stance" toward such agents (sections 4.4.2).

4.2 Judicial character

The justices often have trouble describing their own institutional role without resorting to cliché. This difficulty has far-reaching implications for the justices' discourse, sometimes apparently affecting their reasoning about otherwise unrelated matters. This section considers some such effects, examining first the justices' description of the roles and acts of individual judges and multi-judge panels (section 4.2.1), then the common technique of describing the judicial role by contrast with legislative activity (section 4.2.2).

4.2.1 The "Supreme Wand"

In his sarcastic dissent in the 2014-term case *Young v. UPS*, Justice Scalia accuses the majority of waving "the Supreme Wand" to create the standard they apply (Scalia, 7). The phrase charges Justice Breyer (author of the majority opinion) and the four justices joining him with a kind of trivialized misconduct. Justice Scalia suggests that the majority's potency is an illusion, one that might have tricked the opinion's readers as well, and he performatively demystifies it through his biting epithet.[2] Like many of Justice Scalia's critiques, however, this one has a self-defeating quality. While his comment asserts the illegitimacy of the majority's act, the comment likewise lacks any legal significance.

Many of the justices' efforts to characterize the judicial role, directly or indirectly, are similarly paradoxical. As Chapter 3 explored, it is difficult to describe judges as responsible agents without either acknowledging the judges' subjectivity or imparting unnatural powers to them. Part of what makes judges' activity special is, of course, that judges act within a particular institution, or set of institutions. But judicial descriptions of judicial activity address this aspect of their activity only erratically. The justices often attribute motivations to individual judges and groups of judges indistinguishably. At other times, the justices question the appropriateness of such practices of attribution, as well as the legitimacy of ascribing intentions to other groups, such as legislatures and organizations. The resulting vacillation parallels the alternations between confident mindreading and mindblindness described in Chapter 3. The next section offers examples of these practices from the 2014-term opinions.

4.2.1.1 Panels as people

Intermediate appellate courts in the federal judicial system make most decisions in panels of three judges. If two or three judges agree on the resolution of a case, their decision becomes the court's. Lawyers and other judges almost always describe such decisions as made by a single decision-maker. This description simplifies the way that a panel's "decisions" relate to the panel members' decisions. Members of the panel may agree on an ultimate disposition without agreeing on all of the grounds for it, even when those grounds are interrelated.[3] The possibility of a decision attributable to the group that does not match the decision of any one member is one reason to treat the conclusions of groups as independent of the conclusions of the contributing individuals—to treat the group as an agent in its own right, not just a label for a collection of individuals.

While the U.S. judicial practice of writing reasoned decisions can expose the existence of such disagreements, the practice will not expose all of them, and not all panel decisions are documented in equal detail. It therefore makes some sense that, throughout the 2014-term opinions, the justices attribute the same kinds of mental states to appellate courts as they do to individuals. Sometimes, to be sure, the justices profess a kind of mindblindness in the face of a panel's failure to describe its reasons fully.[4] But usually, the justices do not hesitate to identify the "beliefs" behind a panel's decision. Justices often refer without qualification to matters that lower-court panels or earlier Supreme Court coalitions believed,[5] understood,[6] inferred,[7] or chose.[8]

The justices most commonly attribute mental states to groups of other judges when writing concurring or dissenting opinions, or when justices writing for the majority explain rejection of the position taken in a separate opinion. Justice Scalia's concurring opinion in *Omnicare* goes beyond this to put words in the majority's mouth: "Ah! the majority might say, so a speaker is liable for knowing he lacks *the listener's reasonable basis*!" (Scalia, 5). Sometimes justices qualify such attributions.[9] More often, justices assert confidently that the justice or justices joining a separate opinion are, for example, purporting to do one thing while actually doing another.[10] The justices accuse blocs of other justices of cherry-picking examples,[11] being tired of deciding a particular class of cases,[12] or being motivated by a desire to protect certain interests.[13] Sometimes the criticism is of inaction: ignoring crucial details[14] or sparing not a thought.[15]

Overwhelmingly, the justices treat both other appellate-court panels and groups of Supreme Court justices as intentional agents in their own right, possibly distinct from the individual judges and justices composing the panels. Interestingly, as the next section explains, the justices are far less consistent in their approach to describing the action of the individual judges and justices who make up appellate panels, as well as of trial-court judges. The justices acknowledge but struggle to characterize the role-playing aspect of judicial activity.

4.2.1.2 Judicial role play

Whatever else a U.S. judge's role requires, the justices agree that it requires objectivity. Chapter 2 presented some of the techniques U.S. lawyers and judges use to align their pronouncements and activities with the mind-independent world of fact, and Chapter 3 further considered the structure of "objective" standards and their application. As those discussions suggested, these techniques are not always adequate for the tasks they are asked to perform.

One important aspect of the judicial role that objective standards seem designed to promote is impartiality, or detachment from the judge's everyday interests and the interests of the judge's interlocutors. A 2014-term case that invited the justices to address the judicial role more directly than usual, *Williams-Yulee v. Florida Bar*, revealed the justices' lack of practice in directly describing that role and, in particular, the kinds of relationships—if any—judges may appropriately maintain. The justices also seem to be at a loss when the facts or posture of a case push them to present a positive account of judicial conduct, rather than an account of what such conduct does *not* involve. This section traces the justices' positions on these points through the opinions in *Williams-Yulee* and *Obergefell.*

Williams-Yulee concerned the constitutionality of an ethics rule issued by the Florida Supreme Court. The rule prohibited candidates for election to judicial office in Florida from soliciting donations to their election campaigns. Lanell Williams-Yulee, who was running for a judicial seat, sent out fundraising communications under her own name, and the state bar association disciplined her under the ethics rule. She challenged the discipline as infringing her First Amendment free-speech rights. The Supreme Court had previously held that much political campaign activity is protected by the First Amendment. Nevertheless, in *Williams-Yulee* five justices agreed that the donation-soliciting speech of a candidate for a judicial seat is sufficiently unlike the speech of other political candidates that a state bar may punish judicial candidates for such speech. Despite agreement on this proposition, the case yielded six separate opinions, suggesting significant disagreement among the justices about the reasons for the result.

The *Williams-Yulee* opinions struggle to articulate not only what the judicial role involves but also its significance for the case. Chief Justice Roberts's opinion for the majority focuses on the importance of judicial independence, which he describes almost as isolation. He contrasts judges' independence with the entanglement that links legislators to their constituents, but beyond this, he does not elaborate on the relationship between judges and the judicial system or the bar. The closest he comes to characterizing the judicial role is to quote Alexander Hamilton's famous portrait of the judiciary in *Federalist* No. 78: "Unlike the executive or the legislature, the judiciary 'has no influence over either the sword or the purse; . . . neither force nor will but merely judgment'" (9–10).[16]

The problem with this approach to characterizing the judge's role is that it seems to preclude any action by the judge—it portrays the judge as causally inert. This is a classic approach used by dissenting judges criticizing majority "activism," and it is much more common for separate opinions to invoke this picture than for majority opinions to do so. Two of the other *Williams-Yulee* opinions—those of Justices Breyer, concurring, and Alito, dissenting—take this position, accusing Chief Justice Roberts of misapplying the relevant constitutional standard. The remaining three opinions—from Justices Ginsburg, concurring, and Kennedy and Scalia, dissenting—focus on elements missing from Chief Justice Roberts's account.

Justices Ginsburg and Kennedy both address the effects on the judicial role of judicial candidates' need to campaign in states where judges are elected. Justice Ginsburg describes campaigning as likely to erode judges' neutrality and ultimately disturb the functioning of the adversarial system. Justice Kennedy focuses not on how campaigns affect judges, but on how they affect the public: at least in theory, he maintains, political campaigns are opportunities for public deliberation about judges' role. Justice Scalia's opinion, while more caustic than Justice Ginsburg's or Justice Kennedy's, echoes their emphases on neutrality and populism.[17] All three opinions place judges within a larger political-institutional setting, but all three describe the judge's function within that order as defined by what surrounds it (the invisible-hand-like operation of adversarial disputation, or the processes of public deliberation and political contest).

The *Williams-Yulee* opinions show that the justices are (up to a point) able to agree about what the judicial role is *not*: it is not an opportunity to reward one's friends and punish one's enemies. The justices are less able to agree on what the role *is*. At the most basic level, they do not seem to agree about whether an elected judge is an officeholder of the same kind as an appointed judge. Perhaps one could view the justices' reticence not as a refusal to define the judicial role, but as a kind of rhetorical enactment of the role. Maybe the judge's role is to describe obligations through contrasts and demonstrations, rather than to make forceful positive proclamations. This account would be consistent with most of the *Williams-Yulee* opinions, as well as with many other accounts of the judicial role (e.g., Bickel 1961). But it is ultimately unsatisfying. The "judge-as-negative-space" view makes it hard to tell whether judges are doing their jobs properly. And judges cannot always "act" by refusing to act. For example, judges act affirmatively when they dispense equitable relief.[18] They must also sometimes act when they are asked to decide disputes about constitutional guarantees of individual rights. The *Obergefell* opinions were the term's most vivid illustration of this latter point.

The contentiousness of constitutional controversies often stems as much from the unusual institutional role the Court plays in these cases as from the issues they involve. In such cases, when the Court delivers a new interpretation of a right, the Court is making a judgment that cannot be checked by any other actor (aside from the states, via constitutional amendment). In such cases, the Court cannot define itself as passive unless it fails to act; failing to act is not an option when enough justices are persuaded that there are clear problems with the course taken (sometimes under protest) by the lower courts.

Justice Kennedy's *Obergefell* opinion, seemingly aware of these difficulties, carefully negotiates its appeals to the Court as an institution. He distances the decision from the Court's past practice, referring to the acts of previous Court panels as decisions "it" made rather than decisions "we" issued (8, 11–12). Still, Justice Kennedy presents the majority's conclusion as flowing inevitably from abstract "principles" (3) implicit in the Court's constitutional decisions as well as social practice in the U.S. Justice Kennedy also advances a positive account of the judicial role, which he describes as involving the active "identification and protection of fundamental rights" (10). Yet the active agent he describes is the Court as an institution rather than individual justices, and he does not closely examine how dialogues between individual justices and the judicial apparatus, or between "person" and "State," occur. Like Chief Justice Roberts's *Williams-Yulee* opinion, Justice Kennedy's *Obergefell* opinion seems to describe free human individuals interacting directly with the institutions surrounding them. In *Obergefell*, individuals ask the Court and the states for recognition, and the Court hears and honors their request—but it does so as an institution, not a set of individuals.

More or less explicitly, each of the *Obergefell* dissenters highlights the failure of Justice Kennedy's opinion to clarify the connections among individual justices, the Court as an institution, the states, and individuals seeking government recognition of their marriages. Most of the dissents describe the majority opinion as inappropriately personalized and thus non-judicial. Chief Justice Roberts, for example, depicts the majority as swept away by emotion. His characterization trades on one of the differences between individual and group agents—the fact that the latter cannot have emotional states, at least not as individuals do—to suggest that the majority was acting not as a "Court" but as a group of "[f]ive lawyers" (3).

Justice Scalia also casts the majority as an aggregate of judges, rather than an institutional actor: "Today's decree says that my Ruler, and the Ruler of 320 million Americans . . ., is a majority of the nine lawyers on the Supreme Court" (Scalia, 2; see also 5, 6, 7). Moreover, Justice Scalia suggests, the majority coalition displays disrespect for the other authoritative group actors of U.S. politics; he describes the majority opinion as "a naked judicial claim to legislative—indeed, super-legislative—power" (Scalia, 5). Justice Alito's dissent closes with a similar lament for the contemporary absence of good judicial role models:

> I do not doubt that my colleagues in the majority sincerely see in the Constitution a vision of liberty that happens to coincide with their own. But this sincerity is cause for concern. . . . [I]t evidences . . . the deep . . . corruption of our legal culture's conception of constitutional interpretation.
>
> (Alito, 8)

All of the *Obergefell* dissenters accuse the justices in the majority of acting as individuals, not judges.[19] The dissenters also (with some justification) suggest that the majority failed to present a coherent account of its relationships with the Court as a continuing institution and with other institutions with which it interacts, as well as with the parties in the case and the population at large. This failure is, however, not as surprising or sinister as the dissenters suggest; as the *Williams-Yulee* opinions demonstrate, there is no clearly agreed-upon way for judges (perhaps especially Supreme Court justices) to articulate these relationships affirmatively. The predominant approach to describing the judicial role, when it must be described, is to use negation and contrast, to explain the judicial role in terms of what it is not.

One common such contrast, used by Justice Scalia in the passage quoted above, is with the legislature. This comparison affirms the creative power of legislatures in order to describe courts and judges as properly preference-free and reactive. But it also puts pressure on the writing judge's ability to characterize *legislative* activity—which, like judicial activity, centrally involves linguistic acts—in a coherent way.

4.2.2 The "impetuous vortex"

> The legislative department is everywhere extending the sphere of its activity, and drawing all power into its impetuous vortex.
>
> (James Madison, *The Federalist* No. 48 (1788), quoted by Chief Justice Roberts, dissenting in *Wellness Int'l v. Sharif*[20])

Madison's characterization of the legislature as a kind of passionate maelstrom remains quotable more than two centuries on because it captures features of legislative activity that have endured through those years of U.S. political and legal tradition. On this view, legislation involves value judgments that are not always rationally justifiable, made in a bewilderingly complex setting. Describing legislative activity this way can help judicial activity look better by comparison—more even-keeled, perhaps more responsible. Justices of all stripes draw on this contrast between chaotic legislative and reasoned judicial activity to justify conclusions and attack positions they reject.[21]

Relying on this portrait of legislative activity has a cost; describing the legislature's action as unreasoned makes it difficult for courts to explain why a particular product of the legislative process should have authoritative effect in a given case. It also makes more systematic accounts of legislative action difficult to articulate.

Thus, although the justices often contrast legislative and judicial activity, they also consistently cast legislative activity as intentional, using the very same language they use to describe the intentional acts of individuals, including judges and appellate panels. This practice cuts across ideological divisions. In the 2014-term case *Armstrong v. Exceptional Child Center*, for example, all three justices who wrote opinions—Justice Scalia for the majority and Justices Breyer and Sotomayor, dissenting—use similar language to describe Congress's "intent" (7, 10; Breyer, 1, 2; Sotomayor, 1, 7–8 n.3, 9), as well as its "aware[ness]" (9–10; Sotomayor, 4).

Locutions like these have been the subject of controversy for at least a century; often, the criticism has focused on the legitimacy of ascribing intentionality to the legislature as a group. Much of the recent criticism, of course, has come from Justice Scalia, and many lawyers and law professors seem to believe that Justice Scalia's efforts in this area prompted a fundamental change in judicial attitudes toward legislation and the judicial role (e.g., Gorsuch 2016; Manning 2017; but see Greenhouse 2018). The next section reconsiders this controversy through a critical examination of two 2014-term cases in which it was central.

4.2.2.1 What Congress wants

Justice Scalia's well-known rejection of the notion of "legislative intent" (e.g., Scalia & Garner 2012, xxvii, 29–30) has a long pedigree. Felix Cohen's contemporary Max Radin

(1930) advanced a version of the same argument decades earlier. Radin argued that despite their familiarity, legal references to "legislative intent" are a "transparent and absurd fiction" (870). He based his argument partly on skepticism about the accessibility of any mental states—a kind of mindblindness. But he also argued that individual legislators' mental states are irrelevant to the action of a legislative *body*. Such a body, not being a real "person," cannot have mental states of its own (870–71).

Radin was an individualist (or "eliminativist," List & Pettit 2013, 3–4) on the subject of group agency. He conceived of the legislature as a collection of individuals. Among judges and legal scholars, this conception has arguably prevailed over a competing position that some legal scholars and philosophers proposed as an account of business entities in the early twentieth century (see, e.g., Machen 1911; section 4.3.1). According to that competing "real entity" view, at least some group agents are more than the sum of their parts.

Some consider Radin's skeptical individualist position on the coherence of legislative intent to be the currently orthodox position in the U.S. legal academy (e.g., Manning 2015). At the end of the twentieth century, it did unquestionably become an important plank in the textualist platform. Textualism in statutory interpretation, as Justice Scalia described it, is the position that judicial interpretation of statutes "begins and ends with what the [statutory] text says and fairly implies" (Scalia & Garner 2012, 16; see also Shepsle 1992, 250). To the textualist, information about individuals' preferences and motivations is irrelevant; the enacted text alone matters, and it can be understood and applied without any concern for human beings' or the legislative body's thoughts or wishes. This form of textualism turns the kind of mindblindness discussed in Chapter 3 into an interpretive imperative.

Textualists on the Supreme Court during the 2014 term included, most prominently, Justice Scalia, but also often Justices Thomas, Alito, and Kagan, Chief Justice Roberts, and sometimes Justice Sotomayor. (Justice Gorsuch is also considered a textualist; see Chapter 6.4.) But even though textualists supposedly do not conceive of legislatures as "intentional" bodies, even the most textualist-leaning justices (and their clerks) continue to describe Congress as intending things,[22] as well as

- deciding, choosing, or opting (Justices Alito and Kagan);[23]
- having certain matters in mind, or contemplating them (e.g., Justice Scalia in *Whitfield v. United States*: "The Congress that enacted this [criminal penalty-enhancing] provision may well have had most prominently in mind John Dillinger's driving off with hostages, but it enacted a provision which goes well beyond that" (4));[24]
- and wanting (see Chief Justice Roberts in *T-Mobile South*: "when Congress wants decision-makers to supply reasons, it says so" (3)).[25]

In a 1987 law-review article, linguist Sanford Schane showed that attributions like this are a part of the way speakers and writers of ordinary (nonlegal) English talk about institutional bodies, such as corporations (Schane 1987; see also Petroski 2017). Usage of this kind dates back centuries and remains pervasive in everyday English. But it seems inconsistent with the skeptical textualist position described above, which denies the intentionality of the legislature. The inconsistency in turn seems to reveal a surprising inattention to language use by those justices who, as textualists, insist most forcefully on the importance of textual and linguistic detail. Even if these attributions of intentionality to legislatures (and other groups) are metaphoric, the metaphor seems to undercut the textualists' theoretical position.

A growing number of commentators are questioning the textualist-eliminativist view of legislative activity (see, e.g., Ekins 2012; Nourse 2016; cf. Doerfler 2017). These writers have explained how, contrary to Radin's argument, groups such as legislatures might have "mental" states in a sense that is meaningfully similar (although certainly not identical) to the sense in which individuals have them. This view remains a minority position, but it is better supported than many professors, lawyers, and judges now assume. And its articulation and acceptance by legal actors would be consistent with other trends in the understanding of judges' treatment of legislative output. For example, another emerging scholarly approach to the judicial treatment of legislation addresses judges' and legal academics' lack of understanding of how the legislative process actually works—who drafts legislation, what drafters understand as constraining their choices, where drafters get their marching orders (e.g., Bressman & Gluck 2014; Nourse 2016). This work *could* involve denying the legislature's status as a group agent, but it does not need to do so. The central aim of this approach—although its proponents do not use this vocabulary—is to establish the need for statutory interpreters to take a design stance, as well as an intentional stance, in order to understand legislative activity fully (Dennett 1987; List & Pettit 2013, 82–147).

What these critics have been pointing out is that there is no established legal tradition of analysis of the design dimension of legislative activity. Rather, judges and justices of different theoretical allegiances tend to consider various simplified aspects of legislative process or design. Textualists cite the likelihood of process failures and role defection (or strategic behavior) by legislators to justify their focus on text. At least theoretically, they are less willing to accept descriptions of the legislature as an intentional agent, although as noted above, textualists do often describe the legislature this way. So-called "purposivists" (who do not usually claim that label for themselves) are more willing to assume the good faith of legislators and will consider records of the legislative process.

The opinions in the 2014-term case *Yates v. United States* illustrate these practices. This was the case turning on whether undersized fish qualify as "tangible object[s]." In an opinion for four justices, Justice Ginsburg concluded that the fish were not tangible objects for purposes of the Sarbanes-Oxley Act. Her opinion describes that enactment as a deliberate legislative response to a "stimulus" in Congress's environment: the Enron and Arthur Andersen scandals of the early 2000s (e.g., 6).[26] Justice Ginsburg bases her inferences about what Congress "intended" (6) and "wanted" (18) on inferences about the responses that an intentional institutional agent would plausibly make to these stimuli, as well as on the text of the statute, the way it was incorporated into the U.S. Code, and its legislative history.[27] In fact, in *Yates*, Justices Ginsburg and Kagan both cite legislative history to support their respective (opposed) conclusions (see 6, 12–13 & n.5; Kagan, 6, 11). But neither justice explains why she selected the particular aspect of legislative history she cites.

One could see this back-and-forth brandishing of different aspects of legislative history in *Yates* as confirming the textualist criticism that such materials are too easily manipulated (e.g., Scalia 1998, 29–37). But the possibility of misusing legislative history does not necessarily prove the worthlessness of the materials. It could mean, instead, that lawyers and judges should pay *more* attention to the processes leading to a statute's enactment when they are ascribing intention to the enacting legislature (see Gluck & Bressman 2013; Nourse 2016). Legislative history includes legislators' and staffers' records of the aspects of the environment to which they were responding in proposing and drafting legislation, as well as those individuals' communications with other members of the lawmaking group. In fact, such records give outsiders, like lawyers and judges, more to go on in ascribing intention to groups than they often have in ascribing intentions to individuals. Justice Kagan's use of legislative history in her otherwise textualist opinion in *Yates* suggests that she might grasp its significance in this way.

Nevertheless, Justice Kagan ultimately writes as a textualist in *Yates*. The textualist assumption that legislative history is of suspect reliability rests on the more basic assumption that office holders in organizations generally cannot be trusted—that they will often act not responsibly, but irrationally, unpredictably, or insincerely.[28] Justice Kagan seems to endorse this assumption in *Yates*. She acknowledges that it would be irrational to impose a 20-year prison term on a person for throwing fish overboard after catching them. But she concludes that, if Congress (perhaps because of individual legislators' irrational choices) "wanted" an irrational enforcement scheme, then the Court's job is to effectuate that perverse intention (*Yates*, Kagan, 9 n.2, 15). Her *Yates* opinion recognizes the potential complexity of a group's intention but declines to construe it charitably.

This approach contrasts with that taken by Chief Justice Roberts in his majority opinion in *King v. Burwell*. This was the most significant decision of the term after *Obergefell*, and the term's most challenging statutory-interpretation case next to *Yates*. *King* arose from a suit brought by residents of several states that failed to establish "exchanges" for the purchase of health insurance under the Affordable Care Act (ACA, or Obamacare). The provision at issue in the case, together with a related IRS regulation, authorized tax credits for any person who bought insurance on an exchange "established by the State" (e.g., 5). The plaintiffs argued, plausibly enough, that since they lived in states that did not establish exchanges, they could not purchase insurance on an exchange "established by [a] State," and thus were not entitled to the credits. (This was not a perverse argument because the plaintiffs, if they did not receive the credits, would not be required to buy coverage.)

To the surprise of many observers, Chief Justice Roberts concluded that "established by the State" covered exchanges established by the federal government in states lacking their own exchanges. The Chief Justice justifies this conclusion by explaining that the ACA could not function if states and their residents were allowed to opt out of the ACA's system of near-universal coverage; losing so many enrollees would affect insurers' risk pools and ultimately either patients' premiums or insurers' financial survival. In his opinion, Chief Justice Roberts acknowledges that the process leading to the ACA's enactment was unusual and "unfortunate," resulting in a less-than-consistent text (14–15). But he ultimately treats the ACA as an intentional, if imperfect, response to discernible environmental signals, an effort by Congress as a whole to bring about a different state of affairs: "Congress passed the Affordable Care Act to improve health insurance markets, not to destroy them" (20; see also 4, 15, 18 n.4).

In this case, Chief Justice Roberts ascribes what some philosophers have called "we-reasoning" to the members of Congress who enacted the ACA (e.g., Tuomela 2013). "We-reasons" are goals envisioned from the point of view of, or for the benefit of, a group (be it a legislature or the population it serves). The Chief Justice's opinion in this case exemplifies how judges might describe legislative acts as involving both group-intentional and designed dimensions. This is a much more complex view of intentional institutional activity than the view the Chief Justice offers in *Williams-Yulee*.

In his *King* dissent, in contrast, Justice Scalia describes the ACA as so garbled that it barely qualifies as a product of intentional activity. Although "[l]awmakers do not . . . tend to use terms that 'have no operation at all'" (Scalia, 5), they may well produce texts that contain "mismatches" (9–10) and may have inconsistent "expect[ations]" about what their efforts will accomplish (16), resulting in a statutory text that accomplishes little. Justice Scalia does not acknowledge the possibility of "we-reasoning" in this opinion. Here as in many of his other opinions concerning legislative products, intentional activity occurs in the "I-mode" only. This view is in some tension with other textualist premises, such as the supposition that the text of a statute is authoritative because it is the product of a group process (cf. Doerfler 2017; Nourse 2016). That supposition in turn seems to presuppose the possibility of coordinated activity among members of the group; such activity becomes entirely mysterious, if not incomprehensible, on a view of individual activity that does not acknowledge individuals' ability to mindread, shift perspectives, and share goals. The textualist position thus seems to imply inconsistent accounts of individuals' "I-mode" activity, one that regards individual intentions as generally inscrutable and uncooperative, and another that does not.

Textualist conventions of justification and critique largely keep this inconsistency hidden by directing lawyers' and judges' attention to statutory language. It is not always possible, however, for judges to fall back on the conventions for describing legislative intent that dominate the *Yates* and *King* opinions. The next section considers a 2014-term case that forced the justices to confront both the question of the design of legislatures and the disabling effect of the textualist version of the wordsmith's fallacy.

4.2.2.2 What is a legislature?

In one of the last cases decided in the term, the Court addressed a question it usually avoids: when does a group of people count as a "legislature"? In this case, *Ariz. State Legislature v. Ariz. Independent Redistricting Commission*, Justice Ginsburg wrote for a five-justice majority, and Chief Justice Roberts wrote the principal dissent. Both opinions consider some important aspects of group activity, but both also wrestle with the traditions of judicial avoidance of this issue.

Ariz. State Legislature involved a challenge by the state legislature of Arizona to the formation of the Arizona Independent Redistricting Commission (AIRC). The AIRC was authorized by a 2000 amendment to the Arizona state constitution, accomplished via Arizona voters' approval of a ballot measure proposing the amendment. Once created, the AIRC took over a task previously performed by the Arizona legislature: redrawing the boundaries of districts for the election of representatives to the state and federal legislatures. The Arizona legislature sued to challenge the AIRC's power to perform this task, arguing that it violated the Elections Clause of the federal Constitution, which provides that "[t]he Times, Places, and Manner of holding Elections for Senators and Representatives, shall be prescribed in each State by the Legislature thereof" (Art. I, § 4, cl. 1). The Arizona legislature argued that since the AIRC was not "the Legislature" of Arizona, the AIRC's drawing of district boundaries for the election of federal legislators violated the Elections Clause.

One of the issues dividing the justices was the Court's power to decide the dispute. Justice Scalia wrote separately to state his position that the Court lacks the authority to decide disputes between branches of government. This argument draws on a well-established approach to "political questions," often explained as a method for the judiciary to preserve its impartiality and legitimacy (Bickel 1961). The political-questions doctrine licenses judicial refusal to define the scope of agency of other branches of government; it is a kind of self-imposed judicial blindness to governmental group agency. Like the kinds of mindblindness discussed in Chapter 3, however, it is not a position the Court consistently takes.

In *Ariz. State Legislature*, for example, Justice Ginsburg departs from this position to explain why the Court may properly decide the dispute, despite the Court's refusal to resolve earlier actions brought by individual legislators. Unlike those earlier cases, she explains, this one involves "an institutional plaintiff [the legislature itself] asserting an institutional injury" (12). The Arizona state legislature was not the only institutional agent involved in the case, however. The dispute required the justices to consider the federal Constitution's effect on state-level decisions about constitutional amendment, and thus the extent to which the federal Constitution limits the processes by which states and their inhabitants may amend state constitutions. The case also required the Court to address the relative power, within a state, of the voters as a group, the state legislature as a separate group, and further groups—like the AIRC—generated by the first of these groups over the objections of the second. The case thus squarely posed the question of how state-level group actors are constituted. In part because of the political-questions doctrine, the Court rarely addresses questions like this. In *Ariz. State Legislature*, then, the justices had to answer them without much doctrinal guidance.

Justice Ginsburg resolves the case in the voters' favor. She describes them as "the originating source of all the powers of government" (24) and notes the specific powers granted to voters by the Arizona constitution. A similar premise informs her account of the Elections Clause, to which she ascribes the "dominant purpose" of empowering Congress to "override state election rules" that seem designed to frustrate representative government, not the purpose of "restrict[ing] the way States enact legislation" (25).

Justice Ginsburg also explicitly considers what kinds of state-level actors count as "the Legislature" for Elections Clause purposes. She concludes that the Arizona voters who authorized the creation of the AIRC could count as a "legislature," based on her consideration of the functions a legislature can perform. In her account, federal and state legislatures alike exercise a variety of powers, including "electoral," "ratifying," and "consenting" powers (18), as well as lawmaking powers. According to Justice Ginsburg, the power to redistrict is just another such power, and neither the federal nor the Arizona constitution restricts how it may be exercised. Justice Ginsburg seems to define a legislature, here, as any group agent that (a) exercises some legislative function or functions and (b) is accountable to voters. Since the AIRC satisfied these criteria, its creation did not violate the Elections Clause.

Chief Justice Roberts's objection to this functionalist approach is that it is inconsistent with other legal practices, especially the ratification of the Seventeenth Amendment in 1913. That amendment changed the process for selecting federal senators, reassigning the power to make that selection from state legislatures to "the people" of each state (Roberts, 1). This amendment would not have been necessary, he argues, if "legislature" can mean the same thing as "electorate" (1). More generally, he suggests that Justice Ginsburg's approach is inconsistent with other uses of the term "legislature" in the federal Constitution (10). These other instances, he maintains, can only be read as referring to a "representative body" (19). He presents structure, not function, as the defining feature of a legislature.

Chief Justice Roberts also disagrees with Justice Ginsburg's focus on the voters' role in creating the AIRC. Accountability is important, in his view, but such accountability needs to occur through constitutionally recognized channels. One way to see the disagreement in this case is as disagreement over the role of structure (and perhaps also role performance) in group agency. Justice Ginsburg focuses on the input to and output of the various group agents involved; Chief Justice Roberts considers their internal workings at least as important, and he also suggests that there might be a limited number of ways to arrange those workings. Each perspective addresses features of group activity that other commentators have recognized as important. Justice Ginsburg's approach stresses how such activity is always traceable to—or supervenes on (e.g., Pardo 2015, 1808–10)—individual activity, as well as how the translation of individual into group intentions and acts may occur in multiple ways. But her opinion deemphasizes the possibility that different group designs might lead to different translations of individual into group intentions, the primary (if unelaborated) theme of Chief Justice Roberts's analysis.

The justices exhibit a similar hesitancy about discussing the dynamics of group activity in other contexts. They do so, as the following sections show, even when the questions do not cut quite so close to home, as for example when cases involve the agency of nongovernmental groups. The imperative of judicial impartiality might explain some of the oddities in the *Ariz. State Legislature* opinions, but it does not explain the justices' difficulties in these other areas.

4.3 Groups outside the government

The most controversial group agents recognized by U.S. law are those that we usually consider denizens of the private sector, especially corporations.[29] The Court's recognition of such groups' rights to free speech and the free exercise of religion in *Citizens United v. Federal Election Commission* (2010) and *Burwell v. Hobby Lobby Stores, Inc.* (2014) unleashed a storm of criticism, much of it of the Court's supposed category confusion, in these cases, between corporations and individuals (e.g., Orts 2013, x). (Decisions concerning the action of public-sector actors—like *Obergefell*—also stir controversy, but criticism of these decisions rarely accuses the Court of improperly treating government group actors like individuals.)

During the 2014 term, the Court did not issue any high-profile decisions about corporate agency akin to *Citizens United* or *Hobby Lobby*. But the term's decisions offer many examples of the justices' standard assumptions regarding the status and capabilities of corporations, which those cases simply took to an extreme. Section 4.3.1 outlines some of these assumptions, as illustrated especially by the opinions in *Omnicare*, discussed in Chapter 2.4, and *Commil USA v. Cisco Systems*, a patent case. These cases reinforce the conclusions presented above and the concerns of some commentators: the justices take an intentional stance toward corporate entities but often sidestep questions about the inner workings or "design" of these entities.

Private, for-profit corporations are controversial legal actors, in part, because they are both undeniably powerful and incredibly complex, with many hierarchically organized internal sub-groups (such as shareholder classes and boards of directors) allowing for the diffusion of individuals' responsibility (Tuomela 2013, 168–71). When nonlegal theorists analyze group agency, they often start with much simpler forms of cooperation: taking a walk together, for example, or moving a large piece of furniture (e.g., Gilbert 1989; Tollefsen 2015). American law also recognizes, and polices, such simpler group agents in a number of settings—for example, under the law of conspiracy and accomplice liability (see Kutz 2007) and the law of agency (cf. Binder & Weisberg 2000, 532–35). Such "atomic" group agents are in important respects the building blocks of larger ones, like corporations. Because its doctrines for addressing such smaller group agents are comparatively well developed, U.S. law does contain some resources for the design analysis of group agents, although larger agents are, of course, more than just scaled-up partnerships. Developing this point further, section 4.3.2 below considers the Court's treatment of various sorts of group agents during the 2014 term, especially as illustrated by the opinions in *Henderson v. United States*, a criminal case, and *Alabama Legislative Black Caucus*, a voting-rights case.

4.3.1 Corporate thoughts

The contemporary U.S. legal treatment of corporations as "persons" arguably descends from the medieval European law of municipal and educational corporations (Orts 2013, 127–28). Corporations as we now know them in the U.S. became a part of daily life in the nineteenth century, when state general incorporation statutes started to allow people to organize their enterprises in corporate form without significant government scrutiny of the entities' activity (Orts 2013, 13). Since then, U.S. courts have consistently treated business corporations as legal "persons," able to sue and be sued and to own property.

In what sense, exactly, is a corporation a "person"? Lawyers and scholars have come up with three classic answers, which are basically theories of corporate ontology, or of the sense in which corporations exist. The first, the "fiction" or "creature" theory, views corporations as state-sanctioned creations (Ciepley 2013, 154–55; Orts 2013, 9, 12; Schane 1987, 565–66). This view emphasizes the effects of corporate activity on public interests and usually endorses strong legal scrutiny of that activity. A second approach, the "real entity" or "person" theory, became popular at the beginning of the twentieth century, as U.S. business associations also grew in economic and legal power (Orts 2013, 15–16; Schane 1987, 566–67). This view takes corporations to be a special kind of intentional agent that comes into being when people organize into groups, regardless of state recognition. Such groups have a kind of existence above and beyond the individuals who make them up and before the government authorizes them to act. This view may, but need not, imply a more laissez-faire approach to government control of corporations. The third approach, the "nexus of contracts" theory, is usually considered a more recent development (Orts 2013, 43; Schane 1987, 566). This view regards corporations as made up of many contractual relationships between individuals. The relationships preexist government approval but do not add up to any kind of separate existence beyond the relationships themselves. This approach, too, can support a laissez-faire attitude toward corporate activity.

Each of the three classic perspectives regards corporate persons as in some sense fictions (cf. Orts 2013, 16, 27, 29–33). Under the creature theory, a corporation is a legal fiction in the narrow sense: legal authorities deem the corporation a person. The real entity account treats corporations as cultural (or economic) fictions: when individuals get together and act as if they are part of a larger group intentional agent, they bring that agent into being. In the nexus-of-contracts view, the law treats corporations as "persons" via a kind of shorthand: instead of discussing the complex network of relationships making up a corporation, lawyers and judges talk about the corporation as if it were something simpler, a singular intentional actor. This practice is in some ways similar to the use of theoretical fictions in, for example, the discourse of classical mechanics (e.g., Appiah 2017; Vaihinger 1911). The controversy surrounding corporate rights and responsibilities derives partly from the pairing of these bodies' undoubted influence with their elusive metaphysics. Like mythic figures and superheroes, corporations are created by individuals' intentional, communicative acts, but they also provide a basis for activity that would not otherwise occur. They seem uncannily both to exist and not to exist, and the sense in which they exist is always fluctuating.

Most commentators have concluded that the Court has never fully endorsed any one of the classic corporate ontologies, but has, rather, invoked all of them from time to time (Orts 2013, x; Schane 1987, 569). The 2014-term opinions support this assessment. Passages in Justice Alito's opinion for the majority in *Wynne*, for example (3 n.1), reflect the creature view. Parts of Justice Sotomayor's majority opinion in *Wellness Int'l* (4 n.4, 5) and of Chief

Justice Roberts's dissent in the same case (7) exemplify a nexus-of-contracts approach. The justices' refusal to commit to a particular metaphysics of the corporation is consistent with their usual reluctance to take a "design stance" toward these entities.[30] This hesitation in turn constitutes a kind of "mindblindness"; while attributing intentionality to a corporation could be said to involve a kind of mindreading,[31] refusing to consider the mechanisms of the corporation's activity any more precisely attributes opacity to the corporation, just as the kinds of assertions of mindblindness discussed in Chapter 3 attribute opacity to individuals.

Justice Kagan's majority opinion in *Omnicare* illustrates these vacillations between intentional-stance and design-stance description. This case involved the liability of a corporation, Omnicare, under a statute regulating corporate communications to the public. The statements at issue, contained in Omnicare's registration statement filed with the Securities & Exchange Commission, were uniformly treated by the parties and justices as the utterances of Omnicare itself. The statements described Omnicare's interactions with other groups:

> "We believe our contract arrangements with other healthcare providers, our pharmaceutical suppliers and our pharmacy practices are in compliance with applicable federal and state laws." . . . "We believe that our contracts with pharmaceutical manufacturers are legally and economically valid arrangements that bring value to the healthcare system and the patients that we serve."
>
> (2–3)

Throughout her opinion, Justice Kagan discusses Omnicare's beliefs, opinions, and knowledge (as well as the corresponding mental states of Omnicare's adversary, a pension fund), in mindreading-style language nearly identical to that in the registration statements:

> The two sentences to which the Funds object are pure statements of opinion: To simplify their content only a bit, Omnicare said in each that "we believe we are obeying the law." And the Funds do not contest that Omnicare's opinion was honestly held. . . . What the Funds instead claim is that Omnicare's belief turned out to be wrong—that whatever the company thought, it was in fact violating anti-kickback laws.
>
> (9)[32]

Elsewhere in her opinion, however, Justice Kagan describes Omnicare's actions differently, zeroing in on the individuals responsible for particular decisions and acts (e.g., 4). Throughout the opinion, her language shifts in this way between intentional-stance and design-stance perspectives on Omnicare's conduct. If the intentional stance aligns, roughly, with the real-entity theory of the corporation and perhaps with mindblindness toward individuals, and the design stance with the concession and nexus-of-contracts theories and perhaps with mindreading of individuals, then Justice Kagan's discussion in *Omnicare* might seem to display the kind of ambivalence noted a few paragraphs above as well as a variation of the ambivalence described in Chapter 3.

Such ambivalence need not be seen as problematic. In *Omnicare*, Justice Kagan endorses (or even requires) inquiry into the relations of communication and responsibility within the corporation. In her discussion of Omnicare's liability for omissions, for example, she acknowledges that individuals within a corporation may sometimes fail to communicate their knowledge to one another or fulfill their roles properly. One could defend the slippages in

Justice Kagan's *Omnicare* opinion—between attributing beliefs to the corporation and attributing responsibility to its individual agents—as a matter not of theoretical inconsistency but of acknowledgment that a full understanding of group agents' activity requires taking *both* the intentional stance and the design stance toward them. Justice Kagan does not present her changes in perspective in this opinion as quite so deliberate or motivated, however; the shifts seem unconscious.

In this respect, Justice Scalia's *Omnicare* opinion is more consistent than Justice Kagan's. Justice Scalia rejects the design-stance dimension of Justice Kagan's analysis, arguing that if a corporation "says" it has a belief, then readers—including judges—should take that statement to be sincere and well-informed (Scalia, 3–7). But this embrace of what looks like a real-entity perspective seems, in turn, inconsistent with Justice Scalia's rejection of such a perspective on legislative activity (see section 4.2.2.1), even if it is consistent, as suggested above, with an opportunistic mindblindness toward individuals. It might be possible to articulate a justification for alternating among the three classic conceptualizations of corporate or group personality, but the justices do not seem to perceive any need to do so. Nor do they criticize one another for inconsistency on this point, any more than they criticize one another for opportunistic mindblindness. Nevertheless, the justices' varying positions on the government regulation of business—their positions on the extent to which government actors may appropriately look "inside" private-sector group agents—seem to both arise from and be perpetuated by unarticulated assumptions about the best way to describe both corporate *and* governmental agency.

For all its complexity, *Omnicare* is not necessarily the most extreme 2014-term illustration of such assumptions. Cases involving corporate parties often require the justices to account for multiple levels of group activity. The 2014-term case *Commil* is an example. This case involved a dispute between two corporations: Commil, holder of a patent on a method of managing local wireless networks, and Cisco, charged by Commil with having sold products making it possible for other parties (including corporations) to infringe the patent. A claim like Commil's for "inducement" of infringement may be asserted by one individual against another, if the accused person enabled yet another person to infringe the patent held by the first. This kind of claim alleges a kind of rudimentary group agency, in which the defendant supplies the ingredients for a third party's unlawful act.

In a 2011 case addressing such claims, the Court had held that the enabling defendant's liability depends on that party's mental state: the inducer must "kn[o]w of the patent and that 'the induced acts [of the third party] constitute patent infringement'" (*Commil*, 5–6). In *Commil*, the Court considered the required contents of this mental state—specifically, whether a belief that the patent in question was invalid (i.e., could not be enforced if challenged) could prevent liability for inducing infringement. This question, as considered by Justice Kennedy, for the majority, and Justice Scalia, in dissent, turned on the same kind of interpretive distinction that also arises in case involving individual parties (see Chapter 3.2.2). Like the opinions in *Abercrombie & Fitch* discussed in Chapter 3, the *Commil* opinions assume that this question should be analyzed identically for individuals and corporate parties.

Justice Kennedy's majority opinion espouses what seems like a *de re* reading: an inducement defendant is liable if the defendant knows it is supplying means for infringing an existing patent, regardless of the defendant's beliefs about the patent's validity. This conclusion has convenient implications in inducement cases involving corporate parties, making it unnecessary to determine which (if any) person's belief about the patent's validity needs to be assessed. Justice Scalia, in contrast, concludes in *Commil* that belief in the invalidity of the patent in question is a defense to a claim of inducing infringement. Under this approach, a decision-maker must determine not only what the defendant "thought" the third party might do, and whether or not the defendant knew of a patent covering that party's activity, but also how the defendant conceptualized that patent. Justice Scalia does not address how these determinations are to be made in any detail. But in contrast to his hands-off approach in *Omnicare*, where he suggested that such inquiries would be improper if not impossible, in this case Justice Scalia seems to direct inquiry into the inner workings of corporate "belief."

One way to explain Justice Scalia's apparent shift in position between *Omnicare* and *Commil* would be to note some of the differences between the kinds of group agency involved in the two cases. Unlike *Omnicare*, *Commil* involves a kind of temporary concerted action—inducement—among more permanent private-sector group agents. Such impermanent group agency can arise from the concerted acts of individuals, or from the acts of more permanent group agents, such as corporations, as in *Commil*. Perhaps, then, Justice Scalia is comfortable taking a more intrusive design stance in cases involving impermanent group agents than in cases involving only more permanent private-sector group agents. As the next section will show, this distinction might explain part of Justice Scalia's approach in *Commil*, but the justices (and their clerks) usually do not seem to consider these aspects of their activity in any systematic way.

4.3.2 Dimensions of group agency

Inducing patent infringement creates a kind of ephemeral group agent, one possibly lacking any link between the parties but inducement on one side and infringement on the other. The Finnish philosopher of group agency Raimo Tuomela (2013) calls this kind of group activity "I-mode" action: it involves each member of the group acting on his or her (or its) own behalf, not with the objectives of the group in mind. Tuomela contrasts "I-mode" thinking and acting with "we-mode" action, which is undertaken for the group. We-mode action necessarily involves group members' action in a role or roles (or, as Tuomela puts it, a "task-right" position, 168). Tuomela stresses that group agency can arise from action in either mode. But he also emphasizes the different implications of each mode. We-mode groups, for example, can solve collective-action problems that may paralyze I-mode groups, and we-mode action may also be more efficient than I-mode action in several other ways (2013, Ch. 7).

In the spirit of Tuomela's distinction, this section examines some other dimensions differentiating the kinds of group actors the Court recognized during the 2014 term, along with a few implications of these differences. It turns out that the kinds of group agents that receive the greatest theoretical and legal attention are not necessarily the most important, powerful, or common. As an increasing number of thinkers have been urging, reorientation of our thought and talk about these entities may be among the most crucial cultural and intellectual projects of the twenty-first century, both in and outside law (Ciepley 2013; Orts 2013; Tuomela 2013). The justices' current practices are not equipping new lawyers with anything more than very rudimentary signposts for this task.

One obvious way in which group agents can differ from one another is *size*. The smallest possible group agent involves two members, as in the inducer–infringer relationship in *Commil*. (In *Commil*, both members of the pair were corporations, but they could have been individuals without affecting the legal analysis.) Other common examples of two-member group agents include lawyer–client and principal-and-agent (or, in criminal law, principal-and-accomplice) pairs. The Court often addresses lawyer–client pairs, especially in cases involving prisoners' claims that their lawyers' assistance was constitutionally ineffective.[33] But the highest-profile two-member agent the Court addressed in the 2014 term was the married couple. In *Obergefell*, Justice Kennedy described marriage as "a two-person union unlike any other" (15), one that allows the people who marry to "become something greater than once they were" (28). (Notably, during the same term, a plurality of the Court refused to treat married couples as legal units in the immigration case *Kerry v. Din*. In that case, a U.S. citizen challenged the denial of her non-citizen husband's visa application; Justice Scalia wrote for a plurality that the citizen could not contest her husband's application denial—only her husband could.)

As these examples suggest, the justices often pass judgment on the proper design of such pairs: what their members may and may not do for the group and to and for one another. A more elaborate example appears in the 2014-term case *Henderson v. United States*, discussed as an illustration of the doctrine of "constructive possession" in Chapter 2. Convicted of a felony, Tony Henderson was required to give up possession of his firearms. Henderson asked a judge for permission to deliver the guns to a friend, who, Henderson told the judge, promised not to give Henderson access to the weapons. Justice Kagan, writing for a unanimous Court, concluded that the trial court should honor this request. Justice Kagan analyzes the issue using property-law principles such as "incident[s] of ownership" (3–4). But her opinion also instructs trial-court judges faced with similar requests to ask "whether the felon will have the ability to use or direct the use of his firearms after the transfer" (7)—in other words, whether the defendant and the recipient will form a single-purpose group agent in a kind of "puppeteer[ ]"–"puppet[ ]" relationship (4). In general, as *Henderson* suggests, courts do subject the internal structure of two-member groups to greater scrutiny than the internal structure of, for example, legislatures or corporations, even though these larger groups are in many ways far more consequential.

Group agents can also differ in what might be called *durability* and *fixity*. *Durability* concerns a group's persistence over time, that is, whether it survives changes in the identities of the individuals (or subgroups) making it up. Many two-member groups are not very durable—they are either temporary (like lawyer–client relationships), unable to survive a change in membership (like classic marriages), or both. But some small group agents, like appellate courts, are durable. Larger groups such as legislatures and corporations are more likely to be durable but need not be: examples of large yet temporary group agents include litigation classes and, perhaps, groups of voters.

Fixity concerns a group's susceptibility to change in its features and structure over time as a result of changes in membership. At the limit, a very ephemeral (nondurable) group is likely also to be fixed; if its membership changes, it will no longer exist, much less have the same features. But many smaller group agents, such as casual clubs, are durable yet both accessible to outsiders and highly subject to internal changes upon shifts in membership. Appellate courts are relatively fixed; they survive changes in membership but generally have set numbers of members and stable operating practices. Larger groups may, but need not be, relatively unfixed; groups of voters again provide an example.

Group agents also vary in *self-awareness*: the degree to which the individuals making up the group recognize it as a group agent, and as a result knowingly perform roles within the group. Tuomela (2013) discusses this attribute as, in part, a corollary of the distinction between we-mode and I-mode action (e.g., 46–47). A group whose members act *without* conceiving of themselves as a group might be identified as a unified actor only by observers; such groups might be called "notional" groups (cf. Quine 1965, 177–78). Almost all of the group agents discussed throughout this chapter are, however, self-aware. Lawyer–client and principal–agent relationships usually meet this description, as do, usually, appellate courts, legislative bodies, and corporations. Notional groups, in contrast, include such assemblies as demographic groups. It may be controversial to attribute agency to such groups. But significant bodies of law, such as civil-rights law, are concerned with the interests of members of these groups, and justices sometimes treat them as agents linguistically (i.e., as grammatical agents and as capable of belief, desire, and action), if not as bearers of legal responsibility.

Alabama Legislative Black Caucus, a voting-rights case from the 2014 term, illustrates several of these distinctions. The case arose from a lawsuit brought by the organization named in the case title—"a 'statewide political caucus formed'" with the "'purpose' of 'endors[ing]' [political] candidates . . . who will be responsible to the needs of the blacks and other minorities and poor people" (13). In an opinion written by Justice Breyer, a majority of the justices concluded that the caucus could challenge the state legislature's redistricting plan. The accepted standard for such "organizational standing," which allows a group to be a party to litigation, requires a court to consider the group's relation to the individuals it claims to represent, those individuals' right to sue on their own, and any consequences of letting the organization litigate for the individuals (12). The Legislative Black Caucus is self-aware, durable, and relatively accessible to new members; it also defines itself as the representative of a notional group—"the blacks and other minorities and poor people" of Alabama—to which it stands, more or less, in a relation of agent to principal.[34] Although the Court does not analyze the Legislative Black Caucus in these terms, these characteristics of the group underlie Justice Breyer's conclusion that it had standing to sue in the 2014-term case.

Group agents may also differ with respect to their *system of power allocation* and their *relation to government*. Within any group, control over the group's behavior and commitments may be concentrated, dispersed, or a combination of the two. Tuomela (2013) considers a democratic we-group (in which power is shared equally by all members) to be the "paradigmatic" we-group (31). U.S. law does not favor one kind of power-allocation system over the other, but does seem to regard at least some group agents as defined largely by their systems of power allocation. In employer–employee pairs, for example, employer and employee enjoy different sorts of decision-making power. In contrast, in the eyes of contemporary U.S. law, power is evenly divided between married spouses (although they may choose to depart from that distribution). Many larger groups involve hierarchical power distribution at some locations and egalitarian distribution elsewhere. A corporation's board of directors may take majority votes on certain issues (egalitarian) that then control the actions of all who work for the corporation (hierarchical; see Tuomela 2013, 168). A legislature acts mostly by majority rule (egalitarian), but the matters on which it votes are shaped for its consideration by sub-groups and other actors, such as executive-branch actors and lobbyists (hierarchical) (e.g., Shobe 2014; Sitaraman 2015).

Lobbyists' participation in the legislative process illustrates another axis along which group agents differ: *relation to government*. It is tempting to think of the possibilities here as binary—either a group is part of the government or it is not. The arrangement of the present chapter reflects this conventional carving-up of sociopolitical reality. But lobbyist-drafted legislation, among many other increasingly common practices, complicates that picture (Ciepley 2013; O'Connell 2014). In two cases during the 2014 term, this group attribute was difficult enough to pin down that the Court had to examine it explicitly: *N.C. State Bd. of Dental Examiners* considered the issue at the level of state government, and *Dep't of Transportation v. Ass'n of American Railroads* addressed a similar issue at the federal level. Section 4.4.3 below discusses these cases in more detail; they illustrate how a group agent's location in the private or public sphere can be both disputed and legally consequential. Of all of the dimensions of group agency discussed here, this one might be the most fraught, elusive, and crucial.

Group agents may, finally, be combined in different ways to make up further agents. As suggested by the example of the organizations in *Alabama Legislative Black Caucus*, a group may define itself as acting on behalf of another group. And, as noted above, groups can be embedded within other groups. This embedding may be structured in different ways. Groups upstream in the chain may have the power to direct those downstream, while groups at the same level may function in an egalitarian way, like clones.

Alabama Legislative Black Caucus illustrates how complex a mesh of agency can emerge from these variations. The lawsuit was actually brought by a pair of public-interest organizations, not just the Legislative Black Caucus, to challenge the new boundaries of certain voting districts in Alabama. According to Justice Breyer, the ultimate interests at stake were those of the members of a large, notional, relatively permeable group: the Alabama residents represented by the two plaintiff organizations, the Legislative Black Caucus and the Alabama Democratic Conference (12, 13). In Justice Breyer's account, these organizations made up a litigating unit: "the plaintiffs litigated these cases not as if they [the organizations] were wholly separate entities but as if they were a team" (11). Having recognized the organizations' action as that of a single "team," Justice Breyer could attribute to the team arguments made and evidence presented by each member. This move was critical to his conclusion that the groups had standing, and it also let him reach the merits of their claim that the state legislature had redrawn district boundaries improperly to concentrate African-American voters in particular districts, reducing their voting power statewide.

Justices Scalia and Thomas disagreed with Justice Breyer about whether these various groups could be characterized as agents. Justice Scalia's principal dissent refuses to recognize the plaintiff groups as a litigation team. According to him, the Court should have considered each organization's arguments separately; had it done so, it would have found them deficient. Justice Thomas, in a separate dissenting opinion, questions the recognition of the "notional" groups that the plaintiffs claimed to represent:

> The assumptions underlying this practice of . . . maintaining "safe minority districts"—"that members of [a] racial group must think alike and that . . . they must be provided a separate body of representatives"—remain "repugnant to any nation that strives for the ideal of a color-blind Constitution."
>
> (Thomas, 5–6)

But Justice Thomas does not deny that interest groups may be effective agents. The "repugnant" state of affairs he describes is, in his account, the result of legal reform efforts by the American Civil Liberties Union and factions within the Department of Justice's Voting Rights Division during the 1990s (6–10). The different conclusions reached in the opinions in *Alabama Legislative Black Caucus* thus flow directly from the justices' endorsement of different groups as legitimate or illegitimate actors.

The group agents Justice Breyer recognizes in his opinion are nested: the Alabama electorate "contains" the minority electorate, which is represented by the organizations forming the litigation team. The opinions in the case also acknowledge another set of nested groups on the defendant side of the case, not quite as salient as the plaintiff-side groups but equally crucial. The plaintiffs in *Alabama Legislative Black Caucus* challenged the creation of certain electoral districts by the state legislature—or more precisely, by the legislative redistricting committee that redrew the district boundaries. Justice Breyer does not often refer to this agent as such. Instead, he usually attributes the challenged acts to the "legislature" as a whole (e.g., 9, 16–17, 22–23), or even simply to "Alabama" (2–3, 10, 16, 19, 20). Justices Scalia and Thomas describe the defendant's acts similarly (Scalia, 1, 11; Thomas, 2, 3, 5–13). All three seem to consider such descriptions unproblematic, even when their analyses suggest the possibility of more targeted attributions of responsibility to other groups or individuals (e.g., Thomas, 8, 9). Apart from isolated comments, none of the *Alabama Legislative Black Caucus* opinions consider the structure of the defendant's agency in any detail.

As *Alabama Legislative Black Caucus* suggests, and as the cases discussed in section 4.2 also indicated, the justices seem especially reluctant to take a design stance toward public-sector group agents. One result of this reluctance is that, in disputes involving complex public-sector group agents, disagreements about the appropriate groups to recognize and the ultimate sites of legal responsibility become all but inevitable.

4.4 Personalities in the public sector

Section 4.2 considered two important types of group agents that lawyers universally locate in the public sector: appellate panels and legislatures. As the discussions there suggested, the internal structure of such agents, especially legislatures, can be very complex, but the justices seldom acknowledge those complexities. Instead, the justices treat these two kinds of group agents as conventional carriers of legally significant mental states—stock "characters" of federal law—with complementary and relatively fixed (if sometimes disputed) roles.

These examples notwithstanding, the justices cannot always avoid looking "inside" even governmental group agents. Indeed, the justices seem to understand many areas of constitutional law as requiring them to analyze public-sector group agents' interaction with one another and with the public.[35] The tendency to treat such agents as unanalyzable (as in the justices' discussion of the defendants in *Alabama Legislative Black Caucus*) may contribute as much to the contentiousness of these cases as do the political and moral issues the cases raise. This section develops these points, considering the justices' casual treatment of some other public-sector "personalities" in the 2014 term (section 4.4.1) and how disputes over the distinction between private- and public-sector group agents may push the justices toward design-stance perspectives that they might otherwise be inclined to avoid (section 4.4.2).

4.4.1 Populating the public sector

Lawyers treat the federal Constitution and its state counterparts as having established a number of group agents and set some ground rules for their legal treatment. The Constitution both models and mandates the treatment of certain institutions as intentional actors.[36] But the Court has gone beyond the Constitution's example. Although public-sector group agents, such as states and juries, that the Constitution explicitly recognizes tend to receive special attention in legal disputes, the Court also regularly recognizes governmental groups not mentioned in the Constitution, including regulatory agencies and municipalities. In cases involving challenges to these groups' actions, as suggested in section 4.2, lawyers and judges often conduct their analyses without considering either the internal structure of the groups in question or the roles individuals play within them. This section recounts some manifestations of, and a few departures from, this sort of group-agent "mindblindness" in some of the 2014-term cases.

Both Article III of the Constitution and the Bill of Rights mention juries, but the Constitution nowhere establishes or defines these entities (see Pardo 2015). Consistent with these signals, the justices never hesitate to treat juries as group agents but often keep them at arm's length. *Warger v. Shauers*, unanimously decided in December 2014, reiterated the Court's commitment to a rule of evidence barring testimony from a juror about "internal" jury matters (11). This decision exemplifies the Court's standard practice of treating juries, in particular, as opaque decision-makers. Only occasionally do the justices peek "inside" juries, as in *Davis v. Ayala*, discussed briefly in Chapter 3.3.2, which addressed the process of jury formation. Justice Alito's majority opinion in that case examined the trial judge's approval of the prosecutor's juror strikes in Ayala's trial and described in passing some of the desirable characteristics of a juror. These include not just an open mind and an ability to follow instructions, but also the ability to "get along" with other jurors (18–19; see also 23). Although Justice Alito does not make the point explicit, the characteristics he suggests a juror needs are those required to function as part of a we-group (Tuomela 2013).

The larger and more complex the governmental group agent, the more likely judicial description is to represent it as opaque by abstracting and simplifying the group's agency. Thus, in the 2014 term, justices described regulatory agencies, rather than their personnel, as believing and liking,[37] viewing things a certain way,[38] wanting,[39] feeling,[40] wishing,[41] desiring,[42] deciding,[43] meeting a duty and being sincere,[44] promising or otherwise committing,[45] changing their minds,[46] or "insulat[ing]" themselves from the effect of an otherwise applicable statutory command.[47] When the justices address the internal activity of agencies, they usually do so in general terms. The justices often, for instance, express concern about the ease with which agencies can "change their minds" and the possibility that agencies' power will expand beyond appropriate limits. Very seldom do the justices consider how agencies are structured or the roles played by individuals who work within them.

It is a short step from the justices' portrait of agency activity as both superhuman and nonhuman to accounts of a shadowy "deep state" with unclear contours and suspect motivations. To the extent that the justices' accounts of group agency—especially governmental group agency—adopt only a broad intentional stance toward these agents' activity, the justices are arguably neglecting an important obligation of their role. No other set of governmental officers has the capacity or authority to explain to the public how and why governmental group agents may or may not act in particular ways. By abbreviating their explanations of these matters, the justices may contribute to a wider erosion of governmental legitimacy, including their own.

Michigan v. EPA, one of the final decisions of the 2014 term, illustrates these points. This case concerned the process followed by the Environmental Protection Agency (EPA) in developing standards for regulating emissions from power plants. Like many agency actions, the development of the standards had been ordered by Congress in a statute addressed to the agency. A group of entities affected by the standards, including 23 states, brought a lawsuit arguing that the EPA acted illegally by deciding that regulation was "appropriate and necessary" (a determination demanded by the statute in question), without reaching any conclusion, initially, about how much it might cost power plants to comply with the regulations. (All of the parties and justices agreed that EPA reached no such preliminary conclusions about cost, based on the EPA's communications to the public, which, for purposes of the case, were treated as accurately documenting the EPA's "mental state," e.g., 5.)

In an opinion joined by four justices, Justice Scalia concluded that this decision by the EPA was procedurally unreasonable, so the agency needed to re-start the process of deciding whether to regulate. His opinion offers an extraordinarily simplified account of the agency's actions, explicitly likening its decisions to those of an individual: "By EPA's logic, someone could decide whether it is 'appropriate' to buy a Ferrari without thinking about cost, because he plans to think about cost later when deciding whether to upgrade the sound system" (11). Justice Kagan's dissent criticizes precisely this aspect of Justice Scalia's analysis, stressing the length of time ("more than a decade") and "multiple stages" involved in the EPA's standard-setting process (Kagan, 2; see also 7–8). She asks readers to contemplate the complexity that is necessarily involved in action of this kind by, as it were, putting themselves in the agency's shoes:

> Suppose you were in charge of designing a regulatory process. The subject matter—an industry's emissions of hazardous material—was highly complex, involving multivarious [sic] factors demanding years of study. Would you necessarily try to do everything at once? Or might you try to break down this lengthy and complicated process into discrete stages? And might you consider different factors, in different ways, at each of these junctures? I think you would. You know that everything must get done in the end—every relevant factor considered. But you tend to think that "in the end" does not mean "in the beginning." And you structure your rulemaking process accordingly, starting with a threshold determination that does not mirror your end-stage analysis. Would that be . . . a "reasonable policy choice"?
>
> (Kagan, 16)

Even though Justice Kagan in a sense looks "inside" the EPA's decision-making process in this passage, she too defends the agency's action by likening it to the way an individual actor might approach a problem.[48] In the abstract, she recognizes that the EPA functions as a complex group agent; indeed, the passage above, and others in her dissent, suggest that the tasks the EPA performs could be performed only by a coordinated group of people. But since the 1970s, the agency's annual workforce has been more than 10,000 people strong.[49] Justice Kagan does not consider, for example, how many of these employees might need to contribute to the processes she describes. Her chief objection is to Justice Scalia's oversimplification of the *task* involved, not to his oversimplification of the agency as an agent.[50]

In this respect, the justices' (and lawyers') treatment of agencies resembles their treatment of states. Of course, received understandings of the federal Constitution's allocation of power between state and federal actors encourage federal judges to avoid second-guessing state decision-making. Consistent with this principle, simplified accounts of state agency of the sort found in *Alabama Black Legislative Caucus* (section 4.3.2) are far more common than the more critical analysis found in *Ariz. State Legislature* (section 4.2.2.2). The 2014-term opinions contain countless descriptions of states and their subdivisions as making efforts or attempting to do various things,[51] having "good intentions,"[52] having wishes and wants,[53] having desires and preferences,[54] choosing and deciding,[55] being "reluctant,"[56] manipulating,[57] and ignoring obligations.[58] It is rare for the justices to recount or evaluate the mechanisms by which any of these states of intentionality might come to exist in a particular case.[59] At least as often, the justices explicitly refuse to make such inquiries.[60]

The opinions in *Walker v. Texas Div., Sons of Confederate Veterans* illustrate some consequences of casual ascriptions of agency to entire states. *Walker* involved a challenge to the action of a decision-making panel (the Board) in the Texas Department of Motor Vehicles.

The Board was responsible for approving applications for "specialty" license plates bearing logos or designs submitted by members of the public. The Sons of Confederate Veterans applied for a plate design including an image of the confederate battle flag, a symbol many associate with support for slavery. The Board denied the Sons' application, explaining that "public comments ha[ve] shown that many members of the general public find the design offensive, and . . . such comments are reasonable" (4). The Sons sued the Board, describing this denial as a violation of their First Amendment free-speech right.

As argued and decided, the case turned on determining who, or what, "speaks" via specialty license plates. Had the Sons' application been approved, would their specialty plates have been the speech of the state of Texas, the speech of the Sons as a group, or the speech of drivers who put the plates on their cars? Justice Breyer, for the majority, attributes the "speech" on the plates to the state: "Texas 'has "effectively controlled" the messages [conveyed on specialty plates] by exercising "final approval authority" over their selection. . . .' This final approval authority allows Texas to choose how to present itself" (11, quoting *Pleasant Grove City v. Summum* (2009)). Justice Breyer here equates the Board's decisions with the state's speech. Yet *Summum*, the case Justice Breyer quotes in this passage, involved a municipality, rather than a state or state agency, as a "government speaker." For purposes of First Amendment government-speech analysis, all such group agents seem to be legally equivalent.

From similar premises, Justice Alito draws a different conclusion in his dissent. Although Justice Alito offers a slightly more detailed account of the Board's decision-making than Justice Breyer does, Justice Alito's conclusion about attribution of the specialty-plate "speech" is unrelated to that analysis. His conclusion rests instead on intuitive reasoning about drivers' preferences and attitude toward state power. Like Justice Breyer, Justice Alito treats the attribution of the communications in *Walker* as a straightforward matter, akin to (and sometimes indistinguishable from) "mindreading" an individual.[61] Nowhere does either justice acknowledge the possibility of a difference between individuals' and groups' intentional action or speech. The avoidance of these issues makes the *Walker* opinions—like many of the Court's First Amendment cases—rather imprecise guides to future decision in cases presenting different forms of putative government speech.[62]

In every 2014-term case involving public-sector actors or litigants, the justices refer willy-nilly to individuals, officers, and groups as agents that can interact freely and directly with one another. They discuss the internal structure of group agents casually, if at all, and rarely address the roles individuals play within such agents. This is the standard judicial and legal attitude toward group agency, but it is not inevitable. Occasionally, as the next section will show, the justices encounter disputes that force them to depart from these habits.

4.4.2 Boundary entities

In most cases, the public or private status of a group is a given, even if the matter is not clearly spelled out. But in two cases in the 2014 term, the Court had to locate group agents on one side or the other of the public–private boundary. These disputes reached the Court because the agents in question could defensibly be described as either public- or private-sector entities. In a recent article, law professor Anne Joseph O'Connell (2014) has called agencies of this sort "boundary entities" and documented their proliferation.[63] While such agencies' existence may be troubling for several reasons, their involvement in legal disputes can require lawyers and judges to consider more carefully than usual the agencies' internal structure and relations to other actors, as well as the roles played by individuals within the agencies. Cases like this show that it is feasible for lawyers and judges to attend more deliberately to matters of institutional design and individual role performance in cases involving group agency.

The first of the two cases in question, *N.C. State Bd. of Dental Examiners v. Federal Trade Commission*, was decided toward the end of February 2015. It arose from acts by the N.C. State Board, the professional licensing authority for dentists in North Carolina. In the early 2000s, as Justice Kennedy explains in his majority opinion, North Carolina nondentists began to offer "teeth whitening" services to consumers (2–3). In 2006, the Board "opened an investigation" into the trend and issued "at least 47 cease-and-desist letters" to these nondentists (3). In response, the Federal Trade Commission (FTC) charged the Board with anticompetitive conduct. The question for the series of judges who ruled on the FTC's complaint was whether the Board was a public-sector entity; if it was, it was entitled to "state-actor immunity" under a doctrine permitting state actors to behave anticompetitively (5).

Six justices concluded that the Board could not claim this immunity because it was *not* a state actor. To support this conclusion, Justice Kennedy's majority opinion describes in detail the makeup of the Board and its relation to other state agencies. All nine justices agreed that the applicable legal framework mandated this "design" analysis. This framework makes immunity available to a private-sector actor only when the state has "articulated a clear policy to allow the anticompetitive conduct" by the actor and "provide[d] active supervision of" that conduct (9).

In *N.C. State Bd.*, the active-supervision requirement also led Justice Kennedy to consider the Board's relationships to the state legislature and other state agencies. In describing these relationships, Justice Kennedy touched on the circumstances under which those individuals serving as members of the Board would be able to perform their roles honestly and cooperatively:

> State agencies controlled by active market participants [such as practicing dentists], who possess singularly strong private incentives, pose the very risk of self-dealing [that the "active supervision"] requirement was created to address. . . . This conclusion does not question the good faith of state officers but rather is an assessment of the structural risk of market participants confusing their own interests with the State's policy goals. (13)[64]

Dissenting, Justice Alito argues that the Court should have deferred to the North Carolina legislature's characterization of the Board. As a creature of the state government, empowered by the legislature to regulate practicing dentists, he concludes, the Board was "unmistakably a state agency entitled to . . . immunity" (Alito, 6–7). Focusing primarily on the actions of group agents—the state legislature, the Board, the FTC, Congress, and previous Court panels—Justice Alito dismisses Justice Kennedy's observations regarding the roles of individual Board members as involving speculative inquiries into individuals' motivations.

Legal commentators might describe Justice Alito's approach in this case as "formalist": he considers the form that the state legislature gave the Board, not how it functions (e.g., Strauss 1987). Justice Alito contrasts the certainty this approach promises with the messiness of Justice Kennedy's functionalism: "By straying from th[e] simple path [that the Court established in previous state-immunity cases], the Court has not only distorted [those precedents]; it has headed into a morass" (Alito, 2). This is the classic, basically rule-utilitarian, way that lawyers and judges defend the choice of a formalist over a functionalist standard. Thinking about the formalism–functionalism contrast as a choice between perspectives to take on group agents suggests another way to view the distinction: institutional formalism is conceptually and rhetorically akin to the stereotyping of individuals. Both institutional formalism and individual stereotyping draw conclusions about an agent's behavior and capacities based on limited information concerning the agent's origins and external features, rather than the agent's conduct and interactions. While formalist approaches to institutional analysis do not suffer from the stigma associated with stereotyping of individuals, perhaps they should. Formalism sanctions simplification, and in assessments of intentional agency, simplification is not always appropriate. In the context of assessing the intentional action of group agents, such simplification is arguably an abdication of legal and judicial obligations.

Department of Transportation v. Ass'n of American Railroads, decided less than two weeks after *N.C. State Board* and involving quite different legal issues, nevertheless bears many similarities to the earlier case—perhaps partly because Justice Kennedy wrote the majority opinions in both. *Ass'n of American Railroads* concerned the status of Amtrak as a public or private entity. In a 1970 enactment, Congress created Amtrak but defined it as "not a department, agency, or instrumentality of the United States Government" (2, 6). A later enactment, the Passenger Rail Improvement & Investment Act (PRIIA), commanded Amtrak, along with several other private and public actors, to develop performance standards for the non-Amtrak tracks used by Amtrak trains. The PRIIA also provided that the resulting standards would become part of Amtrak's contracts with other rail carriers. The Association of American Railroads, a trade association representing non-Amtrak railroads, challenged the constitutionality of these provisions. The Association argued that because Amtrak is a private corporation, giving it the power to develop standards binding other actors violated the nondelegation doctrine, which forbids private-sector actors from creating broad legal requirements akin to legislation.

The decision in *Ass'n of American Railroads* was effectively unanimous. All of the justices agreed that for purposes of the PRIIA provisions at issue, Amtrak is a government actor. In this case as in *N.C. State Bd.*, Justice Kennedy, writing for the majority, examines the structure of the entity's governance in some detail, although he devotes relatively little attention to the incentives of and roles occupied by individuals within Amtrak. The case also involved a second, implicit separation-of-powers question: which branch—Congress or the Supreme Court—has ultimate say over Amtrak's status as public or private? Justice Kennedy decided this issue in the Court's favor. Seven justices (including Justice Scalia, who dissented in *N.C. State Bd.*) joined both Justice Kennedy's largely functionalist analysis of Amtrak's status and his more formalist discussion of Congress's power to determine that status.

Justices Alito and Thomas wrote separate concurrences, each expressing suspicion of the good faith of public-sector actors, such as Congress and Amtrak. Justice Alito observes, "When citizens cannot readily identify the source of legislation or regulation that affects their lives, Government officials can wield power without owning up to the consequences" (Alito, 1–2). While he goes on to outline questions for the lower courts to consider on remand, Justice Alito does not explain how "citizens" are to "identify the source of legislation or regulation that affects their lives"; he seems to assume that this identification will almost never be possible. Justice Thomas, in one of several separation-of-powers opinions he issued during the term, likewise focuses abstractly on "power," not on those who wield it. To the extent that individual occupants of government offices figure in the world Justice Thomas outlines, he suggests that they are not to be trusted.

N.C. State Board and *Ass'n of American Railroads* include some of the term's most sustained discussions of the design of governmental group agents, but they are the exceptions tending to prove the rule: most of the justices seem to find it difficult to deal with more than one or two dimensions of group agency, including the roles individuals play within group agents, at a time. Some of the justices seem positively averse to identifying the boundaries of the group agents that populate the legal world, even though the establishment and maintenance of these boundaries is among the chief functions of contemporary legal activity.

4.5 Taking role play seriously

All of the cases the Court decides involve at least one group agent (the Court itself). Most cases involve many more. The justices' prevailing habits of alternately assuming and denying the existence of these agents, and avoiding consideration of their characteristics, generate a host of problems. These habits magnify and extend the negative implications of the justices' inconsistent models of individuals' intentional action discussed in Chapter 3. They also leave judges and lawyers without any obvious way to describe or explain the group agents within which they play their roles and to which they profess fidelity.

As this chapter has suggested, and as a growing number of commentators are pointing out (e.g., O'Connell 2014; Pardo 2015), it is entirely possible to develop a legal framework for the discussion and assessment of group agents and role performance. Most of the necessary elements of such discussions—acknowledgment of the possibility of "we-intentions," the difference between such intentions and the collective intentions of group members, and the changes in perspective required for individuals to perform roles within a group—are already present, at least intermittently, in the way judges and lawyers think and write. These tools are at hand, for example, in the doctrines that handle small-scale group agents (such as the law of agency) as well as larger ones (like the state-actor immunity doctrines at work in *N.C. State Bd.*). The vocabulary of collective intentionality should be, but is not yet, as much part of the common vocabulary of lawyers as the familiar grades of intentionality—recklessness, purpose, knowledge—learned by every U.S. lawyer.

Neglecting the similarities between individual and group agency encourages exaggeration of the differences, a mistake made by Radin and his textualist descendants. The textualist point of view on the linguistic products of group activity, with other intellectual trends of the past few decades, has contributed to an atrophied public discourse that can acknowledge agency only at the individual level. When confronted with bona fide group agency, this discourse is able to conceive of and describe it only as criminal conspiracy or a variation on groupthink. The result is decisions like *Citizens United* (Petroski 2013, 83–85) and, perhaps, also massive public-sector crises such as those marking the Trump administration.

There are at least two important components of a workable conception of group agency. One, emphasized in recent scholarship, concerns the legitimacy of recognizing group agents *as agents* and attributing, for example, responsibility to them (e.g., Gilbert 1989; Tuomela 2013). The second, which is equally important, concerns the interaction between individual agents (human beings) and group agents, and specifically the dynamics of individuals' performance of roles within group agents. This issue was visible to, and considered important by, mid-twentieth-century thinkers (e.g., Hart & Sacks 1958, 1374; Kantorowicz 1957), but it has largely faded from legal awareness.[65] It need not remain dormant, however, and its reinvigoration is not just intellectually desirable but politically and practically urgent. The nonexistence of any public vocabulary for discussing the performance of roles by public officials has, among other things, made very difficult any coherent legal or political response to the Trump administration.

Within legal discourse, the wordsmith's fallacy helps to suppress individual lawyers' and judges' awareness of how legal language models and creates a readiness for particular kinds of role performance in readers and writers. This suppression allows the justices to slip without comment or acknowledgment from an institutional voice to a personal voice, and that slippage teaches readers that there is no difference between the two. It allows the justices to discuss group agents as if they were individual agents and, nearly in the same breath, to deny the equation, making the difference seem arbitrary and merely a matter of description. When these inconsistencies become visible to nonlawyers, as they increasingly are, they breed distrust in lawyers' and judges' good faith, and they contribute to disbelief in the reality and necessity of group activity for human well-being.

Notes

1 Legal academics have taken more notice of this work than of many of the other philosophical currents discussed in this book (e.g., Ekins 2012; Kutz 2007; Orts 2013). But contemporary law students learn about such ideas sporadically, if at all.
2 Conservative justices' 2014-term dissenting opinions drew repeatedly on magic metaphors to disparage majority decisions. See *Ariz. State Legislature*, Roberts, 1; *Brumfield*, Thomas, 14. Justice Kagan's joking reference the Court's "superpowers" in *Kimble* (18) is a rare positive instance of the trope.
3 Christian List and Philip Pettit (2013) call this scenario the "doctrinal paradox" (43); it may arise whenever a group's conclusion is based logically on multiple premises. See also Kornhauser and Sager (1993).
4 See *Reyes Mata*, 6–7 n.3 (Kagan); see also *Dart Cherokee*, 9–12, 13 n.7 (Ginsburg); Scalia, 2, 3.
5 *Lopez v. Smith*, 6–7, 8 (per curiam); *ONEOK*, 15 (Breyer); *Young*, 19 (Breyer); *Rodriguez*, 7 (Ginsburg); *Brumfield*, 8 (Sotomayor); *Johnson*, Thomas, 10.
6 *Davis v. Ayala*, 18 (Alito); *Texas Dep't of Housing*, Alito, 27 n.10; *Omnicare*, 5 n.1 (Kagan).
7 *M&G Polymers*, 8 (Thomas).
8 *Omnicare*, 5 n.1 (Kagan).
9 *Glossip*, Sotomayor, 27; *Ariz. State Legislature*, Roberts, 21.
10 *Kimble*, Alito, 7; *Davis v. Ayala*, Sotomayor, 13; *Clark*, Scalia, 4; *Jennings*, Thomas, 7, 8.
11 *Alabama Dep't of Revenue*, Thomas, 7.
12 *Johnson*, Alito, 1.
13 *Glossip*, Sotomayor, 28–29.
14 *Ariz. State Legislature*, Roberts, 2; *Alabama Legis. Black Caucus*, Scalia, 2.
15 *Brumfield*, Thomas, 27.
16 This passage is also a favorite of Justice Thomas's; see *Perez*, Thomas, 12.
17 These themes reappear in Justice Scalia's *Obergefell* dissent, discussed below, and his dissent in *Alabama Legis. Black Caucus* (Scalia, 3); see also *Davis v. Ayala*, Sotomayor, 5.
18 Equitable relief often involves a judicial command to a party to perform or refrain from performing an act. The 2014-term water-rights dispute *Kansas v. Nebraska* required the Court to order equitable remedies, a task more often performed by trial courts.
19 See *Obergefell*, Alito, 2, 7; Roberts, 22; Thomas, 17–18.
20 Chief Justice Roberts has used this quotation on other occasions, notably in the 2012 Affordable Care Act case *Nat'l Federation of Independent Businesses v. Sebelius*, 567 U.S. 519, 554 (2012).
21 See *MacLean*, 15 (Roberts); *Wynne*, Scalia, 6; *Young*, Scalia, 11; *Baker Botts*, 12 (Thomas). Justice Sotomayor uses the same device in her majority opinion in *T-Mobile South* (13); see also *Yates*, Kagan, 19.
22 In addition to the examples listed in the text and the following notes, see *Woods v. Donald*, 4 (per curiam); *B&B Hardware*, 12, 21–22 (Alito); *Johnson*, Alito, 10; *Kwai Fun Wong*, Alito, 9, 11 & n.3; *T-Mobile South*, Alito, 1; *Texas Dep't of Housing*, Alito, 2, 6, 7, 34; *Coleman*, 6, 7 (Breyer); *ONEOK*, 2 (Breyer); *Young*, 12–13 (Breyer); *Dart Cherokee*, 4–5, 11 n.5 (Ginsburg);

Direct Marketing Ass'n, Ginsburg, 1; *Mellouli*, 5–6 n.3, 11 (Ginsburg); *Mach Mining*, 4 (Kagan); *Kwai Fun Wong*, 4, 5, 7 (Kagan); *Texas Dep't of Housing*, 8 (Kennedy); *MacLean*, 8, 11, 13 (Roberts); *Johnson*, 13 (Scalia); *MacLean*, Sotomayor, 4; *T-Mobile South*, 8 (Sotomayor); *Warger*, 12 (Sotomayor); *Alabama Dep't of Revenue*, Thomas, 7–8; *B&B Hardware*, Thomas, 8, 10; *Caulkett*, 3 (Thomas); *Elonis*, Thomas, 3.

23 See *Texas Dep't of Housing*, Alito, 10; *Kwai Fun Wong*, Alito, 6; *Kimble*, 15 (Kagan); *Kwai Fun Wong*, 5 (Kagan); *Perez*, 9 (Sotomayor).

24 See also *Coleman*, 2 (Breyer); *Harris*, 3 (Ginsburg); *Texas Dep't of Housing*, 15–16 (Kennedy); *Bullard*, 6–7 (Roberts).

25 See also *N.C. State Bd.*, Alito, 3; *Mach Mining Co.*, 4–5 (Kagan).

26 This mode of justifying conclusions about statutory meaning is known as the "mischief" rule because it involves considering the "mischief" prompting legislators to act (e.g., Eskridge 1987, 1508 & n.117). The same intentional-stance conception underlies the justices' frequent practice of asserting that Congress was aware of legal practices in its environment when it acted. See *Kwai Fun Wong*, Alito, 6, 7–8; *Jennings*, 11 (Scalia); *T-Mobile South*, 7–8 (Sotomayor); *Baker Botts*, 8 (Thomas); *Elonis*, Thomas, 7.

27 Justice Ginsburg also justifies her conclusion by suggesting that the provision would have looked different had Congress "wanted" the statute to work differently (16–17; see also 10–11, 12–13). Justices Alito and Kagan use the same technique in their *Yates* opinions (Alito, 3; Kagan, 17–18). For other examples, see *B&B Hardware*, 14 (Alito); *Young*, 13 (Breyer); *Mellouli*, 9–10 n.9, 13 n.11 (Ginsburg); *Michigan v. EPA*, Kagan, 9; *Texas Dep't of Housing*, 12, 15 (Kennedy); *MacLean*, 9–10 (Roberts); *Elonis*, 11 (Roberts); *Baker Botts*, 7 (Thomas); *Elonis*, Thomas, 10; *Integrity Staffing*, 8 (Thomas); *Mellouli*, Thomas, 3.

28 Many recent approaches to statutory interpretation seem to presuppose that office holders will act counter to the interest of other members of the institution and the public (e.g., Scalia 1998; Gorsuch 2016; Nourse 2016).

29 David Ciepley (2013) has argued that business corporations are neither public- *nor* private-sector entities, but a third kind of entity. While a full treatment of this issue is beyond the scope of this book, section 4.4 below will return briefly to this question.

30 Only occasionally do justices discuss chains of communication and noncommunication among employees (e.g., *Abercrombie & Fitch*, 2 (Scalia); Alito, 2), or acknowledge that corporate parties "speak" only via human representatives (*Dart Cherokee*, 3 (Ginsburg)).

31 For examples of confident corporate mindreading, see *B&B Hardware*, 5–6 (Alito); *ONEOK*, 8 (Breyer); *Michigan v. EPA*, Kagan, 10; *Texas Dep't of Housing*, 10 (Kennedy); *Abercrombie & Fitch*, 5, 6 n.3 (Scalia); *Alabama Dep't of Revenue*, Thomas, 10; *Direct Marketing Ass'n*, 3–4 (Thomas).

32 Similar constructions appear throughout Justice Kagan's opinion; see 4, 16 n.11, 18.

33 See, for instance, *Baker Botts*, 6; *Christeson*, 1–3, 5–7; *Jennings*, 2–3; *Reyes Mata*, 2–3.

34 Other examples of notional groups in 2014-term opinions appear in *Wynne*, 11 (Alito) (state voters and taxpayers); *Direct Marketing Ass'n*, Kennedy, 4 (interest groups and advocates); *Obergefell*, 24 (Kennedy) (citizens); *Williams-Yulee*, Kennedy, 4 (citizens); *Obergefell*, Roberts, 26 (voters); *Obergefell*, Scalia, 3 ("the People").

35 Space does not permit extended discussion of a major area of law fitting this description. The federal Constitution requires judges to recognize as agents those entities empowered by Articles I, II, and III, but the Constitution does not define those entities or, significantly, prescribe how to tell whether they are functioning in accordance with constitutional design. In separation-of-powers cases, the justices' job is often to flesh out the "character" of such agents; carrying out this task may involve describing the design of the bodies for the guidance of lower courts and future litigants. Two 2014-term decisions presented dramatic, and characteristically contentious, examples of this activity: *Zivotofsky*, concerning the capacities of the State Department (as an extension of the President) and Congress, and *Wellness Int'l*, concerning the boundaries between the legislative and judicial branches.

36 The federal Constitution describes groups as intentional agents in the same way the Court does. See Epps 2013; Petroski 2017.

37 *Michigan v. EPA*, 9 (Scalia) (EPA).

38 *Perez*, 5 (Sotomayor) (Department of Labor).

39 *Michigan v. EPA*, Kagan, 21 (EPA); *MacLean*, 3 (Roberts) (TSA).

40 *Michigan v. EPA*, Thomas, 4 (EPA).
41 *Horne*, 8 (Roberts) (Raisin Committee).
42 *Perez*, 12 (Sotomayor) (agency).
43 *Mach Mining*, 14 (Kagan) (EEOC); *Michigan v. EPA*, Kagan, 14 (EPA), *MacLean*, 1 (Roberts) (TSA); *Horne*, 2 (Roberts) (Raisin Committee); *B&B Hardware*, Thomas, 11 (TTAB).
44 *Mach Mining*, 3 (Kagan) (EEOC).
45 *Michigan v. EPA*, Kagan, 17, 24 (EPA).
46 *King*, Scalia, 15 (DHHS).
47 *MacLean*, 8 (Roberts) (agencies in general).
48 See also her answer to Justice Scalia's Ferrari analogy, *Michigan v. EPA*, Kagan, 22.
49 See EPA's Budget and Spending, https://www.epa.gov/planandbudget/budget/.
50 The opinions in *Perez*, decided in March 2015, also seem to view agencies as opaque decision-makers whose internal functioning—and their good or bad faith—is indiscernible. When the justices consider how individual civil servants act, the justices more often than not describe them as self-interested or inscrutable; see *Kerry v. Din*, Kennedy, 3; *Perez*, Thomas, 21; *Texas Dep't of Housing*, Thomas, 5–6, 7 n.4. For a counterexample, see *Kerry v. Din*, Kennedy, 4.
51 *Williams-Yulee*, 15 (Roberts); *Glossip*, Sotomayor, 16–17; *Alabama Legis. Black Caucus*, Thomas, 12; *Direct Marketing Ass'n*, 1 (Thomas).
52 *Texas Dep't of Housing*, Thomas, 9–10.
53 *Obergefell*, Alito, 5; *Walker*, Alito, 1, 14; *Walker*, 7–8 (Breyer); *Glossip*, Sotomayor, 27–28.
54 *Horne*, Breyer, 4; *Glossip*, Sotomayor, 27–28.
55 *Walker*, 6 (Breyer); *Ariz. State Legislature*, 27–28 (Ginsburg); *Wynne*, Ginsburg, 2, 6; *Williams-Yulee*, Ginsburg, 5; *Kansas v. Nebraska*, 12–13 (Kagan); *Texas Dep't of Housing*, 5 (Kennedy); *King*, 6 (Roberts); *Obergefell*, Roberts, 2; *Williams-Yulee*, 1, 19, 22 (Roberts); *Alabama Legis. Black Caucus*, Thomas, 11; *Mellouli*, Thomas, 8.
56 *Glossip*, Sotomayor, 31.
57 *Alabama Legis. Black Caucus*, Scalia, 11.
58 *Kansas v. Nebraska*, 16 (Kagan).
59 Exceptions from the 2014 term include Justice Kagan's discussion of Nebraska's organizational failures in *Kansas v. Nebraska*, 2–3, 11–13; Justice Alito's account of the license-plate approval process in his *Walker* dissent, 6–7, 11–12; Justice Sotomayor's account of the selection of midazolam as an execution drug in Oklahoma, *Glossip*, 3; and Justice Breyer's discussion of the redistricting process in *Alabama Legis. Black Caucus*, 17.
60 See *Armstrong*, Breyer, 2; *Wynne*, Ginsburg, 3; *Obergefell*, Scalia, 2; *Obergefell*, Thomas, 14.
61 This is the same opinion in which Justice Alito invited readers into a side-of-the-highway mind-reading exercise, discussed in Chapter 3.3.3.
62 In another First Amendment case from the 2014 term, *Reed*, a different set of justices treat municipalities and their subdivisions very much as they treat states (10, 11, 16 (Thomas); Breyer, 2, 4–5).
63 In two other 2014-term cases, the justices also addressed the contingency of the public–private dividing line: *Taylor v. Barkes*, which involved claims against a state corrections commissioner based on the state's hiring of and failure to supervise a private contractor to provide mental-health screening to prisoners; and *Clark*, tangentially involving a statute requiring some non-government employees to report suspected child abuse to the police. In some cases, the law renders the distinction between private-sector and government actors irrelevant; see *Kimble*, 17 (Kagan); *Kwai Fun Wong*, 16, 17 (Kagan).
64 See also *N.C. State Bd.*, 13–14 (discussing the incentives of municipal officials as opposed to those of members of professional licensing boards).
65 Nourse (2016) dismisses Hart & Sacks's account of the appropriate judicial attitude toward legislative activity; they recommended that judges assume statutory text to be the product of activity by "reasonable persons pursuing reasonable purposes reasonably" (Hart & Sacks 1958, 1374; Nourse 2016, 15). Nourse suggests that this formulation evades inquiry into what actually happens in Congress. The analysis presented here suggests an alternative reading of Hart and Sacks as describing a specific *imaginative activity* on judges' part as an aspect of the judicial role.

5 Virtual realities

5.1 The law world

The previous two chapters showed how, when lawyers and judges write about the intentional acts of people and group agents, they often describe not just the agents' deeds but also their motivations, beliefs, fears, and so on. Another common, and related, legal approach to evaluating action—the subject of this chapter—considers possible alternatives to the action that occurred, describing, for example, what could have but didn't happen. This chapter traces the use of such discussions of possibility through the 2014-term opinions.

The justices' accounts of what is necessary, possible but unrealized, and impossible, both in general and in particular cases, are both descriptive and prescriptive. These accounts purport to describe a shared reality, but they also create the shared professional reality of lawyers by making some possibilities conceivable and articulable and keeping others out of bounds. In this way, the justices' opinions help to establish and maintain a "law world," or a set of such worlds. These worlds exist alongside the "real world" and intersect with the real world at certain points but also possess their own geography and history.

"Traveling" to the law world is in many respects akin both psychologically and ontologically to what happens when we read novels, watch dramatic movies or TV, or discuss the events and people of these alternate "worlds" with others. Paradoxically, accepting this analogy might be easier for nonlawyers than it is for lawyers. The kinds of lawyerly bias discussed in previous chapters encourage lawyers to perceive their words and acts as dealing directly with reality, not constructing a kind of alternative to it, and to resist viewing their work as involving any kind of speculation or imaginative activity.

The law world is both distinct from and integrated into the non-law world. Like the worlds of narrative fiction, the "law world" is part of our shared reality. Like narrative worlds, the law world can only be entered deliberately; unlike those who choose to enter fictional worlds, however, those who choose to enter the law world do not always keep its boundaries in mind. Learning to see the doubled reality involved in lawyers' verbal world does not necessarily lead away from the real world; indeed, it might lead lawyers closer to the real world. We presumably want our law world to reflect and create a real world we want to live in, not to mention a real world worth leaving to future generations. Achieving that goal would seem to require those who construct the law world and inhabit both law-world and real world—lawyers and judges—to be able to navigate both and see clearly how they affect one another. This chapter examines some resources for strengthening this awareness.

The next section of the chapter (5.2) briefly introduces some properties of discourse dealing with the possible (what might be) rather than the actual (what is, "reality") and a quick account of how a partly imagined "world" can be both real and causally significant.

Section 5.3 then looks closely at the Court's 2014-term use of possibility-talk, or modal language. It shows that, despite the justices' consistently critical view of "speculation," they also engage in it relentlessly. Section 5.4 turns to the relation between the justices' rhetoric and more abstract questions of legal constraint and change, suggesting some grounds for qualified optimism about the engagement and self-awareness of legal professionals.

5.2 The importance of the nonactual

The account of the "law world" in this chapter rests on a small group of premises about human thought and communication oriented toward alternatives to perceived reality. These premises are related to matters discussed in previous chapters, but some of the premises have not yet been explicitly introduced. The next two sections perform this introduction. Section 5.2.1 outlines some features of language dealing with possibility (what the justices often call "speculation"), as opposed to actuality. Section 5.2.2 considers the psychological and cultural implications of this kind of language and the thought it reflects and prompts.

5.2.1 How to talk about the nonactual

The ability to imagine things is an important human capability. Imagining alternatives to what we perceive lets us consider and discuss what is possible (or necessary), rather than merely what we encounter as given.[1] Being able to imagine in this way contributes to our ability to draw inferences and to innovate, as well as to tell stories about imaginary events (and to engage in legal reasoning). Even those most skeptical about the value of imaginative activity rarely argue that we could do without these related abilities.

Given the variety of activities underwritten by the imagination, it is not surprising that many scholarly fields focus on imaginative activity and communications about that activity. Humanists study the products of inventive imagination, such as novels. Cultural-studies scholars and some social scientists study the "virtual" worlds of fan culture and engagement with imaginary figures (Jenkins 1992; Saler 2012). Linguists and philosophers study the behavior and implications of statements about possibility and necessity (e.g., Chisholm 1946; Goodman 1947; Harper et al. 1981). At this most focused level, the analysis of modal language and logic addresses how we reason and communicate about degrees of confidence in our beliefs, about our obligations (what we must do), about our sense of what will happen if some contingency occurs, and about our capacity to cooperate.[2]

In all of these contexts, modal language has some characteristic features. Many modal statements involve ambiguity similar to that discussed in Chapter 3. For example, the statement "Ramona might have been at the party" can be read in two ways: it might communicate the speaker's lack of certainty about Ramona's presence at an actual party, or it might communicate that it would have been possible for Ramona to be at a real or hypothetical party, something one might mention while explaining what could have happened had Ramona gone to the party. The first reading is like a *de dicto* or "internal" reading; it takes the modal to express a lack of commitment to the truth of the proposition. The second reading seems more *de re* or "external," proposing an alternative to what actually happened.

Noting this and other features of modal statements, mid-twentieth-century philosophers began considering them more closely. Several adopted an account of such statements as concerning, referring to, or best modeled by "possible worlds" (e.g., Kripke 1963; Loux 1979; Lewis 1986).[3] This approach enabled new ways of describing the relationships among possibility (what might happen), necessity (what must happen), and actuality (what happens to be the case). On a possible-worlds understanding, a statement of necessity addresses what is true "at" all possible worlds (e.g., the statement "1 = 1"), while a statement of possibility addresses what is true at some possible worlds, although not at the world in which the statement is made (e.g., "Ramona might have been at the party," on the second reading).

Literary theorists further developed these ideas. Marie-Laure Ryan (1991) used a possible-worlds model to explain the experience of reading fictional narrative, and in particular, of tracking characters' mental states and perspectives through such a narrative. On her theory, the reader of such a narrative continuously constructs and navigates multiple possible worlds, including the fictional "world" in which the narrative events occur *and* the many partly overlapping "worlds" corresponding to various characters' beliefs, hopes, and plans, each of which will have differently configured contents. Lubomír Doležel (2000) used a possible-worlds framework to explain the linguistic signals that readers of narrative fiction learn to understand as establishing "facts" within the fictional (possible) world of a novel. These approaches to narrative allow us to think of classic narrative elements, such as conflicts between characters, in terms of relationships between the possible worlds making up characters' beliefs, hopes, and fears.

With very few exceptions (e.g., Bruner 1986; Mitchell 2004; Solum 2008; Strassfeld 1992), legal academics did not pick up on this trend. The 1970s and '80s did see influential legal-scholarly investigations of normative "universes"; work by Robert Cover (1983) and James Boyd White (see Chapter 1.4.3) fits into this category, and section 5.4 examines Cover's account further.[4] But Cover and White both discussed the normative "worlds" projected by lawyers as immediately accessible to readers and writers upon processing certain (unspecified) verbal descriptions, and neither of them linked his account with other legal language practices involving the manipulation of modality, such as the pedagogical and persuasive use of hypothetical examples.

This chapter tries to make some of these connections. Markers of modality are everywhere in judicial (and other legal) discourse. As a result, readers of that discourse are constantly engaging in an activity much like that involved in reading a novel—and not just in the sense that they conceive of discourse in a doubled way. Readers of legal discourse are constantly constructing and tracking the relationships among modal universes, or possible worlds. A sense of which possible worlds are and are not accessible and of how to talk about them is a part of American lawyers' mental furniture, although this sense is rarely, if ever, explicitly taught or discussed. Within legal discourse or outside it, modal language works in part to give its readers instructions for a kind of cognitive self-control, a skill they will have learned from the broader cultures they belong to but that is honed in special ways in legal education and practice. Ironically, these self-control mechanisms seem to operate largely beneath lawyers' notice.

5.2.2 Why talk about the nonactual?

As noted above, our imaginative capacities enable other skills we do not normally consider imaginative, such as discussing solutions to real-world problems and figuring out what to do when faced with confusing messages or limited resources. These capacities are not just personal resources; they shape the worlds we share with others. Being able to consider and discuss alternative possibilities—sometimes at length—has been a crucial social skill, as well as a crucial legal skill, as long as the United States has existed.

Human children are like the young members of many animal species in that they seem to be biologically predisposed to engage in play (Bogdan 2013, 77). This behavior helps prepare children to, among other things, assume roles (in groups or organizations, for example), and enjoy make-believe as adults. Examining the development of these skills, the philosopher and cognitive scientist Radu Bogdan explains that playing animals and children "do not confuse normal with playful behavior," but rather "*decouple* their play from their normal goals and the contexts in which they are normally reached, *quarantine* the play in its own sensorimotor envelope, and execute benign variations on (what [will] become) standard behavioral themes" (84). In play, we normally know ourselves not to be acting in earnest and can experiment with actions we might not be willing to take outside the play "envelope." When we do this, we inhabit a kind of possible world.

The most basic function of this activity seems to be to help youngsters learn how their bodies work. But most children also engage in play involving symbolic activity (Bogdan 2013, 85), particularly in scenarios involving standard cultural "scripts" (such as "restaurant," "doctor," and "war") that require addressing others as intentional agents and coordinating activity (Bogdan 2013, 98–118; Tomasello 2001; Schank & Abelson 1977; Sherwin 1994). In such contexts, the "envelope" feature of play enables a kind of perspectival as well as physical quarantining. Such play helps us learn how to think of other minds, how to read them, and what to expect of them. Adult understandings of what is mandatory and possible in social interaction are built on this foundation.

We do not all play in the same way as children, however. Variations in childhood environments and playmates can affect how we come to think of possibility and actuality, as well as more immediate matters like whom to trust and fear. A person's developmental surroundings affect not only the person's actual opportunities, but also what the person *perceives* as opportunities—the worlds possible for that person. That environment also affects (without completely determining) the person's cultivation of more sophisticated skills such as abstraction, strategic thinking, and communication about such matters. And those skills in turn are the building blocks of specifically legal cognitive skills, including the internalization of legal rules and reasoning techniques. Like other forms of expertise, legal expertise requires for its acquisition a kind of "offline" practice analogous to the quarantined play of young animals and children (e.g., Feltovich et al. 2006).

From this perspective, the use of hypothetical problems in legal education (addressed further in section 5.3.3) is a sound pedagogical strategy. Considering a hypothetical scenario prompts a learner to imagine, "offline," entire systems of relation and response between imagined intentional agents. To do this successfully, learners internalize heuristics allowing them to predict the behavior of such intentional agents and the behavior of other members of the lawyerly guild. These heuristic scripts might or might not complement those the student knew of before coming to law school; either way, they are scripts that *lawyers* learn in common, and they leave traces in lawyers' communications, including the judicial opinions that are the subject of this book.

Cultural products, including fictional and nonfictional narrative, can substitute for experiences missing from a person's environments of origin. The mini-narratives that appear in judicial opinions can also serve this function. Narrative cultural products can also themselves become a platform for interaction, supporting the building of communities of commitment that would not exist without the cultural products. Benedict Anderson's (1983) well-known account of the modern nation as an "imagined community" generated through eighteenth-century periodical and fictional discourse described an especially important example of this phenomenon. More recently, competing accounts of political and social events disseminated through social media have prompted discussions of "alternative facts" and alternate political realities in the twenty-first-century United States (e.g., Martinez-Conde & Macknick 2017; Rutenberg 2017).

The building of an imagined community generates insiders and outsiders. The narratives and scripts that drive world building also populate the resulting worlds with personages who count as intentional agents and others who do not (see Cover 1983; Vermeule 2010). Such distinctions can have far-reaching real-world consequences. But both the distinctions and the consequences remain invisible as long as those "running" the scripts are unaware of their constructed nature. Pointing out that a legal or political adversary is not "living in the real world" will not convince the adversary if he or she has already decided that your world is the imaginary one. Recognizing the foundations and scope of perceptions of this kind seems like a precondition for their deliberate change.

Lawyers are not explicitly taught to achieve this recognition, but thoughtful lawyers do achieve it in a sense. Lawyers-in-training learn not only rules, but also how to talk and write about those rules. The ways of talking they learn include idioms for referring to intentional action and causal relations, as well as statements about possibility and necessity; they learn which such statements are legally acceptable largely from Supreme Court opinions and other samples of legal discourse. Although these sources hardly supply templates for all of the situations a lawyer will face, judicial opinions nevertheless provide teachers and students with a shared focus for discussions of the content of law and its relation to other "worlds" and value systems. In these ways, the opinions construct and sustain a "law world" as complex as any other imagined community.

The rest of this chapter examines how some of the 2014-term opinions contribute to this world. It focuses on how the justices discuss the possibilities available within this world, as well as some of the possibilities their discussions omit.

5.3 Virtual realities in the law

Some legal doctrines and argument techniques discourage discussion of nonactual states of affairs. Disparaging an analysis as "speculation" can justify dismissing it. This maneuver is closely related to the use of "fiction" as an epithet discussed in Chapter 2. Some justices use it often. Justice Scalia, in particular, was a fan of such rhetoric. In his opinion for the majority in the 2014-term case *Johnson v. United States*, for example, Justice Scalia used this technique to defend his invalidation of part of a criminal sentencing statute. The provision had to be invalidated, he argued, because its application depended on "judicially imagined" scenarios and on undesirably "speculative" "detach[ment]" from the legal rules at issue (5–6).

Nevertheless, legal discourse is full of "speculation." The following three sections address three dimensions of the justices' explicit use of possibility-talk. Section 5.3.1 examines three 2014-term cases, including *Johnson*, that turned on doctrines demanding judicial hypothesizing. Section 5.3.2 considers other pervasive legal-doctrinal scripts requiring lawyers to analyze alternative possibilities. And section 5.3.3 surveys the function played throughout the term's opinions by an even more widespread practice—the use of hypothetical scenarios in justification.

5.3.1 The dangers of speculation and the "categorical approach"

Johnson was one of three cases decided during the 2014 term involving decisional techniques based on precedent that directs legal decisionmakers to generate and discuss hypothetical scenarios. Although Justice Scalia, writing for six in *Johnson*, cited the speculative character of the technique involved in that case as a reason for striking down a federal sentencing provision, in the other two cases in this group—*Comptroller of the Treasury of*

Maryland v. Wynne and *Mellouli v. Lynch*—the justices in the majority did not question the validity of similar approaches. This section addresses the three cases in the order of their issuance, staring with *Wynne* (May 18, 2015), then moving to *Mellouli* (June 1, 2015)[5] and *Johnson* (June 26, 2015).

In *Wynne*, for the first time in a decade, the Court held that a state tax law violated the federal dormant Commerce Clause, which authorizes judicial invalidation of state legislation on the ground that it "discriminates against" interstate commerce. The case involved a challenge by Maryland residents Brian and Karen Wynne to Maryland's income-tax system. The Wynnes earned income in 39 states via an "S corporation" whose earnings passed directly through to them. Maryland gave the Wynnes credit against their Maryland state income tax for taxes they paid elsewhere, but they did not receive credit for their out-of-state payments against their Maryland *county* tax. Justice Alito's majority opinion agreed with the Wynnes that this part of the Maryland system violated the dormant Commerce Clause.

To explain this conclusion, Justice Alito analyzed the "internal consistency" of the challenged tax (*Wynne*, 7, 18–26). The Court had previously used this approach as part of a more complex assessment of "fair apportionment" of state-tax burdens, not a stand-alone test of constitutionality (Denning 2016, 105–06). In *Wynne*, Justice Alito does not explain his departure from that practice, but simply identifies the "internal consistency" test as uniquely useful. As Justice Alito describes it, the test requires consideration of an imaginary state of affairs: "By hypothetically assuming that every State has the same tax structure, the internal consistency test allows courts to isolate the effect of a defendant State's tax scheme" (19). Explaining how the test applies to the Wynnes' case, Justice Alito inserts simplified hypothetical facts into a schematic version of the Maryland tax system:

> Maryland's income tax scheme fails the internal consistency test. A simple example illustrates the point. Assume that every State imposed the following taxes, which are similar to Maryland's . . . taxes: (1) a 1.25% tax on income that residents earn in State, (2) a 1.25% tax on income that residents earn in other jurisdictions, and (3) a 1.25% tax on income that nonresidents earn in State. Assume further that two taxpayers, April and Bob, both live in State A, but that April earns her income in State A whereas Bob earns his income in State B. . . . April will have to pay a 1.25% tax only once, to State A. But Bob will have to pay a 1.25% tax twice: once to State A, where he resides, and once to State B, where he earns his income.
>
> (21–22)

This explanation of the constitutional problem with Maryland's tax scheme, although it is loosely grounded in the Wynnes' case, is self-evidently unreal. Justice Scalia, dissenting, criticizes the explanation on this basis: "How did this exercise in counterfactuals find its way into our basic charter?" (Scalia, 4). Even so, Justice Scalia also uses his imagination—and recruits his readers'—to rebut Justice Alito's analysis, presenting a competing hypothetical without apology. Justice Ginsburg, dissenting, likewise both criticizes Justice Alito for inventing a new approach to the analysis and uses hypothetical examples to show that the internal-consistency test does not serve the purpose Justice Alito claims. She inserts Justice Alito's "April" and "Bob" characters into a different hypothetical scenario to demonstrate the fairness of Maryland's scheme. Apart from Justice Scalia's "exercise in counterfactuals" remark, none of the justices dismisses such hypothetical reasoning outright; the five justices in the majority indeed seem to mandate its use in similar future cases challenging state tax schemes.

Mellouli, decided a few weeks later, shows what can happen when precedent requires a hypothetical-based analysis. The Court developed the doctrine involved in this case for use in applying statutes that tell judges to take an individual's past criminal convictions into account. (A similar doctrine applied in *Johnson*, discussed next.) The federal statute at issue in *Mellouli* authorizes the deportation of noncitizens convicted of violating "any law . . . relating to a controlled substance (as defined [under federal law])" (2). Moones Mellouli, a noncitizen, was stopped by police for a traffic violation. The police discovered four tablets of Adderall, for which Mellouli had no prescription, in his sock; Mellouli was convicted of violating a Kansas statute banning possession of "paraphernalia to . . . store [or] conceal . . . a controlled substance" (2). Adderall is a controlled substance under both federal and Kansas law, but Kansas law also identifies other substances (not on the federal schedule) as controlled substances, and there is no federal law like the Kansas statute used to convict Mellouli, which criminalizes *possessing* (as opposed to selling) drug paraphernalia and defines paraphernalia to include everyday items that happen to be used in connection with drugs.

The question for the Court was whether the Kansas statute "relat[ed] to a controlled substance," making Mellouli deportable under the federal statute. As Justice Ginsburg explains in her majority opinion, the Court has "historically taken" a "categorical approach" to the application of statutes that attach consequences to a person's previous convictions:

> Because Congress predicated deportation "on convictions, not conduct," the approach looks to the statutory definition of the offense of conviction, not to the particulars of an alien's behavior. . . . An alien's actual conduct is irrelevant to the inquiry, as the adjudicator must "presume that the conviction rested upon nothing more than the least of the acts criminalized" under the state statute.
>
> (5–6)

This approach requires a judge to identify the category of conduct covered by the statute of conviction (thus the "categorical" approach), then to decide whether that conduct "relates to" substances controlled under federal law. As the end of the above passage suggests, this undertaking seems to require the judge to identify all of the varieties of conduct that *might* lead to conviction under the prior statute, and thus to require imaginative activity. Although this task is not unlike the task involved in applying some of the objective standards discussed in Chapter 3.4, as that discussion suggested, it is not a task for which any ready legal models exist.

The lack of such models appears to hamper Justice Ginsburg's analysis. Her conclusion—that the Kansas statute did not "relate to" federally controlled substances—seems defensible, given the breadth of the Kansas statute. As she points out, the Kansas controlled-substance schedules "included at least nine substances . . . not defined" in the federal schedule (9), so the Kansas scheme makes possible some convictions with no link to a federally controlled substance. In this sense, Justice Ginsburg considers whether the set of acts covered by the Kansas statute might include acts not covered by federal law. But she does not explain her conclusion in precisely this way, and she struggles to justify her conclusion clearly: "In short, the state law under which [Mellouli] was convicted categorically 'relat[ed] to a controlled substance,' but was not limited to substances 'defined in [the federal statutory schedule of controlled substances]'" (9).[6]

Justice Scalia joined Justice Ginsburg's *Mellouli* majority opinion. This alignment is notable because just a few weeks later, in *Johnson*, Justice Scalia wrote a majority opinion finding the use of a similar approach to a different statute deeply problematic. The statute at issue in *Johnson*, the Armed Career Criminal Act, authorized increased sentences for defendants with previous convictions for several kinds of offenses, including "any crime . . . that . . . is burglary, arson, or extortion, involves use of explosives, or otherwise involves conduct that presents a serious potential risk of physical injury to another" (2). As Justice Scalia explains, in a 1990 decision, the Court directed that the last part of this provision—the "serious potential risk" part, or the "residual clause"—be applied using a categorical approach like that used in *Mellouli*, one that "assesses whether a [previous] crime qualifies as a violent felony 'in terms of how the law defines the [previous] offense and not in terms of how an individual offender might have committed it on a particular occasion'" (4). Justice Scalia describes this approach as, among other things, "requir[ing] a court to picture the kind of conduct that the [previous] crime involves in 'the ordinary case'" (4). Beyond generating this "judge-imagined abstraction" (6), however, a judge seeking to apply the residual clause must also estimate the risk involved in that "ordinary case" conduct (8) and, on top of that, compare the likelihood and degree of that risk to the "serious potential risk" standard in the statute.

The resulting analysis, according to Justice Scalia, will inevitably generate conclusions varying wildly from case to case:

> [P]icturing the criminal's behavior is not enough; . . . assessing "potential risk" seemingly requires the judge to imagine how the idealized ordinary case of the crime subsequently plays out. *James* [(2007), an earlier residual-clause case,] illustrates how speculative . . . this enterprise can become. Explaining why attempted burglary poses a serious potential risk of physical injury, the Court said: "An armed would-be burglar may be spotted by a police officer, a private security guard, or a participant in a neighborhood watch program. Or a homeowner . . . may give chase, and a violent encounter may ensue." . . . The dissent [in *James*, written by Justice Scalia], by contrast, asserted that any confrontation that occurs during an attempted burglary "is likely to consist of nothing more than the occupant's yelling 'Who's there?' from his window, and the burglar's running away." . . . The residual clause offers no reliable way to choose between these competing accounts of what "ordinary" attempted burglary involves.
> (5–6)

On Justice Scalia's account, people will not agree on what an "ordinary case" involves, much less how much potential risk it poses. Justice Scalia's *Johnson* opinion is entirely preoccupied with the possibility of this runaway speculation; it does not consider some fairly obvious alternatives to invalidation of the clause, such as the possibility that appellate courts could stipulate the degree of potential risk posed by "ordinary cases" of various crimes, crime-by-crime.[7] Justice Scalia's justification for this emphasis seems to rest mostly on the normative, but not precisely legal, principle that legal rules should not encourage, much less require, judges' use of their imaginations.

Judges and justices do not tend to articulate this principle explicitly, but it underlies a number of other legal doctrines, such as the rule against advisory opinions,[8] some of the rules for standing to sue,[9] and the practice of declining to decide questions that the parties did not brief or argue.[10] The contrast between legal reasoning depending on imaginative activity and legal reasoning depending on more solid premises, such as "facts," also serves a more immediate justificatory purpose in many other contexts in the 2014-term opinions (as Chapter 2.3 described from a different perspective). Justices use the contrast between imagined and actual premises to dismiss arguments offered by lower courts,[11] the parties,[12] a dissenting justice,[13] or, especially, a Supreme Court majority analysis with which a justice disagrees.[14] More often than not, these dismissals are summary: no explanation is needed to justify rejection of a position once it has been labeled speculative.

Although nearly all of the justices used such rhetoric during the 2014 term, Justices Alito, Scalia, and Thomas used it especially often. As the discussion above has suggested, their disdain for speculation in the abstract does not keep them from indulging in it and asking their readers to do so as well.[15] Even those justices least given to hypothetical elaboration, such as Justices Ginsburg and Thomas, must sometimes engage in it, not only when taking a "categorical approach," but in more everyday legal reasoning as well.

5.3.2 When speculation is required

Many widely accepted legal rules require lawyers and judges to consider alternatives to what occurred in the past, to what is the case now, or to what might occur in the future, and then to describe at least some of those alternatives in an analysis. Rules of this kind fall into three categories, distinguished by the kind of imaginative activity involved. Each type of imaginative possibility-generation is a flexible mode of reasoning used in many legal areas.

- Some doctrines ask the analyst to subtract an element from what is known to have occurred, then decide whether subsequent events would have differed meaningfully from what actually occurred. Counterfactual analysis of this kind (even if not fully conscious) may be essential to our everyday reasoning about the causes of events (e.g., Byrne 2005; Hart & Honoré 1959; Mackie 1974).[16] This kind of analysis is also basic to the calculation of legal remedies, including monetary damages (see Gallagher 2018; Mitchell 2004; Strassfeld 1992).[17] Some of the justices currently endorse a standard involving this variety of analysis to justify recognition of new fundamental rights. The discussion below will return to this practice.
- Other doctrines ask the analyst to decide whether more than one outcome might result from a given state of affairs, to assess the likelihoods of the outcomes, and to gauge the analyst's confidence in those assessments. Scholars often criticize this practice, arguing that judges' risk assessments are wholly intuitive (e.g., Broker 2016). Justice Scalia's opinion in *Johnson*, the residual-clause case, relied heavily on similar rhetoric. But the generation of forward-looking possibilities in legal analysis is even more pervasive than counterfactual reasoning in the 2014-term opinions. For example, to explain any award of (or refusal to award) prospective injunctive relief, a judge must assess a litigant's "likelihood of success," as Justice Alito notes in this passage from his *Glossip* majority opinion: "The . . . posture of the present case . . . requires petitioners to establish a likelihood that they can establish both that Oklahoma's lethal injection protocol creates a demonstrated risk of severe pain and that the risk is substantial when compared to the known and available alternatives" (13).[18] As described here, the standard requires parties and the judge to assess the risk of pain involved in an execution method, identify alternative methods of (less painful) execution, and determine the likelihood that the judge will reach a particular conclusion upon the presentation of further evidence—to perform at least three forward-looking imaginative assessments.[19]

- A third kind of doctrinally required speculation involves deciding whether more than one path might be traceable from a given cause to a given effect, or whether a given state of affairs might arise as a result of more than one configuration of lower-level phenomena. This kind of speculation may also require deciding how many such causal paths or instantiating sets of circumstances are conceivable and/or comparing them. This might be the most challenging mode of speculation. Like the objective standards discussed in Chapter 3.4, it is highly abstract and therefore difficult to teach, explain, and rebut. When performed by judges, it seems to clash directly with the understandings of the judicial role described in Chapters 2 and 4, according to which judges are to be restrained, not creative. Nevertheless, this type of speculation is pervasive in legal analysis, as Chapter 3.4 suggested.[20] In addition to underpinning many reasonable-person standards, it is also at the heart of the two forms of doctrinal speculation considered at more length in the following sections: means-end review and reversible-error review.

5.3.2.1 Means-end review

U.S. lawyers and judges use means-end analysis in some antidiscrimination cases and in challenges to the constitutionality of legislation (or other government activity). This kind of analysis requires the analyst to think of a statute (or other government act) as a means to an end or aim (i.e., as produced by an intentional agent; see, e.g., Galloway 1988). Usually, the party arguing for the validity of the law, often the government's lawyer, identifies the end the law is taken to serve; this need not be the end lawmakers actually had in mind. The court is asked to decide, first, whether the end is a legitimate one for the government to pursue, and sometimes how important it is; second, how well the law works as a means to that end, an inquiry that may involve asking whether the law does achieve the end (a causal analysis); and sometimes also third, whether the defendant could have chosen better means to the same end—means that are better because, for example, they are more efficient or involve fewer side effects.

In the 2014 term, such means-end analysis played a role in at least eight cases.[21] The discussion here focuses on one, *Holt v. Hobbs*. This case involved a claim asserted by a prison inmate under the federal Religious Land Use & Institutionalized Persons Act (RLUIPA). RLUIPA explicitly requires means-end analysis: if a government rule imposes a "substantial burden" on an institutionalized person's "religious exercise," application of the rule to that person is illegal "unless the government demonstrates that imposition of the burden on that person—(1) is in furtherance of a compelling governmental interest; and (2) is the least restrictive means of furthering that compelling governmental interest" (*Holt*, 3). Gregory Holt, a Muslim inmate in Arkansas's state prison system, wanted to grow a half-inch beard "in accordance with his religious beliefs" (1); he invoked RLUIPA to challenge a "grooming policy" of the state Department of Corrections, which forbade beards more than a quarter-inch long (4).

All nine justices joined Justice Alito's opinion, which concluded that the policy violated RLUIPA. (Justice Sotomayor wrote separately just to clarify a point discussed below.) The justices agreed that the policy was not a good means to the ends identified for it, namely, curbing inmates' smuggling of contraband into prison and preventing prisoners' disguising their appearance to escape. As Justice Alito explains, the grooming policy did not clearly advance these ends. For example, it did not regulate the length of hair on prisoners' heads, leaving them with an equally effective contraband-smuggling method. All nine justices also agreed that the state failed to show that the policy was the "least restrictive means" of achieving these goals. Justice Alito's opinion supports this conclusion by describing other means to the state's ends, including comb searches to find contraband and photographing prisoners with and without beards to address the concern about disguise.

In a concurrence, Justice Sotomayor seeks to limit parties' options in making arguments that depend on the imaginative generation of alternative scenarios:

> [N]othing in the Court's opinion suggests that prison officials must refute every conceivable option to satisfy RLUIPA's . . . requirement. Nor does it intimate that officials must prove that they considered less restrictive alternatives at a particular point in time . . . [T]he Court correctly notes that the Department [in this case] inadequately responded to the less restrictive policies that petitioner brought to the Department's attention . . ., including the more permissive policies used by the prisons in New York and California.
>
> (Sotomayor, 2–3)

Although this passage seems to warn litigants away from overindulging in speculation, it does not involve the kind of anti-speculation rhetoric discussed in section 5.3.1. Justice Sotomayor is, rather, telling readers that they *do* need to consider certain identified but unactualized possibilities. The analyst should focus not on what the prison officials actually did (whether they "considered less restrictive alternatives at any point in time"), but on what they *might have* done (whether they could have used the less restrictive means suggested).

As *Holt* suggests, lawyers and judges conduct means-end analysis almost entirely in modal language—the discussion of possibility, rather than actuality. Means-end analysis of a rule does not concern what actually happened, either during the creation of the rule or as it was applied. Although some statutes (like RLUIPA) have codified means-end analysis, this sort of analysis was originally created by commentators and appellate-court judges (Thayer 1891), and this origin may explain its modal character. Legal commentators, like U.S. appellate-court judges, largely see their job as involving articulation of what should be, rather than what is.

5.3.2.2 Reversible-error review

Appellate judges are likewise responsible for developing another set of speculation-based doctrines: reversible-error review (Greabe 2016). Under these doctrines, once a reviewing court concludes that a lower-court judge made a mistake, the reviewing court must consider whether or not a hypothetical proceeding that did not involve the error would have led to a different result. Sometimes, reviewing judges must also assess their own degree of certainty about this conclusion. These doctrines are more controversial both in theory and in application than means-end review. Yet they are accepted as necessary and are neither obscure nor unusual. Their objective is quite practical: if an error did not make a difference to a case, there is no point in ordering a do-over. In the 2014 term, the justices applied or ordered application of such review in eight cases yielding reasoned opinions.[22]

By the time a case reaches the Supreme Court, it has usually passed through several levels of appellate review, often requiring consideration of several layers of error analysis. The opinions from Justices Alito and Sotomayor in *Davis v. Ayala* illustrate the phenomenon. In this case, Hector Ayala's lawyer objected to the prosecutor's dismissal of several potential jurors from the jury pool. A prosecutor may dismiss a limited number of potential jurors without explanation but may not deliberately tailor the racial makeup of the jury through such strikes. If the defendant's lawyer points out a suspicious pattern of strikes, the judge must ask the prosecutor to explain the strikes and must assess the soundness of the explanation. Ayala's trial judge asked for such an explanation, but Ayala's lawyer was not present when the prosecutor supplied it. After his conviction, Ayala argued that it was reversible error for the judge to accept the prosecutor's explanations without giving Ayala's lawyer a chance to respond.

The state and federal courts reviewing Ayala's conviction all agreed that this was error; they disagreed about whether the error required reversal of Ayala's conviction and sentence. As both Justice Alito (writing for a five-justice majority) and Justice Sotomayor (writing for four) noted, at least three such standards were relevant, each based on a previous Supreme Court decision. The first standard applied on direct review of Ayala's conviction in the California state courts; the second applied on collateral review (habeas review of the constitutionality of Ayala's detention); the third applied to appellate review of the initial habeas decision. Each standard uses slightly different language to describe the required assessment of the severity of the error and the reviewing judge's certainty about the error's effect.

On direct review of Ayala's conviction, using the first standard, a state court concluded that the error was harmless, that is, not grounds for reversal. On collateral review, however, two judges of a three-judge federal appellate panel concluded that under the third standard, the error was reversible. These judges' analysis seemed to focus mainly on how things might have unfolded otherwise in the trial court had Ayala's lawyer been present at discussion of the strikes. Viewed this way, the analysis is similar to a counterfactual causation analysis. A dissenting Ninth Circuit judge, Judge Callahan, maintained that the court should have focused on whether "'fairminded jurists can concur in the [state c]ourt's determination of harmless error,'" that is, whether the conclusion of the state *appellate* courts on direct review was within the set of reasonable appellate conclusions applying the appropriate standard to Ayala's case (8). This approach seems more like an analysis of multiple realizability; it suggests the second-level reviewing court should identify all the different grounds on which other first-level reviewing judges might have "fairminded[ly]" reached the same conclusion.

The Supreme Court opinions reproduced this contrast. Justice Alito's opinion adopts Judge Callahan's approach and assumes that the "fairminded jurist" multiple-realizability standard may be applied without also considering whether things could have played out differently at Ayala's trial without the error. Justice Alito describes this choice as mandated by the applicable legal standard, but he also adopts the state appellate court's counterfactual conclusions (about the effects of the error) as if they were factual findings. This move makes the reversible-error analysis both simpler and less likely to conclude that reversal is required. Justice Alito's simplifying analysis seems driven partly by a violent aversion to speculation; in the same opinion, he upbraids the Ninth Circuit majority for its "flight of fancy" in conducting a counterfactual-causal analysis (24). Justice Sotomayor's opinion, in contrast, does not assume that lower courts' assessments of possibility must be viewed as authoritative. She concedes that the Ninth Circuit panel might have included some unnecessarily vivid details in its opinion but suggests that it is a mistake to focus only on the panel's "flights of fancy." Her more sober alternative account of what might have happened at Ayala's trial demonstrates the possibility of a "fairminded" jurist's disagreement with the state court's conclusion of harmlessness.[23]

In several other 2014-term opinions, including *Wynne* (discussed in section 5.3.1), Justice Alito similarly pairs anti-speculation rhetoric and analytic simplification, on the one hand, with highly specific imagined scenarios, on the other. *Los Angeles v. Patel* provides another striking example. The case concerned a Los Angeles ordinance requiring hotels to keep guest registers and make them available to police upon request. The Court invalidated the ordinance in its entirety as improper under the Fourth Amendment because the ordinance authorized searches at police officers' unlimited discretion. Justice Alito objected to the scope of the majority's holding. As he frames the issue, "[b]efore entering a judgment with such serious safety and federalism concerns [as the invalidation of a '116-year-old ordinance'], the Court must conclude that . . . 'no set of circumstances exists under which the [law] would be valid'" (Alito, 1). Justice Alito then fills more than half of his dissent with a demonstration that several such circumstances exist, presenting five specific hypothetical scenarios in which, he contends, the ordinance could constitutionally apply.

Justice Alito's *Patel* dissent further supports the suggestion, noted in section 5.3.1, that he considers the generation of hypotheticals by at least some Supreme Court justices (as opposed to lower-court judges) to be not "flights of fancy" but legitimate tools for *limiting* lower-court power. The next section will continue to examine Justice Alito's distinctive use of hypothetical examples, as well as some of the patterns in other justices' use of this ubiquitous mode of explanation.

5.3.3 Hypotheticals as how-tos

Unlike the doctrinal rules discussed in the previous sections, which judges often have no choice about applying, hypothetical examples are almost never *required* to explain or illustrate a conclusion. Such examples also depend on modal thought and language. Yet despite the kind of anti-speculation rhetoric discussed in section 5.3.1, hypothetical examples are even more prevalent in judicial discourse, and in the 2014-term opinions, than the kinds of doctrinal speculation discussed above.

These little-studied devices are central to the law world.[24] They are an important part of legal education: U.S. law professors characteristically ask students in class to analyze hypothetical variations on the legal scenarios about which the students have read. Exams both in law school and for licensing purposes ask examinees to render written analyses of constructed scenarios, often flamboyantly unrealistic ones. As suggested earlier, hypotheticals are useful educational devices. They allow students to build a tacit understanding of how particular legal rules work by practicing discussion of the rules' application. Hypotheticals also train students to think modally, since they are often posed in batches that vary only slightly from scenario to scenario.

Supreme Court opinions contribute directly to this process. Even hypotheticals offered just for illustration in Supreme Court opinions may become focal points for and well known to large numbers of law students, lawyers, and judges. The practice is not limited to separate opinions, like Justice Alito's *Patel* dissent. Justice Kagan's majority opinion in *Omnicare*, the corporate registration-statements case, is built mainly of hypothetical scenarios. Justice Kagan introduces the basic scene near the beginning of her discussion and proposes variations on it throughout the opinion:

> Consider th[e] application [of the statute in question] to two hypothetical statements. . . . A company's CEO states: "The TVs we manufacture have the highest resolution available on the market." Or, alternatively, the CEO transforms that factual statement into one of opinion: "I *believe* . . . the TVs we manufacture have the highest resolution available on the market." The first version would be an untrue

> statement of fact if a competitor had introduced a higher resolution TV a month before—even assuming the CEO had not yet learned of the new product. The CEO's assertion, after all, is . . . a determinate, verifiable statement about her company's TVs, and the CEO, however innocently, got the facts wrong. But in the same set of circumstances, the second version would remain true. . . . [T]he CEO really did believe, when she made the statement, that her company's TVs had the sharpest picture around. . . . [A]lthough a plaintiff could later prove that opinion erroneous, the words "I believe" themselves admitted that possibility. . . . That remains the case if the CEO's opinion, as here, concerned legal compliance. If, for example, she said, "I believe our marketing practices are lawful," and actually did think that, she could not be liable for a false statement of fact—even if she afterward discovered a longtime violation of law. Once again, the statement would have been true, because all she expressed was a view, not a certainty, about legal compliance.
>
> (7)

Justice Kagan's opening command, "Consider," and the language appearing throughout this passage—"would be . . . if," and so forth—mark it as about something other than actual statements, beliefs, and so on. Yet the passage presents a serious analysis that is crucial to Justice Kagan's reasoning in the case. The passage also seems very much like an explicit *lesson*: when you encounter situations like these, the passage says to readers, these are the responses it is legally appropriate to have.

Most hypotheticals function in this way as "how-tos." They are fairly blatant articulations of what many cognitive scientists call "scripts" for use in legal activity (Herman 2013; Winter 2003). Scripts are regular, repeated sequences of actions that help us understand one another, respond appropriately in social situations, and act intentionally and strategically. A classic illustration is the restaurant script (Schank & Abelson 1977). When a person in the U.S. enters a restaurant and is shown to a table and given a menu, the person will probably expect, even without any exchange of words, that someone will return to the table to ask about the patron's desired meal. Dennett's account of the intentional stance, discussed in Chapters 3 and 4, can also be understood as a rudimentary script that informs our interactions with one another and permits mindreading (Herman 2013). We use scripts to explain our intuitions about what is possible, necessary, probable, and obligatory, both in and outside of legal culture; in everyday life, we base those intuitions on expectations about physical laws and human behavior that we often describe as matters of "common sense" and that philosophers sometimes call "folk psychology."

The examples in Justice Kagan's *Omnicare* opinion work as lessons partly because the scenario in which she places her CEO fits into a set of scripts shared by many educated U.S. readers concerning corporate behavior and investor inquiry. The examples both reinforce certain broader (although not universally shared) cultural scripts *and* generate more specific scripts for participants in the legal subculture. In this way, the hypothetical examples in the justices' opinions shape the minds of legal initiates by making some inferences and intuitions seem natural and others bizarre.

The justices do not always seem to use these tools with full awareness of their features and implications. The next three sections of this chapter explore three settings in which the justices rely on hypothetical examples especially often: when explaining conclusions about the meaning of disputed language (5.3.3.1); when explaining how to apply (or how not to apply) legal rules (5.3.3.2); and when basing justifications on assertions about what is likely to occur in the future (5.3.3.3).

5.3.3.1 Language, usage, meaning

In the 2014-term opinions, the justices use several kinds of hypothetical to support points about linguistic meaning. One kind presents an example of an act or entity to which a term could apply, that is, a hypothetical demonstration of the application of a statutory term. The passage from *Omnicare* quoted above includes several examples of statements that would, according to Justice Kagan, count as statements of fact, untrue statements of fact, and statements of opinion. A related kind of hypothetical presents a sample of language *use*, often invented by the opinion writer, to show the acceptability (or absurdity)[25] of a proposed interpretation of statutory or other operative language. A third type of linguistic hypothetical discusses a course of action that a lawmaker could have taken but did not take, in support of an argument that, for example, statutory language has a particular meaning.[26]

Although these kinds of hypotheticals are descriptively distinguishable, a single example may perform multiple functions. An example of overlap and apparent confusion appears in Chief Justice Roberts's dissent in *Ariz. State Legislature*, discussed in Chapter 4.2.2.2. Here, the Chief Justice appeals to readers' intuitions about the word "car" to support his argument that a popular referendum vote cannot be considered an act by a "legislature":

> As a matter of ordinary language and common sense . . ., a difference in function does not imply a difference in meaning. A car, for example, generally serves a transportation function. But it can also fulfill a storage function. At a tailgate party or a drive-in movie, it may play an entertainment function. In the absence of vacancies at the roadside motel, it could provide a storage function. To a neighbor with a dead battery, it offers an electricity generation function. And yet, a person describing a "car" engaged in any of these varied functions would undoubtedly be referring to the same thing.
>
> (Roberts, 10)

This passage presents an unusual and only partly worked out metareflection on how nouns operate. The point seems to be that the kind of thing we call a "car" can serve many functions, but that its multifunctionality does not affect its basic identity. From this observation, the Chief Justice suggests the further conclusion that the same logic applies to the kind of thing we call a "legislature." The car analogy does not, however, squarely respond to the point Justice Ginsburg makes in her *Ariz. State Legislature* majority opinion. She does not argue that a legislature stops being a legislature (or being called a "legislature") when it performs a different function. Rather, she reasons that we can apply the term "legislature" to whatever carries out the function of legislating. To challenge *this* argument, it seems that the Chief Justice would need to show that we cannot call a car a "storage unit," and so on—that we could not use language to place a car in the same category with other functionally defined objects. To make the analogy between the word "car" and the word "legislature" work, he might also need to show that some nouns that refer to basic-level concepts like "car" have restricted, non-function-related meanings and that "legislature" is a noun of this kind.

Although the passage seems to enlist its readers' intuitions about language, then, Chief Justice Roberts is, in fact, stipulating a meaning for the term "legislature" here, in a way that resembles the stipulated examples of statements of opinion, and so on, in Justice Kagan's *Omnicare* opinion. Also like that opinion, the Chief Justice's set of examples is itself an exemplary demonstration: a script for stipulating or arguing about meaning.

This kind of discussion exemplifies and reinforces the wordsmith's fallacy by licensing judicial stipulations of meaning alongside casual and only loosely related claims about linguistic regularities.

Similar, and similarly flawed, hypothetical examples of language use appear throughout the term's opinions.[27] The justices seem often to sense that their colleagues' linguistic hypotheticals are flawed, but they seldom criticize problematic examples in great detail. More commonly, a justice asserts the irrelevance of a problematic hypothetical or responds with a counter-hypothetical. This last strategy appeared in three sets of 2014-term opinions.

Two of these exchanges drew on the same cultural background—car use and ownership—invoked by Chief Justice Roberts in *Ariz. State Legislature.* In one case, *Baker Botts,* Justice Thomas appeals to the cultural scripts surrounding car maintenance to support an argument about the kinds of activities by a service provider considered "services":

> A [bankruptcy] professional's preparation of a fee application is best understood as a "[s]ervice rendered" to the estate administrator . . ., whereas a professional's defense of that application is not. By way of analogy, it would be natural to describe a car mechanic's preparation of an itemized bill as part of his "services" to the customer because it allows a customer to understand—and, if necessary, dispute—his expenses. But it would be less natural to describe a subsequent court battle over the bill as part of the "services rendered" to the customer.
>
> (8–9)

Justice Breyer, dissenting, tinkers with the scenario:

> The majority draws an analogy between a fee application and an itemized bill prepared by a car mechanic. . . . But customers do not generally pay their mechanics for time spent preparing the bill. A mechanic's bill is not a separate "service," but rather is a medium through which the mechanic conveys what he or she wants to be paid.
>
> (Breyer, 6–7)

These two justices' respective opinions contain no further analysis of this particular issue, that is, the meaning of "service." The logically isolated quality of the analogies encourages readers to view them as a kind of fact-like "evidence." And it discourages readers from considering whether the generation or comprehension of such examples has anything in common with other aspects of legal reasoning.

A similar back-and-forth about auto maintenance appears in *Michigan v. EPA*, the emission-regulation case discussed in Chapter 4.4.1. Here the dispute concerns the meaning of "appropriate." For the majority, Justice Scalia argues that it was not "appropriate" for the EPA to decide to regulate emissions without first considering costs: "By EPA's logic, someone could decide whether it is 'appropriate' to buy a Ferrari without thinking about cost, because he plans to think about cost later when deciding whether to upgrade the sound system" (11). In dissent, Justice Kagan responds:

> A better analogy might be to a car owner who decides without first checking prices that it is "appropriate and necessary" to replace her worn-out brake-pads, aware from prior experience that she has ample time to comparison-shop and bring that purchase within her budget.
>
> (Kagan, 22)

Here, unusually, Justice Kagan explicitly criticizes Justice Scalia's choice of analogical vehicle, suggesting not only that his comparison is inapt but also that his perspective is elitist.[28]

The justices' widespread willingness to generate hypothetical utterances to support conclusions about language meaning, coupled with their reluctance to analyze such techniques too closely, encourages other legal writers to see the techniques as an acceptable, low-cost, and entertaining way to present arguments about language meaning. The practice perfectly illustrates the self-perpetuating character of the wordsmith's fallacy; as lawyers and judges use this approach more and more, they reinforce their confidence in their own understanding of how language works. The next section considers some other uses of hypothetical examples that contribute to the wordsmith's fallacy less directly.

5.3.3.2 How to apply rules

One of the most basic professional scripts taught to contemporary U.S. law students is that of rule application. Becoming legally trained involves not only learning what legal rules say, but also learning how to explain the implications of the rules in particular situations. The importance of this skill to lawyering (and litigation in particular) is one reason for the ubiquity of hypothetical fact patterns, which provide opportunities to practice such explanation. The application script is relatively fixed and often taught using an acronym, such as "IRAC" (standing for "issue, rule, analysis [or application], conclusion"), or some variation thereon. Learning how to apply a rule includes learning the kinds of situation in which it might apply (when an *issue* concerning it has arisen) and the appropriate kind of *analysis* for the rule in that situation.

Even critics of this paradigm concede its ubiquity and utility (Graham 2015, 691–92, 701, 706). Students internalize the script in part through their reading; appellate opinions, including the 2014-term opinions, rely on it as well. The justices do not just apply legal rules to the case at hand, but often also describe how rules *would* apply in slightly different circumstances. The opinions supply readers with scripts illustrating the correct application of rules ("this is how you write about a situation in which this rule applies") and how to explain when a rule does *not* apply (e.g., "the rule the majority proposes is undesirable because it would not usefully address this common situation"). The opinions also call on cultural scripts readers are probably already "running" (regarding, for example, the perception of similarity between two scenarios) to establish or attack the legitimacy of particular rules ("since scenario A is, as you can see, not meaningfully different from scenario B, the same rule should apply in both").[29] Invented scenarios serving these purposes are everywhere in the 2014-term opinions, and like the language-use hypotheticals discussed in the previous section, they provide readers with lessons about legal consciousness that might not always be consistent with opinion authors' stated positions and goals. The hypotheticals contribute directly, but relatively invisibly, to the construction of a "law world."

Often, the justices' hypothetical examples of rule application are straightforward, as in the following example from Chief Justice Roberts's *Heien* majority opinion. Describing situations in which a police officer's mistake of fact might excuse otherwise unlawful conduct, the Chief Justice explains:

> An officer might, for example, stop a motorist for traveling alone in a high-occupancy vehicle lane, only to discover upon approaching the car that two children are slumped

> over asleep in the back seat. The driver has not violated the law, but neither has the officer violated the Fourth Amendment.
>
> (1)

Similar hypothetical applications of rules appear in many 2014-term opinions written by a variety of justices.[30] Such examples of rule application often accompany instructions to parties for compliance with the standards announced in an opinion.[31]

Even more common are hypotheticals appealing to readers' normative intuitions regarding such matters as fairness and absurdity.[32] Normative-intuition hypotheticals often do double duty, presupposing their readers' access to particular scripts about appropriate behavior or evaluation, but also prescribing the acceptability of those evaluations. In *Williams-Yulee*, for example, Chief Justice Roberts notes, "The identity of the solicitor [of a donation] matters, as anyone who has encountered a Girl Scout selling cookies outside a grocery store can attest" (14). This tactic is formally indistinguishable from more technical hypotheticals, like the one from *Heien*, above, as well as from language-use hypotheticals; each presents the reader with an example (of conduct, understanding, or interpretation) that is both assumed and asserted to be either standard or nonstandard. The parallel encourages readers to regard such normative standards as resources for the invention of illustrative scenarios, not just background assumptions.

Some hypotheticals that appeal to normative intuitions require more investment from readers. In the following passage from his *Williams-Yulee* dissent, Justice Kennedy describes an election contest between two imaginary judges to demonstrate the problems with the majority's conclusion about campaign-donation solicitation:

> Assume a judge retires, and two honest lawyers, Doe and Roe, seek the vacant position. Doe is a respected, prominent lawyer who has been active in the community and is well known to business and civic leaders. Roe, a lawyer of extraordinary ability and high ethical standards, keeps a low profile. As soon as Doe announces his or her candidacy, a campaign committee organizes . . . and begins raising funds. But few know or hear about Roe's potential candidacy, and no one with resources or connections is available to assist in raising the funds necessary for even a modest plan to speak to the electorate. Today the Court says the State can censor Roe's speech, imposing a gag on his or her request for funds, no matter how close Roe is to the potential benefactor or donor. The result is that Roe's personal freedom, the right of speech, is cut off by the State.
>
> (Kennedy, 2–3)

This vignette assumes readers will agree that Doe and Roe should be able to fight for the vacant position on a level playing field. It both presupposes and prescribes a normative script about the desirability of "outsider" access to the political system (cf. Edelman 1977), as well as scripts about judicial virtue and voters' responsiveness to advertising. Extended hypotheticals like this are especially powerful norm-promoting mechanisms.

Hypotheticals demonstrating the application of a rule carry some risk. In his concurring opinion in *Abercrombie & Fitch*, for example, Justice Alito presents a similarly extended example, asking his readers to "[s]uppose" a series of alternative facts about Abercrombie & Fitch's "knowledge" (Alito, 3). Justice Alito ostensibly introduces these alternatives to clarify the problems with the majority's articulation of the standard it applies. But his example seems to attribute to the majority a position that the majority did not take—the majority held that a job applicant does not have the burden of showing that the applicant asked for a religious accommodation, while Justice Alito proposes a scenario in which an employer is mistaken about whether an applicant's practice is religious. The example thus risks not clarifying but rendering unclear the requirement announced by the majority. As Justice Kagan's majority opinion in *Omnicare* also illustrates, absurd-scenario hypotheticals have an unsettling tendency to take on lives of their own in later decisions.[33]

5.3.3.3 *What will be*

Some legal uses of modal language do not concern what could be (or what could or should not be). Some, instead, assert what is possible or probable: what (likely) will be in the future. The justices often offer descriptions of likely future or potential states of the world, either to justify rejection of an alternative (as yielding undesirable consequences) or to justify the rule selected (because, for example, it is expected to create incentives for desirable behavior). Like the normative-intuition hypotheticals discussed in the previous section, these forward-looking statements help to flesh out the law world by cultivating expectations in their readers, regardless of the accuracy of the justices' predictions.[34]

Arguably, judges most directly confront responsibility for the effectiveness of their decisions when they consider the likely consequences of those decisions and discuss the consideration openly (Cover 1983; Posner 2008). Ideally, opinions can chart the kind of doubled awareness this book has described as characteristic of legal attitudes: each opinion is both a deliberately constructed reflection of nonverbal activity and, like a fictional narrative, the creation of a new set of conceptual possibilities. At the same time, as noted at the beginning of section 5.3.2, forward-looking hypotheticals are often criticized as based on little beyond judges' personal experience and intuitions. Judicial forecasts are contestable not just because they are speculative, but also because of their dependence on limited information and on structures of expectations that might not be universally shared.

A good example appears in Chief Justice Roberts's majority opinion in *King*, the ACA case. In that opinion, the Chief Justice explains that the ACA's reforms would be fatally undermined should the plaintiffs' interpretation prevail: exempting entire states full of health-insurance purchasers from the requirement to buy insurance "would . . . likely create the very 'death spirals' [for insurance companies] that Congress designed the Act to avoid" (15).[35] In certain cultures within the U.S., including that of health-insurance executives and, perhaps, many lawyers, the "death spiral" prediction probably seems perfectly sound if not obvious. Outside of those subcultures, interpersonal agreement on what is likely to happen, given a particular set of starting conditions, is likely to be much less robust.

Forecasts may also justify rejecting a rule. Slippery-slope arguments, which describe the ultimately disastrous consequences of a particular choice in order to justify rejecting the choice, are classic legal-rhetorical devices that depend on this kind of reasoning.[36] Such negative forecasts can become quite elaborate.[37] They often appear in separate opinions; indeed, on some accounts, the chief purpose of writing separate opinions is to plant a kind of seed for future decisions addressing similar scenarios in a way that retreats from the majority's resolution (Guinier 2008). By including a negative forecast, a separate opinion can create a kind of trigger for its own reconsideration, should the negative prediction come to pass. The next section will further consider this "seed-planting" practice.

Although hypothetical examples and scenarios take a great variety of forms, they all have the partly didactic effect considered above. They both presuppose *and* establish subcultural agreement among lawyers about appropriate rule-application, kinds of behavior to be expected, kinds of behavior worth describing in a legal setting, and so on. Their ubiquity reveals an important but rarely discussed and never systematized dimension of the Supreme Court's role. That role involves the generation of a significant amount of speculative language that creates the condition for its own claims to acceptability and, ultimately, such truth as lawyers and others ascribe to legal discourse. The Court has created the U.S. "law world" by promulgating these subcultural scripts, many of them in the form of hypothetical examples. It also creates that world by managing the generation of alternative legal worlds, the subject of the next section.

5.4 Possible legal worlds

Robert Cover's "*Nomos* and Narrative" (1983), one of the most-cited law review articles in U.S. legal-academic history, was the Foreword to the *Harvard Law Review*'s survey of the 1982 Supreme Court term. By "nomos," Cover means "a normative universe" (4). "To live in a legal world," Cover writes,

> requires that one know not only the precepts [of the law], but also their connections to possible and plausible states of affairs. It requires that we integrate not only the "is" and the "ought," but the "is," the "ought," and the "what might be." . . .
>
> The intelligibility of normative behavior lies in the communal character of the narratives that provide the context of that behavior.
>
> (Cover 1983, 10)

As this passage suggests, Cover's *nomoi* have much in common with the world constructed by the subcultural scripts discussed in the previous section.[38] "*Nomos* and Narrative" appeared around the time cognitive scientists were starting to discuss such scripts (Schank & Abelson 1977), and when philosophers and literary theorists were also starting to discuss language and metaphysics in terms of possible worlds (Eco 1978; Loux 1979). Cover did not participate directly in these trends, nor did he address the justices' linguistic practices during the 1982 term in great detail, but his foreword concerned phenomena much like those explored in this chapter.

Cover argues that *nomoi* tend to proliferate. Their proliferation yields what Cover calls "polynomia," multiple *nomoi* existing alongside one another. Two people sitting side by side could inhabit different normative worlds in this sense—each requiring its dwellers to consider and act in anticipation of different possible future states of the actual world. Cover regards polynomia as desirable because it allows people to choose the *nomoi* within which they will live. But he also regards the judicial system as designed to reduce polynomia. Courts are "jurispathic," he contends; "judges characteristically do not create law, but kill it" (53). They prefer the mode of necessity to that of possibility (cf. Ferguson 1990). Cover does suggest, however, that although the Court has usually been jurispathic in the past, it need not always be so (41, 67–68).

In their 2014-term opinions, the justices behaved consistently with Cover's account in many ways. But at times the justices also describe their decisions as motivated by a desire to preserve choice among commitments—or even to foster what Cover calls "jurisgenesis," the creation of new *nomoi*. Most of the justices on the Court during the 2014 term thus seem to have a more complex attitude than the blend of alienation and authoritarianism Cover described. Most of them present at least some of their decisions as involving a desire to preserve opportunities for choice at some point. For example, acting under constraint (necessity) now may be justified by the faith that this action will allow for creativity (possibility) in the future; likewise, creative judicial activity now may generate firmer constraints on action in the future.

Obergefell offers an example of this dynamic. According to the dissenting justices, *Obergefell* ended a national debate over the acceptability of same-sex marriage, a state of polynomia that should have been allowed to continue, even if it limited the petitioners' individual freedom. Justice Kennedy's opinion, in contrast, described the Court as fulfilling a duty to simplify the landscape of conflicting state positions in order to protect the dignity and agency of the petitioners and others in their position. The following two sections consider the traces of these two strategies—jurispathy and jurisgenesis—in the 2014-term opinions.

5.4.1 Contemporary jurispathy

Cover offered several explanations for what he saw as courts' (and especially the Supreme Court's) jurispathy. Judges are driven to objectify law, he suggested, because they lack other ways to characterize their action (1983, 44–45, 57). He hypothesized that judges might have a psychological need to fit within a "statist" bureaucracy (58). He also noted that judges themselves classically explain their decisions by reference to the requirement that law be singular so that people subject to the law can know what to expect from it (41 & n. 118).

Although he approved of jurisgenesis, Cover also recognized that jurispathy, or something similar, is sometimes desirable (15–16). Any intentional action involves eliminating options. And the move away from polynomia is not always imposed by the state. Parties to a lawsuit, for example, may agree (stipulate) to a set "universe" of facts, as did the parties in *Patel* (3, 11), or to a particular understanding of the legal provision at issue, taking others off the table, as did the parties in *MacLean* (4). Of course, more often it is judges who impose such restrictions by selecting one of several possible rules or understandings. In the 2014-term opinions, the justices repeatedly acknowledge this dimension of their activity, for example by invoking their duties to eliminate legal ambiguity and to provide guidance to other actors and institutions.

One jurispathic method that the Court self-consciously treats as central to its activity is the resolution of "circuit splits," divergent legal rules generated by different federal courts of appeals (see, e.g., *Sheehan*, Scalia, 2–3, citing the Court's Rule 10). In the terminology of Raimo Tuomela introduced in Chapter 4, the elimination of circuit splits is one of the Court's "we-reasons" for action. Majority opinions often recite the existence of such conflicting norms as the main reason for the Court's decision to review a case.[39] So important is this principle to the Court's account of itself that the justices will explicitly rebuke lower courts and litigants for frustrating its pursuit, as Justice Kagan does in one 2014-term case (*Reyes Mata*, 8).

Although the resolution of circuit splits is exclusively a Supreme Court function, many practices throughout the judicial hierarchy in both state and federal systems pursue the same jurispathic goal. En banc rehearing on intermediate courts of appeals allows those courts to eliminate polynomia within a circuit or to bring their law into line with that of other circuits.[40] The law of preclusion similarly eliminates inconsistencies across time, rather than among simultaneously existing legal systems.[41] The "law of the case" doctrine constrains courts at any level to abide by their own or a higher court's earlier decision at an earlier point in the same case.[42] And, of course, *stare decisis* (discussed further in Chapter 6) is also based on an analogous principle of legal consistency over time.

The elimination of linguistic ambiguity is an even more pervasive mode of apparently jurispathic activity. As Cover recognized, the "[c]reation of legal meaning" involves both generation and a kind of reduction, which he calls "objectification" (45). Another way of putting it would be to say that an ambiguous term creates a kind of small-scale polynomia—the ambiguity allows the same language to motivate different courses of committed behavior, each with a claim to justification. Although circuit splits may arise from linguistic ambiguity, identifying circuit splits is often easier than identifying linguistic ambiguity. Disagreements about whether a split exists are rare, but language that one judge considers ambiguous will not always seem so to another. Because U.S. legal discourse follows no standard approach to detecting linguistic ambiguity (Nourse 2016), the apprehension and resolution of ambiguity is an attractive arena for judicial and scholarly activity (cf. Chapter 1.2.2).

In the 2014 term, disagreements about the presence of ambiguity played a key role in *Yates* (the "tangible object" case) and *King* (the ACA case). In both cases, dissenting justices capitalized on the eye-of-the-beholder quality of ambiguity, responding to the majority's assertion of ambiguity with a denial of its presence (see *Yates*, Kagan, 9; *King*, Scalia, 8). Judges and lawyers share an awareness of the often contestable quality of linguistic ambiguity, which makes such moves predictable. Not only are lawyers always ready to *find* ambiguity in a text or utterance, they also have a set of standard responses to its discovery, including resolution of the ambiguity or simple denial of its existence. These moves are possible because lawyers learn to take a metalinguistic perspective on language, and the internalization of these options for argument helps to reinforce the wordsmith's fallacy.

Controversies over the presence and resolution of ambiguity are most common in cases raising issues of statutory or constitutional interpretation, like *King* and *Yates*. But any form of legal authority, including judicial opinions, may potentially ground multiple *nomoi* and in this sense be ambiguous.[43] Dissenting justices thus sometimes criticize majority opinions as lending themselves to undesirable future uses. Chief Justice Roberts uses this technique in his *Obergefell* dissent: "It is striking," he writes, "how much of the majority's reasoning would apply with equal force to the claim of a fundamental right to plural marriage" (Roberts, 20).

The classic justification for the judicial obligation to eliminate ambiguity is that clarifying the meaning of legal language will provide guidance to those seeking to conform their conduct to the law (Cover 1983, 41 & n.118).[44] A similar justification motivates the classic argument preferring legal rules to standards (Scalia 1998; Sullivan 1992). On this view, bright-line rules (e.g., a speed limit of 35 miles per hour) are preferable to standards requiring consideration of the circumstances (e.g., a sign reading, "Drive at a reasonable speed") because rules are easier to apply and obey and therefore lead to more predictable legal outcomes.

This theme structured the reasoning in several 2014-term cases. In *Kimble*, for example, the majority justified its adherence to a previous decision of the Court in part on the grounds that the rule-like precedent was "simplicity itself to apply" (12). A rule reduces, if it does not eliminate, options for decisionmakers at the point of application. Yet the *establishment* of a rule requires an affirmative selection among options, a firm and often arbitrary decision about the content of the rule. This kind of judicial action can be likened to legislative activity: Justice Alito stressed this point in his *Kimble* dissent (Alito, 1–2).[45] Standards involve more restrained action at the point of articulation; they defer judgment to the moment of application. Justice Breyer self-consciously chooses this approach to apply to claims of excessive force by pretrial detainees in *Kingsley* (9).[46]

In all of the ways explained throughout this section, operative language that can be described as ambiguous or liberating can be redescribed as clear or constraining. The justices are adept at slipping from one to the other of these descriptive perspectives, and they provide their readers with countless lessons in making the same moves. The partly self-conscious engineering of perspectives encouraging the perception of a resolution in one or the other of these ways is as much a part of legal discourse as is jurispathy plain and simple; this movement is closely related to the generation of hypotheticals discussed earlier in this chapter, to the acts of perspective-taking explored in Chapters 3 and 4, and to the more general phenomenon of multistable perception discussed in Chapter 1. The next section considers some additional ways in which the justices describe the contemplation of possibilities—if not multiple *nomoi*—as desirable.

5.4.2 Keeping options open

Cover considers jurispathy generally regrettable. He describes official ("statist") legal orders as unwilling to countenance potentially competing normative orders, such as minority religious communities (26–32) and oppositional readings of legal materials (35–40). And yet, as the latter example suggests, contemporary U.S. legal discourse does glorify the coexistence of at least some competing *nomoi*. The notion of intentional agency that is so fundamental to legal analysis, as described in Chapters 3 and 4, presupposes that responsible agents have the choice to act or refrain from acting. The vision of minimalist judicial action used to argue for rules over standards likewise presupposes the value of keeping open room for future actors' choice.[47] And as the examples discussed in this section show, the justices often refer directly to the importance of preserving options for action by litigants, individuals, firms, and government actors. The justices often also enable such options by providing alternative or redundant arguments supporting a conclusion, or by writing separate opinions planting the "seeds" of *nomoi* that might eventually replace the "imperial" *nomos* (Cover 1983, 13).

A premise of adversary legal systems like that of the U.S. is that parties are free to investigate their cases as they see fit and to choose how to pursue their legal goals. These values were central to the *per curiam* opinion in *Lopez v. Smith*, issued early in the term. This case arose from the prosecution of Marvin Smith for the murder of his wife. Smith defended on the ground that he was physically incapable of the murder. On appeal, Smith contended that he was therefore surprised when the prosecutor told the jury, "[d]uring closing argument, . . . that [Smith] was physically able to wield the log roller that killed Mrs. Smith, but . . . also . . . that, even if [Smith] had not delivered the fatal blow, he could . . . be convicted on an aiding-and-abetting theory" for arranging to have one of his employees commit the murder (2–3). The jury found Smith guilty but did not "specify[ ] which theory of guilt it adopted" (3). Smith challenged the conviction, arguing that he did not receive enough notice that the prosecution was planning to argue that he committed the murder himself. The Supreme Court agreed with the state appellate courts that Smith did receive enough notice and that the prosecution was entitled to keep open the option of arguing for conviction on alternative theories right up to the end of the trial. If Smith could not persuade the prosecution to settle on a single theory, the Court suggested, the appropriate response would have been to prepare an equally multi-pronged defense. The Court in this case expressly rejects the notion that litigants must commit themselves to a single "story" at trial. *Lopez v. Smith* thus illustrates a kind of sanctioned parallel-universe construction within criminal trials, at least up to a point.[48]

The justices also describe their 2014-term decisions as preserving room for choice outside the judicial system. In *Kimble*, for example, Justice Kagan's opinion reaffirming the bright-line precedential rule mentioned in the previous section defends the decision partly by pointing out the many choices it leaves available to contracting parties. Similarly, in *Williams-Yulee*, Chief Justice Roberts justifies the Court's preservation of the Florida ban on judicial candidates' direct solicitation of donations by stressing candidates' other fund-raising options. To present a conclusion as restrained, a judge will often emphasize how the decision safeguards other actors' freedom in this way. Such actors include not just individuals, but also states, municipalities, and their agents, such as prison wardens and police officers,[49] as well as regulatory agencies[50] and other executive-branch actors.[51] Justices also often note the options left open for lower-court judges' compliance with the Court's decisions.[52] When they recognize lower courts' freedom in this way, the justices endorse a kind of polynomia: they create a regime in which different courts might reach incompatible conclusions, many of which could be realized in multiple ways. More broadly, the justices often allude to the unpredictability and even chance inherent in the legal system because of its relationship to the necessarily unruly political process (cf. Chapter 3.3.2). This theme surfaces often in contentious, high-profile cases.[53]

Occasionally, the justices even acknowledge the Court's own unpredictability as a positive feature. Justice Alito presents reasoning of this kind in his *Johnson* dissent. Criticizing Justice Scalia for casually invalidating the Armed Career Criminal Act's residual clause, Justice Alito describes why the existence of judicial disagreement on the clause's application does not prove that the clause is so vague as to be unconstitutional. Justice Alito notes that the Court has been "unable to come to an agreement on many recurring legal questions," not only in ACCA cases but in other important areas as well (Alito, 5). The generation of conflicting decisions, Justice Alito suggests, is inherent in the Court's activity, not a sign of dysfunction. The variation makes it possible for lower-court judges to choose how they wish to justify their conclusions and even to reach different conclusions from the same starting point; these possibilities are a source of redundancy and strength, not just unpredictability.

The justices often incorporate such multiple realizability into the structure of their analyses. Lawyers call this the presentation of "arguments in the alternative." Such arguments take the form "If X, then Y; but even if Z instead of X, Y would still follow." Although it is ubiquitous in U.S. legal discourse, this argument form has not received much scholarly attention. In a brief recent analysis, Kiel Brennan-Marquez (2015) distinguishes arguments that vary the factual premises for a conclusion from those that vary the legal premises, although he does not explicitly address the different rhetorical purposes of these two kinds of variation. Varying the facts allows a lawyer or judge to show the validity of a conclusion under multiple factual suppositions; such an argument shows how robust, how far from questionable, a particular conclusion is. Varying the law, in contrast, lets a lawyer or court show how the conclusion argued for is appropriately restrained. Under slightly different formulations of the rule, such an argument often maintains, given similar facts, the same outcome would result, so there is no need to make the rule more complex to account for such facts.

Brennan-Marquez concludes that lawyers view fact-varying "even if" arguments skeptically. The justices' practice in their 2014-term opinions supports this conclusion; fact-varying "even if" arguments appear about half as often[54] as "even if" arguments turning on legal variations, which play a role in more than 20 2014-term opinions.[55] Law-varying "even if" arguments, which require writer and reader to keep two different legal standards in mind at once, can become quite complex and can generate a kind of ambiguity.

Chief Justice Roberts's dissent in *Wellness Int'l v. Sharif* discusses an example of this phenomenon. In this dissent, the Chief Justice objects to Justice Sotomayor's conclusion that a bankruptcy petitioner may consent to have a bankruptcy judge decide non-bankruptcy claims. Treating consent as a legal issue, he observes that the 2011 decision Justice Sotomayor cites to support her conclusion, *Stern v. Marshall*, addressed consent only in an "even if" argument used to reject the *Stern* dissenters' position (Roberts, 14).

His point seems to be that Justice Sotomayor's *Wellness Int'l* opinion misreads *Stern* by treating an issue not addressed in that case as if it had been part of the rule established by the case. It was the "even if" argument in *Stern* that made this move possible. The example shows how a law-varying "even if" argument may be used by subsequent courts in two contrary ways: as incorporating the counterfactual version of the rule or as not including it. In this way, such arguments create a kind of polynomia, opening the possibility of several future paths for legal development.

Other minimalist justification techniques may have a similar effect.[56] Explicitly labeling a holding as minimalist flags the issue (or issues) underlying the holding for development in future litigation. Such labeling can invite, rather than resolve, circuit splits. The 2014-term opinions contain many examples of such flagging. Sometimes, identifying unresolved issues merely flags a potentially distinguishable factual scenario.[57] But justices also flag issues that are far afield from those decided in the case, especially in separate opinions.[58] Justice Thomas used this technique more often than any other justice in the 2014 term. Chapter 6.4.1 will discuss in a bit more detail his revisionist originalist opinions of the term, which use this approach. But Justice Thomas does not flag only departures from original meaning for future reconsideration (e.g., *Teva*, Thomas, 11–12). Like other devices discussed throughout this chapter, judges across the ideological spectrum use this technique. It also does not appear only in separate opinions, although many separate opinions are apparently written solely for this purpose.[59]

Even when they do not explicitly perform a flagging function, the writing of separate opinions preserves polynomia by planting the seeds of possible future doctrine (Guinier 2008). The justices sometimes, especially in concurring opinions, present these seeds as instructions to lower courts implementing a decision (e.g., *Elonis*, Alito, 5).[60] At other times, judges and justices use dissents to give future readers and justices precedent for more radical legal change. For instance, Justice Thomas has since 2006 been using separate opinions to affirm his commitment to an alternative Confrontation Clause standard, which he reiterated in the 2014-term case *Ohio v. Clark*. Like flagging, this polynomia-preserving technique is not limited to particular justices or ideological blocs.[61] Separate opinions performing this function just explain how the law might be otherwise, sometimes without directly criticizing the result reached in the case at hand. Such discussions both contemplate the possibility that the Court might change its mind in the future and show how to justify any such change.

Practices like flagging and seed-planting suggest that the Court is not always as jurispathic as Cover argued. The justices are often apologists for power, but sometimes a majority takes up a possibility previously only flagged as potential and makes it actual. *Obergefell* was this kind of decision. Such a move is always vulnerable to criticism, but even the criticism may draw on the rhetoric of jurisgenesis: in *Obergefell*, the dissenting justices pounced precisely on the majority's alleged jurispathy in shutting down the national "conversation" on same-sex marriage.

Flagging and seed-planting practices model for legal readers the acceptable ways of conceptualizing what is legally possible: they provide the rhetorical raw materials needed for polynomia within the official legal system and invite the exploration of possibilities even as they constrain the ways such exploration proceeds. Even when the justices apply doctrines requiring the consideration of possibilities, they do so in patterned ways. These scripts for discussing and evaluating normative possibility keep the practice of cultivating and pruning legal possibility under control; they mark the normative boundaries of the "law world," not all of which consist of legal rules.

5.5 Openness in a closed world

The conventions of jurispathy and jurisgenesis discussed in the previous section—from the elimination of circuit splits and ambiguity to the presentation of alternative arguments, flagging, and seed-planting—have been used by lawyers and judges for decades, if not centuries, in their written output. Like hypothetical examples and causal reasoning, they are recurrent elements of legal explanation. The 2014-term opinions teach their readers, by example, how to use these tools.

These tools, as conceptual and discursive "scripts"—comprehensible structures—build on and complement those discussed in earlier chapters, especially the script of intentional action. That script is so basic to legal discourse (and Western discourse generally) that it can be hard to perceive as such. It is woven into U.S. legal thinking and writing at every level. An agent's choice to act or not to act is a necessary component of contemporary U.S. conceptions of legal responsibility as well as of more specific notions of subterfuge and strategic action, unintended consequences, thwarted intentions, and so on, which might all be regarded as variations on the script of intentional agency. This script cannot be articulated or understood without modal language and concepts: it must be *possible*, before the agent acts, for the agent to choose either to act or not to act.

The basic modal contrast between necessity and possibility—what is and what might be—has been, in itself, little discussed by lawyers or legal scholars, yet it structures not only assumptions about the basis for legal responsibility but also more theoretical recurring debates about legal rules and judging, the normativity of law, the possibility of judicial and decisional neutrality, and minimalism. Judges (and lawyers following their model) learn to present their analyses as exhaustive and their conclusions as necessary. This alignment of the legal voice with necessity, obligation, and actuality (cf. Ferguson 1990) drives many of the phenomena discussed in earlier chapters: the dismissal of fiction discussed in Chapter 2, the ambivalence about subjectivity discussed in Chapter 3, the skepticism about speculation discussed in this chapter. But as commentators have long observed, and as the discussions here have shown, that alignment always seems unstable and prone to reversal.

Legal and scholarly arguments that promote particular positions on the basis of their promise of simplicity and certainty are also subject to conventionalized rebuttals. Law students learn that, usually, for every argument advocating a rule over a standard, there is a counterargument explaining why a standard is preferable to a rule. Yet it has proven very difficult to move beyond ping-ponging such arguments back and forth, even in the most sophisticated arenas. One of the goals of this book is to offer an alternative view of these practices, if not an alternative to the practices themselves. The focus on a few specific patterns in legal argument (such as the distinctions between rules and standards, or the potential for ambiguity in a text) blinds legal readers to others and perpetuates a pervasive misconception of the sources of stability in legal discourse. That stability derives not from simplicity and predictability alone, but from lawyers' shared understanding and use of conceptual and compositional scripts, including especially those discussed in this book. These scripts are regularities that keep legal discourse fixed yet flexible, both closed and open—much like natural language. The fixity does not come from agreed-upon anchoring in facts or from the absence of speculation. It comes from shared comprehension of particular patterns—scripts—as meaningful, particularly as they are expressed in discourse.

The law world, and natural language, are closed (fixed, predictable) in that they require initiation or leaning and in that they are regularly structured. Not just any utterance counts as meaningful in natural language; not just any argument counts as legitimate in the law world. Some legal conclusions are unquestionably out of bounds, and some utterances are meaningless. But these systems are also open in that they continue to exist precisely because of the infinite recombinability of the patterns that make them up. These patterns structure the "law world," which is, like natural language, both closed and open to possibility.

Are there patterns in the methods of recombination themselves? The next chapter considers a further component of this world that has remained implicit so far: how the various motifs examined throughout this book are related to one another in legal description, explanation, and analysis. Again as in natural language, the patterns and scripts identified in this book are not just asserted one after another in sequence, but are at least as often stacked or nested hierarchically within one another. A legal rule, for example, may constitute a script that involves multiple elements or steps; the means-end analysis discussed in section 5.3.2 is an example. But within one of the elements of such a script, a legal analyst may call on another script, such as the script of intentional action or one of its variations. In addition, either in sequence or arranged hierarchically, the rehearsal of scripts unfolds in time.[62] Chapter 6 will examine some of the ways the 2014-term opinions exemplify and handle these dimensions of legal meaning.

Notes

1 See, e.g., Bogdan 2013, 49–62; Bruner 1986, 25–29; Byrne 2005, 198–99; Hill 2006, 209–10.

2 Modal terms include auxiliaries (e.g., "could"), adjectives and adverbs (e.g., "possible," "likely"), conditional constructions (e.g., starting with "provided that"), and verbs describing or prompting imaginative activity (e.g., commands to "suppose").

3 The "possible worlds" vocabulary and a more general interest in counterfactuality enjoyed a burst of popularity in several disciplines (as well as in popular culture) toward the end of the twentieth century. The topic was taken up by historians (Climo & Howell 1976; Hawthorn 1991), economists (e.g., Fogel 1964), and other literary scholars, in addition to those mentioned above (e.g., Eco 1978; Pavel 1994; Ronen 1994). Many acknowledged a debt to Gottfried Leibniz, who used the term "possible worlds" in his 1710 *Theodicy*, but they have elaborated the notion far beyond his argument (see, e.g., Gallagher 2018).

4 Bruner (1986) is another example.

5 In a 2012 case involving the doctrine applied in *Mellouli*, *Moncrieffe v. Holder*, Justice Alito and Sotomayor disagreed about whether the categorical approach involves "hypothetical" reasoning; Justice Alito argued that it does not. The discussion in the text adopts Justice Sotomayor's view.

6 Justice Thomas's *Mellouli* dissent advocates an analysis that would not require even the restrained speculative activity implicit in Justice Ginsburg's opinion. Instead of focusing on hypothetical convictable conduct, Justice Thomas considers only the statutes; he describes the appropriate "category" to consider as the category of state statutes implicitly cross-referenced by the federal deportation statute, those state statutes "relating to" the federal statute (Thomas, 8).

7 Justice Alito proposes an approach of this kind in his *Johnson* dissent (Alito, 20).

8 Discussed in *Patel*, Scalia, 2–3.

9 See *Ariz. State Legislature*, 10, 11 (Ginsburg).

10 See *Sheehan*, 12 (Alito).

11 See *Davis v. Ayala*, 19, 24 (Alito); *M&G Polymers*, 10, 11 (Thomas).

12 See *Kingsley*, 12 (Breyer); *Horne*, 15–16 (Roberts); *Baker Botts*, 12 (Thomas).

13 See *Williams-Yulee*, 15 (Roberts); *T-Mobile South*, 10–11 n.3 (Sotomayor).

14 See *Kimble*, Alito, 5; *Rodriguez*, Alito, 1; *Glossip*, Breyer, 24–25; *Alabama Legis. Black Caucus*, Scalia, 3–4; *Glossip*, Sotomayor, 15 n.3; *Omnicare*, Thomas, 3.

15 See *Johnson*, Alito, 12; *Obergefell*, Alito, 6; *Johnson*, Thomas, 3, 5; *Omnicare*, Thomas, 3.

16 See *Texas Dep't of Housing*, 21 (Kennedy).

17 For examples, see *Kansas v. Nebraska*, 15–17 (Kagan); *Horne*, Breyer, 2.

18 See also *Glossip*, 11 (Alito), for a similar discussion.

19 The analysis of contingent property interests also involves prospective speculation. See *Horne*, Sotomayor, 4. For additional examples of doctrines involving such speculation, see *Patel*, 14 n.5 (Sotomayor); *Glossip*, Breyer, 8, 26.

20 See *Woods v. Donald*, 4 (per curiam); *Sheehan*, 6 (Alito); *Young*, 7, 23 (Breyer); *Abercrombie & Fitch*, 1 (Scalia); *McFadden*, 10–11 (Thomas). The conceptual difficulty of the "rational jury" standard, at issue in several of these cases, is attested by the popularity of accounts failing to distinguish between the required speculative assessment (what the rational jury *could* decide, see McNaughton 1955) and the forbidden assessment (what the rational jury *would* decide; see Thomas 2014).

21 These were *Walker*, Alito, 16; *Williams-Yulee*, Alito, 1; *Young*, Alito, 9–10; *Kingsley*, 7–8 (Breyer); *Reed*, Kagan, 6; *Texas Dep't of Housing*, 4, 10 (Kennedy); *Williams-Yulee*, Kennedy, 6; *Williams-Yulee*, 15, 17–18 (Roberts); *Williams-Yulee*, Scalia, 3, 7–8, 10; and *Reed*, 15–17 (Thomas), as well as *Holt*, discussed in the text.

22 These include *Glebe v. Frost*, 2 (per curiam); *Woods v. Donald*, 6–7 (per curiam); *Elonis*, Alito, 8; *T-Mobile South*, Alito, 1–2; *Alabama Legis. Black Caucus*, 5, 17–18, 23 (Breyer); *Kingsley*, 14 (Breyer); *Brumfield*, 8, 10–11, 18 (Sotomayor); *Warger*, 2, 4 (Sotomayor).

23 "[I]t requires little speculation," Justice Sotomayor writes, "to see that defense counsel could have made a powerful argument that [one of the stricken jurors] was equally or even less likely to impose the death penalty than [one of the seated jurors]" (Sotomayor, 10–11).

24 Only a few legal academics have addressed the use of hypotheticals. See Gewirtz 1982; Mitchell 2004; Strassfeld 1992.

25 For examples, see *Carter*, 12 (Alito); *Texas Dep't of Housing*, Alito, 8–9; *Yates*, Alito, 2–3; *Baker Botts*, Breyer, 6–7; *Yates*, 15 (Ginsburg); *Yates*, Kagan, 17–18; *Texas Dep't of Housing*, 16 (Kennedy); *King*, 1–11 (Roberts); *Ariz. State Legislature*, Roberts, 7; *Obergefell*, Roberts, 8; *Alabama Dep't of Revenue*, 8 (Scalia); *Commil*, Scalia, 2; *Zivotofsky*, Scalia, 8; *King*, Scalia, 8; *Michigan v. EPA*, 7 (Scalia); *Warger*, 11–12 (Sotomayor); *Elonis*, Thomas, 11; *Baker Botts*, 7–8 (Thomas); *Ariz. State Legislature*, Thomas, 3–4.

26 For examples, see *Carter*, 9–10 (Alito); *Young*, Alito, 3; *Young*, 13–14 (Breyer); *Yates*, 12–13, 16 (Ginsburg); *Texas Dep't of Housing*, 15 (Kennedy); *Elonis*, 11 (Roberts); *Ariz. State Legislature*, Roberts, 20–21; *Abercrombie & Fitch*, 6 (Scalia); *Young*, Scalia, 7; *King*, Scalia, 5; *Michigan v. EPA*, 12 (Scalia); *Armstrong*, Sotomayor, 10.

27 For other examples, see *Abercrombie & Fitch*, Alito, 4–5; *Johnson*, Alito, 11; *Baker Botts*, Breyer, 2; *ONEOK*, 12 (Breyer); *Bullard*, 6 (Roberts); *Alabama Dep't of Revenue*, 4 (Scalia); *King*, Scalia, 10; *Whitfield*, 2–3, 4 (Scalia); *Zivotofsky*, Scalia, 7; *Elonis*, Thomas, 7–8; *McFadden*, 5 (Thomas).

28 For a third hypothetical-versus-hypothetical battle from the term, see *Yates*, Alito, 1–2; Kagan, 16.

29 See *B&B Hardware*, 17–18, 20, 21 (Alito); *Coleman*, 8 (Breyer); *Kimble*, 6 (Kagan); *T-Mobile South*, Roberts, 7; *Jennings*, 8–9 (Scalia); *King*, Scalia, 9–12; *Omnicare*, Scalia, 4, 6; *Young*, Scalia, 2–3; *Heien*, Sotomayor, 5; *Perez*, 13 (Sotomayor).

30 See *Abercrombie & Fitch*, Alito, 5, 6; *T-Mobile South*, Alito, 1; *Young*, Alito, 4; *Horne*, Breyer, 5; *Kingsley*, 6, 10 (Breyer); *Teva*, 11–13 (Breyer); *Young*, 15–16, 21–22 (Breyer); *Henderson*, 2 n.1, 5–6, 8 (Kagan); *Mach Mining*, 6–7, 9, 14 (Kagan); *Omnicare*, 8, 8 n.2, 12 n.6, 13, 13–14 n.8, 17–18 (Kagan); *Texas Dep't of Housing*, 20–21 (Kennedy); *Elonis*, 8 (Roberts); *Bullard*, 10 (Roberts); *Alabama Dep't of Revenue*, 5 (Scalia); *Abercrombie & Fitch*, 5 (Scalia); *Patel*, 12 (Sotomayor); *T-Mobile South*, 9–11 (Sotomayor); *Integrity Staffing*, 6–7 (Thomas).

31 For other examples from Chief Justice Roberts, see *Heien*, 11; *Horne*, 5. Justices from across the ideological spectrum use intuition-recruiting hypotheticals. See *Walker*, Alito, 1–2; *Kerry v. Din*, Breyer, 9; *Kingsley*, 5 (Breyer); *Michigan v. EPA*, Kagan, 11, 16; *Omnicare*, 12 (Kagan); *Young*, Scalia, 9; *Glossip*, Sotomayor, 26.

32 Consistent with their cautious approach to speculation, only Justices Ginsburg and Thomas did not use any absurd-results hypotheticals during the term. Absurd-scenario arguments appeared in, for example, *Carter*, 12 (Alito); *Christeson*, Alito, 1; *Elonis*, Alito, 6; *N.C. State Bd.*, Alito, 11; *Walker*, Alito, 2, 3–4; *Wynne*, Alito, 14; *Young*, Alito, 6 n.3; *ONEOK*, 13 (Breyer); *Young*, 12 (Breyer); *Henderson*, 7 (Kagan); *Reed*, Kagan, 2; *Davis v. Ayala*, Kennedy, 3; *Obergefell*, 18 (Kennedy); *Zivotofsky*, 27 (Kennedy); *Ariz. State Legislature*, Roberts, 21, 24–25 n.6; *MacLean*, 8 (Roberts); *Alabama Dep't of Revenue*, 9 (Scalia); *Ariz. State Legislature*, Scalia, 3; *Armstrong*, 4–5 (Scalia); *Glossip*, Scalia, 6; *Michigan v. EPA*, 14 (Scalia); *Obergefell*, Scalia, 7–8 n.22; *Omnicare*, Scalia, 3, 7; *Zivotofsky*, Scalia, 14; *Glossip*, Sotomayor, 28.

33 See *Omnicare*, 8 n.1, 13 n.7, discussing a hypothetical example introduced in *Virginia Bankshares, Inc. v. Sandberg* (1997).

34 Forecasts appear to justify rules or holdings in, for example, *B&B Hardware*, 18 (Alito); *Elonis*, Alito, 7; *Clark*, 7, 11 (Alito); *Walker*, 5–6 (Breyer); *Rodriguez*, 7 (Ginsburg); *Kansas v. Nebraska*, 8 (Kagan); *N.C. State Bd.*, 10 (Kennedy); *Texas Dep't of Housing*, 21–22 (Kennedy); *Bullard*, 11 (Roberts); *Williams-Yulee*, 19–20 (Roberts); *Patel*, 11 (Sotomayor); *T-Mobile South*, 7 (Sotomayor); *Armstrong*, 10 (Scalia); *Sharif*, 20 (Sotomayor); *Reed*, 10–11 (Thomas).

35 Chief Justice Roberts bases this forecast on past state-level experimentation with universal health-insurance schemes (*King*, 2–4).

36 A good example appears in Justice Thomas's dissenting opinion in *Jennings v. Stephens*. "[T]he majority's decision," he writes, "will . . . allow[] prisoners to pursue any alternative allegation, no matter how frivolous, that would have justified the same new proceeding awarded . . . below" (Thomas, 9).

37 They may be found, for example, in *Clark*, 11–12 (Alito); *Johnson*, Alito, 7–8; *Texas Dep't of Housing*, Alito, 32; *Walker*, Alito, 10, 14; *Armstrong*, Breyer, 3; *Ariz. State Legislature*, 33 (Ginsburg); *Omnicare*, 16–17 (Kagan); *Reed*, Kagan, 6–7; *Yates*, Kagan, 15 n.6; *Commil v. Cisco*, 10 (Kennedy); *Obergefell*, 26 (Kennedy); *Wellness Int'l*, Roberts, 2; *Williams-Yulee*, 19 (Roberts); *Jennings*, 6 (Scalia); *Zivotofsky*, Scalia, 19; *Omnicare*, Scalia, 3, 6–7; *Armstrong*, Sotomayor, 6, 7, 12; *Heien*, Sotomayor, 4; *Patel*, Scalia, 11–12.

38 Elsewhere, Cover (1983) makes the parallel even more obvious: "A legal tradition . . . includes not only a corpus juris, but also a language and a mythos—narratives in which the corpus juris is located by those whose wills act upon it. These myths establish the paradigms for behavior. They . . . establish a repertoire of moves—a lexicon of normative action—that may be combined into meaningful patterns culled from the past" (9).

39 See *Coleman*, 4 (Breyer); *Kingsley*, 5 (Breyer); *ONEOK*, 9 (Breyer); *Young*, 10 (Breyer); *Rodriguez*, 4 (Ginsburg); *Henderson*, 3 (Kagan); *Mach Mining*, 4 (Kagan); *Reyes Mata*, 3–4 (Kagan); *Obergefell*, 9, 10, 26 (Kennedy); *Bullard*, 4 (Roberts); *Hana Financial*, 3 (Sotomayor); *T-Mobile South*, 13 (Sotomayor).

40 See *Christeson*, 1 (per curiam); *Commil*, 4–5 (Kennedy).

41 See *B&B Hardware*, 1, 8–12 (Alito); *Carter*, 2 (Alito); *ONEOK*, 10 (Breyer).

42 See *Zivotofsky*, Breyer, 1.

43 See *Ariz. State Legislature*, Scalia, 5. The precedent Justice Scalia considers here, *Coleman v. Miller* (1939), exemplifies the "doctrinal paradox" discussed in Chapter 4.2.1.

44 Justices also describe other courts and other government actors as designed to perform the same function. See *Dart Cherokee*, 4, 10 (Ginsburg); *Bullard*, 3 (Roberts); *Perez*, Scalia, 4.

45 See also *N.C. State Bd.*, Alito, 12, making a similar argument.

46 For other examples of rules-versus-standards arguments in the term's opinions, see *Taylor v. Barkes*, 4, 6 (per curiam); *Elonis*, Alito, 1; *Kingsley*, Alito, 1; *Obergefell*, Alito, 2; *Texas Dep't of Housing*, Alito, 31–32, 34–35; *Gelboim*, 8 (Ginsburg); *Yates*, Kagan, 14; *Young*, Kennedy, 3; *Obergefell*, Roberts, 22; *Kerry v. Din*, 15 (Scalia); *Williams-Yulee*, Scalia, 9; *Heien*, Sotomayor, 3; *Horne*, Sotomayor, 10–11; *Abercrombie & Fitch*, Thomas, 8–9; *Direct Marketing Ass'n*, 12 (Thomas); *Mellouli*, Thomas, 1; *Teva*, Thomas, 15; *Zivotofsky*, Thomas, 14.

47 Examples of this kind of argument appear throughout the 2014-term opinions. See *Carroll*, 7 (per curiam); *Woods v. Donald*, 7 (per curiam); *Sheehan*, 14 n.4 (Alito); *Wellness Int'l*, Alito, 1; *Alabama Legis. Black Caucus*, 18–19 (Breyer); *Ariz. State Legislature*, 14 n.2 (Ginsburg); *Texas Dep't of Housing*, 18 (Kennedy); *Zivotofsky*, 17 (Kennedy); *McFadden*, Roberts, 2; *Zivotofsky*, Roberts, 6–7; *Abercrombie & Fitch*, 6 n.3 (Scalia); *Michigan v. EPA*, 3 (Scalia); *Zivotofsky*, Scalia, 5; *Brumfield*, 6–7 (Sotomayor); *Patel*, 10 n.2 (Sotomayor); *Warger*, 10–11 n.3 (Sotomayor); *Brumfield*, Thomas, 21; *Elonis*, Thomas, 17; *Zivotofsky*, Thomas, 29 n.10.

48 In *Glebe v. Frost*, a per curiam opinion issued shortly after *Lopez v. Smith*, the Court reached a conclusion that seems at first to be in tension with the earlier decision. In this case, the defendant's lawyer sought to argue two theories: that the prosecution had not met its burden of proof, and that the defendant acted under duress. The trial judge forbade this tactic on the ground that state law prohibited it, and the Court concluded that this ruling was justified. But interestingly, the Court described the trial court's decision as ambiguous, leaving open the possibility that a future trial judge might accept an argument like Frost's and allow a defendant to make alternative arguments. See also *Armstrong*, Breyer, 4–5; *Harris*, 2 (Ginsburg); *Commil*, 12 (Kennedy).

49 See, e.g., *Wynne*, 26 (Alito); *Walker*, 12, 15–16 (Breyer); *Wynne*, Ginsburg, 6; *Reed*, Kagan, 4; *N.C. State Bd.*, 16 (Kennedy); *T-Mobile South*, Roberts, 2; *Williams-Yulee*, 13, 16 (Roberts); *Patel*, 13 (Sotomayor); *Alabama Legis. Black Caucus*, Thomas, 11.

50 See *Mach Mining*, 11 (Kagan) (EEOC); *ONEOK*, Scalia, 4 (FERC).

51 See *Carter*, 2 (Alito); *Kerry v. Din*, Breyer, 7; *Zivotofsky*, Scalia, 6, 12.

52 See *Christeson*, Alito, 2–3; *Dart Cherokee*, 14 n.8 (Ginsburg); *Gelboim*, 9 (Ginsburg); *Dart Cherokee*, Scalia, 4; *Armstrong*, Sotomayor, 10–11.

53 See *Texas Dep't of Housing* (Alito, 16) and *Obergefell* (Roberts, 25, 27; Scalia, 4; Thomas, 16; Alito, 7).

54 An example of a fact-varying argument appears in a footnote in *Sheehan*: "There is a dispute regarding whether Sheehan was on the ground for the last shot. This dispute is not material: 'Even if Sheehan was on the ground, she was certainly not subdued'" (5 n.2 (Alito)). For other examples, see *Taylor v. Barkes*, 6 (per curiam); *Holt*, 10–11 (Alito); *Walker*, Alito, 12; *Walker*, 16 (Breyer); *Rodriguez*, 8 (Ginsburg); *Kerry v. Din*, Kennedy, 6; *Williams-Yulee*, 11 (Roberts); *Glossip*, Scalia, 3; *Jennings*, 7–8 (Scalia).

55 These include *Carroll*, 4 (per curiam); *Glebe v. Frost*, 2–3 (per curiam); *Lopez v. Smith*, 4–5 (per curiam); *Carter*, 10 (Alito); *Johnson*, Alito, 6, 13; *Kerry v. Din*, 6, 9 (Alito); *Patel*, Alito, 19; *Sheehan*, 13, 16 (Alito); *Texas Dep't of Housing*, Alito, 19; *Teva*, 4–5 (Breyer); *Alabama Legis. Black Caucus*, Ginsburg, 2; *Reyes Mata*, 5 (Kagan); *Kerry v. Din*, Kennedy, 1; *Ariz. State Legislature*, Roberts, 3, 19; *Zivotofsky*, Roberts, 4; *Kingsley*, Scalia, 4; *Davis v. Ayala*, Sotomayor, 14; *Glossip*, Sotomayor, 27; *Warger*, 12 (Sotomayor); *Brumfield*, Thomas, 17 n.8, 22, 24; *Wynne*, Thomas, 3; *Obergefell*, Thomas, 3, 7; *Zivotofsky*, Thomas, 30.

56 In his *Clark* majority opinion, Justice Alito cited an earlier use of this technique in a 2011 case, *Michigan v. Bryant* (6–7).

57 Here is an example from Justice Scalia's majority opinion in *Jennings*: "The State's argument might have force in a case where a district court explicitly imposes (or the appellee asks the appellate court explicitly to impose) a condition governing the details of . . . [a] retrial. But that case is not before us" (6). In *Direct Marketing Ass'n*, Justice Kennedy flagged for litigants the Court's willingness to reconsider a 1967 precedent; South Dakota enacted a law creating the possibility for such a challenge, and the Court overruled the precedent in question in *South Dakota v. Wayfair*, decided in June 2018 (see also Rubin & Stevens 2018).

58 See *Perez*, Alito, 2; Scalia, 4; Thomas, 3 n.1; *Davis v. Ayala*, Kennedy, 5.

59 Other examples include *Ass'n of Am. Railroads*, Alito, 7; *B&B Hardware*, 12 n.2 (Alito); *Elonis*, Alito, 9; *ONEOK*, 16 (Breyer); *Coleman*, 8–9 (Breyer); *Kerry v. Din*, Breyer, 10; *Kingsley*, 6, 12–13 (Breyer); *Dart Cherokee*, 6 n.1 (Ginsburg); *Direct Marketing Ass'n*, Ginsburg, 1–2; *Obergefell*, Roberts, 28; *Perez*, 13 n.5 (Sotomayor); *Davis v. Ayala*, Sotomayor, 6 n.1; *Brumfield*, 17 (Sotomayor); *B&B Hardware*, Thomas, 7 n.3; *Direct Marketing Ass'n*, 13 (Thomas); *Obergefell*, Thomas, 15; *Wellness Int'l*, Thomas, 16, 18; *Zivotofsky*, Thomas, 19–20; *McFadden*, 7 n.2 (Thomas).

60 This kind of seed-planting was encouraged by the Court in *Marks v. United States* (1977), which held that when no rationale receives the endorsement of a majority of justices, "the holding of the Court may be viewed as that position taken by those [justices] who concurred . . . on the narrowest grounds," 430 U.S. 188, 193 (quoting *Gregg v. Georgia*, 428 U.S. 153, 169 n.15 (1976)).

61 Examples occurred throughout the term, including in *Horne*, Breyer, 1; *Obergefell*, Roberts, 29; *Alabama Legis. Black Caucus*, Thomas, 2–3 n.1, 13; *Glossip v. Gross*, Thomas, 1; *Wellness Int'l*, Thomas, 17–18; *Glossip*, Breyer, 2–41, as well as the further examples discussed in Chapter 6.4.1.

62 In the philosophical literature, modality is related not only to intentionality, but also to temporality. The necessary or actual can be conceptualized as what is past (i.e., fixed, not subject to change), while the possible can be conceptualized as what is future (i.e., free, not yet determined; see Loux 1979).

6 Reading the layers of law

6.1 Scripts that use texts as props

The scripts and other patterns considered in Chapter 5 shape lawyers' understanding, communication, and behavior, much as following the "restaurant" script in real life affects both our expectations and our conduct. Being a lawyer, or playing the law game, requires more than just sharing expectations, of course. It requires an appropriate setting and appropriate "props." In U.S. law, these props include legal materials, more often than not texts—hard-copy documents, bound books, electronic files.

The "metalinguistic" perspective Mertz (2007, 135) describes U.S. law students as acquiring is a particular perspective toward language and, crucially, texts. Before law school, she suggests, many students regard documents as largely inert sources of information or entertainment. Law school teaches them also to see documents as potential allies, creators of relationships, and tools for combat. No longer mere windows onto "fact," texts acquire additional dimensions and interrelationships that students, and then lawyers, always keep in mind.

The attitude lawyers acquire toward texts resembles the attitude people take toward make-believe "props" in Kendall Walton's account (1993, 42–54). Walton gives the example of a banana used as a play telephone. As a prop, the banana allows game players to make-believe jointly, redescribing a part of their shared environment, the banana, as a telephone in order to enrich the game. Yet the players remain aware of the prop's dual character: the banana is both a banana and a make-believe telephone.

In law school, students learn about law-specific scripts partly from legal texts, as Chapter 5 explained. Many of the scripts recruited and established by these materials, however, involve text-mediated interaction with other people. So students also learn scripts that require them to use texts as props, and in this capacity the texts acquire the dual character of make-believe props. Lawyers learn how to read language as communicating multiple messages at once to different readers (cf. Dan-Cohen 1993)—sometimes as carrying a metalinguistic, formal–stylistic, or intertextual message to legal readers alongside a referential message to other readers—and how to generate language that achieves the same trick. Lawyers' ability to see texts in both of these ways, and to shift between them, contributes to lawyers' sense of control over the texts themselves and the language making them up.

Exploring these dimensions of the scripts of lawyering, this chapter begins by considering two general formal categories into which most scripts of the law "game" fall. Each form uses texts as props in different ways. The first form has the basic shape of a narrative of action for reasons, or intentional action (section 6.2.1). When lawyers follow scripts of this kind, text-props can function as interventions in the world (performative linguistic acts initiating a state of affairs), instruction manuals (prospectively describing and prescribing future intentional action), or referential accounts of non-textual activity—and sometimes all three. The second form is what this chapter calls the script of the eternal present (section 6.2.2). In this script, text-props function as anchors linking an argument or justification to a normative grounding that does not vary over time.

Most of lawyers' activity draws on both of these forms in yet a third more complex form of script, which combines multiple instances of one or both of the basic forms in a nested or embedded fashion, much like subroutines in computer programs or narrative stories-within-stories. For example, a judicial opinion may describe an earlier authoritative legal act (e.g., the framing of the Constitution) as "containing" a prescription or set of instructions for subsequent legally appropriate intentional activity (e.g., the process for amendment). Lawyers and judges often use one particular configuration of such embedding, described in section 6.3, to explain and justify legal continuity and change. Showing that this and other patterns described throughout this book mark lawyers' verbal activity beyond the Supreme Court, the last section of the chapter turns to describe instances of the same patterns in the opinions issued by then-Judge Gorsuch between October 2014 and June 2015, the period covered by this book (section 6.4).

6.2 Building blocks

Ascribing a mental state or mind to another makes it possible to see that other as acting intentionally. One way of thinking of such ascriptions is to regard them as positing a mind inside the other's body. But the ascriptions can also be conceptualized temporally. The ascriptions are usually driven by observations of the other's behavior, occurring over time. Each such ascription involves seeing a sequence of actions as meaningful (Hutto 2008).

When we see action as intentional, or performed for a reason, we can redescribe it analytically as involving a beginning (where a problem arises for the actor, providing a reason to act), middle (where the actor selects a response and acts to address the problem), and end (where the actor resolves the problem, or conclusively fails to resolve it). Sequences following this basic structure have been studied as instances of narrative since Aristotle (e.g., Binder & Weisberg 2000, 204–05). They can become quite complex. As noted in the previous section, when lawyers and judges enact or identify instances of intentional action following this form, they may use texts as props in a number of ways: as posing the initial problem, as prescribing the actor's activity, as constituting the problem's resolution, or as referentially recounting the intentional action. The discussion below will focus on the second of these functions, the prescriptive one.

It is easy to see action-for-reasons narratives everywhere and tempting to conclude that discourse must take such a form to be meaningful (Bruner 2002; White 1985). But lawyers and judges also use texts as props in their discourse in another equally important way that implies a different play-script. Here is an example of this kind of script from Justice Alito's dissent in the 2014-term case *United States v. Kwai Fun Wong*:

> For well over a century, we have recognized the inflexible nature of the Tucker Act's provision. Since its adoption, we have recognized that the [Federal Tort Claims Act]'s language bears the same meaning as its Tucker Act companion.
>
> (Alito, 9)

These sentences do not present a story. In them, Justice Alito gestures to the text of two statutes and the Court's past statements about them as equivalent linguistic anchors to an unchanging norm. They assert a pattern of nondevelopmental reiteration (cf. Derrida 1988). Lawyers and judges alternate between using texts as this kind of "anchor" prop and using them to motivate and resolve narratives of intentional activity. The next two sections consider some especially vivid examples of these practices in the 2014-term opinions.

6.2.1 Action for reasons: instruction-props

The Court's opinions are instruments for the perpetuation of traditional lawyerly scripts, or sequences of comprehensible behavior, and the creation of newer ones. In part, they serve this function in the way examined in Chapter 5.3.3, through hypothetical examples. But the justices do not just describe acceptable behavior, as in hypotheticals; they also explicitly *prescribe* acceptable conduct in many cases. A significant part of the Court's caseload, for example, consists of cases presenting procedural questions, in which the Court explicitly considers, establishes, and revises litigation-related scripts.[1] More broadly, much of the Court's (and Congress's) output functions to establish sets of behavioral instructions for private-sector actors or actors in other governmental systems.[2]

The disputes that result in Supreme Court litigation often arise from clashes between nonlegal cultural scripts followed by actors from different "worlds." In cases of this sort, the Court may use its opinions to endorse one of the scripts as legitimate, sometimes also prescribing instructions for conduct in similar future clashes. The Court's constitutional criminal procedure cases, which concern police–civilian encounters (often arrests or seizures of evidence), tend to be of this kind. Such cases have been a significant part of the Court's docket for half a century and are often controversial, both because they concern an area of law the Court developed on its own and because of the social, political, and individual significance of the encounters they regulate. Those encounters are characterized by the mismatched perceptions and expectations of the individuals involved. During the 2014 term, those mismatches gave rise not only to eight Supreme Court cases involving police–citizen interactions[3] but also significant public protest activity throughout the U.S.

In all of the term's criminal procedure cases, the justices seem aware of their script-prescribing role. The opinions in *Rodriguez v. United States* are good examples. The police encounter in *Rodriguez* occurred during a traffic stop on a Nebraska highway. The officer making the stop issued a warning to the car's driver, Dennys Rodriguez, for driving on the shoulder, then asked Rodriguez for permission to bring a drug-sniffing dog to the car. Rodriguez refused, but when a backup officer arrived, the first officer nevertheless walked the dog around the car, eventually finding methamphetamine in it. Rodriguez objected to the use of the drugs as evidence against him, arguing that the officer's "exten[sion]" of the stop after issuing the warning made the stop unreasonable and therefore a violation of the Fourth Amendment (4).

Justice Ginsburg's majority opinion resolved the case by invoking behavioral scripts for police officers that the Court had established in previous decisions, and then elaborating on them:

> Like a *Terry* stop [a stop based on "reasonable suspicion," authorized in *Terry v. Ohio* (1968)], the tolerable duration of police inquiries in the traffic-stop context is determined by the seizure's "mission"—to address the traffic violation that warranted the stop . . .,

> and attend to related safety concerns. . . . Authority for the seizure thus ends when tasks tied to the traffic infraction are—or reasonably should have been—completed.
>
> (5)

Justice Ginsburg's resolution of the case relies entirely on a narrative conceptualization of police activity. Her opinion describes each *Terry* stop as a miniature narrative arc with a natural limiting principle (the basis for initiating the stop). This description is also a set of instructions to officers wishing to comply with the law.

Justice Thomas and Justice Alito both dissented in *Rodriguez*, each objecting to this analysis in a different way. Justice Thomas, describing Justice Ginsburg's approach as an arbitrary departure from precedent, advanced an alternative narrative-limiting principle that would keep the Court out of the business of instructing police officers. According to him, as long as an officer starts a stop for any legitimate reason, it is up to the officer when it will end.

Justice Alito's separate dissent in *Rodriguez* is not just deferential to the police perspective in the abstract but affirmatively endorses the officer's behavior in this case. Justice Alito describes Justice Ginsburg's prescription of instructions to police as almost comically formalistic: "The Court . . . holds that the Fourth Amendment was violated . . . simply because of the sequence in which Officer Struble chose to perform his tasks" (Alito, 2). Suggesting that police do not know or care about the Court's decisions, much less such abstract prescriptions as Justice Ginsburg's, he proposes that judges view police officers' behavior as ordinary intentional conduct, not special "police officer" conduct:

> Officer Struble had decided to perform a dog sniff [before calling for backup] but did not want to do that without another officer present. When occupants of a vehicle who know that their vehicle contains a large amount of illegal drugs see that a drug-sniffing dog has alerted for the presence of drugs, they will almost certainly realize that the police will then proceed to search the vehicle, discover the drugs, and make arrests. Thus, it is reasonable for an officer to believe that an alert will increase the risk that the occupants of the vehicle will attempt to flee or perhaps even attack the officer. . . . In this case, Officer Struble was concerned that he was outnumbered at the scene, and he therefore called for backup and waited for the arrival of another officer before conducting the sniff.
>
> (Alito, 2–3)

The free-floating point of view in this passage engages readers in reconstructing what Officer Struble might have thought: Justice Alito attributes his own mindreading of the car's "occupants" to the officer. This passage is nevertheless prescriptive, in the manner of the hypotheticals discussed in Chapter 5.3.3; it provides a script not for police conduct but for the (judicial or lawyerly) drawing of untroubled conclusions about actors' states of mind even at several removes from the actors.[4]

Criminal-procedure cases lend themselves both to the prescriptive instruction mode Justice Ginsburg uses in *Rodriguez* and to the mindreading approach used by Justice Alito. These cases involve small-scale interactions, usually between individuals, and usually turning on the interpretation of behavior, rather than text. Not all cases, of course, fit this mold, and not all cases present explicit instructions to be followed recipe-like by later actors. Even opinions lacking these features can be used as a different kind of prop, the subject of the next section.

6.2.2 The eternal present: anchor-props

> To blind yourself to history is both prideful and unwise. "The past is never dead. It's not even past." W. Faulkner, Requiem for a Nun 92 (1951).
>
> (*Obergefell*, Roberts, 22–23)

Grounding a judicial explanation in accounts of rational action—describing actors' past conduct or prescribing their future acts—helps lawyers and judges establish connections between legal discourse and what lies outside the "law-world." Another way of establishing this connection does not involve narration or prescription. It exploits English speakers' discursive association between that which is past (and linguistically marked as such) and that which is actual (as opposed to merely possible). U.S. lawyers' tendency to regard respect for precedent as a necessary ingredient of any legitimate legal activity (see Waldron 2012) may stem from this verbal cueing just as much as from more frequently noted concerns for consistency, predictability, and respect for authority.

In a study of philosophical and literary possible worlds, Ruth Ronen (1994) investigated the referential effects of verb tense in fiction. In nonfictional discourse, we take sentences using past-tense verbs ("President Trump *nominated* Judge Gorsuch") to be pointing at events that actually occurred in the past. In reading fiction, in contrast, we do not take past-tense sentences to be "anchored" to actual past events; we know that the described events did not occur. Nevertheless, Ronen argues, we still associate past-tense verbs with actually occurring events, and fiction in English capitalizes on this association.[5] In fiction, that is, tense does not mark time as such; it marks modality—the status of events and entities as "actual" (within the fiction) or merely possible (cf. Doležel 2000).

Citation of precedent serves a similar anchoring function in the law-world. Most scholarly discussions of the judicial use of precedent consider the phenomenon in narrative terms, for example, as involving development from one state (establishment of the precedent) to another (its use in subsequent cases; e.g., Waldron 2012). The 2014-term practices discussed next suggest that although the legal treatment of precedent and original understandings does concern the past, that past is not precisely, or not only, the developmental past of historians or "chain novelists" (Dworkin 1986, 229). Lawyers and judges write about the past, and preexisting texts in particular, in two distinct ways, only one of which matches that description.[6]

6.2.2.1 Eternal precedent

In common-law systems, any reasoned judicial opinion may function as guidance in a subsequent dispute (e.g., Watford et al. 2017). Precedential opinions have some similarities to other forms of discursive legal authority, such as statutes and constitutional text.[7] Usually, a reference to precedent refers to the *language* of earlier reasoned, written opinions, which justices analyze and quote in ways that resemble their treatment of statutory and constitutional text (Schauer 1995; Tiersma 2013). According to legal convention, the source of a precedent and the nature of the issue decided determine how a subsequent court may discuss it. These conventions are like the rules of a game dictating how props may be used (Everett 2013; Watford et al. 2017). But a characteristic common to all precedent is that it should sometimes be applied even if the result of applying it seems less than ideal in a particular case. *Stare decisis* commands that what happened before should happen again, in part simply because it happened before.[8]

Although just about every U.S. judicial opinion makes some use of precedent, some opinions address precedent in more detail or with more ambivalence than others.[9] This section focuses on opinions in two 2014-term cases that prompted the justices to handle precedent in a relatively self-aware and complex way. In *Bank of America v. Caulkett*, a bankruptcy case, the Court unanimously followed a questionable precedent. In *Johnson*, examined in the last chapter, a majority nullified some of the Court's previous decisions while following another.

One way of anchoring a decision via precedent is to adopt a previous opinion's assignment of a particular meaning to a statutory term. Justice Thomas followed this approach in several 2014-term opinions, including his opinion for a unanimous Court in *Caulkett*.[10] This case turned on the statutory phrase "allowed secured claim"; specifically, it turned on whether a creditor's claim to a bankruptcy debtor's assets can count as "allowed" and "secured" when the collateral for the loan has zero value (as when the market value of a house is less than the balance on the loan secured by it). A different provision of the Bankruptcy Code defined "allowed secured claim" in a way suggesting that such a claim could not qualify. But, Justice Thomas notes, in a 1992 case, *Dewsnup v. Timm*, the Court had "already adopted a construction of the term "secured claim" in [the "allowed secured claim" provision]" (3).

Although *Dewsnup* addressed a different scenario—in which the value of the property in question was just less than its value at the time of the loan, not less than the loan value—Justice Thomas concludes in *Caulkett* that this detail is irrelevant. Since *Dewsnup* assigned meaning to the very phrase at issue in *Caulkett*, and did not qualify the assignment, *Dewsnup* controls; all the Court can do, according to Justice Thomas, is reiterate its own earlier conclusion.

In a footnote in his *Caulkett* opinion, Justice Thomas explains that *Dewsnup* had long "been the target of criticism" (5 n.†). Justices Kennedy, Breyer, and Sotomayor all withheld their agreement from this footnote; it was the only part of the opinion that did not receive unanimous approval. The abstaining justices' refusal to endorse the footnote is curious. Distinguishing *Dewsnup* or even overruling it would seem to be the more merciful result, since that course would have allowed the debtors in *Caulkett* to exclude the creditors' claims from their estates, reducing their obligations to the creditors. So the abstaining justices do not seem to have been objecting to the footnote's harsh implications. Perhaps they regarded the footnote as a kind of victim-blaming: the footnote might be taken to suggest that the Court would have considered overruling *Dewsnup* had the debtors only made a bolder argument. Another explanation for the justices' abstention, however, might be that they were discomfited by the incongruity between reliance on *Dewsnup* in the text of the opinion and the footnote's implicit projection of a possible future without the precedent.

Several of the opinions in *Johnson* (one of the "categorical approach" cases discussed in Chapter 5.2.1) supply further examples of the discursive pull of reiteration and the need to justify departures from it. Two kinds of precedent played a role in *Johnson*: the Court's 1990 opinion in *Taylor v. United States*, which held that courts should use the "categorical approach" in applying the residual clause; and four post-*Taylor* decisions in which the Court applied that approach to different circumstances. The three major opinions in *Johnson*, from Justices Scalia, Thomas, and Alito,[11] are distinguished by the different attitudes each justice takes toward these two classes of precedent.

Justice Scalia's majority opinion describes *Taylor* as "require[d]" by the residual clause (13) and does not question its authority. But Justice Scalia treats the four post-*Taylor* decisions, to which he objected when they were decided, as "evidence" of the "indeterminacy" of the clause (6, 7). Invalidating the residual clause only, Justice Scalia's opinion in *Johnson* does not explicitly overrule any of these decisions. But *Johnson* had the same effect as an overruling for all of the cases. It nullified the four post-*Taylor* decisions, and it made *Taylor* at least temporarily inoperative, since *Taylor* prescribed a method for applying the clause invalidated in *Johnson*. Justice Scalia's resolution of the case declines to recognize the authority of only the congressional product; formally, it leaves the Court's precedent untouched.

Both Justice Thomas and Justice Alito disagree with Justice Scalia's implicit elevation of precedent over statutory text (and indeed, Justice Scalia's approach does seem to be in tension with his usual reverence for congressionally produced language). Justice Thomas would not have invalidated the residual clause, leaving all five decisions "good law." Justice Alito would have abrogated *Taylor* and the four application decisions, leaving the statutory provision intact. But it is not quite the case that Justice Alito exhibits disregard for judicial precedent in *Johnson*. In explaining why the residual clause is not unconstitutionally vague, he draws on the Court's previous decisions as a source of factual premises that courts might use in applying the sentencing provision. In *Johnson*, he concludes that the lower court correctly applied the residual clause to Johnson because Johnson's prior conviction, for possession of a short-barreled shotgun, was clearly a conviction for a "violent felony": "As we recognized in *District of Columbia v. Heller* . . . (2008), sawed-off shotguns are 'not typically possessed by law-abiding citizens for lawful purposes.' Instead, they are uniquely attractive to violent criminals" (Alito, 17–18).

This use of precedent as a source of "fact" is not unique to Justice Alito or to this case. It has attracted critical notice from commentators (e.g., Faigman 2008; Larsen 2014) and does seem hard to justify on standard accounts of precedential reasoning. But understanding a judicial citation of precedent as a use of an anchoring "prop" can help to explain the practice. All invocations of precedent have the potential to serve an identical rhetorical function: anchoring the Court's current linguistic activity to a past-tense linguistic actuality. Whether that past linguistic act involved pronouncement of an official paraphrase of statutory language (as in *Caulkett*) or authoritative description of real-world regularities (as in Justice Alito's use of *Heller* in *Johnson*), that past act, in theory, bears the same relation to the invoking context—it is past and thus privileged.

6.2.2.2 *The weight of time and access to origins*

Although, in theory, all precedent is equally past and thus equally actual (and authoritative), advocates and judges in practice treat the age of precedent as meaningful. In particular, as suggested by the quotes from Justice Alito's *Kwai Fun Wong* opinion at the beginning of section 6.2, judges stress the age of the precedents they invoke when possible. If a practice or precedent can be described as observed "since time immemorial" (*Walker*, Alito, 10), this is a point in its favor. If a pre-Revolutionary pedigree can be identified for a practice, that is worth pointing out.[12] Anchoring a principle in Magna Carta is similarly desirable,[13] as is noting that a practice or precedent is more than a century old.[14] In these ways, by a peculiar reversal, legal discourse treats the distant past as more "actual"—more certain and powerful—than the more recent past.

But the "time immemorial" invocation of a continuous tradition is not always possible. When the authority at issue involved a deliberate break with the past, for example, a judge or justice may have no choice but to describe it as a break. The justices often use this technique in discussions of constitutional authority, characterizing the framing and ratification of the Constitution as a kind of positive historical rupture. In these references, the constitutional text functions as a prop in two ways at once. The text is the record of an originating performative utterance, an ur-intentional act, and at the same time, as that text comes before us today, it anchors us to past actuality. The justices allude to this double function of constitutional text when they "mindread" the framers in explicating constitutional language. This technique is used by virtually all of the justices; even those who express skepticism about probing lawmakers' intentions will describe what the framers and their contemporaries "understood,"[15] "sought,"[16] were responding to,[17] "knew" and "devised,"[18] "had in mind,"[19] and "believed."[20] This kind of rhetoric both relies on the association of pastness with (graded) actuality and bypasses the usual assumption that the past, if not repeated without change up to the present, is by definition not accessible to us.

Much originalist constitutional interpretation and argument depends on this apparent contradiction. But the technique of mindreading the framers is not limited to originalist opinions. Justice Ginsburg uses it, for instance, in her *Ariz. State Legislature* majority opinion. She concedes that voter-initiative processes did not exist in the eighteenth century but justifies her reading of the Elections Clause partly by reference to the framers' intentions regarding popular democracy:

> As this Court explained in *Arizona v. Inter Tribal Council of Ariz., Inc.*, 570 U.S. 1 (2013), the [Elections] Clause "was the Framers' insurance against the possibility that a State would refuse to provide for the election of representatives to the Federal Congress." *Id.*, at ___ (slip op., at 5) (citing The Federalist No. 59, pp. 362–363 (C. Rossiter ed. 1961) (A. Hamilton).
>
> (25)

In this passage, Justice Ginsburg makes a point about the purpose of the Elections Clause by quoting from a recent opinion (written by Justice Scalia), which in turn cited an eighteenth-century source. This entirely orthodox presentation of the point communicates a dense message about the relationship between time and authority. It demonstrates that she has gained access to information about the framers' objectives through the Court's previous acceptance of this access, via the edited written output of contemporaries such as Hamilton. Through nested citations like this, a judge who is more cautious about mindreading the framers can bootstrap him- or herself into access to the past. Justice Ginsburg's reasoning throughout her *Ariz. State Legislature* opinion takes a similar approach, describing a layering of incremental historical-political activity on top of the unchanging Constitution.

Part of Chief Justice Roberts's criticism of Justice Ginsburg's analysis in *Ariz. State Legislature* is that it is overly complex. Yet the Chief Justice's own argument is not exactly simple. His analysis, for example, stresses the significance of the ratification of the Seventeenth Amendment in 1913. That amendment changed the process for selection of federal senators; Chief Justice Roberts's reasoning depends on treating the amendment as both a component of the Constitution and a deliberate alteration of it. In this account, the Constitution's continued existence as a legal substrate justifies its control over Arizonans' efforts to change their districting system. That substrate originated in a rupturing event—a group-intentional act by the framers and ratifiers—but the continued normative force of the substrate is undisturbed by subsequent acts that might otherwise seem similar to the original event, such as amendment.

This conceptualization of the Constitution is at the heart of Chief Justice Roberts's argument in *Ariz. State Legislature* and, as the next section will explain, many other legal arguments. The layering of legal authority to reconcile otherwise disparate narratives and to jump from one time-scheme to another (from intentional-action narrative to timeless reiteration and back again, for example) is an indispensable part of lawyers' communicative and cognitive toolkit. Indeed, the layered accounts of U.S. law described in the next section might constitute the archetypal narrative form of U.S. legal discourse (cf. Gordon 2017, 139–44).

6.3 Embedding and stories of departure and return

Many commentators have observed that legal discourse in the U.S. is rife with hierarchies of all kinds. Most accounts of this phenomenon, however, associate it with authoritarianism and conservatism (e.g., Balkin 1986; Kennedy 1983). This critical perspective likens legal practices of hierarchical presentation—writers' embedding of levels of authority within one another in legal discourse—to other techniques of hierarchical presentation, such as algorithms, grids, and deductive proofs (e.g., Schlag 2002). This section, in contrast, argues that the experience of reading a legal argument or writing a legal analysis has just as much in common with the experience of reading or composing narrative, especially fictional narrative, as with these more mechanical manifestations of hierarchy, and that this experience does not have any particular inherent ideological implications.

Play, as discussed in Chapter 5.2.2, involves a kind of "embedding" of experience; when we play or make-believe, we interrupt the course of our experience to take a detour into a separate "envelope," from which we will at some point return to the previously interrupted course. Every narrative fiction builds on our capacity to experience such envelopes of separate experience. Many narrative fictions, both verbal and audiovisual, also replicate this structure of experience in embedded narratives or stories-within-stories (see also Doležel 2000; Ryan 1991). Structures of this kind embed one intentional-agency (beginning-middle-end) narrative within another.

Embedding and layering can also coordinate beginning-middle-end narratives with invocations of eternal reiteration. One of the premises of the analysis of literary narrative is the distinction between the "two levels of temporality" such narrative involves (Fludernik 2003, 117): that of the reading process (often called "discourse") and that of the events described ("story"). Narratologists study the ways these two levels may be aligned and pulled apart. As readers move through a narrative, a process that occurs over time, they may be shuttled "back" to earlier events (in flashbacks), or "forward" to later ones. These processes may involve deviating from the overall course of the narrative to follow an account of a significant past event, which the reader will experience as a story within the larger story but also as a retrospectively foundational event. A narrative may also inform readers about events that happened repeatedly *and indistinguishably* in the past; this form of narration is essential to building the "world" of the narrative, establishing basic premises for understanding subsequently narrated events (Sternberg 1979), and it is analogous to the legal use of precedent as an anchor. Understanding a narrative as composed of these two levels—overlaid discourse and underlying story—further presupposes a fixed, permanent sequence of events in the story that are accessed by the "telling" in a variety of ways. The layer of text directly encountered by the reader gives access to a "deeper" layer that the reader constructs in the course of reading; the reader processes that deeper layer as if it remained fixed.

The next two sections of this chapter explore how the 2014-term opinions consistently access a particular underlying "story" of mistaken departure from a set trajectory in order to justify judicial activity (sections 6.3.1 and 6.3.2). The section following (6.3.3) addresses some other contexts, aside from judicial accounts of legal development, in which legal discourse depends on readers' conceptualization of authority as intrinsically embedded.

6.3.1 The "disastrous misadventure" of twentieth-century legal development

Justice Thomas was by far the most prolific author of separate opinions during the 2014 term; he wrote separately in 30 cases.[21] In ten of these opinions, Justice Thomas presented pieces of a single underlying story of the development of U.S. law in the twentieth century. This section addresses this cluster of opinions and the multilayered account of legal history they present.

The ten opinions in question fall into four groups.

- Two describe the twentieth-century growth of "a vast and unaccountable administrative apparatus" (*Ass'n of American Railroads*, Thomas, 27) and, alongside it, the growth of "a doctrine of deference [to agency interpretations of regulations] that has taken on a life of its own" (*Perez*, Thomas, 3). A footnote in *Perez* identifies the beginning of these developments at the start of the twentieth century (19–20 n.6).
- A second set of opinions identifies the effects of these trends on antidiscrimination law. Justice Thomas's opinions in *Abercrombie & Fitch* and *Texas Dep't of Housing* identify the origin of disparate-impact theories of discrimination (see Chapter 3.2.2.2) in the 1960s EEOC.[22] His opinion in *Alabama Legislative Black Caucus* blames on the Department of Justice "the 'disastrous misadventure' of this Court's voting rights jurisprudence" (Thomas, 1, quoting *Holder v. Hall* (1994) (Thomas, J., concurring)).
- A third group of opinions traces a second path of misguided judicial development of various constitutional-law doctrines—including substantive due process and the dormant Commerce Clause—starting in the early twentieth century.[23]
- Most broadly, Justice Thomas characterizes all of these missteps as symptoms of disregard for the original understanding of the constitutional separation of federal powers. He develops this theme most fully in his dissent in *Wellness Int'l* (Thomas, 5–13) but touches on it in several opinions.[24]

The story underlying these opinions is not just a reiteration of the principle that original understandings of the Constitution should control. In fact, Justice Thomas sometimes expresses uncertainty about what those understandings were.[25] In these opinions, rather, Justice Thomas presents a full alternative account of twentieth-century legal development after a point, about a century ago, when a particular set of legal understandings was not yet lost to mainstream legal culture (see Gordon 2017).

In these opinions, Justice Thomas presents the original understanding of the separation of powers as controlling not simply because of its age, but also because that understanding concerns the logically most basic question of institutional authority structuring the system within which federal judges work. A similar inherently hierarchical understanding structures Justice Thomas's repeated but mostly gentle criticism, throughout his 2014-term opinions, of other judges' and justices' misreadings of precedent. In his dissent in *Perez*, for instance, Justice Thomas describes the origin of so-called *Seminole Rock* deference in a moment of sloppiness with respect to authority: "the Court announced [in *Bowles v. Seminole Rock & Sand Co.* (1945)]—without citation or explanation—that an administrative interpretation of an ambiguous regulation was entitled to 'controlling weight'" (Thomas, 2).[26]

Beneath all of these reminders lies a consistent story. Before the early twentieth century, Justice Thomas tells us, U.S. judges understood and applied the Constitution as it was supposed to be applied. Ideally, this state of affairs would have continued indefinitely. But under political pressure, or perhaps through simple slackening of discipline, previous justices lost touch with these practices. Their blundering moved legal development onto a kind of alternative timeline, in which judges began perpetuating their predecessors' mistakes under a possibly well-meaning collective delusion.[27] But we can correct this misguided detour from the practice of endless reiteration of the framers' values. The story implies a metaphysics structured according to the logic of embedding. We are in a false world we didn't realize we had entered, Justice Thomas's opinions say; we need to find our way back to the real world, the one where law is consistent with its governing principles.

While Justice Thomas is an unusually sophisticated and persistent exponent of this narrative, he is, of course, not its originator. Literary critic Catherine Gallagher (2018) has recently described narratives with this general structure as positing a contrast between "our timeline" and an "alternate timeline," and has shown some of their functions in military and political history and novelistic narrative since the eighteenth century. The particular counterfactual political narrative Justice Thomas invokes, presenting "our timeline" as a dystopian departure from original virtue, has the form of a classic jeremiad, "detail[ing] the consequences of the community's failure to stay true to [its] precedent, and promis[ing] a utopia if the community could return to its spiritual roots" (Lee 2014, 33). It is part of a long tradition in Western and U.S. political culture that gained adherents in the legal academy throughout the twentieth century (Sachs 2014; see also section 6.4.2).

Although narratives of "misadventure" are often coupled with conservative and authoritarian political positions, their appeal and utility extend more broadly. In fact, the standard legal foil to this account, a progressive narrative in which the Reconstruction Amendments, New Deal, and civil-rights movements are crucial positive developments, has a similar layered structure. The progressive story describes contemporary legal legitimacy as based on lawyers' and judges' working out of an eternal moral logic that earlier generations, including the framers, did or could not fully realize (Epps 2013; Gordon 2017, 139–44). Although the two accounts involve different views of the extent to which the law-world should remain insulated from cultural change, both rely on the same scripts of persistent principle, mistaken departure, and deliberate rectification, layered in an analogous way.

6.3.2 Stories of mistaken departure in Obergefell

Layering like this appears often in constitutional decisions. It also shows up in many non-constitutional arguments, as when justices accuse one another of misusing precedent[28] or describe enactment of a statute as initiating a regime of what should be consistent judicial reiteration of Congress's will.[29] The most spectacular 2014-term showcases for such narratives are the *Obergefell* opinions, which demonstrate the flexibility of the form and its paradigmatic role in accounts of legal continuity and change. Justice Kennedy's majority opinion in *Obergefell* describes the Court as deliberately realigning the law with natural rights. The dissenting opinions of Chief Justice Roberts and Justices Scalia, Thomas, and Alito lament the majority's thoughtless abandonment of an eternal order.

Justice Kennedy's opinion describes the natural principle in question as the "transcendent importance" of marriage to humans "[s]ince the dawn of history" (3). While this principle has endured, he explains, humans have occasionally set aside various aspects of the tradition, as by substituting companionate marriage for arranged marriages. These changes have not weakened the tradition; they have fortified it by allowing more people to participate in it. *Obergefell* did break with the legal past by repudiating precedent—overruling *Baker v. Nelson* (1971), in which the Court summarily rejected an equal-protection challenge to a state law limiting marriages to male-female unions. But Justice Kennedy presents this repudiation as a delayed realization of a state of harmony between legal rules and nonlegal expectations, an adjustment and correction of the law. In Justice Kennedy's account, the human experience of becoming or being part of a publicly recognized mated pair is the eternal principle, and positive law that interferes with the realization of that principle is the "misadventure."

To stress the importance of this state of harmony, Justice Kennedy's *Obergefell* opinion presents the petitioners' personal stories. These narratives describe the petitioners' lives as violently disrupted by a senseless legal stricture that compounds natural tragedy:

> Petitioner James Obergefell . . . met John Arthur over two decades ago. They fell in love and started a life together, establishing a lasting, committed relation. In 2011, however, Arthur was diagnosed with amyotrophic lateral sclerosis, or ALS. . . . Two years ago, Obergefell and Arthur decided to commit to one another, resolving to marry before Arthur died. To fulfill their mutual promise, they traveled from Ohio to Maryland, where same-sex marriage was legal. It was difficult for Arthur to move, and so the couple were wed inside a medical transport plane as it remained on the tarmac in Baltimore. Three months later, Arthur died. Ohio law does not permit Obergefell to be listed as the surviving spouse on Arthur's death certificate. By statute, they must remain strangers even in death, a state-imposed separation Obergefell deems "hurtful for the rest of time." . . . He suit to be shown as the surviving spouse on Arthur's death certificate.
>
> (4–5)[30]

The law keeps Obergefell from maintaining even a textual connection with Arthur via Arthur's death certificate. Obergefell's description of the effect of this bar ("hurtful for the rest of time") emphasizes the timelessness of the bond that the state has incomprehensibly denied.

The *Obergefell* dissenters respond to Justice Kennedy's narrative with two counter-narratives. One narrative focuses on an alternative nonlegal perspective, according to which *Obergefell* is a repudiation of natural principles. The dissents all emphasize not the variability of the institution of marriage but its previously exclusive heterosexuality, and the consistency of this practice with biological "law."

The other dissenting counter-narrative focuses on the legal rupture caused by Justice Kennedy's opinion. Chief Justice Roberts's elaborate identification of Justice Kennedy's analysis with the "discredited" tradition of *Lochner v. New York* (1905; Roberts, 10–15, 19, 20–21) is structurally akin to the "dangerous misadventure" narrative of Justice Thomas's separate opinions. Both stories suggest the folly of trying to coordinate law and legal rules with anything other than themselves (cf. Lee 2014). The classic critique of *Lochner* invoked by Chief Justice Roberts presents that 1905 decision as a misguided incorporation of flawed economic theory into legal doctrine, an error subsequent Courts painstakingly eliminated from the law (Greene 2016). Drawing on this centrist narrative of twentieth-century U.S. legal development, the Chief Justice responds to Justice Kennedy's story of personal ruptures with an equally intricate but more abstract counter-narrative of doctrinal rupture (Schachter 2016).

Justices Alito, Thomas, and Scalia likewise focus in their respective *Obergefell* dissents on the majority's disruption of legal continuity. Justice Thomas, as in the opinions considered in the previous section, describes the Court's recent due process decisions as out of harmony with original understandings of due process. Justice Scalia attacks the language of Justice Kennedy's opinion, describing it as full of "mummeries and straining-to-be-memorable passages" (Scalia, 4). This criticism is not just criticism of the form of Justice Kennedy's opinion. The *Obergefell* dissenting justices all describe Justice Kenendy's prose and citation practices as irregular to support the dissenters' characterization of the majority opinion as non-legal.

Despite the vehemence of the disagreement in *Obergefell*, there are surprising continuities across the opinions. All present judges' intentional intervention as only occasionally necessary to correct departures from a norm of stability. Justice Kennedy describes the desired stability as resulting from lawyers' and judges' perceptive alignment of legal rules and outcomes with nonlegal expectations. This account necessarily and more or less openly acknowledges the authority of nonlegal expectations. Ideologically and culturally conservative legal narratives of rupture, in contrast, at least in their contemporary form, tend more often to present eternal reiteration of relatively specific legal principles as the desired form of stability. These narratives consider nonlegal expectations more selectively and tend to deny continuities between legal discourse and nonlegal reading and writing practices, while at the same time often asserting a desire for legal simplicity. Such a narrative presupposes a less widely shared, and thus in a sense a less real, "law world."

6.3.3 Lawyering in layers

The narratives just discussed depend on a layered temporality characteristic of legal discourse. In this temporality, one deeper or governing narrative is interrupted by another more superficial or qualified one; that secondary narrative may in turn be interrupted by another. This layered mode of thinking and explanation has a hierarchical structure, in that some layers of the form are prior to and encompass others, but it is dynamic, not a simple materialization of authoritarianism (Douglas 1970; Kennedy 1983; Schlag 2002). As the *Obergefell* opinions suggest, judges can use this form to present an account of legal development that supports progressive as well as conservative conclusions (cf. Levine 2015). Indeed, seeing these hierarchized habits as moves characteristic of the law game, rules for using the verbal and textual props of that game, might help both practitioners and critics avoid exporting the hierarchies inappropriately outside the game.

These layering habits pervade legal discourse; they appear everywhere, from the most sweeping accounts of legal development over time (as discussed in the previous sections) to the most minute and concrete signals of legal discourse, such as citations. As an example, consider this excerpt from Chief Justice Roberts's *Obergefell* opinion, which he offers to support the point that Justice Kennedy's majority analysis departs unacceptably from legal tradition:

> Although the Court articulated the importance of history and tradition to the fundamental rights inquiry most precisely in [*Washington v.*] *Glucksberg* [(1997)], many

> other cases both before and since have adopted this same approach. See, *e.g.*, *District Attorney's Office for Third Judicial Dist. v. Osborne*, 557 U.S. 52, 72 (2009); *Flores*, 507 U.S., at 303; *United States v. Salerno*, 481 U.S. 739, 751 (1987); *Moore v. East Cleveland*, 431 U.S. 494, 503 (1977) (plurality opinion); see also *id.*, at 544 (White, J., dissenting) ("The Judiciary, including this Court, is the most vulnerable and comes nearest to illegitimacy when it deals with judge-made constitutional law having little or no cognizable roots in the language or even the design of the Constitution."); *Troxel v. Granville*, 530 U.S. 57, 96–101 (2000) (KENNEDY, J., dissenting) (consulting '"[o]ur Nation's history, legal traditions, and practices"' and concluding that "[w]e owe it to the Nation's domestic relations legal structure . . . to proceed with caution" (quoting *Glucksberg*, 521 U.S., at 721)).
>
> (Roberts, 14)

The string citation that fills most of the passage formally reiterates the point Chief Justice Roberts makes in the first, substantive, sentence: *Glucksberg* requires a judge to find that a right is "objectively, deeply rooted in this Nation's history and tradition," and state recognition of same-sex marriage cannot be characterized this way. To emphasize the validity of *Glucksberg* (a relatively recent precedent), and at the same time show what it requires, the Chief Justice offers the string citation, which demonstrates that the idea behind the standard is itself "deeply rooted" in the Court's "traditions." The final element in the citation shows, further, that Justice Kennedy himself has endorsed the principle. The attentive legal reader processes this parenthetical as accusing Justice Kennedy of inconsistency: in *Obergefell*, he broke with his past practice, which was consistent with the practice of the institution. The passage presents the *Obergefell* majority opinion not only as faithless to the Court's precedent but also as the product of an author untrue to his own past judicial self, and it conveys the latter message entirely through a citation.[31]

Citation and quotations can suggest a justice's position even more minimally. Here is an example from Justice Sotomayor's majority opinion in *Wellness Int'l*, a case concerning the constitutionality of a bankruptcy judge's decision of certain issues:

> Because "the entire process [of a magistrate judge's consideration of a case] takes place under the district court's total control and jurisdiction," there is no danger that use of the magistrate involves a "congressional attemp[t] to 'transfer jurisdiction [to non–Article III tribunals] for the purpose of emasculating" constitutional courts."' *Id.*, at 937 (citations omitted; alteration in original).
>
> (11)

This passage both describes and physically reproduces a point about institutional layering: the fact that a magistrate judge, like a bankruptcy judge, operates "under the district court's total control." The sentence presents this point by means of a triply embedded quotation. The entire sentence is a quotation (from *Peretz v. United States* (1991)). In its original context, it included one quotation from *United States v. Raddatz* (1980) (the first internal quotation, "the entire process . . .") and another from *Commodity Futures Trading Commission v. Schor* (1986) (the "Congressional attemp[t] . . ." part). The *Schor* passage in turn quoted a concurring opinion from Justice Vinson in *National Insurance Co. v. Tidewater Co.* (1949) (the "transfer jurisdiction . . ." part). Solely through quotation marks, Justice Sotomayor in this passage communicates the reiteration of her point over time (albeit in fragments) and thus also the consistency of her conclusion with precedent.

By omitting the citations, she is able to smooth over the disruption implied by Justice Stevens's stitching together of quotations in *Peretz* and by the use of language from a concurring opinion at the heart of a sequence of majority opinions. The quotation marks signify a temporal embedding. The omission of attributions levels that embedding out into a display of timeless reiteration.

Perceiving the latent presence of these two temporal or narrative orders—timeless consistency and action for reasons—in every scrap of language and act of articulation is part of a skilled lawyer's moment-to-moment practice. Although it is rarely brought to consciousness, it is a basic structural regularity within the U.S. law world, a master rule for handling texts as props. Using and reconfiguring these potentialities in new arguments is playing the law game. The Court's opinions are particularly visible and skilled demonstrations of this phenomenon, but they are by no means unique, as the next section will show.

6.4 Apotheosis of the wordsmith

> In our layered system of trial and appellate courts everyone's assured at least two chances to air a grievance. . . . No doubt our complex and consuming litigation wringer has assumed the shape it has so courts might squeeze as much truth as possible out of the parties' competing narratives. But sooner or later every case must come to an end. After all, that's why people bring their disputes to court in the first place: because the legal system promises to resolve their differences without resort to violence and supply "peace and repose" at the end of it all. . . . For a legal system to meet this promise, of course, both sides must accept—or, if need be, they must be made to respect—the judgments it generates.
>
> (Judge Neil M. Gorsuch, *Ute Indian Tribe of the Uintah & Duray Reservation v. Utah* (10th Cir., June 16, 2015), opening paragraph)

A little less than two years after issuing the opinion containing the passage above, Neil M. Gorsuch became the 113th Associate Justice of the Supreme Court, replacing Justice Scalia, who passed away in February 2016. Commentators were quick to liken the two as talented writers and methodological compatriots (e.g., Palazzolo 2017; Ponnuru 2017). As the passage above suggest, then-Judge Gorsuch's writing style is unorthodox in some ways—in his use of contractions like "that's," for example—but it is entirely consistent with the patterns this book has identified within the justices' writing in many others. Recalling Cover's account of jurispathy, in this passage Judge Gorsuch describes the U.S. legal system as made to call an end to parties' presentation of their "competing narratives." The passage displays Judge Gorsuch's awareness of the system's (and the judge's) role in selecting one of those narratives to prevail and about the gap that may remain between the facts found in a legal dispute and the truth in a more absolute sense; in these senses it articulates what Mertz might call a metalinguistic ideology.

As the following two sections will discuss, this passage is not unusual in its echoing of the themes traced throughout this book. Despite the iconoclasm of then-Judge Gorsuch's style, the 15 published opinions[32] he issued during the period covered by this book—from October 2014 to June 2015—are consistent with the analyses presented in the previous pages. Indeed, some of his opinions take these techniques closer to their logical conclusions than do any of the justices' 2014-term opinions. Justice Gorsuch is a master wordsmith, and his judicial writing shows us what happens when a judge or lawyer's confidence about his or her command over language becomes the practitioner's guiding principle. The next section (6.4.1) briefly surveys Judge Gorsuch's reputation and his opinions from the period; the section following (6.4.2) takes a closer look at two illustrative opinions.

6.4.1 *The "inner grammarian"*[33]

Over the same months during which the Supreme Court issued the opinions discussed throughout this book, then-Judge Gorsuch authored opinions or orders in 48 cases. Thirty-three of these opinions were unpublished; the opinions in another 15 were designated for publication. The latter all bear out Judge Gorsuch's reputation as a thoughtful writer. They depart from orthodoxy in several ways; for example, few follow the standard Roman-numeral-headed section structuring that the justices and Judge Gorsuch's Tenth Circuit colleagues all use (cf. Aldisert 2012). In one case, Judge Gorsuch took the unusual step of writing a separate concurrence to his own controlling opinion for a three-judge panel (*Browder v. City of Albuquerque*).[34] His prose does seem to strive for accessibility and clarity, sometimes to a fault (see Kindy et al. 2017; Whiting 2018). His sentences tend to be short and relatively grammatically simple.

Judge Gorsuch's published opinions from this period also use virtually all of the techniques considered throughout this book. Judge Gorsuch's plain-speaking voice uses down-home language but also often contrasts approved conduct and conclusions with more fanciful positions. In the first published opinion from this period, explaining why the appellate panel could not itself resentence a criminal defendant, he writes, "it is impossible to know for certain what would have happened in a but-for world absent the error [in calculating the defendant's sentence] the government invited" (*Sabillon-Umana*, 1335). Judge Gorsuch's opinion in *United States v. Herrera*, from April 2015, similarly reprimands a trial-court judge for sloppiness in recording its factual findings (575). In the legal universe these opinions describe, facts and findings of fact are the foundation of judicial activity.

Judge Gorsuch also seems comfortable both mindreading individual actors and strategically professing mindblindness.[35] Here, for example, is the opening paragraph of his opinion in a case involving a criminal defendant's Fourth Amendment challenge to the police search that led to the discovery of firearms in his home:

> Steven Denson [the defendant] was on the lam. After his conviction for armed robbery and a spell in prison he quit reporting to his probation officer as his sentence required. For a time, Mr. Denson appeared gone for good. But authorities weren't quick to give up their search and eventually they found his name on a residential Wichita utility account. With an arrest warrant in hand they showed up at the listed address. When a handheld Doppler radar device and other evidence suggested Mr. Denson might be present inside the house, the officers entered. Quickly they found Mr. Denson along with a stash of guns, guns he lacked the right to possess by virtue of his felony conviction.
>
> (*United States v. Denson*, 1216)

Although the first sentence of the passage seems to be looking over the defendant's shoulder, the next sentence initiates a series of descriptions of the mysterious absence of "Mr. Denson." Reminiscent of the account of authorities' well-meaning perplexity offered by Justice Alito in *Sheehan* (Chapter 3.3.3), this passage also resembles many other judicial uses of mindblindness in opinions that ultimately reject civilian challenges to government action, such as *Glossip*.

Judge Gorsuch's opinions from the period display the same variety of positions on the feasibility of group intentionality found in the Court's 2014-term opinions. Like the justices, Judge Gorsuch seems comfortable attributing plans, wishes, and even emotions to groups ranging from the officers in *Denson*[36] and quasi-governmental actors like the Financial Industry Regulatory Agency[37] to state legislatures,[38] the federal Congress,[39] and the framers.[40] On the other hand, while he is not as doctrinaire a textualist as Justice Scalia,[41] Judge Gorsuch does subscribe to the Radin-style critique of legislative consciousness so often cited by textualists.[42] And Judge Gorsuch seems to have seen Justice Scalia as a fellow traveler. In a 2016 lecture on Justice Scalia's legacy delivered at the Case Western Reserve University law school, Judge Gorsuch applauded his predecessor's influence. Discussing the "first opinion the Supreme Court issued after Justice Scalia's passing," *Lockhart v. United States*, Judge Gorsuch commends both Justice Sotomayor, author of the majority opinion, and Justice Kagan, dissenting, for focusing their disagreement not on "views of optimal social policy or what the statute 'should be,'" but on "grammar, language, and statutory structure and on what a reasonable reader in the past would have taken the statute to mean—on 'what the words on the paper say'" (Gorsuch 2016, 907–08). The next section will return to the question of the significance of the trend described by Justice Gorsuch in this lecture.

Judge Gorsuch's opinions also use the kinds of modal discourse and layering explored in Chapters 5 and 6. He sometimes casually dismisses speculative talk[43] but is also willing to acknowledge that the application of a doctrinal test may require the exercise of judicial imagination in the interest of jurispathy.[44] And he often describes imagined alternative courses of action—by parties, by judges, by legislatures, and by future appellate panels of his own court.[45]

The most striking acknowledgment of alternatives in Judge Gorsuch's opinions from this period is his concurrence in *Browder v. City of Albuquerque*, a case in which he also wrote the majority opinion. Majority Judge Gorsuch presents a straightforward analysis of the main issue in the case: individuals' substantive due process right not to be injured by a recklessly driving off-duty police officer (*Browder*, 1078–83). But in both the majority opinion and the concurrence, Judge Gorsuch reprimands the officer defendant for failing to argue that the federal court should have abstained from deciding the case, letting state courts address the officer's state-law tort liability before addressing any federal constitutional issue (e.g., *Browder*, 1079, 1081, 1084–85). This concurrence is explicitly seed-planting: it recommends a course of action to future constitutional-tort defendants (advised to make arguments like this) and future judges (encouraged to accept them). It is also explicitly jurispathic; Judge Gorsuch is offering instructions for preventing a certain class of lawsuit (cf. Kindy et al. 2017).[46]

The instructional tone of this concurrence pervades Judge Gorsuch's opinions from this period. Several rebuke judges or parties for inattention to "the normal course of events" (*Sabillon-Umana*, 1330) or "the normal order of things" (*Cook*, 1093).[47] Judge Gorsuch often criticizes parties, lawyers, lower-court judges, and sometimes his Tenth Circuit colleagues for inattentive reading and/or writing. *United States v. Herrera*, decided in April 2015, is a good example. This appeal concerned whether a district court judge properly refused a criminal defendant's request for an evidentiary hearing; the defendant wanted to show at the hearing that a police affidavit used to get a warrant leading to the defendant's arrest contained false statements from a confidential informant. Judge Gorsuch explains the district court judge's improper parsing of the warrant as follows:

> whether we're talking about acts or omissions the judge's job [in determining the need for an evidentiary hearing in a situation of this kind] is much the same—we must ask whether a warrant would have issued in a but-for world where the attesting officer faithfully represented the facts. . . .
>
> The district court did not follow this order of operations. It didn't ask whether an affidavit corrected for the . . . mistaken impressions it identified would still contain probable cause to support a search warrant. Instead, the district court proceeded to disregard virtually everything the confidential informant said that was included in the warrant application. . . . The district court's chosen course seems to rest on the implicit premise that once any statement of a speaker is found to be false then all of the speaker's other statements must be disregarded. Sometimes . . . this is a fair conclusion. . . . But often people prove reliable truth tellers in some areas even when they are not in some others. And in this case we have little reason to think the confidential informant falls into the first category rather than the second. Indeed, the district court itself never issued a factual finding that the confidential informant was generally untrustworthy—let alone a factual finding that the attesting officer was recklessly indifferent to that possibility.
>
> (*Herrera*, 575)

According to this passage, properly reading the warrant application would have involved several steps: first, identification of non-credible content, then the recording of that identification (and the reasons for it) in a finding, followed by reconsideration of the application with that content "masked." The first and third steps both involve imaginative work: to identify non-credible content, the judge must keep in mind that informants might lie only part of the time and try to "mindread" the informant to detect untruths. Then the judge should adopt the perspective of the official responsible for reviewing the warrant application and ask how that person would have treated the "cleaned-up" application.

The intricacy of this prescription is typical of Judge Gorsuch's opinions from this period. These opinions consistently suggest that litigants' and judges' first and most important task is to be exceptionally disciplined and sensitive readers. Of nearly equal importance, however, is the ability to sequence the resulting conclusions in the appropriate way: to layer readings properly in writing. The next section takes a closer look at two cases from this period in which these concerns structure Judge Gorsuch's analyses.

6.4.2 *Breaking it down*

Judge Gorsuch's instructional opinions often present their subject matter explicitly in terms of layers of meaning. His opinions skillfully regiment precedent, argument, and description into the kinds of strata addressed in section 6.3. This section considers two opinions from this period—*Cook v. Rockwell Int'l Corp.* and *United States v. Rentz*—in which Judge Gorsuch's reasoning appears to be driven by this logic to the exclusion of other potentially relevant considerations.

Cook involved a question of federal statutory preemption of state law.[48] In his opinion, Judge Gorsuch seems to conceptualize this issue in layered terms: state law preexists federal law and applies consistently until the federal Congress decides to create law potentially applying to some of the same actors and conduct. Even after Congress acts, however, "normal state law principles continue to govern unless they conflict with the rules found in" federal law (*Cook*, 1093). Such a conflict gets resolved by preemption.

In *Cook*, Judge Gorsuch coordinates this layered conceptualization of the legal authority at issue with a second set of case-specific layered actions. *Cook* was prompted by the discovery of environmental contamination around a nuclear weapons production facility near Denver. Neighboring landowners sued the facility operators for the damage to their land under state law and the federal Price-Anderson Act (PAA), which limits liability for claims arising from "nuclear incident[s]" (*Cook*, 1090). After a jury verdict in the plaintiffs' favor, the defendants appealed, presenting an argument that Judge Gorsuch describes as, in retrospect, short-sighted: they argued that the judge improperly instructed the jury that they could find the contamination in question to be a "nuclear incident" (1090–91). This strategy was short-sighted because it would have been in the defendants' interest to have the liability-limiting PAA apply. On that first appeal, however, a Tenth Circuit panel accepted the defendants' argument and held that the instructions were too permissive.[49]

In Judge Gorsuch's account, on remand after this decision, the parties disagreed about what was left of the original jury verdict. The plaintiffs argued that their federal claim should "fall away, leaving background state tort law to operate" and that "everything needed for a judgment on the state law nuisance claim already existed[,]" since their complaint had also "sought relief under Colorado nuisance law" (1091). The defendants argued that this nuisance claim was preempted by the PAA and, in the alternative, that the Tenth Circuit's earlier order vacated the entire trial-court verdict and judgment, annihilating the verdict on the plaintiffs' nuisance claim as well as their PAA claim.

Judge Gorsuch rejects these arguments as improper readings of the legal context, on the one hand, and the previous appellate panel's decision, on the other. He rejects the defendants' preemption argument as a "narrative[]" that is "maybe [not] . . . metaphysically impossible," but "more than a little incongruous," particularly compared with the plaintiffs' more "familiar" take on the preemptive scope of the PAA (1094). That more familiar take is the layered narrative described above, according to which state law remains in force in the absence of a conflict with federal law. Justice Gorsuch describes the case-specific narrative in *Cook*—the question of the effect of the earlier Tenth Circuit mandate—as identical in structure. The first panel's order decided only issues related to the PAA claim, he explains, leaving the plaintiffs' state-law nuisance claim, and the verdict on that claim, untouched. As to both the preemption issue and the procedural issue, Judge Gorsuch describes a preexisting regime (state law, the plaintiff's case) as minimally disrupted by the action of a "superior" body (Congress, the first Tenth Circuit panel). Notwithstanding its folksy tone, Judge Gorsuch's *Cook* opinion is oddly rigid in its insistence on the almost surgical precision of the earlier panel's intervention in the case. Recalling his reprimand of the district court for its faulty reading in *Herrera*, passages of this opinion are explicit reading lessons.

Judge Gorsuch's tendency to present his conclusions as blindingly self-evident, at least once he has broken them down, might be clearest in *United States v. Rentz*, an en banc decision from February 2015. The case arose from the prosecution of Philbert Rentz, who wounded one person and killed a second with one gunshot. Prosecutors charged Rentz with two counts of violating 18 U.S.C. § 924(c), a federal statute that imposes a mandatory five-year sentence on "any person who, during and in relation to any crime of violence or drug trafficking crime . . . uses or carries a firearm" (*Rentz*, 1106). Much used by prosecutors, this provision has led to many linguistic and even metaphysical debates (Nourse 2016; Slocum 2016).

Rentz moved to dismiss one of the charges against him, arguing that he committed only one violation of the statute, since he used his gun only once on the occasion in question. The district court agreed, and the government appealed. A Tenth Circuit panel reversed, and Rentz requested en banc rehearing. In an opinion for six of the 11 circuit judges,[50] Judge Gorsuch identifies the issue for decision as the determination of the "statute's unit of prosecution— . . . asking what [is] the minimum amount of activity a defendant must undertake . . . to commit each new and independent violation of a federal statute" (1109). Judge Gorsuch approaches this task as a matter of grammatical analysis. "[T]he feature [of § 924(c)] that draws our immediate attention," he begins, "is the statute's verb" (1109). "This comes as no surprise," he continues, "as the verb supplies the action or doing part of any sentence, statutory or otherwise" (1109). He continues the analysis for several more paragraphs:

> in § 924(c)(1)(A) we find three relevant verbs: uses, carries, and possesses. This alone supplies some evidence that each § 924(c)(1)(A) charge must involve an independent act of using, carrying, or possessing. After all, if a law's verb says it's a crime to *kill* someone, we usually think a defendant must *kill* more than one person to be guilty of more than one offense. . . .
>
> Another linguistic clue points in the same direction. Section 924(c)(1)(A) doesn't prohibit using or carrying or possessing a gun in isolation. . . . Instead, the statute prohibits using or carrying a gun *during and in relation to any crime of violence or drug trafficking crime*. . . . These adverbial prepositional phrases modify the verbs uses, carries, and possesses [sic]. . . . They tell us *which* acts of using, carrying, or possessing Congress sought to punish—explaining that the statute doesn't seek to make illegal all such acts, only the narrower subset the phrases specify. Simplified somewhat, the language looks like this:

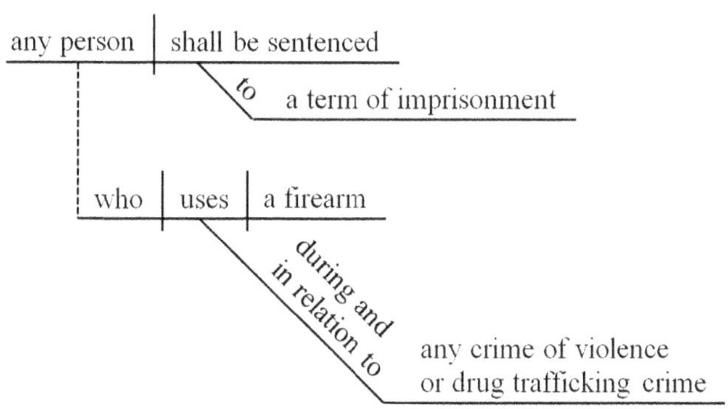

(*Rentz*, 1109–10)

This diagram stands in for argument, much like the language-usage hypotheticals discussed in Chapter 5.3.3.1, a technique Judge Gorsuch also uses in *Rentz*. And like Judge Gorsuch's approach to conceptualizing preemption, the grammatical diagram encourages readers to understand the statutory language as layered. The prepositional phrases and relative clause are subordinate to the words they modify ("person," "uses," and "shall be sentenced"); they mark deliberate sub-choices about the reach of different components of the statute. Having presented the statute's language in this arresting, abstract way, Judge

Gorsuch does not consider the specific reasons drafters or legislators might have made these choices.

Here and throughout his opinions from this period,[51] Judge Gorsuch offers simple explanations as desirable because of their simplicity alone. He encourages his readers to focus on his distillations of a complex and exasperating reality into a clean and often entertaining verbal (or visual) resolution. He does not encourage readers, litigators, or other judges to look beyond the explanation he provides; his readers' direct encounters with written products supply all they need to judge or litigate successfully. In his memorial lecture celebrating Justice Scalia, Judge Gorsuch made clear the centrality of this approach to his judicial philosophy:

> when judges pull from the same narrow toolbox and look to the same materials to answer the same narrow question—what might a reasonable person have thought the law was at the time—we confine the range of possible outcomes and provide a remarkably stable and predictable set of rules people are able to follow. . . . Truly the system is a wonder and it is little wonder [sic] so many throughout the world seek to emulate it.
>
> . . . At the end of the day, we may not be able to claim confidence that there's a certain and single right answer to every legal case, but there's no reason why we cannot make our best judgment depending on (and only on) conventional legal materials, relying on a sort of closed record if you will, without peeking to outside evidence.
>
> (Gorsuch 2016, 917)[52]

Rhapsodist of the law-world as a clean and closed universe, now-Justice Gorsuch can be expected to disseminate similar sentiments to an ever-wider audience of lawyers and lawyers-in-training.[53]

6.5 Off the page

> [A] mandate isn't governed by what's in someone's head; it's governed by what's on the page.
>
> (Judge Neil M. Gorsuch, *Cook v. Rockwell Int'l Corp* (10th Cir. June 23, 2015), 1104 n.7)

The stripped-down, language-focused style of judging that then-Judge Gorsuch so stirringly celebrated in his 2016 lecture is, of course, often associated with Justice Scalia, who is widely credited with having transformed Supreme Court jurisprudence and, accordingly, U.S. jurisprudence as well.[54] From the 1980s forward, this transformation refocused lawyers' and judges' attention on text—the words on the pages of the U.S. Code Annotated, the U.S. Reports, and lawyers' briefs, or on the screen in a legal database—and away from other concerns. Even those who have resisted the shift have been affected by its promotion of simplicity, tangibility, and objectivity, and by its rejection of the speculative, the personal, and the complex. As these values become entrenched, some key aspects of lawyers' activity slip out of sight. These are the aspects that are most characteristically legal—that constitute legal discursive behavior, the "law world"—and yet they also draw on and reconfigure skills almost all humans have and use.

Over the same period, outside the law world, U.S. culture has seemed to fragment into multiple spheres in which the lived experiences of individuals have taken on ever greater cultural significance and at the same time become less mutually comprehensible. In these spheres, individuals' rights to speak their own truths and find their own *nomoi* have been amplified by electronic publication. The ready accessibility of information has, for many, eliminated the need for institutional arbiters of truth, gatekeepers of information, or experts on matters of language and meaning. Over the period during which this book has been written, these trends have seemed to accelerate and to become more pronounced. The election and administration of Donald Trump have disrupted understandings of the status of the United States as a polity. It no longer seems possible to identify any dominant public sphere in the U.S. Instead, the country has come to resemble a swarm of parallel universes inhabited by populations who accept different truths, embrace different values, and envision different and incompatible futures.

Whether or not this is a desirable social state, it poses obvious challenges for legal institutions. While it persists, the allure of a "clean" law world like that of now-Justice Gorsuch is likely only to increase. The aim of this book has been to show that, notwithstanding the compelling simplifying rhetoric of many judges and justices, what is "on the page" is far from simple or self-evident, and that perceiving it as a refuge from an overly complex world is a tempting but ultimately counterproductive mistake. The wordsmith's fallacy builds on the doubled relationship lawyers are trained to develop with language, which becomes both a method of coordination and, at the same time, a flexible tool of simplification. The fallacy is the conviction that this doubled relationship amounts to complete mastery of the tool, a form of hubris that encourages the reductive approach to lawyering exemplified by crude textualism, as expressed in the sentence from Judge Gorsuch's *Cook* opinion that forms the epigraph to this section. In its current form, even lawyers' double vision does not see everything that is on the page, much less everything that is in people's heads.

As understandings of language and its use and comprehension continue to develop in other fields, those who work in such fields have a duty to impart their insights to lawyers and judges. Lawyers, judges, and law professors in turn have a duty to seek out such understandings and incorporate them into their practice. It is very difficult, if not impossible, to determine what a "reasonable reader" would take particular language to mean without an understanding of how reading experiences do and do not vary from person to person, but lawyers and legal scholars do not seem to have been interested in pursuing that inquiry. Likewise, it is impossible to understand a reader's experience in encounters with language without considering what is "in" that reader's head. We worry about what is on the page only because it affects what is in the head. We know about what is in others' heads in part because what is on the page can have meaning to us.

Notes

1 See *Kwai Fun Wong*, Alito, 3, 11; *Kerry v. Din*, Breyer, 5–6; *Gelboim*, 7–8 (Ginsburg); *Reyes Mata*, 2, 5 (Kagan); *Kwai Fun Wong*, 5–7, 11–12 (Kagan); *Commil*, 11 (Kennedy); *Jennings*, 4 (Scalia); *Glossip*, Sotomayor, 22.

2 See *Carter*, 2 (Alito); *Coleman*, 1, 5, 6 (Breyer); *Tibble*, 1 (Breyer); *Mach Mining*, 1, 5–6, 7, 10 (Kagan); *Bullard*, 1, 5 (Roberts); *Perez*, 2 (Sotomayor); *T-Mobile South*, 11 n.4 (Sotomayor); *Direct Marketing Ass'n*, 5–8 (Thomas); *Integrity Staffing*, 2–6 (Thomas); *Jesinoski*, 2–3 (Thomas).

3 Besides *Rodriguez*, discussed in the text, these were *Carroll* (per curiam); *Grady* (per curiam); *Heien*; *Kingsley*; *Patel*; *Sheehan*; and *Taylor v. Barkes* (per curiam).

4 Justice Alito used similar techniques in several other 2014-term opinions (see Chapter 3.3.3). This passage also expresses the kind of ambivalence about the role performance of public servants discussed in Chapter 4.5.

5 English does not have a special tense for written accounts of activity as do, for example, French and German.

6 This same logic appears in other modes of legal treatment of authority; justices invoke similar assumptions in statutory explication (*MacLean*, 4–5 n.* (Roberts)) and discussions of statutory amendment (e.g., *Whitfield*, 2 (Scalia)).
7 Judges and justices also refer to practices other than reasoned judicial opinions as "precedent"; see, e.g., *Zivotofsky*, 14 (Kennedy).
8 See *B&B Hardware*, Thomas, 7 n.4; *M&G Polymer*, 9–10.
9 Commentators often discuss the extension of precedent as a kind of analogical reasoning (e.g., Waldron 2012). That perspective neglects the weight ascribed to precedent on the basis of its pastness alone. For 2014-term opinions addressing extension of precedent, see *Wynne*, 5–6 (Alito); *Walker*, 6–7 (Breyer); *Yates*, 8 (Ginsburg); *Obergefell*, 11–23 (Kennedy); *Texas Dep't of Housing*, 10 (Kennedy); *Heien*, 7–8 (Roberts); *Teva*, Thomas, 8. For opinions rejecting arguments based on previous consideration of the same argument, see *Glossip*, 17 (Alito); *Holt*, 14 (Alito); *Texas Dep't of Housing*, Alito, 14, 15; *Alabama Dep't of Revenue*, 7 (Scalia); *Williams-Yulee*, Scalia, 6; *Patel*, 16 (Sotomayor).
10 See also his opinions in *Integrity Staffing* (5) and *Baker Botts* (7).
11 Justice Kennedy wrote a one-page concurrence that would have vacated Johnson's enhanced sentence without invalidating the residual clause.
12 See *B&B Hardware*, Thomas, 6 n.2; *Armstrong*, 6 (Scalia).
13 See *Kerry v. Din*, 4 (Scalia); *Horne*, 5 (Roberts); *Williams-Yulee*, 9 (Roberts); *Obergefell*, Thomas, 4, 5.
14 See *Elonis*, Thomas, 14; *Davis v. Ayala*, Kennedy, 2; *Patel*, Alito, 1.
15 *Wellness Int'l*, Thomas, 10; *Zivotofsky*, Kennedy, 9; *Zivotofsky*, Thomas, 2, 6, 9.
16 *Kansas v. Nebraska*, 9 n.5 (Kagan), quoting *Cuyler v. Adams* (1981).
17 *Wynne*, 5 (Alito).
18 *Wellness Int'l*, Roberts, 9.
19 *Ariz. State Legislature*, Scalia, 1.
20 *Zivotofsky*, Scalia, 19.
21 Justice Thomas's count (11 concurrences, 19 dissents), was rivaled only by those of Justice Alito (9 concurrences, 13 dissents) and Justice Scalia (4 concurrences, 15 dissents). Justice Thomas's separate opinions were (dissenting unless otherwise noted) in *Abercrombie & Fitch* (concurring in part, dissenting in part); *Alabama Dep't of Revenue*; *Alabama Legis. Black Caucus*; *Ariz. State Legislature*; *Ass'n of American Railroads* (concurring in judgment); *B&B Hardware*; *Brumfield*; *Clark* (concurring in judgment); *Dart Cherokee*; *Davis v. Ayala* (concurring); *Elonis*; *Glossip* (concurring); *Horne* (concurring); *Jennings*; *Johnson* (concurring in judgment); *Kansas v. Nebraska* (concurring in part); *Mellouli*; *Michigan v. EPA* (concurring); *Obergefell*; *Omnicare* (concurring in judgment); *ONEOK* (concurring in judgment); *Perez* (concurring in judgment); *Reyes Mata*; *Rodriguez*; *T-Mobile South*; *Teva*; *Texas Dep't of Housing*; *Wellness Int'l*; *Wynne*; and *Zivotofsky* (concurring in part).
22 See *Abercrombie & Fitch*, 6, 8 n.*; *Texas Dep't of Housing*, Thomas, 1, 10. Justice Thomas was Chairman of the EEOC from 1982 to 1990.
23 Justice Thomas addresses substantive due process doctrine in his dissents in *Obergefell*, Thomas, 7–13, and *Johnson*, Thomas, 12–16. He addresses the doctrine of vagueness in *Johnson*, Thomas, 12–16. He addresses dormant Commerce Clause doctrine in *Wynne*, Thomas, 1–3.
24 *Ass'n of American Railroads*, Thomas, 4–11; *Perez*, Thomas, 5–8; *Zivotofsky*, Thomas, 3–9.
25 For his expressions of uncertainty, see *B&B Hardware*, Thomas, 12; *Wellness Int'l*, Thomas, 12 n.5, 13–14, 18. For expressions of confidence, see *Ass'n of American Railroads*, Thomas, 9, 15 n.5, 22; *Perez*, Thomas, 9–10, 15; *Obergefell*, Thomas, 4–6, 12 n.5, 16.
26 See also *Alabama Dep't of Revenue*, Thomas, 3; *Brumfield*, Thomas, 21–22; *Elonis*, Thomas, 10, 18; *Kansas v. Nebraska*, Thomas, 4, 17; *Rodriguez*, Thomas, 5–6; *Texas Dep't of Housing*, Thomas, 1.
27 Justice Thomas describes many such missteps as the result of carelessness. See *Alabama Legis. Black Caucus*, Thomas, 1; *Ass'n of American Railroads*, Thomas, 12, 22; *Michigan v. EPA*, Thomas, 4–5 (citing *B&B Hardware*, Thomas, 10–14); *Perez*, Thomas, 22; *Wellness Int'l*, Thomas, 12–13; *Texas Dep't of Housing*, Thomas, 11.
28 See *Davis v. Ayala*, 22 (Alito); *Glossip*, 14, 14 n.2, 16 (Alito); *N.C. State Bd.*, Alito, 1–2, 8–9, 13; *Texas Dep't of Housing*, Alito, 21, 27 n.10, 29; *Baker Botts*, Breyer, 5; *Kerry v. Din*, Breyer, 3; *Ariz. State Legislature*, 14 n.3, 29–30 (Ginsburg); *Reed*, Kagan, 5; *Yates*, Kagan, 11; *Wellness Int'l*, Roberts, 12–15; *Alabama Legis. Black Caucus*, Scalia, 5; *Kerry v. Din*, 14 (Scalia); *Kingsley*,

Scalia, 2–3; *ONEOK*, Scalia, 5; *Williams-Yulee*, Scalia, 1, 4; *Zivotofsky*, Scalia, 16–17; *Armstrong*, Sotomayor, 1, 5; *Glossip*, Sotomayor, 24–25, 27; *Horne*, Sotomayor, 12; *Wellness Int'l*, 16 n.11, 17 (Sotomayor).

29 See *Alabama Legis. Black Caucus*, 20–21 (Breyer); *Baker Botts*, Breyer, 4; *Armstrong*, 8 (Scalia); *Jesinoski*, 4–5 (Scalia); *Young*, Scalia, 6; *Wellness Int'l*, 3 (Sotomayor). Progressive counterparts of Justice Thomas's narrative appear in Justice Kennedy's concurring opinion in *Direct Marking Ass'n* (1–3) and Justice Breyer's in *Glossip* (1–2).

30 See also *Obergefell*, 27–28.

31 For another cross-justice parenthetical-citation "conversation," see *Dart Cherokee*, Scalia, 7.

32 These opinions were *ACAP Financial, Inc. v. SEC*, 783 F.3d 763 (10th Cir. Apr. 3, 2015); *Browder v. City of Albuquerque*, 787 F.3d 1076 (10th Cir. June 2, 2015) (majority and concurrence); *Caplinger v. Medtronic, Inc.*, 784 F.3d 1335 (10th Cir. Apr. 21, 2015); *Cook v. Rockwell Int'l Corp.*, 618 F.3d 1127 (10th Cir. June 23, 2015); *David v. Sirius Computer Solutions, Inc.*, 779 F.3d 1209 (10th Cir. Mar. 10, 2015); *Monfore v. Phillips*, 778 F.3d 849 (10th Cir. Feb. 10, 2015); *Myers v. Knight Protective Service, Inc.*, 773 F.3d 1246 (10th Cir. Dec. 22, 2014); *United States v. Alisuretove*, 788 F.3d 1247 (10th Cir. June 8, 2015) (concurrence); *United States v. Denson*, 775 F.3d 1214 (10th Cir. Dec. 30, 2014); *United States v. Herrera*, 782 F.3d 571 (10th Cir. Apr. 6, 2015); *United States v. Nichols*, 784 F.3d 666 (10th Cir. Apr. 15, 2015) (dissenting from denial of en banc rehearing); *United States v. Rentz*, 777 F.3d 1105 (10th Cir. Feb. 3, 2015) (en banc); *United States v. Sabillon-Umana*, 772 F.3d 1328 (10th Cir. Dec. 8, 2014); *Ute Indian Tribe of the Uintah & Ouray Reservations v. Utah*, 790 F.3d 1000 (10th Cir. June 16, 2015); *Williams v. Trammell*, 782 F.3d 1184 (10th Cir. Apr. 10, 2015) (concurrence).

33 This phrase comes from Palazzolo (2017), who noted, "Poorly drafted laws tend to summon his [Judge Gorsuch's] inner grammarian."

34 Judge Gorsuch wrote another separate concurrence in his own majority opinion in *Gutierrez-Brizuela v. Lynch* (Aug. 23, 2016), in which, as in *Browder*, he offered a Justice Thomas–like critique of *Chevron* doctrine (cf. section 6.3.1).

35 For examples of mindreading in Judge Gorsuch's opinions, see *Browder v. City of Albuquerque*, 1077, 1081–82; *Myers v. Knight Protective Serv., Inc.*, 1248; *United States v. Denson*, 1217–19; see also *Williams v. Trammell*, 1219.

36 A group of indeterminate size, *Denson*, 1217–19.

37 *ACAP Financial, Inc. v. SEC*, 765.

38 *David v. Sirius Computer Solutions, Inc.*, 1211.

39 *United States v. Rentz*, 1111; *Caplinger v. Medtronic, Inc.*, 1346; *Cook v. Rockwell Int'l Corp.*, 1095–96.

40 Dissenting in *United States v. Nichols*, 670.

41 Judge Gorsuch consults legislative history to confirm conclusions about the meaning of statutory language in several opinions from this period, almost always following a caveat about the unreliability of the method; see, e.g., *Caplinger v. Medtronic, Inc.*, 1346; *Cook v. Rockwell Int'l Corp.*, 1096–97.

42 See *Caplinger v. Medtronic, Inc.*, 1346.

43 See *Sabillon-Umana*, 1335.

44 *United States v. Nichols*, 672. The same doctrine was at issue in *Ass'n of American Railroads*, the Amtrak case from the 2014 term, and in *Nichols* Judge Gorsuch cites the concurrences of Justices Alito and Thomas in that case, *Nichols*, 670, 671 n.3. For other examples of Justice Gorsuch's embrace of jurispathy in opinions from this period, see, e.g., *Monfore*, 851; *Myers*, 1248–49; *Sabillon-Umana*, 1330–31.

45 E.g., *Nichols*, 676; *Sabillon-Umana*, 1334; *Williams v. Trammell*, 1219.

46 For another example of Judge Gorsuch's advocacy of simplicity from this period, see his concurrence in *United States v. Alisuretove*, 1259.

47 See also *Monfore v. Phillips*, 851–853; *ACAP Financial*, 767; *Herrera*, 575.

48 *Cook* is the only published opinion Judge Gorsuch issued during this period that uses Roman-numeral headings. In all of his other opinions from this period, he separates sections only by asterisks or line spaces.

49 *Cook v. Rockwell Int'l Corp.*, 618 F.3d 1127 (10th Cir. 2010).

50 Four judges concurred in Judge Gorsuch's opinion; only one, Judge Kelly, dissented.

51 See, e.g., Shugerman 2017, criticizing Judge Gorsuch's simplifying approach in a 2016 case, *TransAm Trucking v. Administrative Review Board.*

52 In a footnote toward the end of this lecture, Judge Gorsuch asks, "isn't it easier . . . to assess whether a judge offers a persuasive textualist analysis . . . than to assess a judge's success using some ends-based or efficiency-based methodology, when those methods often rest on contested political or moral convictions or disputed social science data?" (Gorsuch 2016, 919 n.57).

53 On Justice Gorsuch's early opinions for the Court, see, e.g., Liptak 2017.

54 See, e.g., Gorsuch 2016, 905–06 & nn.1–5; Manning 2017.

Appendix

Supreme Court 2014 Term opinions listed alphabetically

Abercrombie & Fitch: see ***Equal Employment Opportunity Comm'n v. Abercrombie & Fitch Stores, Inc.***

Alabama Dep't of Revenue v. CSX Transportation Inc., decided Mar. 4, 2015 **[cited as *Alabama Dep't of Revenue*]**

Alabama imposes sales taxes on railroads' diesel fuel purchases. CSX, a railroad company, sued Alabama for violating a federal statute (the 4-R Act) that forbids states from imposing taxes that "discriminate[ ]" against rail carriers. The district court rejected CSX's claim; the appellate court reversed.

Scalia, J., for 7: In deciding whether a state has violated the 4-R Act, a court should compare the tax burdens on the complaining carrier with the burdens on similarly situated competitors. If the state imposes a different tax on a competitor that is roughly equivalent to the tax imposed on the complaining carrier, then the tax does not "discriminate."

Thomas, J., dissenting (+1): In this case, the carrier cannot show that Alabama's tax singled out rail carriers in comparison to other commercial and industrial taxpayers. So the complaining carrier cannot show that Alabama violated the 4-R Act by discriminating against it.

Alabama Legislative Black Caucus v. Alabama, decided Mar. 25, 2015 (with *Alabama Democratic Conference v. Alabama*) **[cited as *Alabama Legis. Black Caucus*]**

In 2012, Alabama's legislature redrew the boundaries of the state's election districts for federal legislative seats. Organizations representing African-American and Democratic voters sued the state, claiming the redistricting resulted in racially gerrymandered districts in violation of the Fourteenth Amendment. A three-judge federal district court ruled, 2–1, for Alabama on several grounds.

Breyer, J., for 5: A court should analyze racial gerrymandering claims district by district, not by considering the state as a whole. An organization may have standing to challenge district boundaries if the organization can show it has members in some of the districts in question. The goal of maintaining equal population among districts is a background consideration in districting, not a factor to be weighed against the racial makeup of individual districts.

Scalia, J., dissenting (+3): The majority should have deferred to the district court's findings that the plaintiffs lacked standing and had not stated claims for relief.

Thomas, J., dissenting: The Court's voting rights jurisprudence is a jumble that promotes instead of discouraging the consideration of race in districting.

Arizona State Legislature v. Arizona Independent Redistricting Comm'n (AIRC), decided June 29, 2015 **[cited as *Ariz. State Legislature*]**

In 2000, Arizona's voters amended the state's constitution through an initiative that vested redistricting power in the AIRC. The AIRC redrew the state's election district boundaries in 2012. The Arizona legislature, which previously had redistricting power, sued, claiming that the AIRC's control over districting violated the federal constitutional Elections Clause. A three-judge district court dismissed the complaint.

Ginsburg, J., for 5: The legislature has standing to sue in this case. But the creation of the AIRC and its actions did not violate the Elections Clause. The AIRC exercises legislative powers, so it (and the initiative creating it) count as a "Legislature" for Elections Clause purposes.

Roberts, C.J., dissenting (+3): The majority's conclusion conflicts with the meaning of "Legislature" throughout the Constitution. The majority's reading of the Elections Clause, if valid, would have made a 1913 constitutional amendment superfluous.

Scalia, J., dissenting (+1): Disputes between governmental branches are nonjusticiable; the Court should have dismissed this case for lack of jurisdiction. The majority's reading of the Elections Clause is also wrong.

Thomas, J., dissenting (+1): The justices in the majority, who profess respect for popular sovereignty, have not supported popular sovereignty in other recent cases, including *Obergefell*.

Armstrong v. Exceptional Child Center, Inc., decided Mar. 31, 2015 **[cited as *Armstrong*]**

The Medicaid Act requires states to ensure that medical service providers are reimbursed fairly from the state Medicaid plan. Service providers in Idaho sued the state officials administering Idaho's Medicaid plan, asking the court to order the officials to raise the rates paid to the providers. The federal trial and appellate courts ruled for the service providers.

Scalia, J., for 4 on some issues, 5 on others: Neither the Constitution's Supremacy Clause nor the Medicaid Act creates a right for providers receiving reimbursement from a state Medicaid plan to sue for violation of the statute governing reimbursement rates.

Breyer, J., concurring in part and in judgment: The Supremacy Clause is not relevant to this case; the Court only needed to say that the Medicaid Act does not authorize this kind of private action.

Sotomayor, J., dissenting (+3): The plaintiffs have a right to sue state officials for equitable relief. The Medicaid Act does not restrict the traditional equitable authority of the federal courts.

Ass'n of Am. Railroads: see ***Dep't of Transportation v. Ass'n of Am. Railroads***

Baker Botts L.L.P. v. ASARCO LLC, decided June 15, 2015 **[cited as *Baker Botts*]**

ASARCO, a company in bankruptcy, hired a law firm, Baker Botts, to assist it in the bankruptcy proceedings. At the end of the proceedings, Baker Botts applied to the bankruptcy court for reimbursement for the firm's services, including a request for reimbursement for time spent defending the application against ASARCO's objections. The bankruptcy court rejected the last part of the request as not statutorily authorized. The district court reversed this decision; the appellate court agreed with the bankruptcy court.

Thomas, J., for 5 on some issues, 6 on others: The statutory provision in question allows a bankruptcy court to award a firm fees for the firm's assistance of a debtor, but not fees for time the firm spent defending its application for fees.

Sotomayor, J., concurring in part and in judgment: The majority's discussion of incentives for attorneys is irrelevant to the analysis.

Breyer, J., dissenting (+2): The provision in question gives bankruptcy judges discretion to award fees for the time a firm spends defending a fee application, at least when withholding the fees would make an award unreasonably low.

B&B Hardware, Inc. v. Hargis Industries, Inc., decided Mar. 24, 2015 **[cited as *B&B Hardware*]**

B&B Hardware opposed Hargis Industries' application to register its trademark with the federal government, arguing that Hargis's trademark was too similar to B&B's. The Trademark Trial & Appeal Board (TTAB) agreed with B&B. In a separate lawsuit over the same marks, B&B sued Hargis for infringement, and a jury found for Hargis. The court of appeals affirmed this judgment, rejecting B&B's argument that the TTAB's decision should prevent reconsideration of the issue.

Alito, J., for 7: A conclusion by the TTAB that two trademarks are confusingly similar may have preclusive effect in a later case raising the same issue, as long as the ordinary requirements of issue preclusion are otherwise satisfied.

Ginsburg, J., concurring: TTAB decisions about similarity will rarely be preclusive, since the TTAB usually makes these decisions using different information from the information used to decide infringement lawsuits.

Thomas, J., dissenting (+1): The majority improperly treats the TTAB as functioning similarly to a court.

Bank of America, N.A. v. Caulkett, decided June 1, 2015 (with *Bank of America, N.A. v. Toledo-Cardona*) **[cited as *Caulkett*]**

Two individuals separately filed for bankruptcy. Each had a house with a double mortgage and owed more on the second mortgage than the house was worth. The individuals applied to void the liens under a Bankruptcy Code provision allowing debtors to void (i.e., exclude from the bankruptcy estate) liens that are not "allowed secured claims." The bankruptcy courts, district courts, and courts of appeals concluded that the liens could be voided, despite the lenders' citation of a 1992 case, *Dewsnup*, in which the Court held that partly underwater liens could qualify as "allowed secured claims."

Thomas, J., for 9 (with 3 refusing to join a footnote acknowledging criticism of *Dewsnup*): An underwater lien is not voidable if the creditor's claim is "secured" as defined in a different provision. There is no reason to distinguish wholly underwater liens from the partly underwater liens addressed in *Dewsnup*.

Brumfield v. Cain, decided June 18, 2015 **[cited as *Brumfield*]**

Kevan Brumfield was convicted of murder in Louisiana state court and sentenced to death. The Supreme Court then decided *Atkins* (2002), which held that execution of an intellectually disabled adult violates the Eighth Amendment. Brumfield applied unsuccessfully for a hearing at which to present evidence that he was intellectually disabled under Louisiana's standard. On his subsequent federal habeas petition, the district court held that the state court should have granted his application. The federal court of appeals reversed the district court's judgment.

Sotomayor, J., for 5: The appellate court was wrong. The district court correctly concluded that the state court's factual findings (that Brumfield likely could not show he had an intellectual disability), and its resulting refusal to grant Brumfield a hearing, were unreasonable under the relevant statutory standard.

Thomas, J., dissenting (+3 as to all but one section): This petitioner's habeas petition was just the most recent of the petitioner's lifelong series of attempts to avoid responsibility. The majority shows insufficient respect for the state court's findings.

Alito, J., dissenting (+1): Justice Thomas's discussion of the successful life of one of the sons of the petitioner's victim is irrelevant to the legal issues in this case.

Bullard v. Blue Hills Bank, decided May 4, 2015 **[cited as *Bullard*]**

Louis Bullard submitted a proposed repayment plan to the court during his bankruptcy proceedings. The court refused to confirm the plan. Bullard tried to appeal the decision to the Bankruptcy Appellate Panel (BAP), but both the BAP and the court of appeals held they could not review the decision because it was not a "final order."

Roberts, C.J., for 9: A bankruptcy court's order denying confirmation of a proposed plan is not a "final order." Denial of confirmation does not permanently alter any legal relationships or resolve the plan-consideration process; it only gives the debtor an opportunity to revise the plan.

Carroll v. Carman, decided Nov. 10, 2014 **[cited as *Carroll*]**

Andrew and Karen Carman sued Jeremy Carroll, a Pennsylvania police officer, for violation of the Carmans' Fourth Amendment rights after Carroll, seeking a fleeing suspect, entered the Carmans' yard and approached their house from its backyard rather than the front walk. A federal jury returned a verdict for Carroll, but the court of appeals reversed in part, holding that Carroll's method of approaching the Carmans' house violated "clearly established law."

per curiam: The Third Circuit was wrong to deny Carman's qualified-immunity defense. No Supreme Court or Third Circuit precedent clearly established that Carman could not knock at the Carmans' back door.

Carter: see ***Kellogg Brown & Root Servs., Inc. v. United States ex rel. Carter***

Caulkett: see ***Bank of America, N.A. v. Caulkett***

Christeson v. Roper, decided Jan. 20, 2105 **[cited as *Christeson*]**

Mark Christeson was convicted of murder and sentenced to death in state court in 1999. The lawyers appointed to help with his federal habeas petition failed to meet with him before the petition-filing deadline. Years later, they contacted another pair of lawyers for advice in the case; the new lawyers saw that Christeson might apply for permission to file a late petition, but that his earlier lawyers could not represent him now without arguing against their own professional interests. These new lawyers moved twice to allow their substitution as counsel, but the trial court denied the motions, and the court of appeals did not disturb either denial.

per curiam: The district court erred in denying the new lawyers' substitution motions. Christeson's originally appointed counsel faced an irresolvable conflict of interest that prevented them from arguing for tolling of the filing deadline.

Alito, J., dissenting (+1): The Court should have ordered full briefing and argument in this case to avoid confusion about the scope of its holding.

City & County of San Francisco v. Sheehan, decided May 18, 2015 **[cited as *Sheehan*]**

Police officers shot and injured Teresa Sheehan, a mentally ill resident of a group home in San Francisco, when they entered her room forcibly after she refused to open the door for a social worker or the officers. Sheehan sued the officers for violating her Fourth Amendment rights, and she sued the city of San Francisco for failing to accommodate her mental disability under the Americans with Disabilities Act (ADA). The district court granted summary judgment for all defendants; the court of appeals reversed in part, concluding that Sheehan's claims should go to trial.

Alito, J., for 6: Sheehan's claim for violation of the ADA is dismissed as improvidently granted. The officers who shot Sheehan were entitled to qualified immunity on her Fourth Amendment claim. Their conduct was reasonable in the circumstances and did not violate clearly established law.

Scalia, J., concurring in part and dissenting in part (+1): The city's arguments in its briefs on the ADA issue differed from those it presented in its initial petition. By deciding the issue of the officers' qualified immunity, an issue that did not merit certiorari on its own, the Court encourages litigants to file strategic, bad-faith petitions for certiorari.

Breyer, J., did not participate.

City of Los Angeles v. Patel, decided June 22, 2015 **[cited as *Patel*]**

The Los Angeles municipal code required hotel operators to keep guest registries and make them available for police inspection on request. Operators of several hotels sued the city, claiming the provision violated the Fourth Amendment. The lower federal courts held that the hotel operators had no reasonable expectation of privacy in their registries and rejected their Fourth Amendment claims on that basis.

Sotomayor, J., for 5: The provision is facially invalid because it fails to give hotel operators an opportunity to challenge particular search requests in advance.

Scalia, J., dissenting (+2): The searches authorized by the provision are reasonable and therefore constitutional. Hotels are highly regulated, and their operators have no reasonable expectation of privacy in guest identities. The ordinance helps deter crime.

Alito, J., dissenting (+1): The ordinance could be applied constitutionally in many circumstances, including five specific scenarios described in the dissent. Facial invalidation is inappropriate.

Clark: see ***Ohio v. Clark***

Coleman v. Tollefson, decided May 18, 2015 (with *Coleman v. Bowerman*, *Coleman v. Dykehouse*, and *Coleman v. Vroman*) **[cited as *Coleman*]**

Andre Lee Coleman, a prisoner in a Michigan facility, filed three lawsuits challenging his confinement under the federal *in forma pauperis* statute, which waives filing fees when a plaintiff files an affidavit of need, but bars further such suits after three have been dismissed as frivolous. The third of Coleman's suits was dismissed; while it was still pending on appeal, Coleman filed four more complaints with *in forma pauperis* affidavits. The district court denied his requests to proceed *in forma pauperis*, and the court of appeals affirmed.

Breyer, J., for 9: The statutory limit on the number of permitted *in forma pauperis* suits applies after a district court dismisses a third such suit as frivolous, even while the action remains pending on appeal.

Commil USA, LLC v. Cisco Systems, Inc., decided May 25, 2015 **[cited as *Commil*]**

Commil, holding a patent on a method of networking wireless equipment, sued Cisco for inducing infringement of the patent, based on Cisco's sales of equipment that, when networked, infringed the patent. Cisco sought to argue to a jury that it believed in good faith that the patent was invalid and could not be infringed. The trial court did not allow Cisco to make the argument. The court of appeals reversed on this issue.

Kennedy, J., for 5 on all issues, 6 on some: A defendant's good-faith belief in the invalidity of a patent is not a defense to a claim that the defendant induced infringement of the patent.

Scalia, J., dissenting (+1): It is impossible to infringe an invalid patent. A defendant to an induced-infringement claim who believes in good faith that the patent is invalid therefore lacks the state of mind required for liability for inducing infringement: knowledge that the acts induced amount to infringement.

Breyer, J., did not participate.

Comptroller of Treasury of Maryland v. Wynne, decided May 18, 2015 **[cited as *Wynne*]**

Maryland's personal income-tax scheme allows state residents who pay income taxes to other states a credit against their Maryland state income tax, but not against their county tax. Brian and Karen Wynne, Maryland residents who paid income taxes in other states, claimed a full credit on their Maryland tax return for taxes paid elsewhere; the state comptroller denied the credit, and a state tax court affirmed. State trial and appellate courts held, however, that the tax scheme violated the federal Commerce Clause by discriminating against interstate commerce.

Alito, J., for 5: Maryland's tax scheme violates the dormant Commerce Clause by discriminating between residents of Maryland and other states. The scheme fails the "internal consistency test," which assumes that every state has the same tax system and compares interstate and intrastate taxes under that assumption.

Scalia, J., dissenting (+1 as to some sections): The Court's "negative" (dormant) Commerce Clause doctrine is based on a judge-invented principle and gives judges too much discretion in assessing state economic regulations.

Thomas, J., dissenting (+1 as to the first paragraph): The Court's "negative Commerce Clause" doctrine is indefensible and inconsistent with the understandings of the framers and ratifiers of the Constitution.

Ginsburg, J., dissenting (+2): Each state has sovereign power to tax residents' income. This power is absolute, regardless of other states' power to tax income earned within those states, and it is not superseded by the dormant Commerce Clause. The majority overstates and misapplies the "internal consistency" test.

Dart Cherokee Basin Operating Co. v. Owens, decided Dec. 15, 2014 **[cited as *Dart Cherokee*]**

Brandon Owens, representing a class of landowners, sued Dart Cherokee Basin Operating Co. in Kansas court for unpaid royalties on oil and gas leases. Dart removed the action to federal court, stating in its removal papers that the claimed unpaid royalties amounted to $8.2 million (more than the $5 million required for removal). Owens challenged the removal, arguing that Dart did not provide evidence supporting the claimed amount in controversy. The district court remanded the case on this basis; the court of appeals affirmed in a summary order.

Ginsburg, J., for 5: To remove an action, a defendant need not provide evidence supporting its allegations regarding the amount in controversy, unless the plaintiff challenges those allegations.

Scalia, J., dissenting (+2, +3 as to all but final sentence): Since the court of appeals denied review in an unreasoned order, the Court lacked any basis for reversing that court's decision on the ground on which the Court granted review. The Court should have dismissed the petition as improvidently granted.

Thomas, J., dissenting: The Supreme Court lacked appellate jurisdiction over the appellate court's order.

Davis v. Ayala, decided June 18, 2015 **[cited as *Davis v. Ayala*]**

Hector Ayala was convicted of homicide and sentenced to death in a California court in 1989. During jury selection in his case, Ayala's attorney challenged some of the prosecutor's juror strikes, arguing that they might have been racially discriminatory. The trial court judge accepted the prosecutor's justifications for the strikes after conferences from which Ayala's attorney was absent. In postconviction proceedings, the state appellate courts and federal district court concluded that this absence of Ayala's attorney was not constitutional error requiring reversal of Ayala's sentence. The federal court of appeals disagreed and ordered that Ayala be released or retried.

Alito, J., for 5: The Ninth Circuit was wrong to reject the conclusions of the district court and state courts that no error requiring reversal occurred in this case.

Kennedy, J., concurring: Ayala has served most of his 25 years in prison in solitary confinement, an inhumane form of imprisonment. Policymakers should debate and reform the overuse of solitary confinement.

Thomas, J., concurring: Ayala's solitary confinement is not as unpleasant as the conditions of "confinement" of Ayala's murder victims.

Sotomayor, J., dissenting (+3): The trial court's conclusion about the propriety of the juror strikes might have been different had Ayala's attorney been present at the discussion of those strikes. The Ninth Circuit's conclusion was correct.

Dep't of Homeland Security (DHS) v. MacLean, decided Jan. 21, 2015 **[cited as *MacLean*]**

In 2003, Robert MacLean, a federal air marshal, contacted the media to express his concerns about a decision by the Transportation Security Administration (TSA) to reduce air marshal staffing on domestic flights despite a recent briefing about a suspected hijacking plot. When the TSA discovered that MacLean was the leaker, it fired him; he challenged his dismissal under the federal whistleblower statute, which protects federal employees from retaliation for revealing information whose disclosure is not "specifically prohibited by law." The government agency authorized to review MacLean's dismissal rejected his challenge, but the court of appeals held that he was protected by the statute.

Roberts, C.J., for 7: MacLean's disclosure was covered by the federal whistleblower statute and therefore protected. The disclosure was not "specifically prohibited by law," since only TSA regulations, not a statute, prohibited the disclosure.

Sotomayor, J., dissenting (+1): The statute authorizing TSA to promulgate the regulations in question counts as a statute "specifically prohibit[ing]" MacLean's disclosure, triggering the exception to protection for MacLean.

Dep't of Transportation (DOT) v. Ass'n of Am. Railroads, decided Mar. 9, 2015 **[cited as *Ass'n of Am. Railroads*]**

The federal Passenger Rail Improvement & Investment Act (PRIIA) requires Amtrak to help set railway "metrics and standards" potentially binding on other rail carriers. The Association of American Railroads sued to challenge this requirement, arguing that it impermissibly delegated legislative authority to Amtrak, a private entity. The district court rejected the claim, but the court of appeals held that Amtrak was a private entity and could not constitutionally set these standards.

Kennedy, J., for 7: Amtrak is a federal governmental entity for purposes of the PRIIA, despite Congress's statutory designation of Amtrak as a private-sector entity. On remand, the court of appeals should determine whether Amtrak's participation in standard-setting violates any other constitutional clause or principle.

Alito, J., concurring: Amtrak's structure and powers may violate the nondelegation doctrine, the Appointments Clause, the Removal Clause, and other constitutional principles.

Thomas, J., concurring in judgment: The nondelegation doctrine has strayed from its proper form, reflecting the original understanding of the separation of legislative and executive power. As constituted, Amtrak violates the Constitution.

Direct Marketing Ass'n v. Brohl, decided Mar. 3, 2015 **[cited as *Direct Marketing Ass'n*]**

Colorado requires retailers who do not collect sales taxes from Colorado purchasers to notify purchasers of their state-law duty to send sales taxes to the state. The Direct Marketing Association, representing retailers who sell to Colorado residents but do not collect taxes from them, sued the Director of the Colorado Department of Revenue, alleging that this system violated the federal and state constitutions. The district court enjoined enforcement of the system. The appellate court reversed, holding that the federal courts lacked jurisdiction of the case under the Tax Injunction Act (TIA), which bans federal orders restraining "assessment, levy or collection" of state tax.

Thomas, J., for 9: This suit is not barred by the TIA, because the reporting requirement does not concern "assessment, levy or collection."

Kennedy, J., concurring: The Court's decisions holding that a state may not collect taxes from retailers that lack a physical presence in the state are obsolete and should be overruled.

Ginsburg, J., concurring (+1, +2 as to the "first observation"): This suit is not the kind of suit Congress meant to prohibit by means of the TIA. The Court's holding is consistent with other precedent applying the TIA.

Elonis v. United States, decided June 1, 2015 **[cited as *Elonis*]**

Anthony Elonis, using a rapper-style pseudonym, made Facebook posts containing exaggerated threats of violence toward his estranged wife, coworkers, and law enforcement. A jury convicted him under a federal statute criminalizing the transmission of communications containing threats to injure others. On appeal, Elonis challenged the instructions given to jurors, who were told they might find his posts to be threats if they found that a reasonable person would interpret the posts as threatening. The court of appeals held that the instruction was appropriate.

Roberts, C.J., for 7: To convict under the threat statute, the prosecution must show that the defendant had some awareness of the threatening import of his or her words. The statute is satisfied if the prosecution shows that the defendant acted for the purpose of issuing a threat or with knowledge that a statement would be viewed as a threat, but a lesser showing (e.g., of recklessness) might also suffice.

Alito, J., concurring in part and dissenting in part: The majority's analysis does not provide sufficient guidance to prosecutors and judges. A defendant's recklessness as to whether words will be taken as a threat should suffice.

Thomas, J., dissenting: The majority does not provide clear guidance on the mental state required for conviction under this statute. The standard the lower federal courts used was correct.

Equal Employment Opportunity Comm'n (EEOC) v. Abercrombie & Fitch Stores, Inc., decided June 1, 2015 **[cited as *Abercrombie & Fitch*]**

Samantha Elauf applied for a job at an Abercrombie & Fitch store. Abercrombie & Fitch has a dress code for clerks that bans headwear; Elauf is Muslim and wore a headscarf at her interview. A manager decided that she could not be hired because of her attire. Elauf filed a charge with the EEOC alleging that Abercrombie & Fitch failed to accommodate her religious practice in violation of the Civil Rights Act (Title VII); the EEOC litigated the claim for Elauf. The EEOC prevailed in the district court, but the court of appeals reversed, holding that an employer cannot be liable for failure to accommodate unless the employee or applicant gave the employer notice of his or her need for an accommodation.

Scalia, J., for 7: An employer may be liable for failing to accommodate a religious practice even if the applicant does not inform the employer of the practice and need for an accommodation. The applicant need only show that the need for an accommodation was a motivating factor in the employer's decision.

Alito, J., concurring in judgment: For Title VII failure-to-accommodate liability to be imposed on an employer, the employer's action must have been based on the employer's knowledge that the applicant engages in a practice for a religious reason. In this case, it is undisputed that the employer knew or had reason to know that Elauf's headwear was related to her religious practice.

Thomas, J., dissenting: A decision made in compliance with a neutral policy (like the dress code here) cannot give rise to Title VII disparate-treatment liability.

Gelboim v. Bank of America Corp., decided Jan. 21, 2015 **[cited as *Gelboim*]**

Ellen Gelboim and Linda Zacher filed a class action on behalf of buyers of bonds with interest rates tied to the London InterBank Offered Rate (LIBOR). The suit alleged that the bond issuers violated federal antitrust law. A federal multidistrict litigation (MDL) panel consolidated their action with more than 60 others involving LIBOR-related claims. The court hearing the consolidated cases dismissed Gelboim and Zacher's action; they sought to appeal the decision, but the court of appeals held that appellate jurisdiction was lacking, because the dismissal could not be a final order while other cases in the MDL litigation were pending.

Ginsburg, J., for 9: When a lawsuit is consolidated with others for MDL pretrial proceedings, and the suit is then dismissed from the ongoing MDL proceeding, a federal court of appeals has appellate jurisdiction over the dismissed lawsuit.

Glebe v. Frost, decided Nov. 17, 2014 **[cited as *Glebe v. Frost*]**

Joshua Frost was convicted in state court of armed robbery and related offenses. At Frost's trial, his lawyer wanted to argue that the prosecution had not shown beyond a reasonable doubt that Frost participated in the crime, but also that if Frost did participate, he did so under duress. The trial court ruled that state law required Frost's lawyer to choose one of the arguments. On appeal, the state Supreme Court held that the trial-court judge was wrong about the law, but that the error was harmless, not requiring reversal of Frost's conviction. On collateral review, the federal court of appeals held that the error was structural, requiring reversal.

per curiam: No Supreme Court opinion "clearly established" that the trial-court judge's refusal to allow Frost's lawyer to argue alternative theories was reversible error. So the Ninth Circuit was wrong to reverse the state Supreme Court's decision that the trial court's error did not require reversal of Frost's conviction.

Glossip v. Gross, decided June 29, 2015 **[cited as *Glossip*]**

Richard Glossip, Benjamin Cole, John Grant, and Charles Warner, death-row inmates in Oklahoma, moved for a preliminary injunction in federal court, challenging Oklahoma's execution protocol under the Eighth Amendment. Oklahoma planned to use midazolam, a benzodiazepine, rather than an anesthetic, to sedate condemned inmates before injecting them with drugs to paralyze and kill them. The inmates argued that this plan exposed them to a risk of severe pain during their executions. After a three-day evidentiary hearing, the district court denied the motion in an oral ruling based largely on testimony from the state's expert that midazolam could cause prolonged unconsciousness at the planned dose. (Warner was executed before the Court issued this decision.)

Alito, J., for 5: Petitioners did not establish a likelihood of success on their claim that Oklahoma's protocol violates the Eighth Amendment; they did not establish a likelihood of showing that midazolam creates a risk of severe pain that is "substantial when compared with known alternatives." The district court's findings supporting its denial of the inmates' motion were not clearly erroneous.

Scalia, J., concurring (+1): Justice Breyer's arguments for abolition of the death penalty have been made and rejected before. His dissent is not a legal argument.

Thomas, J., concurring (+1): The Eighth Amendment prohibits only punishment "deliberately designed to inflict pain." Oklahoma's execution protocol was not designed for this purpose.

Breyer, J., dissenting (+1): The Court should reconsider whether the death penalty violates the Eighth Amendment. Changed circumstances have rendered it more cruel and unusual since the Court last addressed that basic question in 1976.

Sotomayor, J., dissenting (+3): The district court in this case applied the wrong legal standard and clearly erred in its factual findings. The majority should not have accepted the district court's conclusions.

Grady v. North Carolina, decided Mar. 30, 2015 **[cited as *Grady*]**

Torrey Dale Grady was convicted of sexual offenses in North Carolina state courts in 1997 and 2006. A state statute required that as a recidivist sex offender, he be considered for satellite-based monitoring via a tracking device. When the state court ordered Grady to enroll in the monitoring program, he argued that the order violated his Fourth Amendment rights. The state trial and appellate courts rejected Grady's argument, noting the civil nature of the monitoring program.

per curiam: Even though this monitoring program is civil in nature, the North Carolina courts were wrong to hold that monitoring of a convicted sex offender cannot qualify as a Fourth Amendment "search." On remand, the state courts should determine whether the search of Grady is reasonable under relevant Fourth Amendment doctrine.

Hana Financial, Inc. v. Hana Bank, decided Jan. 21, 2015 **[cited as *Hana Financial*]**

Hana Financial, a California corporation, started using a trademark associated with its name in 1995. Hana Bank, a Korean company, began advertising in the U.S. using the name "Hana" in 1994. In 2007, Hana Financial sued Hana Bank for trademark infringement. Hana Bank argued that it began using the mark before Hana Financial, invoking the "tacking" doctrine, which allows two marks used in succession by the same entity, if similar enough, to be considered one mark for priority purposes. The district court submitted to the jury the question of the marks' similarity for tacking purposes; the jury found for Hana Financial. The court of appeals, affirming, noted a circuit split on the question whether similarity for tacking purposes is a question of law for the judge or one of fact for a jury.

Sotomayor, J., for 9: The question of whether two trademarks are sufficiently similar to be tacked is a question of fact for the jury to decide.

Harris v. Viegelahn, decided May 18, 2015 **[cited as *Harris*]**

Charles Harris III filed for Chapter 13 bankruptcy; after the court confirmed his bankruptcy plan, he had a sum withheld from his wages and sent to his court-appointed trustee, Mary Viegelahn, for distribution to Harris's mortgage lender. When Harris fell behind on his mortgage, the lender foreclosed on his house, but Viegelahn continued to receive money from Harris's wages. Harris then converted his case to a Chapter 7 proceeding, which does not involve a trustee. After the conversion, Viegelahn distributed some of the accumulated funds to Harris's lawyer and creditors, and some to herself. Harris moved to have those distributed funds refunded to him; the bankruptcy court granted the motion, and the district court affirmed, but the court of appeals reversed.

Ginsburg, J., for 9: When a debtor converts a Chapter 13 proceeding to a Chapter 7 proceeding, the debtor is entitled to receive any wages earned following the original petition that were collected by the debtor's Chapter 13 trustee but not yet distributed to creditors as of the date of the conversion.

Heien v. North Carolina, decided Dec. 15, 2014 **[cited as *Heien*]**

Nicholas Heien was riding in a car stopped by a police officer, Matt Darisse, based on Darisse's belief that state law required cars to have two working taillights. Darisse asked for and received consent to search the car and found cocaine in it. Heien moved to suppress evidence of the cocaine at his trial for drug trafficking, arguing that applicable state law did not require cars to have two working taillights. The trial court denied his motion. The state court of appeals agreed with Heien and reversed, but the state supreme court reinstated his conviction, holding that Darisse made a reasonable mistake about the law's requirements.

Roberts, C.J., for 8: The reasonable suspicion required for lawful police stop of a motorist may exist even if the officer making the stop is wrong about the requirements of the law invoked to justify the stop, as long as the officer's mistake is reasonable.

Kagan, J., concurring (+1): An officer's subjective understanding of the law is irrelevant. The type of legal error that justifies qualified immunity will not necessarily justify a stop for Fourth Amendment purposes.

Sotomayor, J., dissenting: Only an officer's reasonable mistakes of fact, not his or her reasonable mistakes of law, can justify a stop under the Fourth Amendment.

Henderson v. United States, decided May 18, 2015 **[cited as *Henderson*]**

Tony Henderson pleaded guilty to a federal drug crime. Federal law prohibits felons from possessing firearms; upon his conviction, Henderson turned his guns over to the FBI. After his release from prison, Henderson asked the FBI, and then the court in which he entered his guilty plea, to transfer the guns to Henderson's wife or to a friend. The district court denied the request, reasoning that the transfer would leave Henderson in constructive possession of his guns. The court of appeals affirmed.

Kagan, J., for 9: The statute barring convicted felons' possession of firearms does not prevent a court from transferring possession of a felon's firearms to a person identified by the felon, as long as the court is satisfied that the recipient will not give the felon control of them or let the felon direct their use.

Holt v. Hobbs, decided Jan. 20, 2015 **[cited as *Holt*]**

Gregory Holt, a Muslim inmate in Arkansas state prison, sought permission to wear a half-inch beard in observance of his religion. Prison officials denied his request, citing a state Department of Corrections (DOC) policy banning beards more than a quarter-inch long. Holt sued the DOC and the warden of his prison for violation of the federal Religious Land Use & Institutionalized Persons Act (RLUIPA), which forbids government actions substantially burdening an institutionalized person's exercise of religion, unless the state shows the action is the least restrictive means of furthering a compelling state interest. Both the district court and the court of appeals held for the state, deferring to its position that the policy helped stop the flow of contraband and prevent prisoners' disguising themselves in order to escape.

Alito, J., for 9: The DOC violated RLUIPA by denying Holt's request to wear a half-inch beard. The DOC's justifications for its policy of permitting only quarter-inch beards did not rationally justify a ban on a half-inch beard.

Ginsburg, J., concurring (+1): This case is unlike *Burwell v. Hobby Lobby Stores* (2014), which also concerned state actions potentially burdening religious exercise, in that Holt's exercise of his religion could not harm any third parties.

Sotomayor, J., concurring: RLUIPA requires deference to the judgments of prison officials where those judgments have any rational basis. The judgments at issue in this case had no such rational basis.

Horne v. Dep't of Agriculture (DOA), decided June 22, 2015 **[cited as *Horne*]**

Marvin and Laura Horne, California raisin farmers, challenged a requirement of the Agricultural Marketing Agreement Act (Act) that U.S. raisin growers set aside part of their crop for disposal by the DOA. The Hornes argued this requirement was a Fifth Amendment "taking" of their property. Between 2002 and 2004, they refused to set aside any raisins and were fined by a DOA officer. The Hornes challenged the fine in district court, but the court held that the requirement was not a physical "taking." After a dispute over appellate jurisdiction resolved by the Supreme Court in 2013, the federal court of appeals affirmed.

Roberts, C.J., for 5 (as to the entire opinion), 8 (as to Parts I & II): The reserve requirement is a Fifth Amendment "taking." Just compensation is required for takings of personal property as well as real property. The ability of raisin growers and handlers to participate in a regulated market for raisins is not just compensation for the taking in this case.

Thomas, J., concurring: It is not clear that the raisin-reserve program involved the taking of raisins for "public use," so there is no need to calculate just compensation in this case. The petitioners should receive the market value of the raisins they were required to reserve under the Act.

Breyer, J., concurring in part, dissenting in part (+2): The Court should remand for determination of the compensation, if any, due to the petitioners for their reserve raisins. It is possible that the marketing order issued under the Act offered the Hornes a sufficient benefit to count as just compensation.

Sotomayor, J., dissenting: The Hornes retained a property right in their set-aside reserve raisins, namely their monetary value, at least part of which the federal government repaid to raisin growers under the Act. Since the Hornes did not lose all rights in the set-aside raisins, but retained a contingent right to at least part of their value in money, the reserve program did not "take" the raisins.

Integrity Staffing Solutions, Inc. v. Busk, decided Dec. 9, 2014 **[cited as *Integrity Staffing*]**

Integrity Staffing Solutions employed warehouse workers for Amazon.com and required them to pass through a security checkpoint before leaving every day. Jesse Busk and Laurie Castro, Integrity employees, sued their employer on behalf of similarly situated Integrity employees in Nevada; the plaintiffs claimed that two federal statutes, including the Portal-to-Portal Act, entitled them to compensation for the time they spent waiting to be screened and being screened. The district court dismissed the complaint, holding that the screening time was "postliminary" and not compensable. The court of appeals reversed in part, holding that postshift activities like screenings may be compensable if they are necessary to employees' principal work and performed for the employer's benefit.

Thomas, J., for 9: The security screenings required by Integrity Staffing Solutions were not compensable overtime activity under the Portal-to-Portal Act.

Sotomayor, J., concurring (+1): These screenings were part of the employees' "egress" from work, so they were not compensable under the Portal-to-Portal Act.

Jennings v. Stephens, decided Jan. 14, 2015 **[cited as *Jennings*]**

After receiving a capital sentence following a conviction for murder in state court, Robert Mitchell Jennings filed a petition for habeas relief in federal court, arguing that his trial counsel gave him ineffective assistance by failing to present mitigating evidence of Jennings's disadvantaged background at sentencing, failing to investigate Jennings's history of potential brain damage, and stating that counsel would not "quarrel with" a death sentence. The district court granted habeas relief on the first two theories. When the state appealed this judgment, Jennings reasserted all three arguments without applying for a cross-appeal on the third. The court of appeals held that it lacked jurisdiction over the argument on the third theory.

Scalia, J., for 6: When a district court grants habeas relief on two of three theories advanced by a petitioner, and the state appeals the grant, the petitioner may argue all three theories on appeal.

Thomas, J., dissenting (+2): An order granting habeas relief is a conditional-release order, unlike an ordinary civil order. A party appealing from such an order may raise only theories that would result in similar conditional-release relief.

Jesinoski v. Countrywide Home Loans, Inc., decided Jan. 13, 2015 **[cited as *Jesinoski*]**

In 2007, Larry and Cheryle Jesinoski refinanced their mortgage with a loan from Countrywide. Three years later, they sent the bank a letter asking to rescind the loan. The bank refused; after another year, the Jesinoskis sued in federal court, seeking a declaration that they had effectively rescinded their loan agreement. The district court held for the bank, reasoning that the federal Truth-in-Lending Act (Act) requires an action for rescission to be filed within three years of "consummation" of the transaction in question. The federal court of appeals affirmed.

Scalia, J., for 9: A borrower's rescission of a loan is timely under the Act if the borrower communicates an intention to rescind to the lender within three years. The Act does not require the borrower to file suit within three years.

Johnson v. City of Shelby, Mississippi, decided Nov. 10, 2014 **[cited as *Johnson v. Shelby*]**

Tracey Johnson, a former police officer in Shelby, Mississippi, sued the city along with other former police officers, claiming that the city board of aldermen violated the officers' due process rights by firing them in retaliation for their exposure of the criminal activities of one of the aldermen. The district court granted summary judgment to the city on the ground that the plaintiffs failed to state a claim for relief by failing to invoke the federal statute creating a cause of action for violations of constitutional rights in their complaint. The federal court of appeals affirmed.

per curiam: The lower courts erred in dismissing the plaintiffs' complaint based on its failure to cite the relevant federal statute. A civil complaint need not specify the law on which the plaintiff's claim is based to survive a motion to dismiss.

Johnson v. United States, decided June 26, 2015 **[cited as *Johnson*]**

Following investigation by the FBI and arrest on suspicion of belonging to a white-supremacist organization planning terrorist activity, Samuel Johnson pleaded guilty to the crime of being a felon in possession of a firearm. The prosecutor requested an enhanced sentence under the Armed Career Criminal Act (ACCA), which authorizes a higher sentence for a defendant with three or more prior violent-offense convictions and defines violent offenses to include those involving "conduct that presents a serious potential risk of physical injury to another" (the residual clause). The prosecutor argued that Johnson's prior conviction for unlawful possession of a shotgun was a violent-offense conviction. The district court agreed and sentenced Johnson under the ACCA; the court of appeals affirmed. After oral argument, the Court ordered reargument on the constitutionality of the residual clause.

Scalia, J., for 6: The residual clause is unconstitutionally vague and cannot be enforced without violating the Due Process Clause.

Kennedy, J., concurring in judgment: The residual clause is not unconstitutionally vague, but Johnson's possession conviction was not a violent-offense conviction, so the district court erred in enhancing Johnson's sentence.

Thomas, J., concurring in judgment: The void-for-vagueness doctrine is closely related to substantive due process doctrine and suspect for similar reasons. The Court should invalidate questionable applications of the residual clause on a case-by-case or crime-by-crime basis.

Alito, J., dissenting: The majority's decision is a rash measure for removing residual-clause cases from the Court's docket. The residual clause is not unconstitutionally vague.

Kansas v. Nebraska, decided Feb. 24, 2105, decree entered Mar. 9, 2015 **[cited as *Kansas v. Nebraska*]**

In the Republican River Compact, approved by Congress in 1943, Kansas, Nebraska, and Colorado agreed to an apportionment among them of water originating in the Republican River Basin. In the mid-2000s, Kansas alleged that Nebraska breached the compact by allowing Nebraska residents to use more than their share of the basin's water. The Court appointed a special master to examine the states' arguments; his report concluded that Nebraska's breach was "knowing," recommended that Nebraska pay $3.7 million to Kansas in damages and $1.8 million as a penalty, and recommended that an appendix to the compact setting out procedures for calculating the states' annual shares of water be judicially revised.

Kagan, J., for 5 (as to all sections), 6 (as to Parts I and III): Nebraska must pay Kansas the value of the excess water Nebraska consumed, plus a penalty for recklessness. The accounting procedures in the appendix are reformed to reflect a more accurate method of calculating the states' use of imported water.

Roberts, C.J., concurring in part, dissenting in part: Although the Court has the power to order disgorgement, the Court's equitable power does not extend to the reformation of interstate compacts.

Scalia, J., concurrence in part, dissent in part: The Court should beware of relying on the American Law Institute's Restatements, including the Restatement (Third) of Restitution and Unjust Enrichment. These resources are not descriptions of the law but proposals for changes in the law.

Thomas, J., concurring in part, dissenting in part (+2, +3 as to Part III): Under ordinary principles of contract law, neither disgorgement nor reformation of the compact is appropriate in this case.

Kellogg Brown & Root Servs., Inc. v. United States ex rel. Carter, decided May 26, 2015 **[cited as *Carter*]**

During the Iraq conflict, Benjamin Carter worked for Kellogg Brown & Root (KBR), a defense contractor. He later filed a whistleblowing action under the federal False Claims Act (FCA) against KBR, alleging that KBR overbilled the U.S. government for its services during the Iraq war. After a series of filings and dismissals, the district court dismissed a third complaint filed by Carter, holding that his suit was barred by the FCA "first-to-file" bar due to the filing of a different lawsuit, and also that it was untimely because Carter filed it outside the six-year FCA filing period. The court also ruled that the Wartime Suspension of Limitations Act (WSLA), which suspends time limits for "any offense" against the federal government, did not apply to civil claims. The appellate court reversed, holding that the WLSA applied and that the first-to-file bar is lifted when a related action is dismissed.

Alito, J., for 9: The WLSA applies only to criminal proceedings; it does not suspend the statute of limitations applicable to a FCA claim that a contractor defrauded the U.S. government. A lawsuit is "pending" for purposes of the "first-to-file" bar only until the suit reaches a final disposition, such as dismissal.

Kerry v. Din, decided June 15, 2015 **[cited as *Kerry v. Din*]**

Fauzia Din, a U.S. citizen, filed a petition for priority immigration status for her husband, Kanishka Berashk, a citizen of Afghanistan and former Taliban civil servant. A consular officer denied the application, citing a federal statute requiring exclusion of noncitizens who have engaged in "terrorist activities." Din sought but was denied a more detailed explanation for the decision; she then filed a federal lawsuit, contending that the denial deprived her of due process. The district court dismissed her claim, but the court of appeals reversed, holding that she had a liberty interest in her marriage entitling her to review of the denial of Berashk's application.

Scalia, J., for 3: Denial of Berashk's visa application without further explanation did not deprive Din of any constitutionally protected due process right.

Kennedy, J., concurring in judgment: There is no need to determine whether Din had a constitutionally protected interest that was infringed in this case; even if she did, the explanation she received satisfied due process.

Breyer, J., dissenting (+3): Din is not seeking a new substantive right, as the majority assumes, but rather procedural protection for her liberty interest in living in the U.S. with her husband. The notice she received of the reasons for denial of Berashk's visa application did not satisfy due process.

Kimble v. Marvel Entertainment, LLC, decided June 22, 2015 **[cited as *Kimble*]**

Stephen Kimble and Marvel Entertainment entered into a contract under which Marvel bought Kimble's patent for a Spider-Man toy and agreed to pay him a lump sum plus a royalty on all future sales. Shortly before the patent was due to expire at the end of the 20-year statutory term, Marvel filed a federal action requesting a judicial declaration that it was not obliged to pay royalties following expiration of the patent, citing *Brulotte v. Thys Co.* (1964), in which the Court held that a patentee cannot receive royalties for sales after a patent's expiration date. The district court granted relief, and the court of appeals affirmed.

Kagan, J., for 6: The bar on post-expiration royalties established in *Brulotte* remains good law. There are no irresistible reasons to overrule *Brulotte*.

Alito, J., dissenting (+2): *Brulotte* was not an interpretation of the Patent Act, but a policy decision. It rested on faulty premises and should be overruled.

King v. Burwell, decided June 25, 2015 **[cited as *King*]**

The Patient Protection & Affordable Care Act (ACA) requires each state to create an "exchange" for residents' purchase of health insurance; it also requires the federal government to establish exchanges in states that fail to establish their own, and provides for tax credits for taxpayers buying plans through "an Exchange established by the

State." The Internal Revenue Service (IRS) issued a rule making tax credits available to those who buy plans on federally established exchanges. Several states, including Virginia, did not establish exchanges. David King, a Virginia resident, did not want to buy insurance and, if not granted the ACA credit, would have been exempted from the ACA requirement to buy insurance. With other Virginia residents, he filed a federal action challenging the IRS's interpretation of the ACA. The district court dismissed his complaint, holding that the ACA made tax credits available to those enrolled through federally established exchanges. The appellate court affirmed, finding the ACA ambiguous and deferring to the IRS's interpretation.

Roberts, C.J., for 6: The ACA provision in question, read with other parts of the ACA, authorizes credits for those who buy insurance on federally established exchanges. Deference to the IRS's interpretation is inappropriate in a case involving an issue of such importance.

Scalia, J., dissenting (+2): The ACA's reference to exchanges "established by the State" is not ambiguous and cannot be read to refer to exchanges established by the federal government.

Kingsley v. Hendrickson, decided June 22, 2015 **[cited as *Kingsley*]**

While Michael Kingsley was in jail awaiting trial on drug charges, officers removed him from his cell and, among other things, stunned him with a Taser. Kingsley sued the officers, alleging that their use of force against him violated his due process rights. The district judge instructed a jury that Kingsley needed to prove that the officers acted "recklessly"; the jury found for the officers. On appeal, Kingsley argued that the proper standard for assessing a pretrial detainee's excessive-force claim is objective unreasonableness and does not require proof of the defendant's state of mind (as a "reckless" standard does). The court of appeals disagreed.

Breyer, J., for 5: To prevail on an excessive-force claim against law enforcement, a pretrial detainee only needs to show that the force officers purposefully or knowingly used was objectively unreasonable. The detainee need not show that the officers subjectively intended to violate the detainee's constitutional rights.

Scalia, J., dissenting (+2): Precedent establishes that intentional punishment of a state pretrial detainee may violate the Fourteenth Amendment, but there is no precedent for the objective standard endorsed by the majority. An officer's intent to punish should be the focus in a pretrial detainee's due process claim.

Alito, J., dissenting: The Court should have dismissed this case as improvidently granted. The proper constitutional rubric for deciding a claim like this is the Fourth Amendment. The Court should not identify new substantive due process rights.

Kwai Fun Wong: see ***United States v. Kwai Fun Wong***

Lopez v. Smith, decided Oct. 6, 2014 **[cited as *Lopez v. Smith*]**

During his trial for murder of his wife in state court, Marvin Smith presented evidence that he was physically incapable of the murder because of a shoulder injury and evidence that one of his former employees committed the murder. The prosecutor argued to the jury that Smith was physically capable of the murder and that even if he had not committed it himself, he had arranged for another person to commit it; the jury was told that it could find Smith guilty on an aiding-and-abetting theory. The state appellate courts affirmed Smith's conviction, rejecting his argument that he had inadequate notice of the prosecution's aiding-and-abetting theory. On collateral review, the federal district court granted Smith's habeas petition; the appellate court affirmed on the ground that the state raised the aiding-and-abetting theory for the first time in its request for jury instructions, and Smith's argument was "indistinguishable" from one accepted in a 1989 Ninth Circuit case.

per curiam: The Ninth Circuit was wrong to reverse the state courts' holding that Smith's rights were not violated by the jury instruction request. No Supreme Court opinion "clearly established" that this practice violates due process.

Mach Mining, LLC v. Equal Employment Opportunity Commission (EEOC), decided Apr. 29, 2015 **[cited as *Mach Mining*]**

A woman who applied for a job as a coal miner with Mach Mining was not hired. As required by Title VII of the Civil Rights Act, before suing for employment discrimination, she filed a charge with the EEOC, which investigated and found cause to believe Mach Mining discriminated. Title VII also requires the EEOC to try to conciliate a dispute before it or an employee may sue. The EEOC sent a letter inviting Mach Mining and the job applicant to participate in informal conciliation; a year later, the EEOC sent Mach Mining another letter stating that efforts to conciliate had been unsuccessful. The EEOC then sued Mach Mining in federal court. There, Mach Mining contended that the EEOC did not try in good faith to conciliate. The district court agreed to assess the EEOC's conciliation efforts but also granted the EEOC immediate leave to appeal. The court of appeals held that the EEOC's obligation to conciliate could not be judicially reviewed.

Kagan, J., for 9: The Title VII conciliation requirement is judicially reviewable. To satisfy the requirement, the EEOC must try to rectify any alleged unlawful unemployment practice through conciliation. "Bookend" letters are evidence of such an attempt, but they are not conclusive evidence of a good-faith attempt if challenged. The EEOC must be able to show that it informed the employer about a specific allegation and gave the employer a chance to remedy it.

MacLean: see ***Dep't of Homeland Security (DHS) v. MacLean***

M&G Polymers USA, LLC v. Tackett, decided Jan. 26, 2015 **[cited as *M&G Polymers*]**

M&G Polymers bought a textile plant in 2000 and at that time entered into collective-bargaining and benefits agreements with the union representing plant employees. The benefits agreement provided that some retirees would receive "full Company contribution" toward their benefits for the duration of the agreement, which was subject to renegotiation in three years. When the agreement expired, M&G announced that it was requiring retirees to contribute to the cost of their benefits. Hobert Tackett and other retirees, on behalf of a class of people affected by the announcement, sued M&G, arguing that the benefits agreement created a right to lifetime contribution-free benefits. The district court dismissed the plaintiffs' complaint, but the court of appeals reversed based on its 1983 *Yard-Man* decision, which the court of appeals interpreted as creating a presumption that parties to a benefit agreement intend benefits to vest for life.

Thomas, J., for 9: Courts should interpret collective-bargaining and related agreements between a union and an employer according to "ordinary principles of contract law," without any presumption that the parties to such an agreement intend benefits to vest in employees for their lifetimes.

Ginsburg, J., concurring (+3): On remand, the Sixth Circuit should apply ordinary principles of contract law to decide whether the parties to this agreement intended the benefits to vest in employees for their lifetimes.

McFadden v. United States, decided June 18, 2015 **[cited as *McFadden*]**

After he sold "bath salts" to a video shop, Stephen McFadden was prosecuted under the federal Controlled Substance Analogue Enforcement Act (Act), which identifies categories of substances similar to those on federal controlled-substances lists and tells courts to treat those substances as controlled substances if they are intended for human consumption. McFadden argued that he did not know bath salts qualified as analogues and asked the district court to tell the jury that the state had to prove that McFadden knew the substance he sold had particular effects on the nervous system. The district court instead told the jury that the state needed to show that McFadden intentionally distributed a substance with effects similar to those of a controlled substance and intended it to be consumed by humans. After McFadden's conviction, the court of appeals affirmed, holding that the Act required the state to show only that the defendant intended the substance sold to be consumed by humans.

Thomas, J., for 8: To convict a defendant under the Act, the state must show that the defendant knew he or she sold a substance regulated by the Act. A showing that the defendant knew of the features of a substance making it an analogue will satisfy this standard, as will a showing that the defendant knew the substance was controlled under the Act, even without knowledge of the substance's features.

Roberts, C.J., concurring in judgment: The Act requires a defendant to know that a substance is controlled, not just the identity of the substance or the features that make it a controlled substance.

Mellouli v. Lynch, decided June 1, 2015 **[cited as *Mellouli*]**

Moones Mellouli, a legal permanent resident of the U.S., pleaded guilty to violation of a Kansas law criminalizing possession of drug paraphernalia, based on his possession of a sock in which he was carrying four stimulant tablets. After Mellouli's conviction, an Immigration Judge ordered him deported under a federal statute authorizing deportation of noncitizens convicted of violating "any law" of a "a State... relating to a controlled substance (as defined in [federal law])." When Mellouli was convicted, the Kansas drug schedules included substances not on the federal schedules. The Board of Immigration Appeals (BIA) affirmed the deportation order, and the court of appeals denied Mellouli's petition for review.

Ginsburg, J., for 7: The federal statute at issue does not require deportation of a person convicted under state law of possessing paraphernalia for the purpose of concealing a controlled substance, when the state law of conviction does not explicitly require proof that the person's conduct involved a federally controlled substance.

Thomas, J., dissenting (+1): The majority's resolution does not provide sufficient guidance to lower courts. As long as a state law "relates to" federally controlled substances, as the Kansas law here does, a conviction for its violation should trigger deportation, regardless of whether the particular conviction related to federally controlled substances.

Michigan v. Environmental Protection Agency (EPA), decided June 29, 2015 (with *Utility Air Regulatory Group v. EPA* and *National Mining Ass'n v. EPA*) **[cited as *Michigan v. EPA*]**

The Clean Air Act (CAA) tells the EPA to regulate emissions of air pollutants from certain installations, such as factories. Before it can regulate power plants under this authority, the EPA is required by the CAA to find that regulation is "appropriate and necessary." In 2000, the EPA announced that it had found power-plant regulation "appropriate and necessary" without considering the cost of regulation, and the EPA initiated the regulatory process. Michigan, with 22 other states, sought review of the rule resulting from that process in the federal court of appeals, which concluded that the EPA acted reasonably in making its decision to regulate power-plant emissions.

Scalia, J., for 5: The EPA interpreted the CAA unreasonably when it decided to regulate power plants without taking the costs of regulation into consideration. The EPA must consider costs, including compliance costs, when making an initial decision about whether regulation is "appropriate and necessary."

Thomas, J., concurring: The Court should justify its doctrine of deference to agency interpretations of statutes or abandon the doctrine.

Kagan, J., dissenting (+3): The EPA did not act unreasonably in deciding to regulate power plants without explicitly calculating costs. The EPA knew it would consider costs later in the regulatory process. The majority should have assessed the entire process EPA engaged in, not just its initial decision.

North Carolina State Bd. of Dental Examiners v. Federal Trade Commission, decided Feb. 25, 2015 **[cited as *N.C. State Bd.*]**

Under state law, the North Carolina State Board of Dental Examiners (Board) is an "agency of the State." In 2006 and 2007, the Board sent cease-and-desist letters to a number of nondentists providing teeth-whitening services, warning them that the unlicensed practice of dentistry is a crime (even though North Carolina law does not classify teeth whitening as dental practice). The Federal Trade Commission (FTC) filed a complaint charging the Board with anticompetitive activity under the FTC Act. An Administrative Law Judge, an FTC panel, and a panel of a federal court of appeals all rejected the Board's argument that it was entitled to antitrust immunity under the "state action" doctrine because it was a state agency.

Kennedy, J., for 6: Because of its structure and operation—composed of industry participants and not actively supervised by the state government—the Board is not a state actor for purposes of antitrust immunity.

Alito, J., dissenting (+2): The Board is a state actor. The majority's conclusion otherwise departs from precedent and relies on an analysis that will be difficult to apply in future cases.

Obergefell v. Hodges, decided June 26, 2015 (with ***Tanco v. Haslam, DeBoer v. Snyder***, and ***Bourke v. Beshear***) **[cited as *Obergefell*]**

James Obergefell and 13 other members of same-sex couples from Michigan, Kentucky, Ohio, and Tennessee filed four suits against officials of their respective states in federal court in each state. They claimed that the officials were violating the Fourteenth Amendment by denying the plaintiff couples the right to marry and refusing to recognize same-sex marriages performed in other states. The district courts ruled in the plaintiffs' favor, but the court of appeals for the circuit embracing all four states consolidated the cases and reversed.

Kennedy, J., for 5: Couples in same-sex relationships have a constitutional right, under the federal Due Process and Equal Protection clauses, to marry on the same terms as any other couples under state law and to have each state recognize same-sex marriages performed in other states.

Roberts, C.J., dissenting (+2): The Constitution contains no right to marry a same-sex partner, and it assigns control over marriage to the states. The Court should have allowed the states to pursue different policies on this issue. The majority's decision will alienate and embitter those with different preferences.

Scalia, J., dissenting (+1): The majority decision is an antidemocratic display of hubris and moral righteousness, written in a "pretentious" style.

Thomas, J., dissenting (+1): The majority relies on a perverse understanding of "liberty" under the Due Process clauses, and a perverse understanding of "dignity." Its conclusion infringes the liberty of as many citizens as it protects.

Alito, J., dissenting (+2): States have a constitutional right to seek to preserve a traditional understanding of marriage as linked to procreation. The majority's opinion will cause persecution of people who hold this traditional view.

Ohio v. Clark, decided June 18, 2015 **[cited as *Clark*]**

Darius Clark was caring for his girlfriend's three-year-old son, L.P. L.P.'s preschool teachers noticed marks on his body and asked L.P. about them; he identified Clark as their cause. At Clark's trial on child-abuse charges, the state offered L.P.'s statements to his teachers as evidence supporting Clark's guilt. L.P. was not allowed to testify under applicable law, and Clark moved to exclude L.P.'s statements to his teachers under the Sixth Amendment's Confrontation Clause. After Clark's conviction on several charges, the state appellate court reversed, holding that the Confrontation Clause made L.P.'s statements inadmissible as evidence against Clark. The state Supreme Court affirmed.

Alito, J., for 9: The use of L.P.'s statements at Clark's trial did not violate the Confrontation Clause, because L.P. did not make the statements for the purpose of creating testimony against Clark.

Scalia, J., concurring in judgment (+1): The majority opinion understates the significance of the break with prior Confrontation Clause doctrine represented by the Court's opinion in *Crawford* (2004).

Thomas, J., concurring in judgment: The majority does not offer clear guidance for Confrontation Clause analysis of statements made to people other than law-enforcement personnel. The Court should assess Confrontation Clause issues by asking whether the statements in question bear sufficient "indicia of solemnity."

Omnicare, Inc. v. Laborers Dist. Council Constr. Indus. Pension Fund, decided Mar. 24, 2015 **[cited as *Omnicare*]**

The Securities Act (Act) requires a company planning to issue securities to file a statement with the Securities & Exchange Commission. Section 11 of the Act allows a buyer of securities to sue an issuer if the statement contains "an untrue statement of a material fact" or "omit[s]" a fact "necessary to make the statements therein not misleading." Omnicare's registration statement contained two statements of Omnicare's belief that it was in compliance with federal and state law. The federal government later sued Omnicare for receiving kickbacks. The Laborers' pension fund, which had bought Omnicare stock, sued Omnicare for violating § 11, pointing to these statements about legal compliance. The district court dismissed the complaint, based on the fund's failure to allege that Omnicare's officers knew they were violating the law. The court of appeals reversed, holding that the officers' belief was irrelevant.

Kagan, J., for 7: A sincere statement of opinion, even if it turns out to be inaccurate, cannot create § 11 liability. But a statement of opinion may imply to a reasonable investor that the maker of the statement inquired into facts underlying the opinion. If a statement of opinion misleads by not mentioning the failure to make such an inquiry, the statement can create § 11 liability.

Scalia, J., concurring in part and in judgment: The only fact implied by a statement of opinion is the fact that the maker of the statement sincerely holds the opinion. A reasonable investor does not believe that statements of opinion are based on any particular factual inquiry.

Thomas, J., concurring in judgment: The majority should not have addressed the issue of liability for omissions (as opposed to untrue statements) under § 11, because the parties did not properly present this issue to the Court.

ONEOK, Inc. v. Learjet, Inc., decided Apr. 21, 2015 **[cited as *ONEOK*]**

Learjet, with other purchasers of natural gas who buy it directly from pipelines, sued ONEOK and other interstate natural-gas pipelines for violations of state antitrust laws, claiming that the pipelines artificially inflated wholesale and retail natural-gas prices. The pipelines removed to federal court and successfully moved for summary judgment on the ground that the claims were preempted by the federal Natural Gas Act (Act). The Act gives the Federal Energy Regulatory Commission (FERC) power to determine the reasonableness of natural-gas rates and practices affecting rates, but limits FERC jurisdiction to practices related to interstate commerce, thus excluding practices affecting retail prices. The court of appeals reversed, holding that the state-law claims sought relief for unreasonable retail prices and were thus not preempted.

Breyer, J., for 5 (as to entire opinion), 6 (as to all but Part I-A): The Act does not preempt the pipelines' state-law claims by occupying the field of gas-rate regulation. There might be a conflict between the Act and the state antitrust laws, but since the parties did not brief this issue, the Court does not decide it.

Thomas, J., concurring in judgment: The Court's previous decisions about the Act's preemptive effect are poorly reasoned, but the majority does not extend them in this case, so its conclusion has limited significance.

Scalia, J., dissenting (+1): The Act preempts these claims. It gives FERC power to regulate practices affecting wholesale natural-gas rates, and there is no reason to distinguish between wholesale and retail rates here. The Act also expressly limits state authority and does not expressly reserve state authority over retail rates.

Patel: see ***City of Los Angeles v. Patel***

Perez v. Mortgage Bankers Ass'n, decided Mar. 9, 2015 (with *Nichols v. Mortgage Bankers Ass'n*) **[cited as *Perez*]**

Between 1999 and 2010, the Department of Labor (DOL) issued several statements addressing whether mortgage-loan officers are exempt from overtime pay under the Fair Labor Standards Act; in these statements, the DOL repeatedly reversed position on the matter. Mortgage Bankers Association (MBA) asked for one of these reassessments of the DOL's position. After the DOL issued a 2010 interpretation taking the position that mortgage-loan officers qualify for overtime, MBA sued the Secretary of Labor, arguing that the interpretation was invalid under *Paralyzed Veterans of America* (1997), in which the D.C. Circuit held that an agency must use the notice-and-comment procedure prescribed by the Administrative Procedure Act (APA) before issuing a new interpretation of a regulation that significantly departs from a previous interpretation. The district court granted summary judgment to the Secretary of Labor, but the court of appeals reversed, applying *Paralyzed Veterans.*

Sotomayor, J., for 5 (as to the entire opinion), 6 (as to all but Part III-B): An agency may revise an interpretive rule without following notice-and-comment procedures. The D.C. Circuit was wrong to hold that revisions of interpretive rules require notice and comment; that requirement applies only to "legislative rules."

Alito, J., concurring in part and in judgment: The D.C. Circuit might have been justifiably concerned about the scope of agency power, since other legal doctrines require deference to agency decisions. One such doctrine, the *Seminole Rock* (1945) rule of heightened deference to agency interpretations of regulations, should be revisited.

Scalia, J., concurring in judgment: The majority decision, like the *Seminole Rock* rule, confers too much power on agencies. *Seminole Rock* should be overruled.

Thomas, J., concurring in judgment: *Seminole Rock* is inconsistent with the original understanding of the judicial, legislative, and executive powers.

Reed v. Town of Gilbert, decided June 18, 2015 **[cited as *Reed*]**

The town of Gilbert, Arizona, had a sign code (Code) regulating outdoor signs. It allowed display of "temporary directional signs" (directing the public to an event) but limited their number and size and required that they be put up and removed within a short time. Clyde Reed, pastor of a church that held services at various locations in Gilbert, posted signs bearing directions to the services but did not remove them within the required time; he and the church were cited for Code violations. Reed sued Gilbert, claiming the Code abridged his and the church's freedom of speech. The district court denied their motion for an injunction against enforcement of the Code. The court of appeals affirmed, reasoning that the Code drew content-neutral distinctions and imposed restrictions reasonably related to safety and aesthetic goals.

Thomas, J., for 6: The Code violates the First Amendment because it regulates speech on the basis of content and lacks a sufficiently close relationship to the advancement of a compelling governmental interest.

Alito, J., concurring (+2): The majority's holding does not imply the invalidity of many other types of sign regulations that could achieve ends similar to those sought by the provision invalidated in this case.

Breyer, J., concurring in judgment: Identifying a government restriction on speech as "content-based" should not lead to its automatic invalidation. The Court should balance the public and private interests affected in each such case.

Kagan, J., dissenting (+2): The majority's analysis threatens the validity of many local sign regulations. If it is not realistically likely that a speech restriction was actually motivated by or is used to discriminate among viewpoints, strict scrutiny of the regulation may not be appropriate.

Reyes Mata v. Lynch, decided June 15, 2015 **[cited as *Reyes Mata*]**

Noel Reyes Mata, a Mexican citizen, was convicted of assault. An Immigration Judge ordered him deported. Mata's attorney filed a notice of appeal with the Board of

Immigration Appeals (BIA) but never filed a brief, and Mata's appeal was dismissed. Through different counsel, Mata moved to reopen the proceedings, arguing that his first lawyer's neglect was an "exceptional circumstance" justifying suspension of the time limit that otherwise applies to such motions. The BIA dismissed the motion; although it had power to excuse Mata's failure to meet the deadline, the BIA declined to do so. Mata appealed to the Fifth Circuit, which dismissed the appeal for lack of appellate jurisdiction, under circuit precedent barring review of BIA decisions not to exercise the authority to excuse deadline violations.

Kagan, J., for 8: A court of appeals has appellate jurisdiction over a BIA rejection of a noncitizen's motion to reopen removal proceedings, filed after the normal deadline for such motions has passed, even if the BIA did not provide a reasoned explanation for its rejection of the motion.

Thomas, J., dissenting: In this case, the Fifth Circuit apparently applied an inappropriately rigid rule requiring "recharacterization" of untimely motions to reopen. This case did not really present a question about appellate jurisdiction. The Court should have held that the Fifth Circuit applied an improper legal rule.

Rodriguez v. United States, decided Apr. 21, 2015 **[cited as *Rodriguez*]**

Morgan Struble, a K-9 police officer, stopped Dennys Rodriguez for driving on a highway shoulder. Struble issued a warning and then, even though Rodriguez did not consent to have Struble's dog sniff the car, Struble brought his dog to the car. The dog's reaction led Struble to methamphetamine in the car. Indicted on drug charges, Rodriguez moved to suppress the evidence from his car, arguing that Struble prolonged the stop without reasonable suspicion in violation of the Fourth Amendment. The district court denied the motion, concluding that the seven or so minutes the dog sniff added to the stop was a "de minimis" intrusion on Rodriguez's rights. Rodriguez entered a conditional guilty plea; the court of appeals affirmed but did not decide whether Struble had reasonable suspicion justifying the dog sniff.

Ginsburg, J., for 6: When a police officer stops a driver for a traffic violation, once the time reasonably required for the officer to complete tasks related to the violation has passed, any extension of the stop to investigate further violates the Fourth Amendment unless it is justified by independent reasonable suspicion.

Kennedy, J., dissenting: Part III of Justice Thomas's dissent addresses an issue not considered by the lower courts (whether reasonable suspicion to support the dog sniff was present). The Court should not address that issue but should let the lower courts consider it on remand.

Thomas, J., dissenting (+1, +2 as to all but Part III): If an officer reasonably executes a traffic stop that was lawful at the outset, there is no Fourth Amendment violation. Struble had reasonable suspicion that justified a dog sniff.

Alito, J., dissenting: The majority unnecessarily addresses a hypothetical question. Struble had reasonable suspicion justifying the dog sniff.

Sheehan: see ***City & County of San Francisco v. Sheehan***

T-Mobile South, LLC v. City of Roswell, decided Jan. 14, 2015 **[cited as *T-Mobile South*]**

The Telecommunications Act (Act) requires a municipality denying a building permit for a cell-phone tower to make the denial "in writing and supported by substantial evidence. . . in a written record." The Roswell city council (Council), after a public hearing, denied T-Mobile South's application for a permit. Two days later, the Roswell zoning division sent T-Mobile a letter communicating the denial and promising that hearing minutes would be available; the minutes appeared on the Council website 26 days later. T-Mobile sued, claiming that the Council violated the Act. The district court agreed that Roswell violated the Act by failing to issue a written decision containing reasons for the denial. The court of appeals, following its own precedent, reversed, noting that T-Mobile had a transcript of the hearing (which T-Mobile arranged to record) and received a denial letter.

Sotomayor, J., for 6: The Act requires a municipality denying a tower-building permit to make the reasons for denial available to the applicant in writing. The municipality must make the reasons available "essentially contemporaneously" with the written notice of denial.

Alito, J., concurring: Municipalities should have some leeway to choose different approaches in their procedures for denying cell-tower permits.

Roberts, C.J., dissenting (+1, +2 as to Part I): The majority's timing requirement is not suggested by the Act and is unnecessary.

Thomas, J., dissenting: The majority's imposition of a contemporaneous-timing requirement is insufficiently respectful of and deferential to municipalities.

Taylor v. Barkes, decided June 1, 2015 **[cited as *Taylor v. Barkes*]**

Christopher Barkes was arrested for violating probation and taken to a correctional institution. An intake nurse evaluated him using a questionnaire designed in part to assess an inmate's risk of suicide. Barkes told the nurse he had a history of psychiatric treatment and disclosed at least one of his four suicide attempts, but said he was not currently suicidal; the nurse did not initiate a suicide-prevention protocol. The following morning, correctional officers discovered that Barkes had hanged himself. His surviving family sued several entities and individuals connected with the facility, claiming they violated Barkes's civil rights by failing to prevent his suicide. The district court denied defendants' summary judgment motion, which argued that they were entitled to qualified immunity as state actors who had not violated clearly established law. The court of appeals affirmed.

per curiam: At the time of Barkes's intake, no Supreme Court decisions "clearly established" that the Constitution gives a person a right to a prison-intake process that will effectively identify whether the person is at risk of suicide. The defendants were entitled to qualified immunity against claims arising from Barkes's suicide.

Teva Pharmaceuticals USA, Inc. v. Sandoz, Inc., decided Jan. 20, 2015 **[cited as *Teva*]**

Sandoz and other firms began marketing a generic version of a multiple-sclerosis drug; Teva owned a patent for a manufacturing method for the drug and sued Sandoz for infringing it. Sandoz countered that the patent was invalid because of the indefiniteness of the term "molecular weight" in the patent claim, noting that there are three accepted methods of calculating molecular weight. After considering expert evidence from both parties, the district court found that a skilled artisan would understand the phrase to refer to weight calculated by one of the methods and concluded that the patent was valid. The court of appeals reviewed all the district court's findings *de novo*, including its finding on the meaning of "molecular weight."

Breyer, J., for 7: An appellate court reviewing a district court's resolution of factual findings subsidiary to the district court's patent claim construction should apply the clear error standard of review, not the *de novo* standard appropriate to questions of law arising during claim construction.

Thomas, J., dissenting (+1): Patent claim construction is an entirely legal activity, involving no factfinding. All conclusions reached by a district court during claim construction should be reviewed *de novo.*

Texas Dep't of Housing & Community Affairs v. Inclusive Communities Project, Inc., decided June 25, 2015 **[cited as *Texas Dep't of Housing*]**

The Fair Housing Act (FHA) forbids denying anyone housing opportunities on the basis of race, color, religion, or national origin. The Texas Department of Housing & Community Affairs (TDH) distributes federal tax credits for low-income housing development. Inclusive Communities Project, a nonprofit that helps low-income families acquire housing, sued TDH for violating the FHA on a "disparate impact" theory, which did not require showing that TDH intended to discriminate, only that its acts had a disparate effect on members of minority groups. The district court held against TDH, concluding that TDH failed to show it had no less discriminatory alternatives for allocating tax credits. The court of appeals agreed that the FHA allows disparate-impact claims but held that the district court applied the wrong standard to decide the claim.

Kennedy, J., for 5: A plaintiff may sue under the FHA on a disparate-impact theory. To prevail, the plaintiff need only show that the defendant's practices have a "disproportionately adverse effect on minorities" and lack a legitimate rationale.

Thomas, J., dissenting: Disparate-impact theories of liability are the illegitimate products of an ideologically motivated campaign by the EEOC during the 1960s, are inconsistent with antidiscrimination statutes, and should be rejected by the Court, both in the FHA context and in other antidiscrimination contexts.

Alito, J., dissenting (+3): The majority improperly extends precedent from other statutory contexts to the FHA, and its conclusion is not compelled by the text of the FHA. Allowing disparate-treatment FHA claims will put municipalities and developers in a double bind.

Tibble v. Edison Int'l, decided May 18, 2015 **[cited as *Tibble*]**

The Employee Retirement Income Security Act (ERISA) imposes duties on employers offering 401(k) plans and allows employees to sue employers for breach of these duties, but it requires suits to be filed within six years of the employer's breaching act or of the last date on which the employer could have fixed its improper failure to act. In 2007, Glenn Tibble, on behalf of himself and other beneficiaries of Edison's 401(k) plan, sued Edison under ERISA, arguing that Edison could have offered lower-priced funds when it added mutual funds to its plan in 1999 and 2002. The district court held that the claims were barred by the six-year limit. The court of appeals affirmed.

Breyer, J., for 9: The ERISA duties of a 401(k) plan trustee include an ongoing obligation to monitor and adjust investments. So the six-year ERISA time limit does not require suit to be filed within six years of the addition of a particular investment to the plan. A plaintiff only needs to identify a failure to monitor or remove imprudent investments within six years before filing suit.

United States v. California, order issued Dec. 15, 2014 **[cited as *United States v. California*]**

In 1947, the Court entered a decree establishing a boundary off the coast of California to clarify the respective rights of the state of California and the U.S. government to offshore lands and natural resources. Between 1966 and 1981, the Court issued three more supplemental decrees regarding various parts of the boundary. In a 112-page order, consisting mostly of longitude and latitude coordinates, the Court "identif[ied] with greater particularity the boundary line between the submerged lands of California and those of the United States."

decree: Motion granted for entry of fifth supplemental decree adjusting California-United States offshore boundary line.

United States v. Kwai Fun Wong, decided Apr. 22, 2015 (with *United States v. June, Conservator*) **[cited as *Kwai Fun Wong*]**

The Federal Tort Claims Act (FTCA) provides that tort claims against the U.S. "shall be forever barred" unless the claimaint meets two deadlines: first, presenting a claim to the appropriate federal agency for review "within two years" after the claim "accrues," and second, filing suit in federal court "within six months" of any agency denial. Kwai Fun Wong and Marlene June each missed one of the deadlines. Wong argued that she missed the six-month deadline because a district court had not let her file her claim until the period expired. June argued that she missed the two-year deadline because the government concealed facts vital to her claim. District courts dismissed both claims, holding that the time bars are not subject to equitable tolling. The court of appeals reversed, concluding that both bars may be equitably tolled.

Kagan, J., for 5: The FTCA filing deadlines are subject to equitable tolling.

Alito, J., dissenting (+3): The FTCA deadlines are jurisdictional requirements for filing FTCA claims and should not be subject to equitable tolling.

Walker v. Texas Div., Sons of Confederate Veterans, Inc., decided June 18, 2015 **[cited as *Walker*]**

Texas offers car owners the option of displaying specialty-design license plates. Designs may be proposed by members of the public but must be approved by the Texas Department of Motor Vehicles Board (DMV). The Texas Division of the Sons of Confederate Veterans and its officers sued the Chairman and the DMV, arguing that the DMV's rejection of the Sons' proposal for a plate showing a Confederate battle flag violated their First Amendment free-speech rights. The district court ruled for the DMV. The court of appeals reversed, holding that the DMV discriminated on the basis of viewpoint in refusing to approve the design.

Breyer, J., for 5: The DMV's denial of the Sons' application did not infringe the Sons' First Amendment rights. Texas's specialty plates are a form of government speech, and the state may choose the content it wants its speech to have.

Alito, J., dissenting (+3): The Texas specialty plates should be analyzed not as government speech, but as a limited public forum, triggering stricter scrutiny of the DMV's justification for denial of this application. The DMV's justifications for this denial—avoiding driver distraction and offense—were insufficient.

Warger v. Shauers, decided Dec. 9, 2014 **[cited as *Warger*]**

Gregory Warger sued Randy Shauers in federal court for negligence after Shauers's truck collided with Warger and his motorcycle. Following a jury verdict in Shauers's favor, one of the jurors contacted Warger's lawyer, claiming that the jury foreperson mentioned, during deliberations, that her daughter had been at fault in a fatal car accident and would have had her life ruined had she been sued. Warger moved for a new trial, arguing that the foreperson lied about her impartiality during jury selection.

The district court denied the motion, holding that Federal Rule of Evidence 606(b), which bars evidence of "any statement made... during the jury's deliberations," barred testimony about the foreperson's statements. The court of appeals affirmed.

Sotomayor, J., for 9: Rule 606(b) forbids a juror's testimony about another juror's admission, during deliberations, of potential bias against a party, even if that testimony would show that the allegedly biased juror lied during jury selection.

Wellness Int'l Network, Ltd. v. Sharif, decided May 26, 2015 **[cited as *Wellness Int'l*]**

Richard Sharif tried to discharge a debt to Wellness International Network in Sharif's bankruptcy proceedings. Wellness asked the bankruptcy court to find that the assets of a trust Sharif claimed to administer were actually his personal property and part of his bankruptcy estate. The bankruptcy court entered judgment against Sharif on the issue. While Sharif's appeal was pending, the Court decided *Stern v. Marshall* (2011), which held that Article III of the Constitution forbids bankruptcy courts' entry of final judgment on certain kinds of claims. Sharif sought to file a new brief in district court arguing that Wellness's claim was a *Stern* claim. The district court declined and affirmed the bankruptcy court's judgment. The court of appeals held that Sharif should have been allowed to make his *Stern* argument and that under *Stern*, the bankruptcy court lacked constitutional authority to enter judgment on Wellness's claim.

Sotomayor, J., for 5–6: A bankruptcy court may adjudicate a *Stern* claim if all parties consent. Consent may be implied by parties' conduct during the proceedings.

Alito, J., concurring in part and in judgment: The majority did not need to and should not have decided whether consent may be implied in this situation. That decision raises additional questions that will need to be answered in future cases.

Roberts, C.J., dissenting (+1, +2 as to Part I): It is not clear that Wellness's claim is a *Stern* claim. A bankruptcy court's adjudication of a *Stern* claim violates Article III of the Constitution, and parties cannot consent to a violation of Article III. The majority decision sets a bad precedent.

Thomas, J., dissenting: The Court should have remanded this case for determination of whether Wellness's claim is a *Stern* claim. The Constitution assigns the judicial power to Article III tribunals, with only a few exceptions, and does not allow individuals to consent to violations of the separation of powers.

Whitfield v. United States, decided Jan. 13, 2105 **[cited as *Whitfield*]**

Larry Whitfield, having unsuccessfully tried to rob a bank, entered the home of 79-year-old Mary Parnell and guided her a few feet within the house; she then died of a heart attack. Whitfield was convicted in federal district court of, among other things, violating a federal statute prescribing enhanced penalties for anyone who "forces any person to accompany him without... consent" while committing or fleeing from a bank robbery. The court of appeals held that Whitfield's actions satisfied the statute, rejecting his argument that the statute requires "substantial" movement.

Scalia, J., for 9: The provision at issue applies whenever a robber forces a person to move with the robber, even over a short distance measured in feet.

Williams-Yulee v. Florida Bar, decided Apr. 29, 2015 **[cited as *Williams-Yulee*]**

Florida is one of 39 U.S. states where voters elect judges. The Florida Supreme Court adopted a rule (the Canon) as part of its Code of Judicial Conduct, providing that candidates for election to judicial seats "shall not personally solicit campaign funds."

Lanell Williams-Yulee, during her campaign for a seat as a state judge, mailed and posted online a letter soliciting contributions to her campaign. The Florida Bar disciplined her for violating the Canon. Yulee argued that the First Amendment protects her right to personally solicit campaign funds. The state Supreme Court upheld her disciplinary sanction, concluding that the Canon is narrowly tailored to serve the state's compelling interest in preserving public confidence in the integrity of the judiciary.

Roberts, C.J., for 4, 5 (as to all but Part II): The Canon does not infringe candidates' First Amendment free-speech rights. It is justified by Florida's interest in preserving public confidence in the integrity of the judiciary and is tailored appropriately to advance that interest.

Breyer, J., concurring: The Court should treat the strict-scrutiny analysis that it applies in cases like this one as a guideline rather than a mechanical test.

Ginsburg, J., concurring in part and in judgment (+1): Strict scrutiny (requiring a compelling government interest and a narrowly tailored means of advancing it) should not apply to the Canon. States should have wide latitude to regulate judicial elections.

Scalia, J., dissenting (+1): The Canon is a content-based restriction on speech and is not narrowly tailored to target concerns about the appearance of impartiality, so it should have been held unconstitutional.

Kennedy, J., dissenting: Strict scrutiny is especially important in the context of election-related speech, and the Canon fails strict scrutiny.

Alito, J., dissenting: The Canon is not narrowly tailored. The majority's narrow tailoring analysis sets a bad precedent for future cases requiring strict scrutiny.

Woods v. Donald, decided Mar. 30, 2015 **[cited as *Woods v. Donald*]**

With four other men, Cory Donald robbed a drug dealer, who eventually died of injuries sustained during the robbery. Donald was prosecuted in state court for felony murder and armed robbery, and tried along with two of the other men involved in the robbery. At trial, the government offered as evidence a chart showing phone calls among three of the robbers, not including Donald. Donald's lawyer did not object. The judge admitted the chart and took a recess; Donald's lawyer did not return to the courtroom until after proceedings involving testimony about the chart had resumed. The jury found Donald guilty on all counts. On appeal, Donald argued that he was entitled to a new trial because his lawyer's absence during part of the trial denied him his constitutional right to effective assistance of counsel. The state appellate courts rejected his claim. A federal district court, however, granted him habeas relief, and the court of appeals affirmed.

per curiam: The court of appeals was wrong to hold that a criminal defendant's attorney's absence from the courtroom during trial testimony concerning other codefendants necessarily amounted to constitutionally ineffective assistance of counsel. No precedent "clearly established" this rule.

Wynne: see ***Comptroller of Treasury of Maryland v. Wynne***

Yates v. United States, decided Feb. 25, 2015 **[cited as *Yates*]**

During an inspection of a fishing ship in the Gulf of Mexico, a deputy federal agent found undersized fish, in violation of federal conservation law, and told the captain, John Yates, to separate those fish from the rest of the catch until his return to port.

Instead, Yates had a crew member throw the fish overboard. The government charged Yates with violation of 18 U.S.C. § 1519 (part of the Sarbanes-Oxley Act), which authorizes a sentence of up to 20 years for any person who "alters, destroys, mutilates, conceals, covers up, falsifies, or makes a false entry in any record, document, or tangible object with the intent to impede" a federal investigation. At trial, Yates argued that "tangible object" covered only objects used to store information. The district court rejected the argument, and a jury found Yates guilty. The court of appeals affirmed, concluding that fish are "tangible object[s]."

Ginsburg, J., for 4: This provision was part of a legislative response to accounting fraud and was meant to deter future fraud of the same kind. It covers only objects used to record or preserve information, not objects such as fish.

Alito, J., concurring: The textual features of the provision support the majority's restricted reading of "tangible object."

Kagan, J., dissenting (+3): The Court should apply "tangible object" according to its ordinary meaning, which would include objects other than those used to record information, such as fish.

Young v. United Parcel Service, Inc., decided Mar. 25, 2015 **[cited as *Young*]**

The Pregnancy Discrimination Act (PDA) requires employers to treat pregnant employees "the same for all employment-related purposes... as other persons not so affected but similar in their ability or inability to work." Peggy Young, a driver for United Parcel Service (UPS), was advised by her doctor not to lift more than 20 pounds during her pregnancy. UPS told Young that she could not work while under this restriction, and Young sued UPS for violating the PDA by refusing to accommodate her restriction, pointing to UPS policies for reassigning employees unable to perform their usual duties for other reasons (such as being injured on the job). The district court granted judgment for UPS based on a finding that the other employees UPS accommodated were not "similar" enough to pregnant employees. The court of appeals affirmed.

Breyer, J., for 5: To prevail on a PDA claim, a plaintiff must show that she was pregnant, sought accommodation for her pregnancy, and was not accommodated, and that others who received accommodation were "similar in their ability or inability to work" to her. If the employer presents an apparently neutral accommodations policy, the plaintiff may try to show that the policy is pretextual by showing that it imposes a significant burden on pregnant workers and that the justifications the employer offers for the burden are insufficiently strong.

Alito, J., concurring in judgment: The clause of the PDA containing the phrase "similar in their ability or inability to work" has independent significance from other parts of the provision and justifies the framework set out by the majority.

Scalia, J., dissenting: The majority's framework, and Justice Alito's reading of the provision, depart from the PDA's text.

Kennedy, J., dissenting: Young cannot show that she would have been accommodated had it not been for her pregnancy, so UPS was entitled to judgment. Pregnancy discrimination is, however, a problem, and the PDA is only one of several important protections for female and pregnant employees.

Zivotofsky v. Kerry, decided June 8, 2015 **[cited as *Zivotofsky*]**

A provision of the Foreign Relations Authorization Act (FRAA) instructed State Department officials to record the place of birth of "a United States citizen born in the city of Jerusalem" as "Israel" "upon the request of the citizen or the citizen's legal guardian." Menachem Zivotofsky was born in Jerusalem to U.S. citizens. His mother asked embassy officials to list his place of birth as "Israel" on his U.S. passport. The officials refused, citing the executive branch's longstanding position that the U.S. does not recognize any country as having sovereignty over Jerusalem. Zivotofsky's parents sued on his behalf, invoking the FRAA. The court of appeals held the FRAA unconstitutional based on its contradiction of the executive branch's exclusive power to recognize foreign sovereigns.

Kennedy, J., for 5: The FRAA provision unconstitutionally infringes the President's exclusive power to recognize (or withhold recognition from) foreign sovereigns.

Breyer, J., concurring: This dispute presents a political question and should not be resolved by the judicial branch. Given the Court's previous decision that the issue is justiciable, however, the majority reaches the right conclusion.

Thomas, J., concurring in judgment in part, dissenting in part: The FRAA is unconstitutional to the extent that it lets consular officials contradict presidential policy on passports, but it is not unconstitutional in directing consular officials to identify Israel as the place of birth of Jerusalem-born citizens on consular reports of birth abroad. These reports, unlike passports, do not involve the exercise of a power constitutionally assigned to the President.

Roberts, C.J., dissenting (+1): The majority's approach deviates from the established framework for assessing the legitimacy of presidential action and dramatically expands the scope of presidential power relative to Congress.

Scalia, J., dissenting (+2): The Constitution assigns powers relating to foreign affairs to both the President and Congress. The FRAA provision does not concern recognition and does not conflict with the President's recognition power.

Bibliography

Adamson, Robert E., Functional Fixedness as Related to Problem Solving: A Repetition of Three Experiments, 44:4 *Journal of Experimental Psychology* 288–91 (1952).

Aldisert, Ruggero, *Opinion Writing* (3d ed., Carolina Academic Press, 2012).

Amsterdam, Anthony G. & Jerome Bruner, *Minding the Law* (Harvard Univ. Press, 2000).

Anderson, Benedict, *Imagined Communities: Reflections on the Origin and Spread of Nationalism* (Verso, 1983).

Anderson, Jill C., Misreading Like a Lawyer: Cognitive Bias in Statutory Interpretation, 127 *Harvard Law Review* 1521–92 (2014).

Anscombe, G.E.M., Pretending, 32 *Proceedings of the Royal Aristotelian Society Supp. Volume* 279–94 (1958).

Appiah, Kwame Anthony, *As If: Idealization and Ideals* (Harvard Univ. Press, 2017).

Austin, J.L., *How to Do Things with Words* (1962; 2d ed., Harvard Univ. Press, 1975).

Azzouni, Jody, *Talking About Nothing: Numbers, Hallucinations, and Fictions* (Oxford Univ. Press, 2010).

Balkin, Jack M., The Crystalline Structure of Legal Thought, 39 *Rutgers Law Review* 1–110 (1986).

Balkin, Jack M., *Constitutional Redemption: Political Faith in an Unjust World* (Harvard Univ. Press, 2011).

Banfield, Ann, *Unspeakable Sentences: Narration and Representation in the Language of Fiction* (Routledge, 1982).

Barthes, Roland, *S/Z: An Essay* (1970; Richard Miller trans., Hill & Wang, 1975).

Baron-Cohen, Simon, *Mindblindness: An Essay on Autism and Theory of Mind* (MIT Press, 1995).

Baum, Lawrence, *Judges and Their Audiences: A Perspective on Judicial Behavior* (Princeton Univ. Press, 2006).

Berger, Eric, *Gross* Error, 19 *Washington Law Review* 929–1004 (2016).

Bickel, Alexander M., The Supreme Court, 1960 Term—Foreword: The Passive Virtues, 75 *Harvard Law Review* 40–79 (1961).

Binder, Guyora & Robert S. Weisberg, *Literary Criticisms of Law* (Princeton Univ. Press, 2000).

Bobbitt, Philip, *Constitutional Fate: Theory of the Constitution* (Oxford Univ. Press, 1982).

Bogdan, Radu J., *Mindvaults: Sociocultural Grounds for Pretending and Imagining* (MIT Press, 2013).

Boudreau, Cheryl, Matthew D. McCubbins, & Daniel Rodriguez, Statutory Interpretation and the Intentional(ist) Stance, 38 *Loyola–Los Angeles Law Review* 2131–46 (2005).

Brennan-Marquez, Kiel, *For Argument's Sake*, N.Y.U. School of Law Public Law & Legal Theory Research Paper Series, Working Paper No. 15–45 (2015).

Bressman, Lisa Schultz & Abbe R. Gluck, Statutory Interpretation from the Inside—An Empirical Study of Congressional Drafting, Delegation, and the Canons: Part II, 66 *Stanford Law Review* 725–802 (2014).

Broker, Tyler, Essay, First Amendment Speculation and Conjecture, 51 *Gonzaga Law Review* 561–72 (2016).

Bruner, Jerome, *Actual Minds, Possible Worlds* (Harvard Univ. Press, 1986).
Bruner, Jerome, *Making Stories: Law, Literature, Life* (Harvard Univ. Press, 2002).
Byrne, Ruth M.J., *The Rational Imagination: How People Create Alternatives to Reality* (MIT Press, 2005).
Calvert, Clay, Emma Morehart, & Sarah Papadelias, Rap Music and the True Threats Quagmire: When Does One Man's Lyric Become Another's Crime?, 38 *Columbia Journal of Law & the Arts* 1–28 (2014).
Camerer, Colin, George Loewenstein, & Martin Weber, The Curse of Knowledge in Economic Settings: An Experimental Analysis, 47:5 *Journal of Political Economy* 1232–54 (1989).
Caracciolo, Marco, Blind Reading: Toward an Enactivist Theory of the Reader's Imagination, in *Stories and Minds: Cognitive Approaches to Literary Narrative* 81–105 (Lars Bernaerts, Dirk de Geest, Luc Herman, & Bart Vervaeck eds., Univ. of Nebraska Press, 2013).
Chisholm, Roderick M., The Contrary-to-Fact Conditional, 55 *Mind* 289–307 (1946).
Ciepley, David, Beyond Public and Private: Toward a Political Theory of the Corporation, 107:1 *American Political Science Review* 139–58 (2013).
Climo, T.A. & P.G.A. Howell, Possible Worlds in Historical Explanation, 15:1 *History & Theory* 1–20 (1976).
Cohen, Felix S., Transcendental Nonsense and the Functional Approach, 35 *Columbia Law Review* 809–49 (1935).
Cohn, Dorrit, *Transparent Minds: Narrative Modes for Presenting Consciousness in Fiction* (Princeton Univ. Press, 1984).
Cohn, Dorrit, Signposts of Fictionality: A Narratological Perspective, 11:4 *Poetics Today* 775–804 (1990).
Constable, Marianne, *Our Word Is Our Bond: How Legal Speech Acts* (Stanford Univ. Press, 2014).
Corasantini, Nick, On Social Media, an Outpouring of Support, *New York Times*, June 26, 2015.
Corley, Pamela C., The Supreme Court and Opinion Content: The Influence of Parties' Briefs, 61:3 *Political Research Quarterly* 468–78 (2008).
Cover, Robert, The Supreme Court, 1982 Term—Foreword: *Nomos* and Narrative, 97 *Harvard Law Review* 4–68 (1983).
Culler, Jonathan, Omniscience, 12:1 *Narrative* 22–34 (2004).
Currie, Gregory, *The Nature of Fiction* (Cambridge Univ. Press, 1990).
Dames, Nicholas, *The Physiology of the Novel: Reading, Neural Science, and the Form of Victorian Fiction* (Oxford Univ. Press, 2007).
Dan-Cohen, Meir, Decision Rules and Conduct Rules: On Acoustic Separation in Criminal Law, 97 *Harvard Law Review* 625–77 (1993).
Dan-Cohen, Meir, *Rights, Persons, and Organizations: A Legal Theory for Bureaucratic Society* (2d ed., Quid Pro, 2016).
Daston, Lorraine and Peter Galison, *Objectivity* (Zone Books, 2007).
Davidson, Donald, *Subjective, Intersubjective, Objective* (Oxford Univ. Press, 2001).
Davis, Kenneth Culp, An Approach to Problems of Evidence in the Administrative Process, 55 *Harvard Law Review* 364–425 (1942).
Delgado, Richard, Storytelling for Opportunists and Others: A Plea for Narrative, 87 *Michigan Law Review* 2411–41 (1989).
Dennett, Daniel C., *The Intentional Stance* (MIT Press, 1987).
Denning, Brandon P., The Dormant Commerce Clause ~~Wynnes Won~~ Wins One: Five Takes on *Wynne* and *Direct Marketing Association*, 100 *Minnesota Law Review Headnotes* 103–25 (2016).
Derrida, Jacques, *Limited Inc* (Jeffrey Mehlman & Samuel Weber trans., Northwestern Univ. Press, 1988).
Deutsch, Harry, Making Up Stories, in Anthony Everett & Thomas Hofweber eds., *Empty Names, Fiction, and the Puzzles of Non-Existence* 149–82 (CLSI Publications, 2000).
Doerfler, Ryan D., Who Cares How Congress Really Works?, 66 *Duke Law Journal* 979–1044 (2017).
Doležel, Lubomír, Mimesis and Possible Worlds, 9:3 *Poetics Today* 475–96 (1988).
Doležel, Lubomír, *Heterocosmica: Fiction and Possible Worlds* (Johns Hopkins Univ. Press, 2000).
Donnellan, Keith, Speaking of Nothing, 83:1 *Philosophical Review* 3–31 (1974).

Dorf, Michael C., Symposium: In Defense of Justice Kennedy's Soaring Language, SCOTUSblog, June 27, 2015.
Douglas, Mary, *Natural Symbols: Explorations in Cosmology* (Barrie & Jenkins, 1970).
Dovey, Ceridwen, Can Reading Make You Happier?, *The New Yorker*, June 9, 2015.
Dworkin, Ronald, *Law's Empire* (Harvard Univ. Press, 1986).
Eco, Umberto, The Myth of Superman, 2:1 *Diacritics* 14–22 (1972).
Eco, Umberto, Possible Worlds and Text Pragmatics: "Un drame bien parisien," 19/20 *Versus* 6–72 (1978).
Edelman, Murray, *Political Language: Words that Succeed and Policies that Fail* (Academic Press, 1977).
Ekins, Richard, *The Nature of Legislative Intent* (Oxford Univ. Press, 2012).
Elfenbein, Andrew, *The Gist of Reading* (Stanford Univ. Press, 2018).
Eskridge, William N. Jr., Dynamic Statutory Interpretation, 135 *Univ. of Pennsylvania Law Review* 1479–1556 (1987).
Epps, Garrett, *American Epic: Reading the U.S. Constitution* (Oxford Univ. Press, 2013).
Everett, Anthony, *The Nonexistent* (Oxford Univ. Press, 2013).
Faigman, David L., *Constitutional Fictions: A Unified Theory of Constitutional Facts* (Harvard Univ. Press, 2008).
Fallon, Richard H. Jr., Fact and Fiction About Facial Challenges, 99 *California Law Review* 915–74 (2011).
Fallon, Richard H. Jr., The Meaning of Legal "Meaning" and Its Implications for Theories of Literary Interpretation, 82 *University of Chicago Law Review* 1235–1308 (2015a).
Fallon, Richard H. Jr., Taking the Idea of Constitutional "Meaning" Seriously, 129 *Harvard Law Review Forum* 1–10 (2015b).
Feigenson, Neal, *Experiencing Other Minds in the Courtroom* (Univ. of Chicago Press, 2016).
Feltovich, Paul J., Michael J. Prietula, & K. Anders Ericsson, Studies of Expertise from Psychological Perspectives, in *The Cambridge Handbook of Expertise and Expert Performance* 41–67 (K. Anders Ericsson et al. eds., Cambridge Univ. Press, 2006).
Ferguson, Robert A., The Judicial Opinion as Literary Genre, 2 *Yale Journal of Law & the Humanities* 201–20 (1990).
Fludernik, Monika, *The Fictions of Language and the Languages of Fiction* (Routledge, 1992).
Fludernik, Monika, Chronology, Time, Tense, and Experientiality in Narrative, 12:2 *Language and Literature* 117–34 (2003).
Fogel, Robert, *Railroads and American Economic Growth: Essays in Econometric History* (Johns Hopkins Univ. Press, 1964).
Frankfurter, Felix & James M. Landis, The Supreme Court under the Judiciary Act of 1925, 42 *Harvard Law Review* 1–29 (1928).
Fuller, Lon L., Positivism and Fidelity to Law—A Reply to Professor Hart, 71 *Harvard Law Review* 630–72 (1958).
Fuller, Lon L., *Legal Fictions* (Stanford Univ. Press, 1968).
Gaines, Philip, *From Truth to Technique at Trial: A Discursive History of Advocacy Advice Texts* (Oxford Univ. Press, 2016).
Galanter, Marc, *Lowering the Bar: Lawyer Jokes and Legal Culture* (Univ. of Wisconsin Press, 2005).
Gale, Richard M., The Fictive Use of Language, 16:178 *Philosophy* 324–40 (1971).
Gallagher, Catherine, The Rise of Fictionality, in 1 *The Novel: History, Geography, and Culture* 336–63 (Franco Moretti ed., Princeton Univ. Press, 2006).
Gallagher, Catherine, *Telling It Like It Wasn't: The Counterfactual Imagination in History and Fiction* (Univ. of Chicago Press, 2018).
Galloway, Russell W., Means-End Scrutiny in American Constitutional Law, 21 *Loyola of Los Angeles Law Review* 449–96 (1988).
Garrow, David J., A Revolutionary Year: Judicial Assertiveness and Gay Rights, in *A Year at the Supreme Court* 55 -70 (Neal Devins & Davison M. Douglas eds., Duke Univ. Press, 2004).

Genette, Gérard, *Narrative Discourse: An Essay in Method* (1967–70; Jane E. Lewin trans., Cornell Univ. Press, 1983).
Gerrig, Richard J., *Experiencing Narrative Worlds: On the Psychological Activities of Reading* (Yale Univ. Press, 1993).
Gewirtz, Paul, The Jurisprudence of Hypotheticals, 32 *Journal of Legal Education* 120–26 (1982).
Gilbert, Margaret, *On Social Facts* (Princeton Univ. Press, 1989).
Gluck, Abbe R., Imperfect Statutes, Imperfect Courts: Understanding Congress's Plan in an Era of Unorthodox Lawmaking, 129 *Harvard Law Review* 62–111 (2015).
Gluck, Abbe R. & Lisa Schultz Bressman, Statutory Interpretation from the Inside—An Empirical Study of Congressional Drafting, Delegation, and the Canons: Part I, 65 *Stanford Law Review* 901–1026 (2013).
Goldman, Alvin M., Imagination and Simulation in Audience Responses to Fiction, in *The Architecture of the Imagination: New Essays on Pretense, Possibility, and Fiction* 41–56 (Shaun Nichols ed., Oxford Univ. Press, 2006).
Goldsmith, Jack, *Zivotofsky II* as Precedent in the Executive Branch, 129 *Harvard Law Review* 112–46 (2015).
Goodman, Nelson, The Problem of Counterfactual Conditionals, 44:5 *Journal of Philosophy* 113–28 (1947).
Goodman, Nelson, *Fact, Fiction, and Forecast* (Harvard Univ. Press, 1955).
Gordon, Robert W., The Geologic Strata of the Law School Curriculum, 60 *Vanderbilt Law Review* 339–70 (2007).
Gordon, Robert W., *Taming the Past: Essays on Law in History and History in Law* (Cambridge Univ. Press, 2017).
Gorsuch, Neil M., Of Lions and Bears, Judges and Legislators, and the Legacy of Justice Scalia, 66 *Case Western Reserve Law Review* 905–22 (2016).
Graham, Laura P., Why-Rac? Revisiting the Traditional Paradigm in Writing About Legal Analysis, 63 *Kansas Law Review* 681–716 (2015).
Graziano, Michael S.A., *Consciousness and the Social Brain* (Oxford Univ. Press, 2013).
Greabe, John M., The Riddle of Harmless Error Revisited, 54 *Houston Law Review* 59–124 (2016).
Green, Mitchell, How and What We Can Learn from Fiction, in *The Blackwell Companion to Philosophy of Literature* 350–66 (Garry L. Hagberg & Walter Jost eds., 2010).
Greene, Jamal, Pathetic Argument in Constitutional Law, 113 *Columbia Law Review* 1389–1482 (2013).
Greene, Jamal, The Meming of Substantive Due Process, 30 *Constitutional Commentary* 253–94 (2016).
Greenhouse, Linda, Justice Scalia's Fading Legacy, *New York Times*, March 15, 2018.
Grice, H. Paul, *Studies in the Way of Words* (Harvard Univ. Press, 1984).
Guinier, Lani, The Supreme Court, 2007 Term—Foreword: Demosprudence Through Dissent, 122 *Harvard Law Review* 4–138 (2008).
Harmon, Louise, Falling off the Vine: Legal Fictions and the Doctrine of Substituted Judgment, 100 *Yale Law Journal* 1–72 (1990).
Harper, W.L., G.A. Pearce, & R. Stalnaker eds., *Ifs: Conditionals, Belief, Decision, Chance, and Time* (Springer, 1981).
Harrison, Bernard, What Are Fictions For?, 25 *Midwest Studies in Philosophy* 12–35 (2001).
Harshaw (Hrushovski), Benjamin, Fictionality and Fields of Reference: Remarks on a Theoretical Framework, 5:2 *Poetics Today* 227–51 (1984).
Hart, H.L.A., Positivism and the Separation of Law and Morals, 71 *Harvard Law Review* 593–629 (1958).
Hart, H.L.A., *The Concept of Law* (1961; 3d ed. Oxford Univ. Press, 2012).
Hart, H.L.A. & Tony Honoré, *Causation in the Law* (Oxford Univ. Press, 1959).
Hart, Henry M. Jr., & Albert M. Sacks, *The Legal Process: Basic Problems in the Making and Application of Law* (1958; William N. Eskridge, Jr. & Philip P. Frickey eds., Foundation Press, 1994).

Hawthorn, Geoffrey, *Plausible Worlds: Possibility and Understanding in History and the Social Sciences* (Cambridge Univ. Press, 1991).

Heider, Fritz & Marianne Simmel, An Experimental Study of Apparent Behavior, 57:2 *American Journal of Psychology* 243–59 (1944), DOI: 10.2307/1416950.

Hempfer, Klaus W., Some Problems Concerning a Theory of Fiction(ality), 38:3 *Style* 302–23 (2004).

Henderson, M. Todd, Citing Fiction, 11 *Green Bag* 2d 171–85 (2008).

Herman, David, *Storytelling and the Sciences of Mind* (MIT Press, 2013).

Hill, Christopher S., Modality, Modal Epistemology, and the Metaphysics of Consciousness, in *The Architecture of the Imagination: New Essays on Pretense, Possibility, and Fiction* 205 (Shaun Nichols ed., Oxford Univ. Press, 2006).

Holland, Norman, *The Dynamics of Literary Response* (W.W. Norton, 1975).

Holmes, Oliver Wendell, Jr., *The Common Law* (1881; rev. ed. Dover, 1991).

Hutto, Daniel D., *Folk Psychological Narratives: The Sociocultural Basis of Understanding Reasons* (MIT Press, 2008).

Iser, Wolfgang, *The Act of Reading: A Theory of Literary Response* (Johns Hopkins Univ. Press, 1980).

Jenkins, Henry, *Textual Poachers: Television Fans and Participatory Culture* (Routledge, 1992; rev. ed. 2012).

Kahan, Dan M., David A. Hoffman, & Donald Braman, Whose Eyes Are You Going to Believe? *Scott v. Harris* and the Perils of Cognitive Illiberalism, 122 *Harvard Law Review* 837–906 (2009).

Kahneman, Daniel & Amos Tversky, The Simulation Heuristic, in *Judgment Under Uncertainty: Heuristics and Biases* 201–08 (Daniel Kahneman & Amos Tversky, eds., Cambridge University Press, 1982).

Kantorowicz, Ernst, *The King's Two Bodies: A Study in Medieval Political Theory* (1957; Princeton Univ. Press, 2016).

Kearney, Joseph D. & Thomas W. Merrill, The Influence of Amicus Curiae Briefs on the Supreme Court, 148 *Univ. of Pennsylvania Law Review* 743–856 (2000).

Kennedy, Duncan, *Legal Education and the Reproduction of Hierarchy: A Polemic Against the System* (NYU Press, 1983).

Kidd, David Comer & Emanuele Castano, Reading Literary Fiction Improves Theory of Mind, 342 *Science* 377–80 (2013), DOI: 10.1125/science.1239918.

Kindy, Kimberly, Sari Horwitz, & William Wan, Simply Stated, Gorsuch Is Steadfast and Surprising, *Washington Post*, Feb. 18, 2017.

Kripke, Saul, Semantical Considerations on Modal Logic, 16 *Acta Philosophica Fennica* 83–94 (1963).

Kripke, Saul, *Naming and Necessity* (Harvard Univ. Press, 1980).

Kornhauser, Lewis A. & Lawrence G. Sager, The One and the Many: Adjudication in Collegial Courts, 81 *California Law Review* 1–60 (1993).

Kutz, Christopher, *Complicity: Ethics and Law for a Collective Age* (Cambridge Univ. Press, 2007).

Langer, Ellen J., The Illusion of Control, 32:2 *Journal of Personality & Social Psychology* 311–28 (1975).

Larsen, Allison Orr, The Trouble with Amicus Facts, 100 *Virginia Law Review* 1757–1818 (2014).

LaPiana, William L., *Logic and Experience: The Origin of Modern American Legal Education* (Oxford Univ. Press, 1994).

Lazarus, Richard J., Back to "Business" at the Supreme Court: The "Administrative Side" of Chief Justice Roberts, 129 *Harvard Law Review* 33–93 (2015).

Lee, Michael J., *Creating Conservatism: Postwar Words that Made an American Movement* (Michigan State Univ. Press, 2014).

Levine, Caroline, *Forms: Whole, Rhythm, Hierarchy, Network* (Princeton Univ. Press, 2015).

Levinson, Sanford, The Rhetoric of the Judicial Opinion, in *Law's Stories: Narrative and Rhetoric in the Law* 187–205 (Peter Brooks & Paul Gewirtz eds., Yale Univ. Press, 1996).

Levitin, Daniel J., *Weaponized Lies: How to Think Critically in the Post-Truth Era* (rpt. ed., Dutton, 2017).

Lewis, David, Truth in Fiction, 15 *American Philosophical Quarterly* 37–46 (1978).

Lewis, David, *On the Plurality of Worlds* (Blackwell, 1986).

Liptak, Adam, The Lackluster Reviews That Lawyers Love to Hate, *New York Times*, Oct. 21, 2013.

Liptak, Adam, Supreme Court Ruling Makes Same-Sex Marriage a Right Nationwide, *New York Times*, June 26, 2015.

Liptak, Adam, Confident and Assertive, Gorsuch Hurries to Make His Mark, *New York Times*, July 3, 2017.

List, Christian & Philip Pettit, *Group Agency: The Possibility, Design, and Status of Corporate Agents* (Oxford Univ. Press, 2013).

Loux, Michael J. ed., *The Possible and the Actual: Readings in the Metaphysics of Modality* (Oxford Univ. Press, 1979).

Machen, Arthur W., Jr., Corporate Personality, 24 *Harvard Law Review* 253–67 (1911).

Mackie, J.L., *The Cement of the Universe: A Study of Causation* (Oxford Univ. Press, 1974).

Maine, Henry Sumner, *Ancient Law: Its Connection with the Early History of Society and Its Relation to Modern Ideas* (1861; Dorset, 1986).

Manjoo, Farhad, *True Enough: Learning to Live in a Post-Fact Society* (Wiley, 2008).

Manning, John F., Inside Congress's Mind, 115 *Columbia Law Review* 1911–52 (2015).

Manning, John F., Justice Scalia and the Idea of Judicial Restraint, 115 *Michigan Law Review* 747–82 (2017).

Mar, Raymond A., Keith Oatley, Jacob Hirsh, Jennifer dela Paz, & Jordan B. Peterson, Bookworms Versus Nerds: Exposure to Fiction Versus Non-Fiction, Divergent Associations with Social Ability, and the Simulation of Fictional Social Worlds, 40:5 *Journal of Research in Personality* 694–712 (2006).

Marmor, Andrei & Scott Soames eds., *Philosophical Foundations of Language in the Law* (Oxford Univ. Press, 2011).

Maroney, Terry A., The Persistent Cultural Script of Judicial Dispassion, 99 *California Law Review* 629–82 (2011).

Martinez-Conde, Susana & Stephen L. Macknick, The Delusion of Alternative Facts, *Scientific American*, Jan. 27, 2017.

McNaughton, John T., Burden of Production of Evidence: A Function of a Burden of Persuasion, 68 *Harvard Law Review* 1382–91 (1955).

Meinong, Alexius, Über Gegenstandtheorie [On the Theory of Objects], in *Realism and the Background of Phenomenology* 76–117 (1904; I. Levi, D.B. Terrell, & R.M. Chisholm trans., Roderick Chisholm ed., Free Press, 1960).

Mellinkoff, David, *The Language of the Law* (Little, Brown & Co., 1963).

Mertz, Elizabeth, *The Language of Law School: Learning to "Think Like a Lawyer"* (Oxford Univ. Press, 2007).

Meyer, Philip N., *Storytelling for Lawyers* (Oxford Univ. Press, 2014).

Miller, Alan D. & Ronen Perry, The Reasonable Person, 87 *NYU Law Review* 323–92 (2012).

Miller, Sidney T., The Reasons for Some Legal Fictions, 8 *Michigan Law Review* 623–36 (1910).

Mitchell, Gregory, Case Studies, Counterfactuals, and Causal Explanations, 152 *University of Pennsylvania Law Review* 1517–1608 (2004).

Moore, Michael S., The Semantics of Judging, 54 *Southern California Law Review* 151–294 (1980).

Moran, Mayo, *Rethinking the Reasonable Person: An Egalitarian Reconstruction of the Objective Standard* (Oxford Univ. Press, 2003).

Nagel, Thomas, *The View From Nowhere* (Oxford Univ. Press, 1984).

Newton, Brent E., Law Review Scholarship in the Eyes of the Twenty-First Century Supreme Court Justices: An Empirical Analysis, 4 *Drexel Law Review* 399–416 (2012).

Nichols, Shaun & Stephen P. Stich, *Mindreading: An Integrated Account of Pretence, Self-Awareness, and Understanding Other Minds* (Oxford Univ. Press, 2003).

Note (2015a), Administrative Procedure Act—Changing Interpretive Rules—*Perez v. Mortgage Bankers Ass'n*, 129 *Harvard Law Review* 291–300 (2015).

Note (2015b), Armed Career Criminal Act—Residual Clause—*Johnson v. United States*, 129 *Harvard Law Review* 301–10 (2015).

Note (2015c), Article I—Dormant Commerce Clause—Personal Income Taxation—*Comptroller of the Treasury of Maryland v. Wynne*, 129 *Harvard Law Review* 181–90 (2015).

Note (2015d), Article I—Elections Clause—Legislative Control of Redistricting—*Arizona State Legislature v. Arizona Independent Redistricting Commission*, 129 *Harvard Law Review* 191–200 (2015).

Note (2015e), Article III—Separation of Powers—Bankruptcy Jurisdiction—*Wellness International Network, Ltd. v. Sharif*, 129 *Harvard Law Review* 201–10 (2015).

Note (2015f), Article VI—Private Rights of Action—Equitable Remedies to Enforce the Medicaid Act—*Armstrong v. Exceptional Child Center, Inc.*, 129 *Harvard Law Review* 211–20 (2015).

Note (2015g), Clean Air Act—Cost-Benefit Analysis—*Michigan v. EPA*, 129 *Harvard Law Review* 311–20 (2015).

Note (2015h), Eighth Amendment—Death Penalty—Preliminary Injunctions—*Glossip v. Gross*, 129 *Harvard Law Review* 271–80 (2015).

Note (2015i), Fair Housing Act—Disparate Impact and Racial Equality—*Texas Department of Housing & Community Affairs v. Inclusive Communities Project, Inc.*, 129 *Harvard Law Review* 321–30 (2015).

Note (2015j), Federal Threats Statute—Mens Rea and the First Amendment—*Elonis v. United States*, 129 *Harvard Law Review* 331–40 (2015).

Note (2015k), Fifth Amendment—Takings Clause—Regulatory Takings—*Horne v. Department of Agriculture*, 129 *Harvard Law Review* 261–70 (2015).

Note (2015l), First Amendment—Freedom of Speech—Government Speech—*Walker v. Texas Div., Sons of Confederal Veterans, Inc.*, 129 *Harvard Law Review* 221–30 (2015).

Note (2015m), First Amendment—Freedom of Speech—Judicial Campaign Speech—*Williams-Yulee v. Florida Bar*, 129 *Harvard Law Review* 231–40 (2015).

Note (2015n), Fourteenth Amendment—Equal Protection Clause—Racial Gerrymandering—*Alabama Legislative Black Caucus v. Alabama*, 129 *Harvard Law Review* 281–90 (2015).

Note (2015o), Fourth Amendment—Search and Seizure—Reasonable Mistake of Law—*Heien v. North Carolina*, 129 *Harvard Law Review* 251–60 (2015).

Note (2015p), Fourth Amendment—Standing—Facial Versus As-Applied Challenges—*City of Los Angeles v. Patel*, 129 *Harvard Law Review* 241–50 (2015).

Note (2015q), Passenger Rail Investment and Improvement Act—Nondelegation—*Department of Transportation v. Association of American Railroads*, 129 *Harvard Law Review* 341–50 (2015).

Note (2015r), Religious Land Use and Institutionalized Persons Act—Religious Liberty—*Holt v. Hobbs*, 129 *Harvard Law Review* 351–60 (2015).

Note (2015s), Sarbanes-Oxley Act—Destruction of Evidence—*Yates v. United States*, 129 *Harvard Law Review* 361–70 (2015).

Note (2015t), Sherman Act—State Action Immunity—*North Carolina State Board of Dental Examiners v. FTC*, 129 *Harvard Law Review* 371–80 (2015).

Nourse, Victoria F., *Misreading Law, Misreading Democracy* (Harvard Univ. Press, 2016).

O'Connell, Anne Joseph, Bureaucracy at the Boundary, 162 *Univ. of Pennsylvania Law Review* 841–928 (2014).

Ogden, C.K., *Bentham's Theory of Fictions* (1932; Routledge, 2000).

Orts, Eric W., *Business Persons: A Legal Theory of the Firm* (Oxford Univ. Press, 2013)60.

Oscamp, Stuart, Overconfidence in Case-Study Judgments, 29:3 *Journal of Consulting Psychology* 261–65 (1965).

Palazzolo, Joe, Supreme Court Nominee Takes Legal Writing to Next Level: Judge Neil Gorsuch Strives for Accessibility in Opinions, *Wall Street Journal*, Jan. 31, 2017.

Palmer, Alan, *Fictional Minds* (Univ. of Nebraska Press, 2008).

Palmer, Alan, *Social Minds in the Novel* (Ohio State Univ. Press, 2010).

Pardo, Michael S., Group Agency and Legal Proof: Or, Why the Jury Is an It, 56 *William & Mary Law Review* 1793–1858 (2015).
Paskins, Barrie, On Being Moved by Anna Karenina and *Anna Karenina*, 52 *Philosophy* 344–47 (1977).
Pavel, Thomas G., *Fictional Worlds* (Harvard Univ. Press, 1994).
Petroski, Karen, Does It Matter What We Say About Legal Interpretation?, 43 *McGeorge Law Review* 359–401 (2012).
Petroski, Karen, Texts versus Testimony: Legal Uses of Non-Legal Expertise, 35 *Univ. of Hawai'i Law Review* 81–128 (2013).
Petroski, Karen, What a State Wants: The Language of Another Legal Fiction, 3 *Savannah Law Review* 71–93 (2017).
Ponnuru, Radesh, Neil Gorsuch: A Worthy Heir to Scalia, *National Review*, Jan. 31, 2017.
Popper, Karl, *Objective Knowledge: An Evolutionary Approach* (Oxford Univ. Press, 1986).
Posner, Richard A., *How Judges Think* (Harvard Univ. Press, 2008).
Posner, Richard A., Comment on Professor Gluck's "Imperfect Statutes, Imperfect Courts," 129 *Harvard Law Review Forum* 11–15 (2015).
Posner, Richard A., *Divergent Paths: The Academy and the Judiciary* (Harvard Univ. Press, 2016).
Pronin, Emily, Daniel Y. Lin, & Lee Ross, The Bias Blind Spot: Perceptions of Bias in Self Versus Others, 28:3 *Personality & Social Psychology Bulletin* 369–81 (2002).
Putnam, Hilary, Meaning and Reference, 70:19 *Journal of Philosophy* 699–711 (1973).
Quine, W.V., Quantifiers and Propositional Attitudes, 53:5 *Journal of Philosophy* 177–87 (1965).
Radford, Colin & Michael Weston, How Can We Be Moved by the Fate of Anna Karenina?, 49 *Aristotelian Society Supp. Vol.* 67–80 (1975).
Radin, Max, Statutory Interpretation, 43 *Harvard Law Review* 863–85 (1930).
Rescher, Nicholas, *Hypothetical Reasoning* (North-Holland, 1964).
Ristroph, Alice, State Intentions and the Law of Punishment, 98 *Journal of Criminal Law & Criminology* 1353–1406 (2008).
Robbins, Joel & Alan Rumsey, Cultural and Linguistic Anthropology and the Opacity of Other Minds, 83:2 *Anthropological Quarterly* 407–20 (2008).
Rodes, Richard E., *De Re* and *De Dicto*, 73 *Notre Dame Law Review* 627–36 (1998).
Roese, Neal J. & James M. Olson, eds., *What Might Have Been: The Social Psychology of Counterfactual Thinking* (Lawrence Erlbaum, 1995).
Ronen, Ruth, *Possible Worlds in Literary Theory* (Cambridge Univ. Press, 1994).
Rosenberg, Anat, The History of Genres: Reaching for Reality in Law and Literature (review of Ayelet Ben-Yishai, *Common Precedents: The Presentness of the Past in Victorian Law and Literature* (2013)), 39:4 *Law & Social Inquiry* 1057–79 (2014).
Rubin, Richard & Laura Stevens, Supreme Court Case on Sales Tax Rattles Merchants on Amazon, *Wall St. Journal*, April 15, 2018.
Russell, Bertrand, On Denoting, 14:56 *Mind* 479–93 (1905).
Rutenberg, Jim, "Alternative Facts" and the Cost of Trump-Branded Reality, *New York Times*, Jan. 22, 2017.
Ryan, Marie-Laure, *Possible Worlds, Artificial Intelligence, and Narrative Theory* (Indiana Univ. Press, 1991).
Ryan, Marie-Laure, Postmodernism and the Doctrine of Panfictionality, 5:2 *Narrative* 165–87 (1997).
Sachs, Stephen E., The "Constitution in Exile" as a Problem for Legal Theory, 89 *Notre Dame Law Review* 2253 (2014).
Sainsbury, R.M., *Fiction and Fictionalism* (Routledge, 2010).
Saler, Michael T., *As If: Modern Enchantment and the Literary Prehistory of Virtual Reality* (Oxford Univ. Press, 2012).
Scalia, Antonin, Support Your Local Professor of Administrative Law, 34 *Administrative Law Review* xvii–xxii (1982).

Scalia, Antonin, *A Matter of Interpretation: Federal Courts and the Law* (Amy Gutmann ed., Princeton Univ. Press, 1998).
Scalia, Antonin & Bryan A. Garner, *Reading Law: The Interpretation of Legal Texts* (Thomson/West, 2012).
Scarry, Elaine, *Dreaming By the Book* (1999; Princeton Univ. Press, 2001).
Schachter, Jane S., *Obergefell's* Audiences, 77 *Ohio State Law Journal* 1011–38 (2016).
Schaeffer, Judith, The Constitution Has Everything to Do with It, SCOTUSblog (June 26, 2015).
Schane, Sanford A., The Corporation Is a Person: The Language of a Legal Fiction, 61 *Tulane Law Review* 563–610 (1987).
Schank, Roger C. & Robert P. Abelson, *Scripts, Plans, Goals, and Understanding: An Inquiry into Human Knowledge* (Lawrence Erlbaum, 1977).
Schauer, Frederick, Opinions as Rules, 62 *Univ. of Chicago Law Review* 1455–76 (1995).
Shen, Francis X., Matthew R. Ginther, Richard J. Bonnie, Morris B. Hoffman, Owen D. Jones, René Marois, & Kenneth W. Simons, The Language of Mens Rea, 67 *Vanderbilt Law Review* 1327–72 (2014).
Scheppele, Kim Lane, Facing Facts in Legal Interpretation, 30 *Representations* 42–77 (1990).
Scheppele, Kim Lane, Manners of Imagining the Real, 19:4 *Law & Social Inquiry* 995–1022 (1994).
Scheppele, Kim Lane, Autocratic Legalism, 85 *Univ. of Chicago Law Review* 545–84 (2018).
Schiffer, Stephen, Language-Created Language-Independent Entities, 24:1 *Philosophical Topics* 149–67 (1996).
Schlag, Pierre, The Aesthetics of American Law, 115 *Harvard Law Review* 1047–1118 (2002).
Schneider, Valerie, In Defense of Disparate Impact: Urban Redevelopment and the Supreme Court's Recent Interest in the Fair Housing Act, 79 *Missouri Law Review* 539–84 (2014).
Scholl, Brian & Patrice Tremoulet, Perceptual Causality and Animacy, 4:8 *Trends in Cognitive Sciences* 299–309 (2000), DOI: 10.1016/S1364-6613(00)01506-0.
Searle, John R., The Logical Status of Fictional Discourse, 6:2 *New Literary History* 319–32 (1975).
Searle, John R., *Expression and Meaning: Studies in the Theory of Speech Acts* (Cambridge Univ. Press, 1985).
Shepsle, Kenneth A., Congress Is a "They," Not an "It": Legislative Intent as Oxymoron, 12 *International Review of Law & Economics* 239–56 (1992).
Sherwin, Richard K., Law Frames: Historical Truth and Narrative Necessity in a Criminal Case, 47 *Stanford Law Review* 39–83 (1994).
Shklar, Judith, *Legalism: Law, Morals, and Political Trials* (Harvard Univ. Press, 1964).
Shobe, Jarrod, Intertemporal Statutory Interpretation and the Evolution of Legislative Drafting, 114 *Columbia Law Review* 807–78 (2014).
Shugerman, Jed Handelsman, Neil Gorsuch and the "Frozen Trucker": The Judge's Infamous Dissent Reveals He May Not Have the Temperament to Serve on the Supreme Court, *Slate*, Mar. 21, 2017.
Simon, Herbert, *The Sciences of the Artificial* (MIT Press, 1969).
Sitaraman, Ganesh, The Origins of Legislation, 91 *Notre Dame Law Review* 79–132 (2015).
Slocum, Brian G., *Ordinary Meaning: A Theory of the Most Fundamental Principle of Legal Interpretation* (Univ. of Chicago Press, 2016).
Smith, Murray, Film Spectatorship and the Institution of Fiction, 53:2 *Journal of Aesthetics & Art Criticism* 113–27 (1995).
Smith, Peter J., New Legal Fictions, 95 *Georgetown Law Journal* 1435–96 (2007).
Solan, Lawrence M., *The Language of Judges* (Univ. of Chicago Press, 1993).
Solum, Lawrence, Constitutional Possibilities, 83 *Indiana Law Journal* 307–37 (2008).
Spencer, A. Benjamin, The Law School Critique in Historical Perspective, 69 *Washington & Lee Law Review* 1949–2066 (2012).
Spolsky, Ellen, *Contracts of Fiction: Cognition, Culture, Community* (Oxford Univ. Press, 2015).
Spriggs II, James F. & Paul J. Wahlbeck, Amicus Curiae and the Role of Information at the Supreme Court, 50 *Political Research Quarterly* 365–86 (1997).

Stern, Simon, *R. v. Jones* (1703): The Origins of the Reasonable Person, in *Landmark Cases in Criminal Law* 59 -79 (Henry Mares, Ian Williams, & Phil Handler eds., Hart, 2016).
Strassfeld, Robert N., If…: Counterfactuals in the Law, 60 *George Washington Law Review* 339–416 (1992).
Sternberg, Meir, *Expositional Modes and Temporal Ordering in Fiction* (Univ. of Indiana Press, 1979).
Strauss, David, Common Law Constitutional Interpretation, 63 *Univ. of Chicago Law Review* 877–936 (1996).
Strauss, David, *The Living Constitution* (Oxford Univ. Press, 2010).
Strauss, David, The Supreme Court, 2014 Term—Foreword: Does the Constitution Mean What It Says?, 129 *Harvard Law Review* 1–61 (2015).
Strauss, Peter L., Formal and Functional Approaches to Separation-of-Powers Questions—A Foolish Inconsistency?, 72 *Cornell Law Review* 488–526 (1987).
Su, Anna, Judging Religious Sincerity, 5 *Oxford Journal of Law & Religion* 28–48 (2016).
Sullivan, Kathleen M., The Supreme Court, 1991 Term—Foreword: The Justices of Rules and Standards, 106 *Harvard Law Review* 22 (1992).
Sunstein, Cass R., Incompletely Theorized Agreements, 108 *Harvard Law Review* 1733–72 (1995).
Tamanaha, Brian Z., *Beyond the Realist–Formalist Divide: The Role of Politics in Judging* (Princeton Univ. Press, 2009).
Tamanaha, Brian Z., *Failing Law Schools* (Univ. of Chicago Press, 2012).
Taylor, Marjorie, Conceptual Perspective Taking: Children's Ability to Distinguish What They Know From What They See, 59:3 *Child Development* 703–18 (1988).
Thayer, James Bradley, The Origin and Scope of the American Doctrine of Constitutional Law, 7 *Harvard Law Review* 129–56 (1891).
Thomas, Suja A., Summary Judgment and the Reasonable Jury Standard: A Proxy for a Judge's Own View of the Sufficiency of the Evidence?, 97 *Judicature* 222–27 (March–April 2014).
Tomasello, Michael, *The Cultural Origins of Human Cognition* (Harvard Univ. Press, 2001).
Thomasson, Amie, *Fiction and Metaphysics* (Cambridge Univ. Press, 1999).
Tiersma, Peter S., The Textualization of Precedent, 82 *Notre Dame Law Review* 1187–1278 (2013).
Tollefsen, Deborah Perron, *Groups as Agents* (Polity, 2015).
Tribe, Laurence H., Equal Dignity: Speaking Its Name, 129 *Harvard Law Review Forum* 16–32 (2015).
Tuomela, Raimo, *Social Ontology: Collective Intentionality and Group Agents* (Oxford Univ. Press, 2013).
Twining, William, *Rethinking Evidence* (1994; 2d ed., Cambridge Univ. Press, 2006).
Vaihinger, Hans, *The Philosophy of "As If": A System of the Theoretical, Practical, and Religious Fictions of Mankind* (1911; C.K. Ogden trans., Harcourt Brace, 1925).
van Inwagen, Peter, Creatures of Fiction, 14:4 *American Philosophical Quarterly* 299–308 (1977).
Vermeule, Blakey, *Why Do We Care About Literary Characters?* (Johns Hopkins Univ. Press, 2010).
Waldron, Jeremy, Stare Decisis and the Rule of Law: A Layered Approach, 111 *Michigan Law Review* 1–32 (2012).
Wallace-Wells, Benjamin, Police Shootings, Race, and the Fear Defense, *The New Yorker*, July 12, 2016.
Walton, Kendall, *Mimesis as Make-Believe: On the Foundations of the Representational Arts* (Harvard Univ. Press, 1993).
Wang, Amy B., "Post-Truth" Named 2016 Word of the Year by Oxford Dictionaries, *Washington Post*, Nov. 16, 2016.
Watford, Paul J., Richard C. Chen, & Marco Basile, Crafting Precedent (review of Bryan A. Garner et al., *The Law of Judicial Precedent* (Thomson Reuters, 2016)), 131 *Harvard Law Review* 543–81 (2017).
Wechsler, Herbert, Toward Neutral Principles of Constitutional Law, 73 *Harvard Law Review* 1–35 (1959).

Weisberg, Richard, What Remains "Real" About the Law and Literature Movement?: A Global Appraisal, 66:4 *Journal of Legal Education* 37–43 (2016).
White, James Boyd, *The Legal Imagination* (1973; abridged ed., Univ. of Chicago Press, 1985).
Whiting, Amanda, Law Twitter Is Having a Fun Time Mocking Neil Gorsuch's Writing Style, *Washingtonian*, Mar. 21, 2018.
Williams, Patricia J., *The Alchemy of Race and Rights: Diary of a Law Professor* (Harvard Univ. Press, 1992).
Wimmer, Heinz & Josef Perner, Beliefs about Beliefs: Representation and Constraining Function of Wrong Beliefs in Young Children's Understanding of Deception, 13 *Cognition* 103–28 (1983).
Winter, Steven L., *A Clearing in the Forest: Law, Life, and Mind* (Univ. of Chicago Press, 2003).
Yoshino, Kenji, A New Birth of Freedom?: *Obergefell v. Hodges*, 129 *Harvard Law Review* 147–80 (2015).
Yoshino, Kenji, Appellate Deference in the Age of Facts, 58 *William & Mary Law Review* 251–84 (2016).
Zipursky, Benjamin C., Reasonableness in and out of Negligence Law, 163 *Univ. of Pennsylvania Law Review* 2131–70 (2015).
Zunshine, Lisa, *Why We Read Fiction: Theory of Mind and the Novel* (Ohio State Univ. Press, 2006).

Index

For Product Safety Concerns and Information please contact our EU representative GPSR@taylorandfrancis.com Taylor & Francis Verlag GmbH, Kaufingerstraße 24, 80331 München, Germany

Batch number: 10726294

Printed by Printforce, the Netherlands